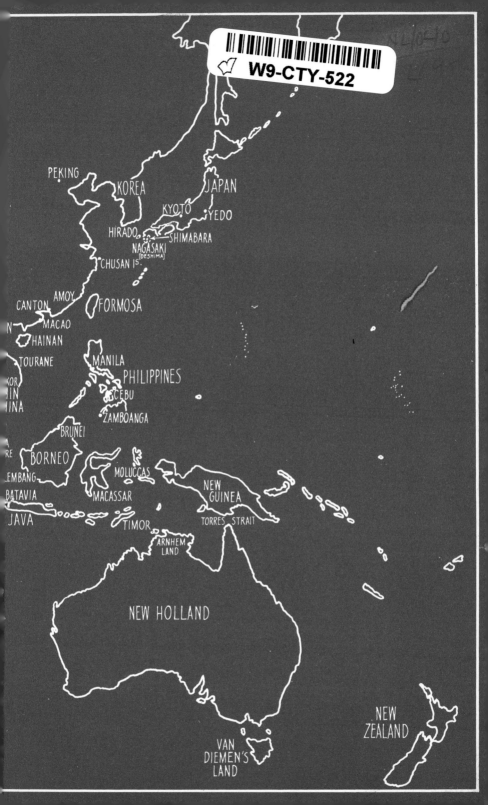

SOUTHEAST ASIA

SOUTHEAST ASIA

ASIA

Past and Present

NICHOLAS TARLING

F. W. CHESHIRE

Melbourne   Canberra   Sydney

Contents

Maps

Introduction

TERRA AUSTRALIS INCOGNITA: the notion of a southern continent excited explorers like Drake and Dampier and publicists like Dalrymple. Torres and Tasman started to delineate it. The mystery began to be fully revealed only with Cook's voyages to New Zealand and to the attractive east coast of New Holland and the subsequent inauguration of white settlement. These ventures coincided with the beginning of vast political, economic and social changes in the lands to the north as a result of the industrial revolution and the establishment of British predominance.

Hitherto the areas had shared little of their history. The contacts of the southern lands with the north had been slighter even than their own experience. The Australian population was related to peoples of whom merely traces remained in the Archipelago. Only a few of the later Malay peoples contacted Australia's northern coast, and none at all the more distant, if more hospitable, shores of the Land of the Long White Cloud, colonised from the Pacific. The early Europeans explored some of the western and northern coasts of New Holland and hit upon Van Diemen's Land and New Zealand: they inaugurated no colonies, neither European nor Asian nor African slave.

The impact of common world forces in the late eighteenth and nineteenth centuries still did not produce a common history. The unknown south land was seen and, settled, saw itself as Austral-Asia. But it forged no substantial links with the north, for the British did not foster any commercial ties and did not establish a political control in the islands that might have associated them with the colonies that monopolised the south. Their command of the sea preserved their Austral-Asian settlements, but did nothing to connect them with Asia. On the contrary, European migrations produced a severance rather

Introduction

than a development of contacts with Asia; and Australasia became merely a convenient term for Australia and New Zealand. Contacts with Europe, or rather with Britain, predominated, and it was in relation with them, or in reaction to them, that Australia and New Zealand sought individuality and gained self-consciousness. The colonial lands of tropical Asia were *Terra Septentrionalis Incognita*.

The twentieth century saw some growth in economic contacts, increasing commerce, for instance, between Australia and the Netherlands Indies, between Australia and North Borneo. But the revolution was a political one. It was the result of the decline of British preponderance, the rise of Japan, the collapse of the colonial structure in Southeast Asia. The Australasian Dominions, as they had now become, had to develop a new political relationship with Southeast Asia, in the context, furthermore, of the joining of a world struggle for power that at times focused on the same area, in the context, too, of the emergence of a powerful and populous China. Australia, moreover, came to share a common frontier in New Guinea with the largest of the new Southeast Asian states. The extent to which the Dominions should readjust their policies became a matter of controversy in the diplomatic and military fields. But still deeper issues were raised. The immigration restrictions of the nineteenth and early twentieth centuries were brought into question. And attempts were made to overcome the emotional gulf between Asian and Australasian societies, and to remedy ignorance of the unknown north.

Faced suddenly with the splendour, tragedy and excitement of the Southeast Asian picture, Australians and New Zealanders might well be bewildered. Attempts to understand it involve attempts to master unfamiliar names and unfamiliar concepts, to comprehend societies quite different from an urban democratic norm. The kaleidoscopic character of the picture, its enormous variety, the intensity of its chiaroscuro, are also challenging. The author is painfully aware of the limited extent to which he may be able to help meet that challenge, aware of the risks taken in discussing so vast an area, substantially yet spasmodically covered by authoritative writings, aware that his own ignorance may in fact exaggerate the extent to which the area is unknown. But this readiness to apologise for attempting a concise history of Southeast Asia is slightly tempered by his belief that Australasians may prove in the event to be relatively well equipped to understand it. He hopes, too, that it will

x

interest those in other parts of the world concerned with the past and present both of Southeast Asia and Australasia.

Southeast Asia is here taken to include present-day Vietnam, north and south, Laos, Cambodia, Thailand, Burma, the Philippines, Malaysia, Indonesia, and the Andaman and Nicobar islands (part of the Indian Republic). It is indeed a vast area by European if not by Australian standards. It is indeed marked by an astonishing diversity in all the fields of human activity, diversity in language, religion and culture, diversity in economic, social and political organisation, diversity so copious it scarcely needs illustration. One has only to contrast the peasant masses of central Burma and east and central Java with the fishermen of the seven thousand typhoon-struck islands of the Philippines; the temples of Bangkok with the long houses of the Borneo Dayaks or the blocks of government flats in Singapore; the dark forests of rubber and the open sores of tin mines in western Malaya; the rudimentary government of the Andamans with the parliament in Kuala Lumpur or the People's Democracy in Hanoi; the wealth and the squalor that are marked by cultural dichotomies also; extremes of westernisation and remnants of the stone age.

For the general historian the central problem of abridgment is here at its keenest. The simplest method has always been continuous and direct reference of the past to the present: historians have been, to borrow words Marc Bloch used of Renan and Taine, 'obsessed with origins'. But such a historiography may not help towards a genuine understanding even of the present, such as Australasians may seek of Southeast Asia. There is, however, one theme that facilitates the presentation of its history without doing violence to the validity of the past, that avoids over-simplification and promotes a deeper understanding. The area has always been, as C. A. Fisher puts it, marked by 'demographic immaturity';[1] while, at the same time, its geographical location places it across some of the world's most important routes and adjacent to some of its most complex civilisations. Some parts of the area are by now highly developed, some scarcely at all. The great rice-growing valleys, the mineral areas, the trading foci, have become centres of population: in other regions the physical obstacles have been too great; and mountain, jungle, and swamp have cut off one centre from another.

The area may be seen as throughout its history a frontier area, variously populated by immigrants whose distinctness was preserved, even enhanced by its regionalisation. The second major feature of the area is its geographical position. It has been peopled in great part overland from the north, a movement impeded and filtered by the jungle and high mountain chains of that region. Only in North Vietnam is the geographical boundary with China relatively open. That with the Indian subcontinent is defined, if uncertainly, by the jungle and swamp familiar to the soldiers of the Burma campaign, soldiers of the Commonwealth and the would-be Japanese invaders of India. To the southeast lies the also uncertain jungle frontier of New Guinea and the sharper inhospitability of the North Australian coastline. But if largely, though in places ambiguously, cut off by land, the area is immensely open by sea and it stands at the confluence of great world routes. This further diversified the peoples and influences that reached it. The area has a unity in its very diversity: a theme for its history may be found in a survey of the interactions between outside influences and given conditions; and inasmuch as the adjustment continues, disturbing and fructifying, that history may especially help in understanding the complexity of contemporary Southeast Asia.

If this theme makes it possible, even desirable, to discuss the history of Southeast Asia as a whole, and disposes of the criticism that Southeast Asia is an unsatisfactory unit of historical study, it also helps to justify the use of the term 'Southeast Asia'. The Japanese and Chinese saw a unity in the area and respectively called it 'Nan-yo' and 'Nanyang', the 'southern seas', the latter appellation later borrowed by the Europeans in naming the 'South China Sea'. Others called the area, for instance, 'Further India'. These terms, however, emphasise particular aspects of the diversity of the area, contemplating it as a province of Chinese or Indian cultural influences. The term 'Southeast Asia', one that came into use in the second world war, though not then including the identical area (Mountbatten's command included Ceylon also), is paradoxically a more neutral one and thus preferable. Equally, if the area is not to be seen merely in relation to India and China, its development is not a study of 'East-West relations'. The significance of these connexions can only appear as part of the general history of the area, which must be structured in the least misleading way.

The theme suggests other cautions in approaching the history of Southeast Asia. Clearly it would be unhelpful to deal throughout with the history of the countries as known today one by one. This would deprive us of some of the benefit of treating the area as a whole and impose the (indeed insecure) structure of the present too heavily upon the fluctuations of the past. By the nineteenth century, on the other hand, it may be more helpful to deal individually, if comparatively, with countries that had by then assumed a more recognisable form.

Another problem is that of terminology. The sort of history written and read today has long been primarily a European phenomenon, and the terms it uses carry overtones of the European past. In applying them to Southeast Asian history, we have continuously to remember the different course of its social and political development. Categories like church and state, nobility and bourgeoisie, bureaucracy and local authority, town and peasantry, may be necessary; but their inexactitude must be borne in mind.

Linked with this problem is that of chronology. Even if the Christian calendar is employed for the sake of convenience, that must not mean imposing a periodisation that, initially also a convenience, ends by obstructing understanding. Most of our schemes of periodisation, including the Marxist, have been built about peculiarly European developments, the fall of the nobility and the rise of the bourgeoisie, the struggle of church and state, Renaissance and Reformation, the rise of modern science. To apply such categories to Asian history — Indian, Chinese, or Southeast Asian — is quite misleading. Was not Pegu in Lower Burma a great city for the early sixteenth century Bolognese visitor Ludovico di Varthema? And at Malacca, reported Dirck Pomp, 'all exquisitenesses are . . .'[2] Here were cities that awed visitors from Renaissance Europe. Their remarks are evidence of a medieval phase in Europe, not in Asia.

Our sources for early periods of Southeast Asian history are indeed scanty. Much of the available documentary material is the work of outsiders, especially of Chinese annalists, for Indian writers were little concerned with mundane things. Though, for instance, Vietnamese annals exist that date from the thirteenth century, the shifting character of political power in Southeast Asia, and disasters heaven-made as well as man-made, tended to prevent the preservation of documents in archives or centres of learning. Archaeological and epigraphical evidence is more ample, though, perhaps paradoxically, its testimonies of greatness were uncovered and interpreted largely again by outsiders, by Europeans from Raffles to Winstedt, from Mouhot to Groslier. But again climate, insects, mould, rainfall, alluvium, exuberant and destructive vegetation eliminate traces of man's influence; and if the temples of Borobudur or Angkor remain, there is little trace of the royal but wooden cities that surrounded them, still less of peasant villages that supported them.

The other European temptation is to divide Southeast Asian history into colonial phases, Indian and Chinese, Portuguese or Iberian, Dutch and British. But this tendency was again criticised by Europeans, such as van Leur, even before the crisis of European colonialism produced a more general change in the climate of opinion (a sufficiently rare tribute to the academic, whose expanding researches often remain within traditional interpretative bounds). 'With the arrival of ships from western Europe', van Leur complained in reviewing a general history of Indonesia,[3] '. . . the Indies are observed from the deck of the ship, the ramparts of the fortress, the high gallery of the trading-house . . .' More recently, with the challenge to colonialism itself, the controversy has intensified. Perhaps the consensus would confirm his denial that the history of the Indonesian area — still less that of Southeast Asia — can be described in the sixteenth, seventeenth and eighteenth centuries in purely Dutch terms, as if Dutch colonialism were the only significant activity; and his belief that the predominantly European sources of the period have to be used with caution. On the other hand, historians would not underestimate the impact of European influences in particular areas and fields of activity.

In the period from the late eighteenth century European influences greatly augmented. European travellers now differed from Ludovico di Varthema and Dirck Pomp and found Southeast Asia often decayed and corrupt, poor, unprogressive. James Brooke, for instance, believed the Archipelago to be in 'a state of anarchy and confusion, as repugnant to humanity as it is to commercial prosperity',[4] and the future king Mongkut of Siam he thought 'a highly accomplished gentleman, for a semi-barbarian'.[5] Even so, colonial history does not comprise the history of Southeast Asia, and our system of periodisation must not encourage a misinterpretation that, moreover, could in turn promote a misunderstanding of the contemporary situation.

In this book some periodisation is attempted. It is broken into three parts, with the late eighteenth century, or more specifically the 1760s, forming a major dividing date. Firstly, some remarks on the geography and resources of the area precede a brief account of its history up to 1500 A.D., and then follows an account of the sixteenth, seventeenth and eighteenth centuries. The second part comprises a discussion of the long period of substantial change stretching from the late eighteenth to the early twentieth century, and a concluding section attempts to deal with the contemporary phase of Southeast Asian history inaugurated by the Japanese invasions. These periods are not to be labelled Indian (still less medieval) or Dutch or British. The aim is rather to provide a framework for conveniently appraising the interaction of external influences and given conditions that forms the theme of a book about a frontier area.

Such a theme is perhaps especially appropriate for an Australasian essay in Southeast Asian history. Australians and New Zealanders may see their history in frontier terms also, though the interaction of external influences and given conditions has left them with a much less complex picture than that of Southeast Asia; yet with dead as well as live cities, with shifting cultivation and impermanent settlement; and with a chiaroscuro even sharper and contrasts — between outback and opera house, Yirrkala and Canberra, the boomerang and the Boeing — even more abrupt. If comparisons provoke wonder rather than generate analysis, a history of contacts between the regions seems to afford even less scope. But perhaps for this very reason, there is less cause to fear that a survey that sees Southeast Asia as *Terra Septentrionalis* will distort as much as one that sees it as the Nanyang, as Further India, or even as a field of European colonial activity. It may be, indeed, that Australians and New Zealanders are able to free themselves from the tyranny of European terminologies and chronologies without flying to an 'anti-colonial' extreme, and so promote a wider understanding of Southeast Asian history. If on the other hand, the shortness of their history and the tightness of their British connexion commits them to some sort of love-hate relationship with European influences (such as the Russian intelligentsia indulged), this itself may help them to comprehend, say, the attitudes of Indonesian intellectuals towards the Dutch legacy. Australians may give warning by example, too, of the way such a relationship may produce a violent reaction and extreme nationalist interpretations of the past — a historiography that in fact was the more 'colonial' for being so determinedly nationalist. If Australians and New Zealanders may share apprehensions of China felt in Southeast Asia, and uphold restrictive immigration policies directed originally against the Chinese, they ought, in view of their own background, to understand the Nanyang

Chinese community drawn, as C. P. FitzGerald has pointed out, not from the upper-class of their homeland, yet not the less loyal to its traditions and its culture.[6]

It seems possible then that Australasians may find in their own experience some means of understanding the Southeast Asian picture. The author hopes that he will be able to aid in this by identifying some common as well as by noting many diverse factors in the different histories of these regions. He also believes that, for related reasons, Australasian historians may be able to make a special contribution to scholarly research on Southeast Asia at a time when students in one-time imperial centres may be less attracted.

PART ONE

Southeast Asia to about 1760

1 Geographical Survey

IF THIS presentation of Southeast Asian history is to stress attempts to overcome physical obstacles and to build civilisations and centres of political power, the first concern of a preliminary geographical survey is with the resources of the area. Its second concern is with the position of Southeast Asia in relation to the rest of the world, in relation to China and Japan, India, Europe, America and Australasia, and with the ways peoples and cultures have reached this frontier area from outside.

In the physiographic as in other spheres, Southeast Asia is complex. Older mountain ranges form the core of the Indo-Chinese peninsula, and beyond them there are two axes of folding, one approximately latitudinal, one predominantly longitudinal, trending towards the eastern parts of the Indonesian Archipelago. In present-day Burma, for instance, the old mountains lie to the east, while on the west side of the Irrawaddy valley, between it and the Bay of Bengal, the folds of the Arakan Yoma tend to divide off Arakan from the rest of the country. These folds proceed south in two ridges, then bend eastward, running through the Andamans, west Sumatra, Java, Bali, the Lesser Sunda and Banda islands, and in some regions are yet, as the Balinese know to their cost, volcanically active. The other, more longitudinal, line of folds creates the peaks of the Philippines, and in the Moluccas and beyond produces extraordinary contours, vast ocean depths and high mountain peaks. The core on the Indo-Chinese peninsula itself fans out in a mass of rugged malarial ridges dividing off the principal river basins. One series of ranges runs down the narrow Malayan Peninsula — narrowest in the Kra region — to present-day Johore, and just beyond the mainland ceases.

Characteristic of the volcanic mountain structure of the area are its mineral riches. The Indo-Malayan mountains contain not only lead, silver, zinc and antimony, but the greater part

3

of the world's tin and tungsten, more easily worked further south, in Malaya, Bangka and Biliton, because heavier rains have washed it down in alluvial mud. There are scattered deposits of iron in eastern Malaya, in the Philippines also, and in the Riau-Johore area there is bauxite. Gold lured early Indian traders to Malaya; and gold was a welcome resource in the Philippines in the depression of the 1930s. The area has little good coal, but considerable mineral oil, in upper Burma, in Sumatra, and in Borneo (both in present-day Kalimantan and in Brunei).

Important also are the effects of relatively more recent geological developments, such as volcanic outpourings. Sumatra is an instance: but here the ejecta have been largely acidic in character, and in only a few areas, for instance the region of Medan on the east coast, are there ejecta basic in character and forming fertile soils. The Lampongs in south Sumatra were fertilised by the great explosion of the Krakatau volcano in the last century. In Java volcanoes have produced basic and fertile soils, and farmers press riskily close to the summit of Merapi. The other source of particularly fertile soils in Southeast Asia is the alluvial deposits created by the great rivers, the Irrawaddy, the Menam Chao Praya in Thailand, the Red River in northern Vietnam, the Mekong in the south, the Solo in Java. The high rainfall means considerable erosion, especially where, as in central Burma, it is preceded by a period of drought. Hence the rivers carry considerable deposits, borne far abroad in time of flood. The delta of the Irrawaddy, though eroded by the sea, expands some three miles per century; the deltas of the Solo in Java and the Mekong expand more rapidly still. The shallow seas of the 'Sunda Shelf' and the mangroves help to retain the silt. In the Philippines, both sources of fertile soils are present: the soil is renewed by streams in the Cagayan valley, by ash on Negros.

These processes produce areas of great fertility, but generally the soils of Southeast Asia are poor, sterile, red laterites, created by the leaching action of heavy rainfall which, with low organic content, has washed the silica away and left clays. This process is, of course, least noticeable in the drier areas, where indeed evaporation may draw up plant nutriments into the soil, for instance in east Java or central Burma. Upon laterites an elaborate vegetation may exist — there are in the Archipelago alone, it is thought, some 45,000 species of flowering plants — and its luxuriance has often misled visitors as to the fertility of the soils. In fact this vegetation is the result of a delicate balance, and it lives off its decaying self rather than from the soil. Excessive destruction of this vegetation may lead to erosion and further impoverishment. Heavy rainfall, dense vegetation, and the existence of a continental shelf, mean that there are many swamps in Southeast Asia — in eastern Sumatra, west and south Borneo, south-west New Guinea — the greatest of all obstacles to settlement.

The rainfall in most areas is over eighty inches a year. It is, however, not uniform. In the equatorial belt there is no true dry season and there is no real variation in temperature. To the north there is a seasonal rhythm, varied, in the Philippines (in Luzon and the Visayas) by the high incidence of typhoons. The differences are indeed partly the work of the winds, pressing south in the northern winter months, north during the rest of the year. Other variations are produced by relief and aspect. The sunshine period is relatively low: but in areas where there are long sunny periods, as in the dry season in Java, extensive rice farming is encouraged.

The other factors to be considered are those that relate the position of Southeast Asia to the rest of the world. Overland it is clearly difficult to enter Southeast Asia. Most peoples have, it seems, originally come over the northern mountain ridges, but the obstacles are great, and help to account for the relatively slight population of Southeast Asia till recent times: even about 1830 the total was probably around only 25,000,000, while that of China has been estimated at 350,000,000. No great mountains divide off the Red River delta from the south China littoral, however, and these areas were peopled by the same movement. 'Tonkin' has long been open to Chinese influence. The mountains rise only in central Vietnam. Another Southeast Asian boundary — that of Arakan with the Indian sub-continent, with Bengal — is better defined, though somewhat ambiguous. Far away to the southeast, New Guinea, poor and isolated, has been almost to the present day 'the dead end of the archipelago',[7] while remoteness or inhospitability or both have isolated Australasia from most of the population movements to the north. The Philippines have been peopled from the Chinese mainland — across a seaward frontier — but chiefly from the south, from within Southeast Asia.

No area, not even Europe itself, compares with Southeast Asia in the high proportion of coast to land area; and the high rainfall and numerous rivers — though they often have bars across where the tides do not scour away alluvial muds — add to the accessibility of the region from the sea. This accessibility

5

is particularly marked in the Peninsula and Archipelago, which project, furthermore, across major sea-routes linking Europe and Southeast Asia with East Asia and the Pacific, and thus additionally became centres for the diffusion of overseas influences.

In what ways have peoples originating overland or overseas exploited the resources of the area, at once contending, even into modern times, with malaria and cholera and the cruel diseases of the humid tropics? After the most primitive phases emerged the practice of shifting cultivation or swidden agriculture, in which temporary clearings in the jungle are utilised, then abandoned. The practice still continues mostly in remote areas, enabling a modest population to live off poor soils which more intensive exploitation damages. It is an agriculture that inserts itself in the self-renewing process of the jungle and can, unless delicately managed, itself lead to erosion. Examples are the *ladang* cultivation of rice in many parts of Indonesia, the system of *ray* in Vietnam, of *taung-ya* in Burma, of *caiñgin* in the Philippines. In more fertile areas, enjoying also, perhaps, other favourable circumstances, such as a long sunshine period, more intensive cultivation of rice was undertaken by sedentary farmers, and further intensification produced by irrigation and the control of flood waters — and of human labour. So were gradually developed the great rice-growing centres of central Burma, of the Red River and the Menam valleys; so emerged the contrast between the *sawah* lands of east and central Java and the *ladang* of west Java and still more of Sumatra.

Inshore, and on lakes, canals and swamps, the waters of Southeast Asia early afforded fine fishing. In time the sea and rivers offered other resources. River-mouth settlements were particularly well-placed to take advantage of trade passing through Southeast Asian waters as well as of trade involving Southeast Asian products. Overseas demand led to the production of spices for export, fitted into the shifting pattern of agriculture, to the collecting of jungle produce, even to the exploitation of alluvial tin. But it was only in a quite recent phase that new crops — like coffee and rubber — were fitted into the pattern, and that minerals, oil as well as tin, were exploited on a major scale; at the same time as new methods were promoting an intensive rice agriculture in the delta regions, as in southern Burma or southern Vietnam, or inserting sugar into the *sawah* pattern of east and central Java, or creating processing and light industries. These vast changes of scale, and of practice, belong to the nineteenth and twentieth centuries.

In the early centuries of the Christian era, nevertheless, some of the fertile regions of Southeast Asia had become major centres of population and power. But masters even of these, faced by physical obstacles and poor communications, could with difficulty control wide areas or establish integrated kingdoms. Nor, equally, could there be any unity among these regions scattered over Southeast Asia, none of them able to exercise a unifying influence and each of them going their several ways. The Irrawaddy, Menam, Mekong and Red River centres were isolated one from another by mountain barriers. The other early centre of population, in east and central Java, was too peripheral decisively to affect the future of the whole area.

Other early centres of power were the trading foci. Their power was clearly relatively greater in the Malay Peninsula and the Archipelago than on the mainland, where that of the river-valleys was more influential. For a similar reason, their power was less in east and central Java than elsewhere in the Archipelago. But again river-mouth settlements could scarcely exercise a powerful integrating control upon the tribes of the interior: the fissures in Archipelagic society again existed from an early period. Moreover, among these petty states there was no real source of unity, though there were attempts to create commercial empires in the Archipelago, centred generally in the Straits of Malacca, held together only with difficulty by obligations more often breached than observed. What was needed was power backed up by the possession of rich agricultural territory. Such existed in east and central Java, but it was too peripheral to assert a continuously effective control over the major trading centres even of the Archipelago.

Political organisation was unable to overcome the obstacles raised by geographical and cultural division to integration and unification. Political units were unstable, political change part of a continuous adaptation to changing conditions. Political forms were imprecise and political boundaries were fluid. A further reflection of the demographic immaturity of the area was the flexible relations between states. There might be occasional conquests by one state of another, irregular tribute from one state to another. But tribute might be paid by an inferior state to more than one superior state as a matter of expediency, and imperial relationships might merely mean a tangle of sometimes conflicting customary obligations.

The increase in economic development and in the power of the state from the late eighteenth century could perhaps have created a greater unity in Southeast Asia: some of the geographical, some of the cultural divisions might have been over-come. But the establishment of European power in Southeast Asia was to bring the establishment of European political divisions: if the British predominated, they saw in their world-wide policies reason for permitting, while it was still theirs to permit, the fragmentation of almost all the area among European empires. The focal point of Singapore was given some of its potential command in Southeast Asia with the resources of the British and British Indian empires. But elsewhere other colonial powers created new political units, the French basing themselves on the developing Mekong basin and then on the delta of the Red River, the Dutch basing themselves on the fertile lands of east and central Java, a cradle of Archipelagic empire-makers. European notions — and European rivalries — also led to attempts to delineate boundaries with a European precision hitherto alien to Southeast Asia. Even within these boundaries the Europeans did not generally seek cultural or ethnic unification. Furthermore, the great economic changes of the period presented the Southeast Asian peoples with immense problems of adaptation, and many opportunities in a time of opportunity were absorbed by migrants from India, but above all from China, coming to Southeast Asia not unprecedentedly but in unprecedented numbers.

The nineteenth and twentieth centuries did not solve — indeed they amplified — the problems created by geography and history in the Southeast Asian area. They were handed on, as it were to the nation-states of the contemporary period, the product of yet another — and an imported — system of political relations in the area. With the results of this process, at a time, too, when world-forces were in fact impinging more than ever upon the area, Australia and New Zealand are much concerned. Their nineteenth and twentieth century history runs a different course: their political unity and their independence were ensured sooner; they were able to limit, if not solve, the problems of ethnic and cultural integration. But this was in part because their earlier history ran a different course. And if the Australians and New Zealanders of today seek an understanding of the unknown north, they must seek it in the history of its more remote as well as its more recent past.

2 Early States and Population Movements

IN PREHISTORIC TIMES the general movement of population in the Southeast Asian region was, it seems, southwards from southwest China, penetrating thinly through difficult mountain territory. It is possible that the Australoid people evolved in Southeast Asia and that the Negrito peoples came from India, while the Melanesoid peoples may derive from a mixture of the two. But the southward movement predominates and persisted into historic, even into recent times. Some of the migrations continued into Australia, leaving traces behind in Southeast Asia. Southeast Asia is, indeed, an ethnic museum, 'an anthropologist's paradise', as its chief historian calls it.[8] Its peculiar geographical features allowed the preservation of isolated primitive peoples and inhibited their absorption by those of more advanced cultures. Thus traces of the Australoid peoples may be found yet among the hill peoples of Flores and Timor. The Negritos include the Semang of Malaya, the Orang Akit of Sumatra, the Aeta of Luzon, the Tapiro of New Guinea, and the Andamanese. The Melanesoid are represented by the Bali Aga in remoter parts of Bali, by the Alfurs of the Moluccas, and above all by the Papuans.

Once, no doubt, more widespread, these peoples of the palaeolithic and mesolithic periods yielded in more accessible areas to the Nesiot peoples, with their neolithic culture, and the Pareoeans, creators of the Dongson or iron and bronze culture. These, it has been suggested, represent not two distinct migrations, but a series of southerly movements of 'progressively more Mongoloid peoples'.[9] Nesiot characteristics are marked among hill peoples of the mainland: the Wa and Palaung of Burma, the Kha of Laos, the Pnong of Cambodia, the Moi of Vietnam, the Jakun of the Malay Peninsula. They are marked, too, among some of the inland peoples of the Archipelago, like the Bataks of Sumatra, the Sasaks of Lombok, the Dayaks of Borneo, the Toradja of Celebes, the Bontoc and Ifugao 'Igorots'

9

of the Philippines, and the Nicobarese. They characterise also, it seems, the *orang laut,* the sea-gypsy peoples of the Archipelago. The Pareoean peoples include those that came to dominate the

richer lands, the accessible coasts and river mouths, and in course of time were to become themselves somewhat differentiated, as the Javanese and Sundanese are today, as are the

Bugis and the Balinese and the Achehnese. On the other hand, on the mainland, the related Pareoean peoples — such as the Mons of Burma and Siam, the Khmers and the Chams — were to be substantially absorbed or overwhelmed by later Pareoean peoples, like the Burmans, the Thais, Laos and Shans, and the Vietnamese.

Before these developments, however, Southeast Asia's seaward contacts with the outside world had been amplified by the expansion of trade that occurred in the early centuries of the Christian era. To some extent this had a European origin: Rome unified the shores of the Mediterranean and inaugurated through the Middle East and India a demand for Southeast Asian products, gold, spices, scented woods, resins. Furthermore, nomadic disturbances in the pre-Christian era had closed the routes through Bactria to Siberian gold, and Indian merchants thus again looked to Southeast Asia. But it is evidence also of a Chinese commercial interest that we find in Chinese records reference to one of the earliest states of Southeast Asia, to which this commercial impulse must have helped to give birth. The Chinese called it Funan and it occupied the Mekong delta. Its port, Oc Eo, has been investigated by French archaeologists.

The first reference to the state of Champa — the country of the Cham tribes — appears to put its foundation at about the late second century A.D., and its centre was then somewhat south of modern Hué. The Chams were sea-raiders, but colonised the fertile pockets in the mountains of present-day central Vietnam at the expense of more primitive tribes. Their state faced immense difficulties in trying to assert political unity in so unfavourable a terrain, and in meeting the invasions of other peoples, the Khmers and the Vietnamese.

A number of river-valley political units appeared in the Malay Peninsula at this time, for instance Lankasuka, whose existence is confirmed by the Malay and Javanese chronicles. It was situated in the region of modern Patani, while other states appear to have lain to the north.

The position of all these states was clearly determined in part by the routes of trade between India and China. Clearly, too, the traders preferred to cross the isthmus, rather than risk the route through the yet undeveloped areas surrounding the Straits of Malacca and Singapore. States flourished in the isthmian region, and indeed this induced Funan to establish its supremacy there in the third century. Lankasuka was to revive with Funan's decline in the late fifth century.

This trade route perhaps also attracted the Khmers, who

11

lay to the north of Funan on the lower and middle Mekong in what is now northern Cambodia and the southern part of the kingdom of Laos. In the seventh century they established a new kingdom with a capital near the present city of Kompong Thom. In the ninth century the Khmer kingdom, 'Cambodia', was refounded by Jayavarman II and endowed with a new capital at Angkor — which may have been bigger than ancient Rome — by a successor, Yasovarman I, and by Suryavarman II. In subsequent centuries the Khmers continued to expand westward, contending with the Mons who had founded the kingdom of Dvaravati, centred at the present city of Nakorn Pathom, and with the Thais of the Menam valley. They waged campaigns against the Chams, too, and in the late twelfth century, under Jayavarman VII, builder of Angkor Thom and the Bayon monument, established a loose sway over their kingdom. Finally, they also fought with another opponent of Champa, the kingdom of Dai Viet to the north.

In the Archipelago the expansion of trade was leading to new political possibilities. The decline of Funan led in the seventh century to the first of several attempts to the south to create a commercial empire, centralising the trade of a number of petty river-mouth statelets or levying exactions upon it, and creating a fragile political structure thus dependent on command of the sea. The empire was Sri Vijaya, centred near the present-day city of Palembang in south Sumatra, then a good position for controlling the Straits of Malacca and of Sunda. At this stage, however, it was still important to control the isthmus, which had not entirely yielded its position in Asian trade, and this remained an important object of Sri Vijaya policy under its Sailendra dynasty. 'The Sailendra thalassocracy was made up of a confederation of trading ports on the fringe of the primeval forest', and land routes were unimportant save on the isthmus.[10] The empire had no great resources of fertile land and population to back up its fragile claims. Such there were in the Archipelago only in east and central Java, where some shadowy kingdoms existed from the early centuries A.D. It was once thought, indeed, that Sri Vijaya secured control over central and eastern Java in the eighth century. But the Sailendras ruling central Java at that time, whose wealth is illustrated by the Borobudur remains, seem not to have ruled Sri Vijaya, where the Sailendra dynasty appears only after it has fallen in Java. There is no territorial connexion. Among the areas over which Sri Vijaya did establish the sort of supremacy a maritime empire could expect to maintain were the regions of Jambi and

Panei on the east coast of Sumatra, that of Acheh to the north, the Nicobar islands, and the isthmus and Kedah. It was the latter region not surprisingly that attracted the Chola raiders from India in the eleventh century. From their attacks Sri Vijaya was to recover, but not in Kedah.

Meanwhile the centre of the Javanese kingdom was moved from central to east Java, and this brought its rulers in closer touch with the trade between the now developing regions to the eastward and the Straits. It brought also in the late tenth century a struggle with and defeat by Sri Vijaya, striking at a potential rival commercial empire. The Javanese kingdom collapsed in the face of this external threat, coupled as it was with internal regional dissension. However, before the middle of the eleventh century, the great statesman Airlangga had pulled together a new kingdom, and weakened Sri Vijaya accepted its sharing in the trade between the further parts of the Archipelago and the Straits. The successor of this state, the kingdom of Kediri, also controlled much of the trade to the east, and Ternate in the Moluccas was a vassal state. In turn it collapsed in 1222, to be reconstituted as the kingdom of Singosari. Of this the last and greatest king, Kertanagara, planned to make the resources of Java tell throughout the Archipelago. The despatch of a powerful expedition abroad, however, gave discontented vassals a chance to rebel. A new king was set up, overthrown by Kertanagara's son-in-law as a result of a Mongol invasion, and a new capital then created in the lower Brantas valley at Majapahit. Another attempt was made at once to hold together a Java kingdom in face of regional obstacles and to use its rather peripheral position but substantial resources to create an empire in the Archipelago. Rebellion and division delayed the imitation of Kertanagara, but Gaja Mada, chief minister from 1330, was able to adopt a policy of expansion. Bali was conquered, and Majapahit's supremacy established over coastal parts of Sumatra and Borneo. The extent of 'Great Majapahit' has indeed been a matter of historical controversy. C. C. Berg has strongly criticised the more extravagant notions of fourteenth century Javanese hegemony presented in Prapanca's poem *Nagarakertagama* as a flattering court myth. But legend and actuality might also be reconciled by emphasising the necessarily loose control Majapahit must in face of given conditions have exercised in the Archipelago. There may have been a wide empire, but it must also have been a fragile empire.

This period saw a development of the southern parts of the

13

Malay Peninsula, coinciding with the shift from the isthmian to the Straits route. In the late fourteenth century Majapahit claimed supremacy over the largest state there, Pahang, and over Tumasik, or Singapore, in the extreme south, which had controlled the 'Keppel Harbour' passage between Pedro Branca and Karimun for most of the century. On Keppel Harbour itself was a community of *orang laut,* sea-gypsies not absorbed, controlled or civilised by the new political structure and committing outrages on junks that visited the port. The city consisted of temples and other important buildings on the hill, which was cut into terraces, structures of atap and bamboo on brick and stone foundations; and on the plain, the dwellings of the citizens, surrounded by rampart and ditch. Civil war in Majapahit in the early fifteenth century weakened its position in the Archipelago. On the Peninsula the way was open for the rise of a new state, Malacca, whose fortunes were to be associated with the rise of Islam. But the Thais had also been pressing into the Peninsula during the fourteenth century.

The Peninsula was indeed in some sense a boundary between the Archipelago and the mainland. In the Archipelago, the Pareoean peoples were increasingly becoming differentiated. On the mainland, there were, on the other hand, major new population movements, including those of the Thais and the related Laos and Shans. The existence of empires in the Archipelago may have helped to restrict these movements to the mainland. Also undoubtedly important were the resistance of existing Mon and Khmer and Cham peoples, and the divisions among the later peoples, between the Shans and the Burmans, for instance.

The Tibeto-Burmans had been descending the Irrawaddy valley probably since the later centuries B.C., but shortly before the eleventh century A.D. they began to enter the lowlands of the dry zone and by 1054 were sufficiently numerous to establish the first truly Burman dynasty at Pagan. Hitherto 'Burma' had been populated by Pyu and Mon peoples. In lower Burma the Mons were in contact with Mon states in the valley of the Menam: the kingdom of Dvaravati in lower 'Siam' was indeed the centre of Mon power. Of the Pyus, less is known: lying more to the north, they were perhaps a vanguard of the Burmans, subsequently merged or submerged. The Burmans made use in the dry zone of an irrigation system already developed by the Mons, and gradually pushed south displacing that people from political power. The first king of Pagan, Anahwrahta (1044-77), united under his sway most of Burma Proper, with northern Arakan, mostly inhabited by Burmans,

14

and lower Burma, the Mon country. His conquest of the Mon kingdom of Thaton inaugurated the long struggle of the Burmans, based on the central dry zone, to bring the Mons of the south into subjection. The Pagan kingdom was held together only with difficulty, and external stress, as with Java, brought about internal disruption. In the 1280s Mongol invasions brought about its collapse: northern Arakan proclaimed its ultramontane independence; and the Mons of the south rose in rebellion.

The second population movement on the mainland — that of the Vietnamese — was again one that spanned centuries of the historic period. They originated with a mixture of Chinese and earlier Pareoean tribes settled in the kingdom of Nan Yueh or Nam Viet which, in the second century B.C., extended from Kwangsi and Kwangtung through Tonkin to the north Annam coast. In 111 B.C., the region was annexed to China by the emperor Wu Ti, a few years before he conquered another outlying realm, Korea; and from that date Nan Yueh became an integral part of the Chinese empire as the province of Giao-chi, despite some attempts at securing independence led by families of Chinese origin or remnants of the old feudal aristocracy. In 679 the southern part of the province was reorganised as the prefecture of Annam. Its inhabitants seized a new opportunity to gain independence with the decline and collapse of the Tang dynasty in the tenth century, and Ngo Quyen founded the national dynasty of the Ngo (939-68). The new kingdom was difficult to hold together, for geography was only partly on its side. Geography, too, exposed it to its great neighbour, though to some extent these problems cancelled out. For instance Dinh Bo Linh was in the 960s able to unite the kingdom, now called Dai Co Viet, in face of a threat from the Sung dynasty. A third feature of Vietnamese history was the continued southward movement, a movement of conquest backed by colonisation. The Ly dynasty fought Champa in the eleventh century, and the victorious Ly Thanh-tong was to proclaim himself emperor of Dai Viet. The conflict weakened Champa in its struggle with Cambodia. But during the fourteenth century it continued to resist Dai Viet, especially under the indomitable Che Bong Na. The Vietnamese did not deliver the death blow till 1471 — it was delayed by Chinese incursions — but in that year Le Thanh-tong, greatest of the Le dynasty, took the capital Vijaya, after which only a diminutive Cham state remained. And Dai Viet came into closer contact — and intenser conflict — with the Khmers, at odds also with the Thais. The related Shan-Thai-Lao peoples had been moving down the Salween and Menam valleys under constant Chinese pressure in the early centuries A.D. Early in the twelfth century tiny Thai states appeared in the upper Menam valley, and

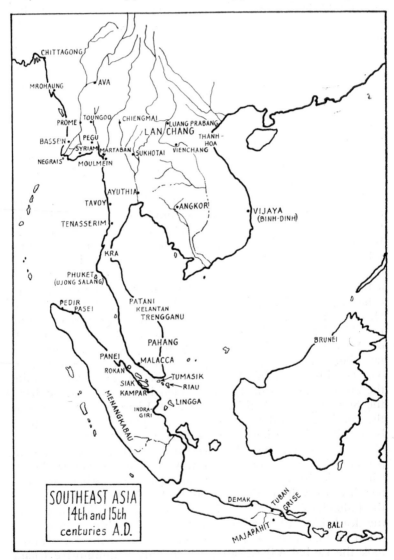

SOUTHEAST ASIA
14th and 15th
centuries A.D.

other Shan states appeared in this region and in 'Burma' early in the thirteenth century. The weakening of Khmer power through constant struggles with Champa and through megalomaniac building projects helps to explain this. The principal movement of the Lao-Thai-Shan peoples was, however, caused by Kublai Khan's destruction of the kingdom of Nanchao in Yunnan in 1253. A last great dispersal ensued and Thai military ruling classes took control in new regions in the Irrawaddy and Menam valleys.

The Burmans presented an obstacle to this movement in the former region, and the Shans were to be largely confined to the plateau country. It was true, however, that during the chaos following the Mongol sacking of Pagan in 1287, Shan dominion was for a while widely extended over the plains, and the Mongol withdrawal from upper Burma increased Shan activity there in the fourteenth century. In the anarchy and disorder of Burma itself Shan chieftains and the old dynasty played a part. Finally one of the Shan chiefs founded a new capital, Ava, more central to the dry region, and began to reduce the country to obedience. The kingdom remained Burman, though the king was a Shan. Meanwhile, following the collapse of Pagan, the Mon kingdom of Pegu had established its independence. The kingdom of Ava's chances of pursuing the traditional Burman policy of suppressing the Mons were, however, limited in the fourteenth century by the threat of the Shans on the northern and north-eastern frontiers. In 1385, Mingyi Swasawke took Prome and carried the fighting into the Mon country, but he failed to take Pegu. Further incursions into the Mon territory in about 1415 were brought to a halt by the Shan threat from the north. Again outside threats pointed up a kingdom's weakness: feudal chiefs allied with Shan chiefs; and the king of Arakan, which had been hitherto a field of conflict between Burmans and Mons, gained complete independence after 1430, established a new capital at Mrohaung and later took Chittagong. The divisions among the Shan chiefs assisted the survival of the Burman kingdom itself, as did the Shans' differences with the Chinese, but by the beginning of the sixteenth century they had virtually destroyed Ava.

The Mon-Khmer peoples of the Menam basin offered less resistance to the Thais than did the Burmans to the Shans, or even the Mons of the Irrawaddy valley to the Burmans. The southward advance here was marked by the occupation of a series of river-valley settlements, each in turn a forward capital. In the 1290s, a new Thai kingdom centred at Chiengmai replaced an old Mon state in that region. A Thai chief at Sukhothai, Rama Khamheng, conquered the Mons of the Menam valley. The subsequent decline of Sukhotai left the way open

17

for the creation of a new Thai state, and its centre, significantly in the south, was at Ayuthia on an island in the Menam where the king was crowned in 1350. To the north, meanwhile, the Lao states were welded by Fa Ngoum into the kingdom of Lan Chang in 1353. But the kingdom of Ayuthia characteristically spread its influence southward, and it gained control over much of the Malay Peninsula, including the isthmus and Tenasserim and Tavoy. The movement of their capital south intensified the Thais' struggle with Cambodia: warfare ensued between Ayuthia and Angkor, and soon the Khmers were hard pressed by the Thais and also by the still active Chams. The Ayuthia kingdom faced the problem of maintaining Thai unity: Sukhothai attempted to maintain independence; and Chiengmai was openly hostile for several centuries. Early in the fifteenth century there were, nevertheless, new invasions of Cambodia, but the attempt to make that state into a vassal was a failure. In 1438 Sukhotai became a province of Ayuthia, and the king-dom was reorganised. Continued trouble with Chiengmai, how-ever, weakened Ayuthia's hold on the Peninsula. This aided the rise there of the new Archipelagic power of Malacca.

If the re-establishment of Archipelagic empire was a further guarantee against southward movement from the mainland — though it was to prove no guarantee against invasion from the sea — on the mainland itself movement continued. Some of the hill tribes of today — the Karens, Chins, Kachins of Burma, the Miaos and Lolos of Laos and northern Vietnam — undoubtedly arrived at the same time as or soon after the Burmans and the Thais. Some, on the other hand, are relatively recent, almost contemporary arrivals. But those who came earlier remained in the hills, as indeed did some of the Thai tribes, thanks no doubt not only to geographical obstacles, but also to the oppo-sition of the Burmans and the Thais. It was only in the nine-teenth century that the Karens, who probably arrived in Burma before 1000 A.D., moved into the lowlands.

3 Trade and Society

IF up to the turn of the fifteenth century, the major population movements were overland, outside influences, perhaps even migrations, were reaching Southeast Asia by sea, placed as it was at the confluence of world routes. Certainly the area was commercially linked with China and with India and the Middle East and thus indirectly with Europe from the early centuries A.D. The nature of the overseas connexions that developed can be understood only after some appraisal of this commerce and the societies that it linked. The economies of India and China and of the great rice-growing areas of Southeast Asia — indeed of most parts of Southeast Asia — were and remained primarily subsistence economies. This did not mean that there was no regional trade. Nor did it mean that there was no foreign trade. But it did mean that international trade was limited in quantity, that it was not normally the bulk traffic in everyday commodities with which we are more familiar, that it was more a luxury traffic. Southeast Asia came to be both a commercial route and itself a source of supply. In the latter capacity, it provided tin, spices, ivory and ebony, gold and aromatics for India, and thus in part for Europe, in return receiving high-quality Indian piece-goods. To China, in return for silk, porcelain and lacquer ware, parasols and objects of ceremonial use, it supplied precious metals, jewels, cotton fabrics, betel nut, and aromatics.

Within Southeast Asia, the major agricultural areas of this period, central Burma, the Red River basin, the Menam valley, and east and central Java, came to support relatively dense and organised populations, a richly-developed village life providing the substructure for aristocratic and bureaucratic kingdoms. In relation to more primitive, or even sometimes closely related peoples in the hills, these kingdoms exercised often only a frail authority, based on occasional expeditions, not assimilation, and on feudal suzerainty rather than integrating political control: tribal structures were utilised rather than displaced. But in the core of the kingdom the king would seek greater political unity. He had still to contend with the forces of localism, aided by geography, and most of the kingdoms witnessed a struggle between feudal and anti-feudal principles of relating superstructure and substructure.

In Dai Viet the Chinese domination before 939 had worked against feudalism, and subsequent monarchs sought to maintain the Chinese system of a hierarchy of civil and military officials and of examinations for entry into it (though open only to those with titles or grades). This had, however, to be modified by other practices, for instance Ly Thai-tong (1028-54) gave fiefs to particular supporters, great officials receiving the right to levy taxes and *corvée* services on families in the villages of certain areas. In principle the right reverted to the state on the death of the official, in fact this did not always happen. But the monarch generally sought to make a more direct contact with the people through his bureaucracy and also to inhibit the development of landed magnates, thus increasing the tax yield of the peasantry and ensuring the state's command of its military service and *corvée*. On the other hand, a decree of 1266 allowed the nobles to recruit the vagabonds and workless for cultivating waste lands, and this helped them to build up latifundia. Wars, heavy taxes, natural disasters, also promoted the tendency to enserfment, while recovery from such crises was generally associated with new assertions of monarchical principle. Thus emperor Le Thai-to liberated Dai Viet from the Ming invaders in the 1420s and established a new capital called Dong-kinh (hence 'Tonkin'). He carried through a redistribution of land, in particular expropriating those who had joined the Ming. The bureaucracy was opened to sons of the people as well as to mandarins. Under his great successor, Le Thanh-tong, the official hierarchy received salaries, though also a share of revenue and harvests. Hereditary domains were still handed out as a reward for especially meritorious service. Generally, however, the desire to maintain maximum taxability led the monarchy to attempt to minimise the growth of landowning, to avert enserfment, to preserve communal village land through (non-equalising) repartition among villagers, and to limit slavery, the fate of criminals and prisoners-of-war, to the service of the palace and high mandarins.

Outside the expanding territories of Dai Viet, the state structures bore a less Chinese, but still not a feudal character. The example of the early Khmer kingdom was strong in the attempts made to centralise the Thai kingdom after the foundation of Ayuthia and again in the fifteenth century reign of Boromotrailokanat. In Trailok's kingdom privilege depended on office, not heredity, though the sons of officials had good chances of succession. Officials received a grant of land and a number of clients, but these could be withdrawn. As patrons, the officials had the right to exact *corvée* from the peasantry on their own behalf and the duty of organising the state's share. Slavery existed again, as in Dai Viet, for prisoners-of-war, and also for debtors, but their position was not greatly different from that of the freemen. In practice the system in Ayuthia was perhaps like that in Pagan. There the court authenticated the claims of the *myothugyis*, or hereditary township leaders, who combined the duties of police officer, minor judge, tax collector, and army recruiter. Certain sections of the population — under hereditary *myothugyis* — were set aside for the special support of the court. In Java, if the system bore any resemblance to that of the nineteenth century Mataram, there was apparently a somewhat similar dichotomy. One part of the state was in hereditary hands, one set aside for the support of the court. In this latter area, the ruler's relatives or high officials might receive revocable transfers of the right to levy taxes and services. But appanages were not allowed to become fiefs. Everywhere, in fact, a feudal structure was avoided.

Monarchs in the fertile regions of Southeast Asia sought in these ways to establish their power over the hill tribes and over the peasant villages. In relation to neighbouring states, they generally attempted to assert claims of suzerainty recognised by presentation of gifts and enforced by catastrophic intervention. Yet a fourth sphere of their political relations was with trading towns.

Essentially the trading towns of Southeast Asia were rivermouth settlements, engaging in the traffic between the interior and the outside world. In some areas — in Burma, in the Menam and Red River valleys, for instance — the interior would be relatively highly developed, and the political question would be the extent of the independence that the coastal town might acquire of the territorially-based state up-river. In large parts of the Peninsula and Archipelago, on the other hand, the interior was only superficially developed and *ladang* predominated. The trading settlements at the river months might be politically more advanced than the interior, and would seek to exercise some sort of control over the often more primitive peoples upstream, rather as the mainland states sought the vassalage of

21

the mountain peoples without contriving to assimilate them. In Sumatra, indeed, the inland kingdom of Menangkabau assumed a great eminence after the late thirteenth century. But the situation in Java was characteristically much more ambiguous. East and central Java were early the scene of intensive agriculture, relatively dense population, bureaucratic monarchy. The coastal towns, on the other hand, enjoyed, as the Archipelago's trade developed, greater relative power than those in mainland Southeast Asia. At times the Javanese monarchies, as has been seen, sought to control the trade of the Archipelago. At other times the trading towns were to direct the future of the monarchies.

There were other attempts at empire in the Archipelago besides the Javanese. The trading towns often originated, no doubt, in the local ex-tribal aristocracies along the coast and in the activities of energetic rulers who sought to participate in and develop the commerce along the river and live off it by duties or monopolies. In some cases they might compel the population, enslaved or subjected to *corvée*, to deliver spices, collect jungle produce, or mine tin. The development of these political structures produced some civilisation among the coastal Malay peoples. The settlement at Singapore has already been described. Even there, however, there were *orang laut*, not fully assimilated to more regular commercial and political activities, and ready to impede the trade of the port or, no doubt, to serve the purpose of political adventurers.

These petty principalities could scarcely contact each other overland: they could on the other hand be linked by the sea. It was this that made possible a larger form of government among them, the creation of Archipelagic empires composed of a number of principalities. The object of an empire-builder was the concentration of the trade of a number of rivers in a single entrepot and/or the exaction of duties or customs or services from the local rivers which might be farmed out more or less hereditarily to members of the imperial aristocracy or form appanages of the great officers of the empire. In this way larger political structures might rest upon the trade between the Peninsula and Archipelago and the outside world. The centralisation of the commerce of a vast but undeveloped area offered economic advantages. But the sort of control an imperial capital could maintain over dependent rivers was loose and required continuous effort. Continuous exertion of marine strength − 'un perpétuel recours à la force'[11] − was also required to direct international trade to the chosen port.

Sri Vijaya, the first of these empires, benefited from the position of its capital in the Straits: but its prosperity was based also on the enforced stapling of the international trade of Southeast Asia; and for this military and maritime power was unhesitatingly used. Of the inhabitants a Chinese author wrote in 1178: 'in fighting on land or on water none surpass them in impetuosity of attack . . . If some foreign ship, passing this place [Palembang], should not enter here, an armed party would certainly come out and kill them to the last'.[12] Their methods probably became more violent in the days of Sri Vijaya's decline. As for its tributaries, many acknowledged its supremacy only by paying yearly tribute and by sending warriors to fight for the empire in time of need, and constant predatory expeditions were required to keep them in hand. Maritime empires of this sort were thus fragile, impermanent, ill-defined, dependent on a number of factors human as well as geographical. One of Sri Vijaya's major drawbacks was lack of population in the poor lateritic lands of Sumatra and Malaya which were its centres. Majapahit was better provided in that respect, but its empire-building was hindered by the peripheral character of Java. The coastal towns of Java indeed tended to be politically oriented towards the Straits and the further east.

In the context of a relatively limited commercial development, and of geographical obstacles, political structures were based upon continuous attempts to assert control over human and economic resources often by the most forcible means. This also explains the nature of political change. If a prince determined to found an empire, if an adventurer sought to make himself a prince, if rebels sought to overthrow a prince, if a dependent principality sought independence, the outcome turned upon the mastery of the rivers, of the sea, of their commerce; upon marine warfare. This was indeed the dynamic political force of the Peninsula and Archipelago, the way change was effected, opportunities sought, ambitions realised, a legitimate process in the given conditions. The frequency of political change is not surprising, for change was an essential element in a political system adapted to those conditions. Thus one legitimate monarchy legitimately succeeded another. Thus new states and dynasties were founded by adventurers who found or forced their way into the system and whose unruly *orang laut* followers might in the process be absorbed into the growing civilisation of new port centres. Some might remain piratical: but it would be a mistake to apply such a term, especially with the minatory overtones it assumed relatively late even in Europe, to marine warfare, part of a legitimate because necessary process of political change.

There has been considerable controversy as to the character of the traders in the towns of mainland and Archipelagic Southeast Asia, and their influence on the polities of the area. Van Leur insisted on the pettiness of the traders themselves. 'One is constantly struck by the large numbers of traders, the bustle on shipboard . . .'[13] In reference to the Archipelago he drew a distinction between them and the money-holders, essentially aristocratic in origin, the ruling class who were the real traders. The 'peddlers' were of many nationalities, Malays and Javanese and those from further afield, Indians and Chinese, for instance. In Palembang, there were certainly separate quarters for each nationality, and contacts between the rulers of Southeast Asian states and the alien groups were generally maintained, it seems, through the recognition of headmen or Capitans. But some of the merchants were by no means peddlers. They engaged in substantial overseas traffic on their own. If there are suggestions that in the earliest centuries, Malay peoples engaged in overseas traffic, certainly by the fifteenth century, and probably long before, it was dominated by alien merchants, Indians, Chinese and Arabs, dealing mostly with the local aristocracy. The more local trades, the 'peddling', were occupied by Indonesians and Malays; there was no indigenous middle-class group; and even locally the Chinese were already adept middlemen. Some of the greatest overseas merchants no doubt assimilated themselves to the ruling groups, just as they were also broached by war and adventure. In the trade-oriented states of the Archipelago such merchants were likely to have more political influence than on the mainland. There power was likely to rest with the monarch and his bureaucracy. Before the end of the fifteenth century, however, a Chinese merchant, a native of Fukien, is known to have become a ranking official in Ayuthia. In the Archipelago, van Leur's thesis is certainly open to modification.

These considerations indeed assist an approach to the problem of Indian and Chinese influence in Southeast Asia in this period. Van Leur was concerned in particular with the Indianised states that covered much of the area from Funan onwards. Scholars had long attributed their Indianised culture and political life to some sort of Indian colonisation. Mookerji, in *Indian Shipping* (1912), pictured a Hindu imperialism occupying 'Farther India' from about the fourth century A.D. up to the Muslim invasions of India: 'swarms of daring adventurers from Gujarat ports, anticipating the enterprise of the Drakes and Frobishers, or more properly of the Pilgrim Fathers . . .'[14] This extreme view was not shared by Dutch historians like Krom, and his compatriot van Leur reacted even further against it. Arguing that commerce was in the hands of petty traders, he denied that they could have spread Indian culture. Its introduction must therefore have been the work of indigenous monarchs and aristocracies imitating the harbour principalities of India. If modifications of van Leur's views on Southeast Asian trade are acceptable, then his views on Indianisation must be modified also by the suggestion that they apply more completely to the mainland than to the Archipelago.

Indian influences reached Southeast Asia primarily overseas. The land connexion was substantially barred by mountainous jungle that formed a sort of frontier for Southeast Asia. The influences came along trade routes, brought by merchants and missionaries (the warlike Cholas of the eleventh century were raiders, anxious to break Sri Vijaya, and achieved nothing permanent). Some princes invited Indianisation, others, influenced by Indians or of Indian origin, promoted it. Why? In India princes called on the Brahmans who were trained in writing and administration. 'Their services were enlisted to assist the prince in the formal organisation in the Hindu manner of his patrimonial bureaucratic rule and status structure, and to consecrate the prince as a legitimate Raja or Maharaja . . .'[15] In Southeast Asia the organisation of administration and the legitimation of monarchy would help to preserve the state in difficult frontier conditions. Thus Indian culture — and not merely Hindu — colonised a frontier area. It spread into other fields, into crafts and customs; but created no caste system. Indian influence was especially evident in public architecture, in court ritual, in astrology and official religious observance.

In these ways, therefore, and to this degree, the states of Southeast Asia assumed their Indianised culture. D. G. E. Hall gives an account of the legend of Brahmanic inspiration used to explain the origins of the Funan dynasty, and later adopted by the Khmers. The Pyu and Mon rulers in early Burma were provided with legendary ancestors dating from the time of Buddha himself. Sri Vijaya was a Buddhist kingdom and the expansion of the Mahayana cult in the eighth century may have been associated with its imperial designs. The Sailendra dynasty in Java were Buddhist, their predecessors Saivite: and their success was marked by the building of Borobudur, the work, as Stutterheim showed, of Javanese stonemasons and

sculptors, influenced by indigenous religious ideas and practices that continued strongly among the people. The fall of
the Sailendra was associated with the revival of east Javanese
Saivism; and one of the new kings was responsible in his triumph
for the monuments of the Prambanan group. The eleventh
century kingdom of Airlangga, controlling central as well as
east Java, mixed Saivism and Mahayana Buddhism. Kertanagara
practised the cult of Siva-Buddha. Majapahit was the last of
the great Hindu-Buddhist kingdoms in this region.

On the mainland, meanwhile, the development of religious
cults had equally reflected political change. The foundation of
Angkor was marked by the adoption of a new Hindu cult, that
of the Deva-raja, the god-king, and in subsequent years the
great temples arose that were the glory of the region. The
Angkor Wat, built in the early twelfth century, marked the
acceptance of Vaisnavism: the central shrine deified the king
as Vishnu. In Burma the king of Pagan, Anahwrahta, undertook the establishment of Hinayana Buddhism among the
Burmans. In time the related Theravada Buddhism of Ceylon
was to become the most powerful factor in Burman religious
life, without destroying 'indigenous' animism. Indeed it affected
the greater part of the mainland. But in Dai Viet other factors
came into play.

The influence of China in Southeast Asia was for several
reasons of a character different from that of India. Its own
political structure essentially differed from that of India. No
doubt this helped to make its example less susceptible of
imitation by Southeast Asian princes, and the cultural influence
of Chinese merchants, even if they were politically important,
less effective. Undoubtedly Chinese merchants in the area were
numerous, and probably there were settlement and intermarriage. There were Chinese tin-miners at Phuket under Thai
administration from the fourteenth century. But the political
influence of China was felt in other ways.

In Southeast Asia, given the great physical obstacles, the
effect of superior power could make itself felt only irregularly:
a lesser state might be brought under the control of a greater
only to a limited extent, through occasional warlike expeditions
and a vague tie of vassalage rather than through any organised
system of political hegemony. Generally the states of Southeast
Asia were in this position in regard to the Chinese empire.
Sporadically China made her power directly felt in the region
with catastrophic impact. One period of vigorous activity was
connected with the creation of the Mongol empire, and under

the Mongol emperors there were incursions into Southeast Asia. Champa was attacked and Vijaya taken in 1283. The threat of Kublai Khan's expedition brought Kertanagara and the kingdom of Singosari to a sudden end in 1292. The Mongol conquest of Pagan five years before had a deep effect on the history of Burma: the Shans entered the Burman region in the succeeding period of disorganisation. The succeeding Ming dynasty also wished to make itself felt in Southeast Asia, and in the early fifteenth century a memorable series of voyages was undertaken mostly by the famous eunuch admiral Cheng-ho. Between 1405 and 1433, in some seven voyages, he visited Champa, Java, Sumatra, India and Ceylon, and even Arabia and east Africa. These voyages, apart from any commercial objects, were undoubtedly a more peaceful means than that of the Mongol dynasty of reaffirming the general supremacy China assumed over Southeast Asia. The states sent embassies to the celestial empire and acknowledged its overlordship.

In some cases Southeast Asian rulers could turn the interest of China in their affairs to good account. A promise to accept Kublai Khan's overlordship over Java secured the founder of Majapahit the assistance of Mongol troops. The fourteenth century king of Burma, Mingyi Swasawke, was recognised as 'Governor of Burma', and the two powers co-operated to some extent against the Shans. Thai diplomats who needed to be subtle saw the possibilities especially clearly. Sukhotai sent missions to Peking in the Mongol period, and the Thais had the support of China as a splinter movement in the Khmer empire: the traditional policy of the Chinese towards the 'southern barbarians' was indeed one of fragmentation, and was thus perhaps a further element in the kaleidoscopic politics of the area. Ayuthia became strong in the fourteenth century in part perhaps because of the weakness of the Mongols, and with the accession of the Ming dynasty the situation changed. The Thais, however, were alive to this, and sent frequent embassies to the Ming capital at Nanking to cultivate friendly relations.

The Burmans and the Thais no doubt acquired a smattering of Chinese culture as they entered Southeast Asia. But one part of that area is especially open to penetration by land. In Dai Viet the Chinese exerted a special influence. Before it became independent, it had been substantially sinicised. Paradoxically, it was this that helped Dai Viet to secure and maintain its independence of China (rather as Japan was later to ensure its independence of the West by westernising). Some of the rulers after independence sought to cultivate Buddhist bonzes

27

as an antidote to suspect Confucianists. But by the later eleventh century the kingdom increasingly relied on a Confucianist élite, and the influence of Buddhism gave way in the fourteenth century. The Chinese example was followed so far as it could be as the best means of stabilising and unifying a kingdom especially exposed to the Chinese. The adoption of intensive Chinese agricultural methods not only supported the kingdom's economy, but enabled it to strengthen itself by expanding southwards at the expense of other peoples. Yet another means of defence against the Chinese was a politic recognition of the supremacy of China, afforded for instance as early as 972.

Nevertheless there were struggles with Chinese invaders. The Mongols sought to cross Dai Viet in order to attack Champa. This led to the great battles of the 1280s, terminating in Mongol defeats, but also in an offer of tribute from Dai Viet as a means to ensure peace. Dai Viet recognised the Ming in 1369, but this did not avert disaster. Exhausting wars with Champa and the decline of the Tran dynasty marked the close of the century. A usurper attempted to strengthen the kingdom but alienated a nobility whose land and power had grown in the preceding decades. A new war with Champa, 1400-3, and a Cham appeal to China, precipitated Ming intervention. In 1407 the province of Giao-chi was re-established and the policy of assimilation was renewed. But a great landed proprietor, Le Loi, led a war of liberation from the south (Thanh-hoa), and secured victory by 1427. It was then that he became emperor Le Thai-to and created his capital of Dong-kinh. A Cham invasion of 1470 was encouraged by the Ming, but it led to Dai Viet's capture of Vijaya and the reduction of the Cham kingdom.

In Dai Viet the scholars, like their Chinese exemplars, remained Taoist or Confucian: the mass of the people mixed Buddhist and indigenous cults. Elsewhere the importation of Indian cults up to the twelfth century was very much an affair of rulers and princes and did not greatly affect the peasants. Existing cults persisted, and even at higher levels, syncretism marked, as it has continued to mark, religious observance in Southeast Asia. In Airlangga's kingdom in Java, it was common practice for the kings to be worshipped after death in the form of Vishnu; and ancestor-worship, although outwardly Hindu or Buddhist, represented a survival from the pre-Hindu past. Kertanagara's cult of Siva-Buddha easily adapted itself to the Javanese ancestor-cult. In Cambodia it is clear that the adoption of Hinduism affected only court circles: animism and ancestor-worship continued to be the real religion of the mass of the

people. Anawrahta of Pagan built pagodas: yet his chief monument, the Shwezigon pagoda, begun in 1059, had a set of shrines
to the 37 Nats, testifying to the persistence of Burman animism.
But Anawrahta's work ensured the ultimate triumph of Theravada Buddhism, and this was to spread through mainland Southeast Asia as a popular religion, reaching the peasants, though
not the tribesmen. A Mon monk, Chapata, established a chap-
ter of Theravada Buddhism in Burma in 1190. The Theravada
teachings were taken by missionary monks to the states of the
Menam valley, and ultimately to Cambodia itself. The effects
were revolutionary. For unlike Saivism, Vaisnavism, and
Mahayana Buddhism, the new doctrine was preached to the
people and stimulated a popular movement which led the
Khmers and others into the Hinayana fold. It spread to the
Thais also. 'Its missionaries were monks who prescribed austerity,
solitude and meditation, and were devoted to a life of poverty
and self-abnegation. Unlike the hierarchy at the capital, they
were in direct contact with the people, and they undermined
completely the old state religion and all that went with it . . .'[16]
In fact Hindu influence persisted in court ceremony, and the
Thais imported Khmer court Brahmans and the appurtenances
of Khmer royalty. But one of the ruler's main roles became
the protection of Buddhism, and, on the other hand, it became
one of the main props for the unity of the state. The spread
of Theravada Buddhism on the mainland had another important
effect. The population movements of the tenth and subsequent
centuries did not penetrate much beyond the isthmus, as has
been seen; and thus created some division between the mainland and the Archipelago. Now Theravada Buddhism was to
provide, as a popular religion, a barrier against the penetration
of Islam which had no parallel in the Archipelago. But the
different geographical features of the regions and their different
sources of political power help also to explain this new religious
dichotomy.

The penetration of Islam from outside Southeast Asia again
raises the question of cultural imperialism: how did it come?
how was it spread? Undoubtedly Muslim traders were known
in the area before the spread of Islam in the thirteenth and
fourteenth centuries. Arab merchants had been following the
route to China from the earliest times, and after the seventh
century they were Muslims. There were colonies of them in
the trading cities. Islam is thus known on the west coast of
Sumatra about 674; but it began to exert a wider influence only
in the fourteenth century. In part this was the result of a

29

general movement of proselytisation begun in the thirteenth century, perhaps a repercussion of the Mongol wars, the capture of Bagdad, the fall of the Muslim caliphate, and the penetration of Christian missionaries into the Asian lands of the Khans. One aspect of this movement was the foundation of the Sufi orders.

So far as the spread of Islam in the Archipelago is concerned, while Sufism was prepared to build upon the past, no doubt an important factor was the attraction Islam held for those who found the old animism or the old cults unsatisfying in lands to which the princes had not summoned the Ceylon Buddhists and where Theravada doctrine had not been preached. But without discounting religious motivation, other motives may be reckoned alongside, even in one individual. If Islamisation involved in the earlier stages a missionary phase, if indeed its penetration among the people at large was thereafter the continuing missionary work of centuries, nevertheless the movement was spurred on in the interim by politico-commercial incentives. It was associated with adventurers and traders who founded new states or who procured or promoted a shift in allegiance among rulers of existing states or disrupted commercial empires.

The connexion with trade had a greater political force in the Archipelago than on the mainland. Islam was associated with the dynamism of the Archipelago but not with that of the mainland. Not only the popularity of Theravada Buddhism but also the different political structure — the different relationship between trading towns and the centres of power — helped to produce the religious dichotomy between mainland and islands. Traders, Islamic or otherwise, had no such influence on the continent as they had in the Archipelago. Only in despairing Champa, and during the last stages of its struggle with Dai Viet, did Islam gain a hold on the mainland.

Some of the small harbour principalities of northern Sumatra, for instance Pasei and Pedir, turned to Islam at the end of the thirteenth century: they were in close touch with western India, where Islam was triumphing, and they were anxious to escape the hegemony of Sri Vijaya. The ruler of newly-founded Malacca accepted it in the early fifteenth century: it put the new entrepot in the Straits in amicable connexion with newly Islamised principalities in India; but it was also a state-supporting ideology and one that could be used to create an Archipelagic empire to rival or replace that of Hindu-Buddhist Majapahit.

The peripheral position of east and central Java in terms of island empire has already been mentioned. The populated rice areas offered a basis for extending influence in the Archipelago, but a basis hard to build upon. The coastal towns of Java had, on the other hand, greater influence than those related to similar polities on the mainland. The ricelands themselves were hard enough to hold together, and fifteenth century Majapahit was deeply affected by civil war in Java. But the coastal towns were particularly open to centripetal attraction, inasmuch as their commercial interests led them to look to the Straits and to the Moluccas as much as to Java itself. Such an attraction was fostered by Malacca, interested especially in the rice that the towns also sent to the eastward. There was clearly more than one motive in Malacca and in the towns alike for the adoption of Islam in defiance of the empire of the inland regions. In the port of Tuban a native ruling house was converted to Islam. Elsewhere — in Demak, Japara, Cheribon, Grise — Islamic merchants assumed power. And thence Islam spread to the Moluccas, since the twelfth century source of spices, market for rice and Indian piece-goods.

On the Peninsula Islam was turned to account in the struggle with the Buddhist Thais — on the frontier within Southeast Asia — and both sides incidentally invoked the Chinese. The isthmian state of Patani was converted from Malacca in the later fifteenth century, but Malacca did not establish political control, and Thai influence remained strong. Kelantan received Islam as a dependency of Patani, Trengganu as a vassal state of Malacca. The first Muslim ruler of Pahang was a son of the Sultan of Malacca. The coastal states on neighbouring Sumatra — Rokan, Kampar, Indragiri, Siak — went over to Islam in the course of the fifteenth century. Characteristically many of the interior tribes were not converted, any more than by Buddhism on the mainland, by Islam in the Archipelago. The Bataks of Sumatra were never Islamised, nor were the Dayaks, nor most of the other interior tribes of Borneo. The coastal towns of Borneo, including Brunei, seem, on the other hand, to have been converted by Javanese or Malaccan merchants also in the fifteenth century.

Malacca had begun in no unorthodox way with the activities of 'piratical' adventurers, drawn from the Bugis tribes of Celebes, it seems, led by a renegade Sumatran or Javanese. Its success developed a more legitimate trade. It had no agricultural base and prosperity yet depended upon control of the Straits, and, despite its fine position, was assured only when Iskandar Shah fitted out a fleet of boats, manned by 'Cellates' — or *orang laut* — to force vessels to call. Also from the dependent states of Sumatra, the Peninsula, and the Riau-Lingga Archipelago, a tribute of men and export products was exacted. Commerce became the lifeblood of Malacca, a strategic point on the great route westward, a port where a monopoly of the spices required in Europe could be established, an entrepot for trade in general. It distributed Indian textiles from Gujerat, from Bengal and Coromandel, it imported rice (hardly a luxury for Malacca), it collected the spices of the Moluccas, it obtained tin from the Peninsula, it traded in Borneo camphor and Javanese krisses.

The town itself was characteristic. The present St Paul's Hill was a royal precinct, and a palisade later surrounded it. The pole-raised dwellings of the immigrant Malays occupied the lower slopes, *orang laut* huts lay against the shore, wealthier merchants resided outside the town. Many foreigners lived there, Bengalis, Gujeratis, Klings, Parsees, Arabs: 84 languages were used, says the Portuguese Pires. Government was by the Sultan, in theory autocratic, though in fact much power was left to the great officers, especially the Bendahara. Shabandars represented the merchants of each nation, and helped to estimate customs and gifts owed to the aristocracy. The Sultan was the chief charterer of junks, the high officials, often foreign in origin, extensive traders; but the Malay nobility was generally still a warlike element, claiming 'feudal' loyalty from the commoners, the type represented by the Laksamana Hang Tuah, a folk hero. The commoners were seamen, rarely traders, the *orang laut* fishermen and followers on warlike expeditions.

This wealthy entrepot was obviously attractive to the Portuguese. A century that in Southeast Asia began with the astonishing assertions of Chinese influence in the voyages of Cheng-ho, that witnessed the effective introduction and spread of Islam, that saw the greatest days of the greatest of the Malay commercial empires, was to close with the advent of the Europeans, whose impact again was to differ in the Archipelago and the mainland. Yet it is hard to maintain that the Portuguese seizure of Malacca struck down a state that might have brought unity to Southeast Asia. In face of geographical and cultural obstacles, that was a most unlikely achievement, though it might have brought unity to the Peninsula. Indeed there was yet a further region in Southeast Asia where the Europeans were to have yet a different effect.

The islands of Luzon and the Visayas had been in commercial contact with China, and had possibly afforded a field for migration. But, perhaps not surprisingly, this had not led to the setting-up of advanced political structures. On the other hand, the islands had lain apart from the main stream of Archipelagic commerce, penetrating from the isthmus to the Straits and beyond, apart also from the cultural influences that came, by whatever means, along with it. The islands remained as it were in an early phase of political development. In the interior, in mountainous regions like the Sierra Madre and Zambales mountains in Luzon, there were primitive Negrito peoples. On the coast trading settlements at the river-mouths were linked with China and with Borneo to the south. Politically the islands were a mass of petty states, *barangay*, ruled by clan chiefs or *datus*, with great men or *maharlika*, free men or *timagua*, and slaves. None exerted a wide authority. The fragmentation was geographical, political, and also linguistic. The development of commerce in the eastern parts of the Indonesian Archipelago and in Borneo in the fourteenth and fifteenth centuries brought Malay empire-builders and then Islam to the south. The sultanate of Sulu emerged, a loose structure resting upon hereditary aristocratic *datus*. Its attempts at imperialism and proselytisation were to be both excited and inhibited by the Europeans.

4 The Portuguese

THE ORIGIN and motives of the Portuguese and Spanish voyages of 'discovery' have been the subject of much controversy. This extraordinary movement is certainly not explained by reference to expanding capitalism or industry. Portugal and Spain were by no means the most commercially advanced of the European states: the former in particular was a poor country with a population of only one million in 1500. In England and the Netherlands, there was a flourishing cloth industry, but these countries did not at first play a major part in the overseas voyages, and when they did, their cloth exports were largely unsuccessful.

Equally it is not possible to explain the voyages by alluding to the advance of technology or geographical knowledge. The striking facts are the great geographical ignorance of the early voyagers and the absence of any significant technical advance in relation to the preceding period. Navigation in the early voyages was haphazard. On his first voyage round the Cape to India in 1498, Vasco da Gama landed several times simply in order to correct his reckoning. Nor was there any preliminary development of geographical knowledge. In early medieval maps allegory and lesson-giving prevailed, as in the *Mappaemundi* and in the geographical writings of Orosius and Rabanus Maurus. This was gradually displaced by the effects of practical experience, evidenced in the late medieval rutters and *portolani*. But such referred only to already explored and travelled routes, and could hardly aid voyages of 'discovery'.

In the course of the sixteenth century these voyages were, of course, to lead in Europe to improvements in technology and advances in geographical learning, the result of new and wider experience. The knowledge of them was to spread more rapidly as a result of printing. The voyages of the late sixteenth century thus had an advantage over the earlier. Men's minds had been exercised, too, over the navigational problems the earlier voyages had raised. In England, for instance, Digges and Stevin argued over the ways of determining longitude. Problems of cartography were tackled by Nunez, the Portuguese mathematician, and by Mercator of Louvain. Attempts to determine the compass variation more accurately stimulated mathematicians like Rotz and Dee. The voyages of discovery began in fact to affect the movements that culminated in the scientific revolution of the seventeenth century. Galileo tried to make the movement of the tides the climax of his system, and Gilbert tried to reach a new synthesis starting from the compass variation. But all this does not explain the early voyages.

Even in this later period the theoreticians behind the voyages — the Hakluyts in England and others there and elsewhere — were very much scholars, very much concerned with books and ledgers, with authority as well as experience: they were still men of the Renaissance. Some of the authorities of the past, respected in the Renaissance, indeed represented a regression of geographical knowledge in the light of medieval experience and knowledge derived from the Arabs since the twelfth century. The Renaissance recovery of learning cannot be utilised in this way to explain the voyages. Renaissance ignorance rather than knowledge influenced Columbus. On one theory, he was influenced by the classical geographer Marinus, who thought that the discovered world was even bigger in relation to the undiscovered than had the classical geographer Ptolemy. Classical evidence was adduced for the existence of *Terra Australis;* and since three-quarters of the world were supposed to be under water, this was another reason for doubting the existence of a western continent: America could not exist because Australia did. Columbus would not have 'discovered' it had he not been led to believe that it was not there.

Clearly the voyages were all the more acts of courage and endurance. The accounts of the voyages tell the tale of tension with quarrels and disputes, mutinies and harsh discipline. There was an appalling loss of life, above all occasioned by the insanitary condition of the Portuguese and Spanish ships. From da Gama's first voyage 55 men returned to Portugal: 170 had left.

What were the powerful motives that induced men to proceed on such hazardous undertakings? The essential motive was the acquisitive urge: and in the discussion the Renaissance does play a part. The later Middle Ages saw a period of great prosperity among the Italian cities, especially in Venice, arising from the general European recovery after the Black Death, the growing connexion with the Mediterranean, and the developing trade with the East across Egypt and Arabia. On this prosperity the Renaissance was built: it financed the attempts to recapture the glories of antiquity. The new culture that in fact resulted in the city states was the envy of European states outside Italy, in northern Europe and the Iberian peninsula, realms still cast for the most part — especially that of Portugal — in a feudal form. The achievements of Renaissance Italy held out great prospects, in art and culture and in the sources of political power. What was needed was wealth, and this need contributed to the voyages of discovery.

The Renaissance was important to the voyages not because of any technological contribution to their achievement, but because it offered vast new opportunities for using wealth. Without this inspiration men's courage and endurance might have failed in face of tremendous obstacles: without their success many of the achievements of Renaissance Europe would have been impossible. Spain, with the wealth of Mexico and Peru, became the greatest state of Renaissance Europe. Portugal, calling in the aid of the Genoese, rivals of the Venetians, built

Renaissance Lisbon and created the culture that produced Camoens' *Lusiads,* picturing da Gama as a new Aeneas watched over by Venus.

The men of the time had before them a picture of the wealth of the East painted by Marco Polo and by Italian merchants and missionaries, missionaries sent to the Mongols like John of Monte Corvino and Odoric of Pordenone and Jordanus who wrote a work called *The Wonders of the East,* merchants of the fifteenth century like the Venetian Nicolo de Conti and the Genoese Hieronomo de Santo Stefano who visited Burma in the 1490s. In the fifteenth century the Portuguese had been slowly exploring the west African coast in search of the Rio de Ouro. Only in 1487 did Diaz round the Cape, and this, and the succeeding voyage of da Gama opened up a new prospect, a participation by that route in the trade between Europe and Asia, in competition with the Egyptians and the Venetians using the overland route. But this trade, drawing above all spices to Europe, drew precious metals from Europe, since there was little that Europe's industry could provide that could find a market in India or China or Southeast Asia. There was nothing that Portugal could provide. The Portuguese object came to be to trade within Asia, to attempt to monopolise the more important products, and to remit the profits of empire to Europe in the form of spices, then 'a chief ingredient in apothecary and kitchen alike',[17] thanks to the state of medical science and to the lack of refrigeration and of winter cattle-fodder.

The initial effort of the Portuguese was on the western side of the Indian Ocean, where their success dated from the defeat of the Egyptians at Diu in 1509. Hormuz and Goa were acquired and control of Malabar pepper sought. In 1518 they established themselves at Colombo in search of cinnamon. They also went to Pulicat, Negapatam and St Thomé in order to participate in the textile trade to Southeast Asia. And Southeast Asia had already attracted their attention as a source of articles in Asian trade, including spices, and a route for intra-Asian trade. In particular they realised the significance of Malacca, which was taken by Albuquerque in 1511. An expedition was sent to the Moluccas, source of nutmeg and clove. From Malacca there were missions to China. After 1557 the Portuguese occupied Macao, participating thence in the trade to Southeast Asia and to Japan, where they were welcomed as suppliers of firearms.

These early successes of the Portuguese were indeed often aided by local political factors, like the civil war in Japan or the divisions among the princes of India and the Archipelago.

It is possible that they had initially, not only the advantage of singleness of purpose and the element of surprise, but also a certain superiority in weapons and in naval and military techniques. But their opponents were likely, as it were, to catch up, and their empire reached its greatest extent early. Perhaps the only advantages that remained to the Portuguese were the heavy armament that could be put on their great ships or *naos*, and their Asia-wide organisation.

Their empire indeed had in many respects a feudal character. Van Leur speaks of 'a conglomeration of nobles and *condottieri* each with his own retinue of henchmen bound to him by a vassal's loyalty or a lust for gain; often the officials in authority provided their own equipment and carried out exploitation for their own benefit by means of offices bestowed on them, frequently on a short term basis . . .'[18] Nevertheless there were centralist elements and there was a bureaucracy. Attempts were made to assert a spice monopoly for the government, or later for the *fidalgo* to whom, or organisation to which, the government auctioned the voyages, and to control smuggling and levy duties on general commerce through a pass system. But the monopoly was never complete, nor the pass system entirely effective. The profits fell, and expenses became more burdensome, as rivals 'caught up'. Distance made corruption difficult to restrain, and the fall in revenue opened the way to private trade still further, since salaries could not be paid, and this involved a further decline of monopoly and profit.

The decline of the Portuguese empire in Asia in the latter half of the sixteenth century was marked by an increase in missionary activity. It is true that in 1500-1 Cabral had carried a piously worded letter from King Manoel to the Zamorin in Calicut, suggesting that God had ordained the miraculous feats of the Portuguese not only for 'traffic and temporal profits . . . but also the spiritual of souls and their salvation to which we are more bound'.[19] No doubt — as in the Crusades against the Moors of which the Spaniards and the Portuguese regarded their voyages and conquests as in some respects a continuation — the acquisitive urge and the missionary spirit were mixed. It was only in the days of their decline — also, admittedly, the days of the Counter-Reformation and of Jesuit militancy — that the Portuguese became 'more bound' to the latter. The Christian endeavour was naturally in the given state of European relations with Asia closely tied to Iberian enterprise, and the Portuguese king enjoyed extensive clerical patronage. But some of the activities of the missions — their participation in trade, their growing intolerance, the disputes between Jesuits and Franciscans — did not assist the Portuguese. And if it was hoped that missionary enterprise would shore up the empire in its latter days, it should have been remembered that the Portuguese adventure operated on both sources of the expansion of Islam. It threatened Islam as a whole, as had the earlier Christian contacts with the Mongols: and the Portuguese involvement in local politics tended to stress the local motives for the spread of Islam. Some rulers opposed to Islam turned to the Portuguese, but Islamic rulers gained a new motive for promoting the Muslim cause. To stress missionary endeavour in such circumstances, while it might convert primitive tribes where the Portuguese could retain control, would in general only weaken their position and embroil them more deeply.

The rivals of the Portuguese at the close of the century, especially the Dutch, were to take advantage of this situation and avoid missionary activity. But their triumph reflected not simply the weakness of the Portuguese policies in Asia and the existence of many rivals: it essentially reflected the relative commercial position of the two powers in Europe. The Dutch indeed were aiming at Venice as well as at Lisbon. In fact the Portuguese had by no means destroyed the overland trade. They had secured for themselves a share in the trade between Europe and Asia, which in fact expanded during the sixteenth century with the general expansion resulting above all from the Spanish import of precious metals from America. And in Asia they were one among a number of politico-commercial powers, though with characteristics of their own.

5 The Archipelago in the Sixteenth Century

By a great effort the Portuguese had taken Malacca, the centre of the flourishing empire of island Southeast Asia. They attempted to create a new empire that differed by its more organised political connexion with other parts of Asia though using methods by no means unknown to the Archipelago. 'The years were filled with piracy and naval warfare by the Portuguese, defense against assaults, and attacks on trading ships, war fleets, and fortresses, guerilla warfare with a strong element of vendetta to it.'[20] And so they created a commercial empire of great instability, constantly menaced by rivals and competitors. There were shifts in political power, but not a change in its nature; new states, but not different sorts of states.

Malacca had been fostering the independence which the coastal trading cities of east and central Java were attempting to secure of the control of Majapahit. That empire indeed appears finally to have disintegrated between 1513 and 1528 before a coalition of the Muslim states composed of Madura, Tuban, Surabaya and Demak, and the Sultanate of Demak became the most powerful state in Java. It controlled the northern rice-growing plains from Japara to Grise, exporting rice to Malacca and trading to the Moluccas. The Portuguese gained a foothold in west Java by agreement with the ruler of the petty state of Pajajaran at Sunda Kelapa (Jakarta). By 1527 the neighbouring ruler of Bantam, forcibly acquired in the name of the Sultan of Demak as an outpost against the Portuguese, had taken over. Bantam was to become in 1568 an independent Sultanate, extending over all west Java and to the Lampongs and south-west Sumatra, its swidden lands becoming a great source of pepper.

The independence of the Sultanate was achieved as a result of a struggle in east and central Java which, however, ultimately created a new empire in the later sixteenth century. The collapse of Majapahit had left the interior of Java a political chaos, but a new dynasty arose, that of Mataram, which ultimately succeeded in subjugating the coastal principalities. Initially Mataram was a small district under the ruler of Pajang, itself part of Demak. In 1582 an official of that ruler, Senapati, an adventurer of low origin, was able to usurp the government of Pajang, and in 1586 he shifted its seat of government to the age-old heart of the Javanese region at Mataram. Mataram made itself felt among the coastal towns taking part in international trade, which were perhaps weakened by their struggle with the Portuguese. Conceivably it was on the way to creating another Javanese empire in the Archipelago, though at Senapati's death in 1601 it was still an inland state. Its success was not prevented by the Portuguese: it was by the Dutch.

The Portuguese — more or less as a corollary of their weak

position in Java — were not as strong as is sometimes thought in the Moluccas. The Javanese towns continued to have a wide influence not only in western Borneo, source of diamonds, and in Timor, Aru, Ceram and Kai, but in the spice islands themselves. Their colony at Hitu on Ambon — a key to the clove islands — was early a centre of resistance to the Portuguese. The

THE PHILIPPINES, THE MOLUCCAS, JAVA and DAI VIET
16th, 17th, and 18th centuries A.D.

Portuguese never occupied Banda, the source of nutmeg and mace, and they met Javanese as well as Spanish and local opposition in Tidore and Ternate, centres of commercial empire in these regions. Ternate at first welcomed the Portuguese while Tidore welcomed the Spaniards, but struggles in the 1560s forced the former to move to Tidore. In succeeding years the ruler of Ternate became 'Lord of the 72 islands', claiming parts of Celebes, the Sula islands, Sumbawa and Buton, while Tidore claimed suzerainty over southern Halmahera and north-west New Guinea. The Portuguese had, however, established themselves more firmly at Ambon, to which competition spread the cultivation of cloves. The struggle with Mataram somewhat diverted the effort of the Javanese towns.

To the westward the Javanese traded to the Straits, south Sumatra, and the Gulf of Siam. They attempted to stay the Portuguese not only by building up Bantam, but also by attempting to capture Malacca itself, on which they made vain attacks in 1513, 1535, 1551 and 1574. But in this region there were other native powers, whose existence indicated the nature of the Portuguese position, but whose rivalries tended to preserve it.

Some of the traders of Malacca fled on its conquest to Acheh in north Sumatra. European sources tell us little of the subsequent attempt to create a new empire in the Straits that anticipated Mataram's attempts in Java. Possibly the use of Portuguese weapons was an important factor. In the first half of the sixteenth century Acheh extended its control over the pepper-producing ports of Pedir and Pasei, and over part of Menangkabau, and in search of pepper it stretched down the west coast as Bantam stretched up it. The Portuguese were driven south from Pasai, and had to obtain their pepper from central east Sumatran ports like Indragiri, Kampar and Jambi. Furthermore, Acheh attacked Malacca several times, for instance in 1537, 1539, 1547, 1568, 1573, and 1575, and it endeavoured to establish a control over the petty states of the Peninsula, like Kedah and Perak, sources of tin, attempting as had Sri Vijaya to control both sides of the Straits. But these attempts at commercial empire did not meet the opposition of the Portuguese alone.

The conquest of Malacca had not destroyed the influence of the Malacca dynasty. Sultan Mahmud fled to Pahang. In 1521 he moved to the island of Bentan, south-east of Singapore island, and from here he sought to re-establish his commercial and political position. He was repeatedly attacked by the Portuguese, but in 1523 and 1524 beat them off with heavy loss and even sent a force to lay siege to Malacca. In 1526 his capital was destroyed, but a new capital was established in Johore, until the Portuguese enforced its removal to Muar in 1536. The power of Johore brought it into conflict with Acheh, and this paradoxically helped the Portuguese to survive. In 1539 the advance of Acheh in eastern Sumatra — it captured Deli — provoked a clash with Johore because of the old Malacca claims

there: and Johore, with Perak and Siak, defeated the north
Sumatrans. In 1564, on the other hand, the Sultan of Acheh
sacked Johore and this inaugurated a period of great enmity.
Thus when Acheh followed up with a great attack upon
Malacca, Johore came to the aid of the Portuguese. In 1582 the
Portuguese helped the Johore Sultan to beat off an Achehnese
attack. Then these two fell out, Johore besieged Malacca,
Malacca destroyed Johore, and Acheh rejoiced. If the Portuguese were assisted in one quarter by the rivalry of the Javanese
coastal towns and the rising Mataram, here they were helped
by the rivalry of Acheh and Johore. Thus economic warfare
continued, the Johore ruler using the *orang laut* or 'Cellates'
as in earlier struggles for empire, affording an outlet for their
predatory traditions.

Other traders flying Portuguese Malacca settled in Patani on
the Peninsula, in Macassar in Celebes, and in Brunei and Sulu,
and a new Sultanate emerged in Mindanao. But there, as in
the Moluccas, the Spaniards were also concerned.

In the Archipelago, it appears, the Portuguese were able to
make some political impact. As elsewhere, the greatest successes
were the initial ones: afterwards others caught up, as with
Acheh. The fragmentary nature of political power in the region,
its disunity, assisted them to secure a foothold; and indeed
their very weakness led them to make the most of it, especially
when faced by rival Spaniards as in the Moluccas. Furthermore,
at that particular time, the Java-based empire of Majapahit was
on the point of utter collapse, weakened by the centripetal interests of the coast towns abetted by Muslim Malacca. The
Dutch were to establish themselves before the empire was reconstituted by Mataram, and meanwhile both Portuguese and
Dutch were aided by its struggle with the coastal towns. Such
factors decreased the resistance to the Europeans. Elsewhere
other lesser empires appeared, in Acheh, Johore, even in Borneo
and Sulu, more peripheral than Malacca, with less potential
for unity, and their rivalries helped the Portuguese to survive.
Certainly the latter established no political unity in face of
the many obstacles, geographical and otherwise. It is indeed a
question whether this period of disruption and fragmentation
did not witness an increase of 'privateering' and a decrease of
stability.

In the sixteenth century, the volume of trade between Europe
and Asia expanded, and so, no doubt, did that of Southeast
Asia. Within Asia, moreover, the Portuguese effected some new
commercial contacts and opened some new routes. The develop-

ment of pepper on the swidden lands of Sumatra and the Peninsula represented a shift from concentration on the Malabar coast in part the result of Portuguese activity. The more widespread production of cloves has already been mentioned. But in the Archipelago the trade of the Portuguese was exceeded many times in quantity by that carried on by Chinese and by Indians from Coromandel, Gujerat and Malabar. The Chinese traded to Sulu, to Johore, to Patani, to Macassar, and to the Javanese towns. They came also to Malacca, but the Portuguese had not succeeded in either displacing or canalising their trade, though they no longer went to the Moluccas. As for the Indians, probably a very large part of their trade was done at Acheh, but by no means all.

The towns of the Archipelago were, of course, as cosmopolitan as ever, if not more so. At Bantam there was 'great resort of divers Countries and nations', each 'nation' living in its quarter inside the wall or in its suburb outside.[21] Even in the spice islands the situation was not dissimilar: in 1609 in Banda there was still a Gujerati quarter. There was room still for the exercise of alien Asian influences.

The influence of China, apart from the exceptional case of Dai Viet, had, however, been exerted largely through general assertions of supremacy backed by occasional expeditions. In Dai Viet in this period, despite its internal division, Chinese intervention was relatively limited. The weakness of the Ming also affected the position in the Archipelago. The lack of assertion there may be explained less by the arrival of the Portuguese than by mounting troubles elsewhere. When Sultan Mahmud lost the battle for Malacca, he sent an emissary to China beseeching aid against the 'Franks'. The Ming emperor replied that with a war against the Mongols to fight, too, he was in no position to fight the Portuguese. Again the Portuguese were aided by adventitious political circumstances in Asia.

Indian influence had penetrated along the trade routes, still substantially occupied by Indians. In India these were the decades of Muslim triumph, the climax being the expansion of the Moghul empire by Akbar in the last thirty years of the century. The prestige of Islam in India and the presence of Indian traders partly account for the advance of Islam in the Archipelago. But the Portuguese incursion strengthened Muslim determination in general, and the policy of the Portuguese in the Archipelago, especially the missionary activity of their declining years, helped to spread Islam.

The religious dimension of the struggle in the Archipelago

43

is apparent. The Portuguese obtained facilities at Sunda Kelapa from the Hindu Raja of Pajajaran: this prompted the founding of the Muslim state of Bantam by a fanatical zealot called Faletehan in the name of the Sultan of Demak. In east and central Java, Mataram finally followed the lead of the coastal towns and chose the way of the Prophet. It was, as Benda puts it, 'confronted by the combined strength of Islamized principalities claiming suzerainty over the wealthy coastal regions and of the Muslim sultanate of Bantam in West Java. The ruler of Mataram in the end chose conversion to Islam as the best means of realizing his ambitions . . .'[22] It was not surprising that the interior of Java should at last follow the lead of the towns and so amplify the religious dichotomy between mainland and Archipelago. Only Bali preserved its Hindu culture intact.

Elsewhere the spread of Islam east of Java received a new impulse. Bandjermasin in south Borneo was converted to Islam about the middle of the sixteenth century as a result of its connexion with the Muslim state of Demak. In the Moluccas, again, Islam was stimulated by the Portuguese threat and encouraged by its failure. The expansion of Ternate after 1575 was associated with the expansion of Islam. So also the substantial extension of Brunei during the sixteenth century was associated with the *jihad* or holy war.

In the west of the Archipelago, Acheh 'after the middle of the sixteenth century became the most important centre for the transit trade of the western Asian and Indian Muslims with the archipelago. Evincing strong Muslim sympathies, successfully attempting to expand in Sumatra, at the same time spreading Islam, it developed into the centre of religious study in the archipelago as well'.[23] Acheh was nearest India, nearest Mekka, and was a centre of Islamic reaction to the Portuguese. The league against Malacca in the 1560s was indeed backed by gunners, guns and ammunition from Turkey, and the Sultan was in close touch with Muslim princes in India. Acheh, as Schrieke puts it, was 'one of the main channels through which spiritual life on Java . . . was given nourishment from Muslim India and the Holy Land . . .'[24] Moghul practices spread to the Achehnese court. Islam's hold increased and it strengthened the state organisation in face of frontier conditions. In 1539 the Sultan of Acheh began war on the Bataks in the interior to force them to go over to Islam, though the struggle was vain. Islam did not provide a political unity among states: Muslim Johore and Muslim Acheh were as much rivals as either rivalled the Portuguese at Malacca. But the reaction to the Portuguese and the spread of Islam did help to effect a greater cultural and religious unity in the Archipelago, though that in a sense meant a deeper division within Southeast Asia as a whole. One area of contrast and contact was the Peninsula where Muslim Malays faced Buddhist Thais. But the Thais were restrained in the sixteenth century by the Burman menace, and this, incidentally, assisted the Portuguese, too.

The character of the Islam spread in the Archipelago varied from area to area and from class to class. In some regions, scarcely affected by Hindu civilisation and especially open to Islamic influence, such as Acheh and Bantam, Islam had the most profound effects and appeared in its least conciliatory form. In east and central Java, on the other hand, it had to adapt itself to old traditions, partly indigenous, partly Hindu-Buddhist, and it lost much of its doctrinal rigidity. Thus, while the adoption of Islam by Mataram promoted the religious unity of the Archipelago, it was, on the other hand, a long time before Islam brought about radical changes in religious and social life in Java. Islam, too, came mostly via India, and its orthodoxy was modified by mysticism. But 'its success in Indonesia is indicative of a rather superficial degree of Hinduisation' — there were no lasting divisions between Hindus and Muslims as in India — and 'Javanese Islam in the early centuries was a wedding of Sufi and indigenous mysticism rather than of Islam and Hinduism proper'.[25] Even syncretic Javanese Islam, however, represented a symbol of opposition to the Europeans, and their activities continued to promote the Islamisation of society.

The missionary endeavour of the Portuguese could on the whole only advance the cause of Islam. It represented an attempt to fill the gaps in their political and commercial system, and it waxed with their wane. Xavier spent eighteen months in the 'Islands of Divine Hope', and the Portuguese attempted to assure their hold on Ambon by the conversion of the population. The attempt to establish Christian communities prompted violent Islamic reaction, however, and their fortunes were involved in the long struggles with Ternate. The increased missionary effort of the Portuguese in the days of their decline prompted their further decline by stimulating the opposition of the native princes, but some of the last remnants of their empire owed much to missionaries. The Portuguese had long shared with the Javanese and others in the trade upon Timor and the Lesser Sundas. From about the middle of the sixteenth century, they had settled on Solor, largely thanks to the Dominicans, who in 1566 built a fort to protect their Christian converts which became a centre for traders. Later the White Friars had a fort at Pulau Ende on Flores, and that island became a Portuguese centre — with a fort at Larantuka — early in the seventeenth century when a native rebellion on Solor was followed by a Dutch conquest. It was from Larantuka that the Portuguese were to spread to their last stronghold, the island of Timor. The Dominicans began work there in the 1640s, but the Dutch took over their fort at Kupang in 1653. The Governor of Larantuka established a new post at Lifao in 1702.

Thus — where they anticipated Islam in converting peoples of more primitive religion — the Portuguese created more or less recognisably Christian communities in the Moluccas and the Lesser Sundas (though they failed at the other extreme of the Archipelago, in the Nicobars). The settlement at Larantuka was largely populated by 'Black Portuguese', and their other legacy to the cultural diversity of the Archipelago was the creation of the first Eurasian communities. Portugal was thinly populated: it always had difficulty manning its ships, in the eighteenth century more and more filled by negro slaves from Mozambique. The settlers in the East were encouraged by trading privileges which helped to erode the state monopolies. Their multiplication was encouraged by intermarriage with Asian women. As the empire fell apart, the Indies Portuguese were increasingly left to look after themselves. As a Dutch observer remarked in the seventeenth century: 'For the Portuguese and their descendants the situation is completely different from that for our burghers and the Company's trade . . . the larger number consider the Indies as their fatherland, no longer thinking of Portugal; they trade with it little or not at all, and sustain and enrich themselves from the advantages of the Indies as though they were natives and did not have any fatherland.'[26]

In some ways therefore the most lasting changes brought by the Portuguese were marginal and dated from their decline. Otherwise their empire had enjoyed only initial and very partial success and had provoked rather than destroyed opposition. But what ensured their defeat was the rise of Dutch commerce.

6 The Dutch and the Archipelago, 1600—1640

THE RISE of the maritime and commercial power of the Dutch was closely associated with economic developments in Europe. Up to the early sixteenth century they had been important in the commerce of the North Sea, the Channel and the Atlantic, carrying fish and grain to the Iberian and Mediterranean countries, and cloth from Flanders to the eastward. Spain's imports of silver from Mexico and Peru greatly affected this commerce. In Spain there were no industries for such wealth to fertilise. The wealth was expended in political and religious expansion and in importation even at the expense of indigenous resources. The Dutch were the principal carriers of the trade thus promoted, and paradoxically their wealth enabled them to revolt against Spanish political and religious hegemony, and create the Republic of the United Provinces, often loosely called Holland by the name of the largest province.

Spain remained dependent very largely upon the commercial services of the rebels who continued to draw away the profits of its empire-building in America. Their success meant that they were in a position to venture into the Asiatic trade, and various Dutchmen who had been in the service of the short-handed Portuguese — the most famous was van Linschoten — as also the persecuted Portuguese Jews, could supply information upon the Portuguese empire in Asia, its weaknesses and the strength of Asian opposition to it. The decisive moves were not made till the king of Spain, having become also king of Portugal in 1580, tried in the early 1590s to close Lisbon to the Dutch rebels. The struggle against the Portuguese in Asia now became also an aspect of the struggle for independence of the Habsburgs. The extent of the success of the Dutch may be largely ascribed to their superior economic assets. The ships of the Portuguese were perhaps superior to those of the Dutch: but they were fewer in number, and Portuguese resources were used less skilfully and their leadership was poorer.

In some respects the organisation of the Dutch venture was also superior to that of the Portuguese. The first few voyages were characterised by the localism of the Dutch Republic. In 1595 the first Amsterdam company for trade in the Indies sent out a fleet of four ships under Houtman, and an enlarged version sent out a fleet of eight ships in 1598. In the latter year a Flushing merchant sent out two ships and a Middelburg company three, and others were sent from Rotterdam. 'The genesis of the Company was not due to the subscribers' wish for it, but to the interference of the Government.'[27] The United Company was formed in 1602 because the States-General wanted a financially strong organisation that could wage a war in India without any expense on the part of the Government. The new Company obtained a charter granting it exclusive rights of trade, shipping, and exercise of authority in the territory between the Cape of Good Hope, the meridian a hundred miles east of the Solomon islands, and the Bering Straits. Regional interests remained powerful; and the existing companies became chambers in the United Company, delegates from these forming the Court of Directors or Heeren 17. The financial structure was old-fashioned and the book-keeping confused. But it was an advance on the Portuguese, and in particular there was — initially at least — less of the private trading which had so sapped Portuguese attempts at monopolising certain products and at exacting revenue that alone could uphold the empire.

The venture of the Dutch did not involve a transformation of the commercial relationship between Europe and Asia. They followed the example of the Portuguese in seeking a share of the commerce within Asia as a means of supporting a one-sided trade to Europe and in selectively seeking monopolies of some of the more important products. In so doing they opened some new routes and connexions, but their trade followed many traditional patterns. Thus the Dutch early realised the importance of a share in the age-old textile trade from the Coromandel coast to the Malay Archipelago, and in 1605 they planted commercial 'factories' at Masulipatam and Petapoli. They also established themselves at Cambay in Gujerat, the other great textile area, while later Surat became an important station for purchasing the textiles of northern India. Their exploits in the Archipelago must indeed be seen in the context of their activities elsewhere in Asia. In Ceylon, despite Portuguese opposition, they early obtained a share in the cinnamon trade. In the Far East, the Dutch were less successful. An attempt to drive the Portuguese from Macao in 1622 failed. They gained a footing in the Pescadores, but had to leave under threat of attack by the Chinese Governor of Amoy. The Dutch Company later moved to Formosa (1624), but it never established any trading factory on the mainland. In Japan the Dutch obtained a factory at Hirado in 1609.

The influence the Dutch possessed in the Archipelago in the period 1600-40 has sometimes been exaggerated. Any attempt to consider it a 'colonial' period must be qualified, for instance, by noting the existence of local powers who might assist the Dutch against the Portuguese at first and then turn against them.

The early Amsterdam fleets traded at Bantam, the Portuguese at Malacca vainly attempting to induce the Bantam Regents to refuse the Dutch permission. The 1598 fleet established a factory on Lonthor in the Banda islands and also visited Ternate, and a 1599 Amsterdam fleet, unable to subdue the Portuguese fort at Ambon, erected a Dutch fortress, the Castle Afar, and closed some contracts for the delivery of spices. A later 1599 fleet abandoned the castle and was unable to trade at Acheh, and the 1600 fleet vainly attempted to overmaster the Portuguese at Tidore. Middelburg ships of 1601 established a factory at Acheh and one at Patani, found Bantam blockaded by the Portuguese, and failed to trade at Ambon. In 1603 a factory was established in Johore.

After the formation of the United Company there were more energetic attempts to develop Dutch commerce in the Archipelago. The first fleet sent out was of 15 ships and within three years 38 ships had been despatched to the East. In 1609 the Dutch appointed a Governor-General with control over all the forts, factories, and business of the Company. The appointment of Coen as Governor-General in 1618 began a period of yet more vigorous Dutch extension in the Archipelago.

In 1606 the Dutch had destroyed the Portuguese fleet off Malacca, but failed to take the city. Instructions from the Heeren 17 of 1610 ordered the acquisition of a central rendezvous at Johore, Bantam, or Jakarta. The choice fell on the last, for the ruler was only 'a nobleman ruling over a small coastal town without much trade and a small hinterland which could yield only a limited amount of pepper';[28] yet the position, midway between the two focal points of Archipelagic power, the Straits and east and central Java, was superb. In Coen's period the new city of Batavia was created on the site. But it was at once threatened by the ruler of Bantam, and in Coen's second term as Governor-General (1627-9), it was threatened by the empire of Mataram. The great Sultan Agung had gradually been conquering the Javanese coastal towns, in 1621, for instance, Tuban, in 1622 Grise, weakened as they must have been by European competition. In 1624 he ravaged Madura and in 1625 conquered Surabaya. As 'Susuhunan' ('he to whom all are subject') he claimed overlordship over the whole island of Java. In 1626 he prepared to attack Batavia, and in 1629 laid siege to it with a vast force, defeated because it could not be supplied with food overland, and the Dutch had command of the sea. After this the energy of Mataram was concentrated against native powers to the eastward. Bali yet contrived to maintain its independence and its Hinduism, though the Balambangan region of eastern Java was conquered in 1639. Mataram's influence had spread to western Borneo: in 1622 it destroyed Sukadana and forced Bandjermasin to submit. The Europeans had indirectly assisted Mataram in its struggle with the coastal towns of east and central Java, but prevented its controlling western Java and, perhaps, conquering Bali.

In the Straits, Malacca yet remained in Portuguese hands, and this was also a period of great prosperity for Acheh. In 1607 Iskandar Shah seized the throne and expanded Acheh's control over the pepper and tin-producing areas of the Straits, over the coastal regions of Sumatra and over the Peninsular states of Pahang, Kedah and Perak. In 1629, however, the Achehnese fleet was defeated by the united forces of Malacca, Johore and Patani, and this setback began a period of decline which the Dutch capture of Malacca was to accelerate. In their final successful attempt on Malacca, the Dutch were assisted by the Sultan of Johore, who had joined them earlier in the vain attack of 1606.

The previous period had seen Indian trade in the Archipelago curtailed, if Indianised Islam spread. The Dutch had more impact on the Chinese traders. Initially the Dutch in the western half of the Archipelago had concentrated on Bantam, the great source of Indonesian pepper, more important to the Company than that of Malabar. At Bantam the Chinese were established as middlemen and Chinese junks also visited the port. The Dutch tried by force to secure pepper collected for the junks. Then they moved to Jakarta and blockaded Bantam. Some of the Chinese middlemen moved to Batavia, and the Dutch tried to attract the junks there, too. Other Chinese junks shifted to Jambi, where middlemen tapped the pepper coming downriver from Menangkabau, and others still went to Bandjermasin. But more and more the Dutch sought, if not to eliminate the junk trade, to concentrate it at their entrepot, and Chinese middlemen activities became more closely associated with the Dutch colonial enterprise. The Dutch pursuit of pepper and spices was aided by the weakening of Bantam and the Javanese towns in the course of their struggle with Mataram. But if pepper also embroiled the Dutch in Sumatra, the finer spices had already led them to the Moluccas, still mostly a preserve of the Javanese.

The position of the Dutch in the Moluccas and the eastern parts of the Archipelago in the period 1600-40 — and indeed the situation in Java and especially vis-à-vis Bantam — cannot be considered without reference to the enterprises of the English, their main European rivals aside from the Portuguese, and notwithstanding the newly-founded French and Danish East India Companies. In the sixteenth century English merchants had sought routes to the East not obstructed by the Iberian powers or others: but no N.E. or N.W. passage was found; and the Muscovy and Levant Companies failed to develop trade with India through Russia and Syria. The only practicable route was round the Cape of Good Hope, and the decline of the Portuguese seemed to offer an opportunity to the English as to the Dutch. Drake had visited the Moluccas in his voyages of circumnavigation in the late 1570s, and Cavendish's voyage across the Pacific took him to the 'Philippines' and the south-west coast of Java. But in 1591 an expedition under James Lancaster was sent round the Cape, and from Sumatra and Penang he was able to raid Portuguese commerce passing through the Straits of Malacca. The success of the first Dutch venture stimulated a new enthusiasm. In 1600 the East India Company obtained a charter granting it a monopoly of English trade in the region between the Cape of Good Hope and the Magellan Straits. The resources of the English were slimmer than those of the Dutch and their Company less well organised. It had difficulty in acquiring specie to send to the East and attempted to dispose of English cloth manufactures. And the Dutch were likely to oppose its wish to share the trade within Asia.

The first expedition, under Lancaster, left in 1601, reached Acheh in 1602, and obtained permission to build a factory at Bantam. Very quickly relations with the Dutch deteriorated. But relations among the powers in Europe frequently influenced their impact in Southeast Asia, and if the organisation and posture of the Dutch were affected by their relations with Spain, and indeed by the relations between Spain and Portugal, their policies in Asia were also modified by their need of English support in the European struggle with the Habsburgs. On the

51

other hand, England had a stake in the independence of the Netherlands, for it was from this part of the Continent, especially if occupied by a major European power, that the island could most easily be attacked. In the East these mutual interests tended to be obscured by local rivalries. There the English were an obstruction in the way of the Dutch Company's capturing the spice trade from the Iberians, the Javanese and others. The second voyage of the English Company was aimed at opening up direct relations with Ambon and Banda. But the Dutch prevented Middleton from trading at Ambon, which they had just taken from the Portuguese. On proceeding to Tidore, he was followed by the Dutch, who captured it, but he obtained a cargo at Ternate. Subsequently the third English voyage found the Dutch driving the Spaniards out of Ternate and Batjan.

In Europe the Dutch upheld the legality of their monopoly contracts with native rulers, challenged by the English as made under pressure, and pointed out the expense of their operations. At this juncture — the period of the twelve-year truce with Spain — they could afford to be unconciliatory. In the Archipelago Coen's first Governor-Generalship saw outright conflict. The English came within an ace of taking Batavia, and were only restrained by a deployment of Bantamese troops. But Coen was concentrating on the Moluccas, where the English had established a fortress at Pulau Run.

While the English in the East resisted the Dutch attempts to impose a monopoly by force, the approaching end of the truce produced a settlement in Europe. An agreement of 1619 provided that the English should be allowed to establish factories alongside the Dutch ones, obtain one-third of the fine spices and one half of the pepper and bear one-third of the costs of the Dutch garrisons. But the expenses were heavy, and even in 1622 the English were doubtful about continuing the spice trade in the Moluccas. Coen meanwhile decided to complete the conquest of Banda. In 1621 he occupied Lonthor and the English were forced to leave their post at Run. The inhabitants of Banda were wiped out, and the spice lands parcelled out to Company's servants to cultivate with slave labour. Ceram was treated to 'a dose of the same medicine'.[29] The erosion of the English position was not completed without bloodshed either: the famous massacre at Ambon of 1623. The English now concentrated, as the Directors had already envisaged, on pepper, using a factory in independent Bantam, and trading also at Bandjermasin and Patani. But they 'smuggled' other spices via Macassar.

In the Moluccas the Dutch made a determined effort and, meeting with no major native government, drove out the overburdened English, left the Spaniards with only footholds in Tidore and Ternate, and eliminated much of the competition from the already weakened Javanese towns. From the time of the brutal conquests of the Banda islands they were able to fix the price of nutmeg, and at great expense of life and treasure they were on the way towards a monopoly of spices other than pepper. Cloves were secured at Ambon by forced deliveries at fixed prices.

The Dutch empire in the Archipelago had been built, like the Portuguese, as part of a commercial network in seaward Asia as a whole. Like the Portuguese, too, the Dutch followed older Archipelagic empires in their attempts to centralise commerce in certain entrepots and to monopolise certain products. They differed in the elaborate contractual basis they attempted to give their monopolies and commercial agreements — in the attempt to envelop the Archipelago in an improvised legal system, sanctioned by maritime power. They differed from those who had previously exerted maritime power in the Archipelago by their greater method and perhaps by their greater ruthlessness. Already they seemed more firmly established than the Portuguese. If their position was maintained, still more if it was strengthened, the effects on Indonesian commerce and political power were likely to be permanent. Chinese and Indian trade to the Archipelago might not be eliminated, but it might be canalised, and the creation of rival indigenous empires would become impossible.

Nevertheless even in the Archipelago the Dutch operated no overall power at this point. In Celebes, in Acheh, in Jambi and elsewhere, they were one trader among many. After the conquest of Malacca, the Heeren 17 stressed 'the peaceful trade throughout the whole of the Indies [that] the kitchen at home must smoke of . . .' The Company's trade must be 'based on the common right of all peoples, consisting in freedom of commerce, the which being granted in neutral places by free nations where We find laws and do not have to bring them, We may not appropriate the aforesaid trade according to our own ideas and constrain such nations thereto by force . . .' But Van Goens, a member of the Council of the Indies, commented that the Dutch were 'deadly hated by all nations . . . so that in my judgment earlier or later war will have to be the arbiter . . .'[30] The conflict had indeed already been joined.

7 The Dutch and the Archipelago, 1640—1700

In the period after 1640 there was a shift in the European situation that affected Dutch policy in Asia. This was above all a result of the decrease in the importation into Europe of precious metals from Spanish America, which fell rapidly about this time and produced a period of economic recession that contrasted with the expansion of the previous century. With it, too, are associated the decline of Habsburg predominance in Europe, and the rise of a state that found its power in its military and diplomatic resources, the France of Richelieu and Louis XIV. France marked its recovery of a major position in European affairs by promoting new commercial ventures in Asia: the French China Company was set up in 1660 and Colbert's Compagnie des Indes in 1664. But this was also the period that saw the founding of the Société des Missions Etrangères (1659), and it was characteristic of the nature of its power that France should concentrate in Asia on diplomatic and missionary activities. Rome had been seeking to disengage the Catholic cause overseas from the declining Portuguese, and in 1622 the Propaganda (the Sancta Congregatio de Propaganda Fide) had been founded. The French initiative was welcome.

The political changes were to face the Dutch Republic with a threat from France in place of that from the Habsburgs. The recession also profoundly affected the position of the Dutch. It produced an access of mercantilism among other European countries directed against their hold on the carrying and colonial trades. Their reaction in Asia was to seek more stringent monopolies of the important products, to drive down the prices of others by political means, to eliminate Asian as well as European competition in the more profitable trades.

This determination was reflected in their policies outside the Archipelago. On the Coromandel coast they took Negapatam, and a treaty of 1644, following the regaining of its independence of Spain, gave Portugal only a respite in Ceylon. By 1663 the

Portuguese had lost all their possessions there, and all but Goa and Diu in India. Any hope of Portugal's revival after the peace of 1661 was dashed by the raids on its East African settlements by the Arabs of Oman. In the Far East, as ever, the Dutch were less successful. The disturbed Japan of the sixteenth century had sent traders southwards and brought European traders and missionaries northwards. But in the early seventeenth century the Tokugawa Shoguns ended the long civil wars, and as a guarantee of internal peace sought seclusion from external influences. The Spanish and Portuguese missionaries were driven out and the Dutch traders confined to Deshima. Governor-General van Diemen sought compensation in a more determined pursuit of Chinese trade and in 1642 drove the Spaniards from Formosa. But Koxinga, one of the Ming leaders cast out of the mainland by the Manchus, in turn forced the Dutch to abandon their factory.

In the Archipelago, on the other hand, the Dutch greatly strengthened themselves after 1640. From 1633 they had instituted a blockade of Portuguese Malacca, intensified into a siege in 1640 with help from Johore. At last in mid-January 1641 it fell, and the capture of this important town affected not only the position of the European rivals of the Dutch, but that of the native states in the western part of the Archipelago. The Dutch were able more effectively to pursue a command of pepper and of tin.

In 1641 itself a commercial contract was made with Palembang on the opposite side of the Straits, backed up by the visit of seven ships the following year, 'a terse contract . . . fulfilled more out of respect than love'. In 1643 a pepper contract was made with the neighbouring state of Jambi. 'The aim of the contracts was to obtain a monopoly for the Company, eliminate the Chinese buyers, prevent price inflation by setting a fixed price, and impose limitations upon Jambinese competition in shipping . . .' Several 'disciplinary actions' (1657, 1661) and new contracts (1662, 1678) proved to be necessary to assure the Company's position in Palembang.[31]

The pursuit of a pepper monopoly affected Acheh: so did the Company's interest in tin. In 1642 the Dutch made an agreement with Kedah for the delivery of half its production, and the following year Ujong Salang (Junk Ceylon or Phuket) promised the whole of its production. Kedah had to be blockaded but was never fully coerced. Perak remained under Achehnese suzerainty, but in 1650 the Dutch extorted from the queen of Acheh a treaty whereby the Company was to share the Perak tin trade equally with her to the exclusion of all other traders. In 1651, however, the Dutch factory was attacked and plundered, and at the end of the decade a Dutch blockade of Perak and Acheh produced an agreement granting the Company two-thirds of the Perak trade.

Dutch attempts to capture the pepper trade of the west coast of Sumatra also promoted the decay of the Achehnese empire. The pepper, like that of the east coast ports, came down from the interior regions of Menangkabau. The Dutch displaced Achehnese supremacy on the west coast, and under the Painan contract of 1663 a number of rulers in the Padang region granted the Company 'an absolute monopoly over the pepper trade'.[32]

Johore, after assisting the Dutch to destroy the Portuguese at Malacca, attempted also to make capital out of the defeats they inflicted on its rival, Acheh. The Sultan in fact was able in the 1640s and 1650s to extend his power over Siak and Indragiri, also pepper ports on the east coast of Sumatra. But this brought conflict with Jambi, and also the intervention of the Dutch, who used the opportunity to strengthen their monopoly of the newly discovered tin of Siak.

East of Java the Dutch sought to consolidate their monopoly of clove and nutmeg, and the independence of Macassar was disagreeable because their competitors found there a base for 'smuggling'. The prosperity of the south Celebes port began with the arrival of Malays from Malacca after the Portuguese capture. From the late sixteenth century Portuguese and Chinese and English merchants visited it, especially after the establishment of Javanese and, later, Dutch influence at Bandjermasin, and Mataram's oppression of the coastal towns tended to drive Javanese trade to it. The capture of Malacca by the Dutch made Macassar more important to the Portuguese, and the Dutch Governor-General commented that the local ruler 'is attempting to expand his dominion more and more, so that, in time, in order for it not to become too big it will need to be stopped, either by dexterity or open violence'.[33] In 1660 the Sultan agreed to prohibit all sailings to the Moluccas and expel the Portuguese, but he failed to carry out the undertaking. In 1667 he was finally defeated by a Dutch force under Speelman, aided by Bugis from the Celebes state of Boni, and he signed a treaty by which he accepted Dutch suzerainty, agreed to dismantle his forts, granted the Company a monopoly of trade and undertook to expel all non-Dutch Europeans. Shortly after south

Celebes was placed under a Dutch Governor. The Portuguese were left in Flores under the treaty of 1661.

In the Moluccas themselves, the Spaniards evacuated Tidore in 1663, and Speelman forced its ruler to follow the Sultan of Ternate in accepting Dutch overlordship. 'What Acheh had practised on the pepper coast, what the Portuguese applied in the Moluccas, what the rulers of Ternate and Tidore were accustomed to carry on against each other – *hongi* expeditions were now elevated by the Dutch Company to a system'. These fleets of large praus or *cora-cora* 'served first of all to punish the wicked violators of the monopoly contracts for selling spices to the foreign traders and by intimidation to make trade impossible for competitors, in the second place to maintain the spice prices by limiting production (destroying plantings)'. The policy meant revolt and increasing poverty in the islands, but it meant that for the Company 'the gross profit from the spices became overwhelming, often more than 1000%'.[34] In the last decades of the century the Dutch Company could fix the prices of clove and nutmeg in Europe and Asia. Too high a price might stimulate competition, however, and in pepper, despite the conquest of Malabar and the advances in Sumatra, the Dutch position was much weaker.

Pepper was in fact distributed far more widely than nutmeg or clove, and it was for this reason that the Dutch found it more difficult to obtain a monopoly. Their attention now turned to the independent state of Bantam, visited still by Chinese, Indians, English, French, and by the ships of the Danish East India Company, reorganised in 1670. The Dutch were assisted by a succession dispute, in which they aided one party with troops. As a result the victor made an agreement with them in 1684, surrendering his claim to Cheribon, paying the Company's war-costs, granting it an exclusive right to trade, and agreeing to expel all non-Dutch Europeans. The fortress of Speelwijk was constructed nearby. Bantam had partly existed on the pepper trade of south and south-west Sumatra, and the English, on leaving Bantam in 1682, had obtained permission to settle there, and ultimately founded a fort at Benkulen in 1685.

The advance of Dutch power in the western parts of the Archipelago deeply affected Mataram. The ruler had reached out and opened relations with Palembang, Jambi and Acheh. He sought also to prolong the resistance of Malacca by shipping it food supplies, and had sent an embassy to Goa in 1633. Soon after the fall of Malacca, the Dutch and the Susuhunan made the treaty of 1646, under which the Company received freedom to trade in his dominions and his subjects were forbidden to trade to the Moluccas. The Susuhunan sought to contain this most powerful of coastal towns, Batavia, by establishing a rice monopoly, but this produced rebellion elsewhere and Amangkurat I had to ask the Dutch for assistance. The dynasty was saved only by making important territorial concessions to the Company in 1678, including territory south of Batavia, the port and district of Semarang, and various coastal towns. Amangkurat's successor, Amangkurat II, was crowned with the ancient crown of Majapahit, but only as a result of Dutch troop movements. So far from creating a new Majapahit in the Archipelago, Mataram continued to yield to the commercial empire of the Dutch Company, and its monopolies of the sale of cloth and opium in the Susuhunan's dominions completed the ruin of Javanese commerce. Java 'now became more and more the land of enforced market crops'.[35] Already in the 1640s the Dutch had tried to supply the European market with sugar from Batavian estates. The loss of Formosa meant a strengthening of Javanese sugar on the Company's Asian markets, especially in Persia and north-western India.

In this period 1640-1700 Dutch power clearly increased in Java as in other parts of the Archipelago. There, as elsewhere, the Dutch benefited from their maritime resources and from the divisions of their opponents and from succession disputes. But their victories in Java suggest also their military superiority. In the capture of one of the rebel strongholds in Mataram in 1680, the Company had one man wounded and its allies, the Susuhunan's forces, lost only thirty, although the rebels had felt capable of resisting all attacks. The Dutch were vulnerable only to surprise and *amok*.

8 The Dutch and the Archipelago, 1700—1760

THE CHANGES in Europe in the period 1700-60 again much influenced developments in the Archipelago. Growing wealth expressed itself with new demands for Asian goods — for Bengal textiles and for China tea — and a new ability to supply them. Spices, on the other hand, became, with the provision of winter cattle-fodder and culinary changes, relatively less important. The Dutch were faced with problems of adaptation, adaptation to new areas and new products, adaptation more generally to the expansive conditions of the eighteenth century as distinct from the recession of the seventeenth. They were faced also with the competition of the English, whose mercantilism had proved remarkably successful and contributed to a 'commercial revolution'.

In the case of the new European demand for Indian textiles — the 'Indian craze' — the Dutch had some initial success. At the turn of the century these products occupied a dominant position in the goods received in the Netherlands from the East. The textile trade of the Coromandel coast, on which the Dutch had concentrated for the supply of the traditional Southeast Asian markets, had suffered from local civil wars, and with this new European demand they had taken the initiative in developing trade in Bengal. They were, however, soon left behind by English commercial competition there: and in the first third of the eighteenth century the English definitely took the lead.

The Dutch failure to compete was even clearer in the case of tea, then Chinese alone. The Dutchman Valentijn indeed opposed this novelty: 'People who study hard and use their brain diligently should take good care not to drink tea, as they are enfeebled by the work of their brain in advance and therefore should not strive after further exhaustion . . .'[36] But the various East India Companies flung themselves into the trade. In the late seventeenth century a Russian trade developed overland. The Chinese admitted the sea-trade of other nations at

Canton. The Dutch had never established a direct trade with China and were at a disadvantage in these new conditions. They attempted to compete with the English at Canton rather by attracting Chinese junks to Batavia, where they could be supplied with cinnamon, pepper, and other jungle and marine products in exchange for tea, silk, alum, and tutenag. In the 1730s a direct trade from the Netherlands began, supplemented by Batavian ships carrying Archipelago goods to lessen the demand for specie. The sales of tin and pepper greatly increased in the 1740s and 1750s. 'As a whole', however, 'the Dutch Company during these years lost ground in the European race for China tea. The English competing company had . . . become the greatest importer.' [37]

Furthermore, even in the acquisition of Archipelagic goods for the China market, which did not yet absorb European manufactures, the English became supreme. Their success in the trade in tin, jungle and marine products undermined the Dutch position in the Peninsula and in many parts of the Archipelago. English resources and enterprise gave England command over this aspect of the trade within Asia. The spice monopoly remained an object of the envy of the English. Yet it may be that the Dutch devoted so much attention to maintaining it that they neglected the new opportunities that opened up. In one respect they did adapt. They turned their position in Java to account by promoting coffee cultivation there and attempting to compete in the expanding European market with the supply from Arabia and from other colonial sources. Perhaps the major effect of these changes in the Archipelago, indeed, was to strengthen the Dutch in Java, and thus further to differentiate its development from that of the other islands.

In Java at the opening of the century the Dutch possessed a belt of territory stretching from coast to coast between Mataram and Bantam. In East Java, Surapati, a Balinese adventurer, began to carve himself a kingdom out of the territory of Mataram, but when Amangkurat III appeared to be in league with him, the Dutch installed his uncle as Susuhunan as Pakubuwono I (1705). For this he paid with further territorial concessions, dropping all claims to Cheribon, the Preanger and eastern Madura, and accepting a Dutch garrison at his capital at Kartasura. In 1706 the Dutch defeated Surapati and in 1707 drove Amangkurat III into exile. The death of Pakubuwono I led to a succession dispute among his sons and to Dutch intervention. Further territory was exacted from Pakubuwono II in 1743. He surrendered all his claims on Madura and the north coast of Java became a Dutch province centred at Semarang. Yet further military action followed in 1749-57. Mangku Bumi, his brother, opposed the Susuhunan, and when his successor received the crown from the Dutch as Pakubuwono III, most of the Mataram chiefs joined Mangku Bumi and for a time the Dutch were hard pressed. The solution was the partition of Mataram.

In 1755 Mangku Bumi accepted Pakubuwono III as ruler of the eastern half of the kingdom, centred at Surakarta, while he received the western half, with a capital at Jogjakarta and the title of Sultan Amangku Buwono. Two more years' fighting were required to subdue his nephew. At the same time the Dutch were involved with Bantam. There Governor-General van Imhoff intervened in a succession dispute and produced a rebellion which lasted till the next Governor-General reversed his policy. The new (and rightful) Sultan then in 1752 ceded the Company control over the Lampongs in south Sumatra. With his recognition of its suzerainty, too, the Company was now after much effort master of Java, save for the territory in the extreme east of the island, where, until 1772, the Balinese supporters of Surapati still caused trouble. The Dutch had been assisted not only by a technological superiority, but also by the divisions between the coastal towns (above all Bantam) and the inland empire, and by divisions within that empire.

The Dutch had first prevented Mataram's imitating Majapahit, and then virtually displaced Mataram in Java itself. Their Asia-wide empire, as it were, contracted upon the Archipelago, and upon Java, the potential centre of an Archipelagic empire. But the Dutch were committed in Europe also, and their immediate, and always a prominent concern was not with empire-building as such, but with dividends. At this point, therefore, Java was important to the Dutch Company in its efforts to meet the competition of the English and other Companies in Asian trade as a whole. It attempted, for instance, to grow tea there, as ordered by the Directors in the 1720s. But the great achievement of the period was the successful introduction of coffee, especially in the swidden areas of the Batavian highlands, the Preanger and Cheribon. The great break-through of Java coffee on the European market came in the 1720s. Hitherto the Archipelago had supplied goods for the trade within Asia or goods with a monopoly position in the European market. The situation in Java was exceptional in that coffee was directed to Europe in competition with 'colonial' sources of supply. But it was procured by old-fashioned methods not strange to the Archipelago, by the use of the growing political power of the Dutch.

The cultivation of coffee was originally arranged by Governor-General Zwaardekroon, whose contracts offering fivepence a pound promoted a rapid expansion. The Directors lowered the price, and this reduced the number of trees. As a result coffee was increasingly produced by 'forced deliveries'. The cultivators had to grow and deliver at a fixed price much to their disadvantage. Furthermore, a share went to the local aristocracy through whom the Dutch operated. In the 1740s waste land was sold in the Batavian highlands to private farmers who were given seigniorial rights over the peasants in order to ensure them a labour force and in return they sold the produce to the Government at a fixed price. But in most of the cultivation districts the Dutch worked through the Regents and other native officials. In some sense this was 'the traditional pattern of compulsory labour supervised by local officials for the benefit of lords and princes'.[38] But the power, the method and the continuity of the Dutch tended in the long run to emphasise the seigniorial and communal elements in Javanese village life and to set it in a more rigid pattern.

Outside Java the Dutch found it less and less possible or worthwhile to enforce their monopoly contracts in many parts of the Archipelago. In the Moluccas they sought still to retain their command of clove and nutmeg, and the success of their methods, including the *hongi* expeditions and the control of food supplies, continued to bring dividends, as well as to reduce the islands to poverty and entirely to destroy the greatness of Tidore and Ternate. But even in these regions there was 'smuggling' and elsewhere the Dutch position deteriorated still more, for instance on the west coast of the Peninsula. On the one hand, this was the work of the 'Country Traders', English merchants resident in Asia whose trade had first become important during the disorganisation of the London Company in the 1650s and in favour of whom it subsequently renounced much of its claim to monopoly of the trade within Asia. By the early eighteenth century their most successful field was the Peninsula, especially the western side, and by the 1740s they had made deep inroads on the Dutch preserves. But they were assisted also by the Bugis who, in these days of Dutch decline, were able to build up a network of trading posts linking the Straits with Borneo and beyond without establishing a more formal empire, and whose enterprise indirectly aided that of the English Country Traders. The Bugis of Boni had helped the Dutch against Macassar, but then Dutch monopoly had fallen upon them, and they reacted to this, and to the ruin of the Moluccas, by intensifying their activities further afield, initially by privateering, but also by trading and governing.

In the eastern part of the Archipelago, they established their influence at Pasir — with the sort of indirect rule they preferred — and developed a commercial centre at Pontianak. The Dutch on the other hand sought to protect the approaches to the Moluccas by concluding a new trade agreement with the Sultan of Bandjermasin in 1756. But it was in the western part of the Archipelago — where the English Country Traders were strongest, and where the Straits formed the main overseas approach to increasingly important Java — that the battle was joined most intensely.

The early years of the eighteenth century had been marked in Johore by a succession dispute which permitted the expansion of Dutch influence. The last Sultan of the Malacca line was murdered in 1699, and he was succeeded by his chief minister, the Bendahara. But in 1717 the throne was seized by the Menangkabau ruler of Siak, Raja Kechil, who ruled the Johore dominions from Riau. The deposed Sultan intrigued with Daing Parani, a Bugis adventurer, and in 1722 the Bugis placed his son on the throne, with a Bugis as viceroy enjoying the real power the Bendahara had enjoyed in earlier days. Already from the 1680s there had been Bugis settlements on the Klang and Selangor estuaries, and now Bugis influence expanded from Riau. Attempts were made to control Kedah and Perak in face of Menangkabau opposition and a Bugis Sultan of Selangor was set up. The Dutch tried to strengthen their position. In 1745 they began to rebuild a fort at the Dindings. They were also assisted by the growing restiveness of the Johore Malays under Bugis tutelage, and in 1755 made a treaty with the Sultan promising him help against the Bugis in return for the tin monopoly of Selangor, Klang and Linggi. The Dutch were involved in open war with the Bugis and in intervention in Siak. The importance of the Straits to them exceeded the importance of their tin monopolies or of the general threat of Riau, which the Country Traders used as an entrepot. Malacca, attacked by the Bugis in 1756, was in some sense an outwork for Java.

The Dutch position was weakening in many parts of the Archipelago in the phase 1700-60. The effect of this, however, can only be appraised if the impact of the Dutch in the whole period since 1600 is reconsidered. Their effect had not been — as had that of the Portuguese — simply to displace the centres of wealth and power in the Archipelago. Their influence had been exerted more continuously and effectively in seeking control of the spices upon which the empires of Ternate and Tidore were built and the pepper and tin upon which Acheh and Johore had been built in the days of Portuguese retreat. The result was clearly the decline, if not the destruction of these empires. Yet the Dutch did not entirely replace them, and they tended to remain in suspended animation, restless centres of aristocratic disappointment and tyranny, for which the subsequent relaxation of the marine control of the Dutch only gave greater scope. The rain forest had been destroyed, the secondary forest grew, lower, tangled, congested, and no trees came to maturity. The expansion of the Dutch in Java destroyed another commercial empire of the same vintage, Bantam, and acquired them the dominance of east and central Java. But they were not yet seriously applying the resources of this old centre of empire to the stabilisation of the Archipelago.

The other sources of power and possible stabilisation in the latest phase were the English Country Trade and the Bugis. But the Dutch contended with them and no new equilibrium was reached in the Straits or the Johore regions. The Bugis found no scope — even if they had inclination — for an empire on the old pattern. Nor did the Country Traders represent a politically constructive element (for such traders, for instance, the entrepot practices of the Sultanate of Acheh were an inconvenience), and the English Company so far had displayed little wish openly to break into Dutch preserves.

Neither the old Dutch maritime policing nor the new British or Bugis commercial enterprise reached north Borneo and Sulu, and the empires there faced also the rivalry of Spain. It was not surprising that these last regions in particular — but also Johore — became the especial strongholds of what the Europeans tended to classify as piracy but which had more complex origins than the mere desire to rob at sea.

9 Indian and Chinese Influence in the Archipelago after 1600

ISLAM continued to be associated with the resistance to the Europeans throughout the period from 1600. The decline in Javanese merchant activities made Mataram an isolated, inland and agrarian state, and increasingly Javanese Islam was forced 'to turn inward and to operate within the framework of traditional religious beliefs'. Nevertheless, Islam was 'a rallying point of identity' and symbolised 'separateness from, and opposition to, foreign, Christian overlords'.[39] The European impact tended still further therefore to domesticate what had once been another alien influence. The Dutch Company not surprisingly took measures against the Muslim 'popes', and not surprisingly every effort to resist the expansion of the Company's power took on the character of a holy war. The intensifying influence of the Dutch in Java in the eighteenth century, associated as it was with the native Regents, had a rather differentiating effect. The ruling élite, or *priyayi,* had long distrusted the growing influence in Javanese society of the Muslim teachers and scribes, the *kiyayi* and *ulama,* and feared the erosion of traditional custom or *adat.* This was additional reason for association with the Dutch, but that in turn only expanded the influence of the *ulama* in the village and tended to dissociate the *priyayi* from Indonesian Islam.

In other parts of the Archipelago, Islam was connected with the maintenance of independence and with the active and adventuring, even piratical, elements in Indonesian life. 'The treatment received by Mataram and Bantam at the hands of the Dutch "infidels" caused many Mohammedans to take up arms in defence of their religion, and for a time a pirate fleet under a fanatical Malay of Sumatra, who assumed the name of Ibn Iskander ("Son of Alexander the Great"), terrorised the Java Sea until in 1686 a Dutch squadron under Krijn de Rode destroyed it.'[40] In the eighteenth century, when Dutch control was relaxing but no new political structures were replacing the old, adventurers who tried to seize power by piracy and might attain limited political success were often Sharifs, with the sanction of Islam, enjoyed, indeed, by some earlier empire builders.

Only in the Moluccas did the Dutch seriously attempt to expand Christianity: they were concerned, for instance, to turn the Portuguese Catholic converts on Ambon into Calvinists of some sort. Elsewhere they realised the obstacles among Islamised coastal populations, and they had hardly penetrated to the interior, save in Java.

Islam in this period, especially in Java, was, however, more cut off from the centres in India and Arabia than previously. It seems likely that the trade of the Indians to the Archipelago had been further reduced by the Dutch attempts both in India and in the Archipelago to control the age-old trade between the two. Indian trade was probably rather confined to Acheh and the western parts of the Archipelago; and there, too, it met the competition of the English Country Traders.

The commercial activities of the Chinese changed in direction and in some degree in scope. In the seventeenth century the Dutch, seeking a monopoly of pepper, had competed with the Chinese merchants in Bantam, in Jambi and elsewhere. The object of the Dutch in the case of overseas trade with China, however, was generally to attract junks to their ports, as distinct from native, and much less to attempt a monopoly of trade with China where they had no settlement. The impact of the Dutch in Java opened up new opportunities for the Chinese. Sugar developed round Batavia in the later seventeenth century: 'from the very first . . . , plantations and mills had mainly been run by Chinese people'.[41] The fostering of the junk trade in the early eighteenth century greatly increased the number of Chinese in Batavia. As early as 1706 the Dutch issued stiff regulations against those 'without means of existence who became roving beggars and a menace to law and order'. In July 1740 stronger measures were decided upon: 'all Chinese unable to prove that they were suitably employed were to be deported to work in the cinnamon gardens in Ceylon'.[42] Resistance followed the unfair operation of these decrees, and the resistance was followed by a bloodbath of the Chinese.

The Chinese were, however, making themselves more and more indispensable to the Dutch colony: they were craftsmen and revenue farmers, as well as tea-traders and sugar-cultivators. Some middleman activities were indeed theirs even before the establishment of the Dutch, and in this sphere the impact of the latter tended to be of a quantitative rather than of a qualitative nature, though in time the qualitative change emerged from the quantitative. It is also true that Chinese resorted to areas where Dutch influence did not prevail. Alexander Hamilton found a thousand families settled in the Johore dominions in the early eighteenth century, and Chinese miners were invited by the Sultan of Sambas in west Borneo to work his goldmines. The Sultan of Palembang had also invited Chinese to work the tin of Bangka island, but this was in 1724, two years after he had signed an exclusive contract with the Dutch.

If the Chinese communities grew in size, this did not mean that they exerted a greater influence on the indigenous population. Perhaps on the contrary. They were frontiersmen, organised for protection in *kongsis,* in groupings according to their different places of origin in southern China, in secret societies. Communications were such that few Chinese actually achieved the objective of returning home in affluence, while few women came to join them. But the tendency to racial assimilation was somewhat countered by the restrictive aspects of Dutch policy (the Chinese, for instance, were excluded from the Preanger districts, in order to prevent infringements of the Company's monopoly and, it was said, to protect the natives from the quick-witted immigrants), by the barrier of the Islamic religion, and by the very determination of the frontiersmen to maintain their Chinese culture. And local governments — native and Dutch — left the communities more or less autonomous, adopting the practice of appointing a Chinese headman or Capitan, often no doubt the head of a powerful secret society.

The Chinese government asserted no political influence in the Archipelago in this period, which was, no doubt, a further factor in Dutch favour. In the seventeenth century the alien Manchus had displaced the Ming dynasty. But their insecurity, and their awareness of the Europeans, led them to reduce contacts with outside, especially with the Archipelago. An edict of 1712 prohibited trade in the Nanyang and requested governments there to repatriate the local Chinese for execution. The Nanyang Chinese communities were, in fact, hotbeds of anti-Manchu sentiment, deeply ensconced in the secret society structure. At about the same time, the Tokugawa régime in Japan also sought seclusion, but with more complete success. But the Japanese of the sixteenth century had traded not to the Archipelago, but to the mainland and the 'Philippines'.

10 The Mainland
1500—1760

WHILE AN EFFECT of the period from 1500 was further to differentiate developments in Java from those in the rest of the Archipelago, it also saw a greater differentiation between the Archipelago and the mainland. Indeed neither the Portuguese nor
the Dutch effected such changes among the states built upon
the great rice-bowls of the mainland as they did among the
commercial centres of the Archipelago and ultimately in ambivalent Java.

If the activities of the Portuguese in the Archipelago became
in their decline increasingly those of adventurers, proselytisers
and private traders, on the mainland they were such from the
beginning. Their influence there was less affected by the erosion
of their government superstructure. They were above all missionaries and mercenaries for the rulers of the region.

In Dai Viet the immediate successor of Le Thanh-tong, the
conqueror of Champa, was Hien-tong, who proved an able ruler,
but subsequent monarchs were incapable. An old pattern of
politics repeated itself. With the decline of the central power,
great territorial magnates built up their strength, and in the
growing strife obtained clients and created private armies. A
period of bloody chaos produced the accession of Mac Dang
Dung as emperor in 1527. A descendant of the Le sought the
intervention of the Chinese, but Mac bought them off in 1540.
But the Le, with their generals Nguyen Kim and then his son-
in-law Trinh Kiem, recovered the provinces of Thanh-hoa and
Nghe-an in the early 1540s, and the following decades saw
struggles that culminated in the defeat of the Mac in the early
1590s by Kiem's younger son, Trinh Tung, and the emperor
Le The-tong entered the capital Dong-kinh in 1593. But the
Le were now powerless: and under their nominal sovereignty
the Trinh dominated the north, and the Nguyen built their
power on the newly conquered lands to the south. The Mac
continued to provide yet a further divisive element: supported

by the Chinese, they remained in the province of Cao-bang for three generations. This threat to Dai Viet no doubt helped to induce the Trinh to continue the Le dynasty: a usurpation might have provoked a further intervention. And it gave a semblance of unity to a realm where there were now two centres of power, a realm that was difficult to control from the north as it extended into southern regions, themselves difficult to control, as the Chams had found.

The Lao kingdom of Lan Chang in the northern valley of the Mekong had been forced in the late fifteenth century to pay tribute to Dai Viet. But the subsequent disorders seem to have led to a long period of peace during which the Lao kingdom prospered as a result of commercial relations with the cities of the Menam valley, more accessible than the lower Mekong. The centre of the kingdom was moved down from Luang Prabang to Vienchang.

The Laos were indeed involved in the attempts of the Thai king of Ayuthia to gain control in Chiengmai which continued in the sixteenth century. In 1545 the Lao king placed his own candidate on the Chiengmai throne, and the Laos routed the intervening Thais in 1547. There appear to have been Portuguese soldiers-of-fortune serving in the Ayuthia army.

The Portuguese also acted as mercenaries in Burma on various occasions. The Ava kingdom had been able in the fifteenth century to maintain some semblance of authority only when China was pressing on the Shans who threatened it. Divisions among the Shans also assisted the preservation of the Burman kingdom; but on the other hand they threatened to involve the Burman king or give his vassals a chance to rebel. In 1527 Ava was finally sacked by the Shans, and the remaining rulers up to 1555 were all Shan chiefs. At that point Ava was incorporated in a new Burman kingdom. A small state had maintained a precarious existence — during the long struggle between Ava itself and the Mons — at Toungoo in the Sittang valley. The chaos in Ava afforded the able prince Minkyinyo (1486-1531) opportunity to expand his dominions, and by 1527 he was 'the most powerful ruler in Burma'.[43] Then he made preparations for an attack upon the rich and cultivated Mon kingdom of Pegu which had been independent since the Mongol destruction of Pagan in 1287. His son, Tabinshwehti, fell upon the delta region in 1535 and in a very short time had reduced the whole kingdom once more: Bassein was taken in 1535, though Pegu held out till 1539. In 1541 Tabinshwehti took Martaban, another Mon trading port, 'with an army reinforced by Mon levies and

69

a contingent of Portuguese mercenaries under João Cayeyro'.[44] Moulmein surrendered, and so the whole Mon kingdom down to the Thai frontier at Tavoy fell into Burman hands. Tabinshwehti then turned northward and captured Prome, winning a decisive victory against the Shan ruler of Ava with the help of Portuguese gunners. Then he was crowned in Pagan, but his capital remained in the south, at Pegu.

This was because Tabinshwehti had designs upon the Menam valley, once also a Mon region, now controlled by the Thais. His invasion of Ayuthia in 1548 began a long struggle between the Burmans and the Thais for the southern provinces and the north of the Malay Peninsula. The murder of the Burman king in 1550 put an end to these expeditions for the moment, and the kingdom fell into chaos. His son-in-law, Bayinnaung, was however crowned in Toungoo, and in 1551 'with a mixed force of Burmese and Mons, and a Portuguese detachment led by Diogo Soarez de Mello',[45] he reconquered Pegu. In 1555 he defeated the Shan chiefs to the north and captured the city of Ava. He was then in a position to renew the attacks upon the Thais, to join again the struggle of the Burman and the Lao-Thai-Shan peoples. Bayinnaung attempted, in face of opposition from Vienchang, to establish his control over Chiengmai. This was but a step towards his chief object, the conquest of the greatest of the Thai states, Ayuthia, and the vast expedition of 1563-4 succeeded in establishing a vassal ruler there.

The fragility of Bayinnaung's régime was illustrated by the Mon revolt that occurred during his absence. In 1568-9, however, a second expedition was sent to maintain control of Ayuthia, but an attempt to take Vienchang failed, and in 1570 Bayinnaung retreated. Ayuthia remained under Burman control for fifteen years, but attempts to establish control in Vienchang ended with Bayinnaung's death in 1581.

His death meant a crisis for an empire so much the creation of force and will as that of Bayinnaung. His successor, Nanda Bayin, was faced with rebellion in the north centred on Ava. Furthermore, having built up their strength in repelling the Cambodians — who were trying under Ang Chan to take advantage of Ayuthia's weakness, while relatively free of interference on the other hand because of the civil wars in Dai Viet — the Thais were tempted to regain their independence of the Burmans. In December 1584, therefore, Nanda Bayin invaded 'Siam' through the Three Pagodas Pass. Ayuthia was besieged in 1587, but the invasion ended in a disaster that might have been worse but for a Cambodian invasion of Siam. By 1593 Nanda

Bayin had failed in five full-scale invasions of Siam, and it was the turn of the Thai king Naresuen to invade Burma. First, in 1593-4, he dealt with Cambodia. Then he turned on southern Burma, acquiring first Tavoy and Tenasserim, and then, with the help of Mon rebels, Moulmein. In 1595 Chiengmai came again under the suzerainty of Ayuthia, and the same year the Thais threatened the city of Pegu. And now Nanda Bayin's kingdom finally collapsed, for his brothers revolted and the central government disappeared. Ayuthia retained lower Burma from Martaban southwards.

In the crisis of the Burman kingdom, the Arakanese played a part. Their kingdom had secured independence in 1430, taking advantage of its peculiar position in relation to the centres of Burman power, of the weakness of the Ava dynasty, and of the weakness also of the Bengal régime, which enabled it to seize Chittagong. The Toungoo dynasty planned to restore Burman authority over the Arakan Yoma, and Tabinshwehti led a vain expedition to Mrohaung. The succeeding struggle at once to hold down the Mons and defeat the Laos, Shans and Thais engaged the further attention of the Toungoo kings, though Bayinnaung was about to attack Arakan upon his death in 1581. In the event the Arakanese were to be the aggressors, seizing the chance offered by Nanda Bayin's difficulties. In 1599 a powerful fleet seized the port of Syriam, and this the Arakanese retained, placing it under the control of one of their Portuguese mercenaries, Philip de Brito. The kingdom of Arakan had for some decades past had Portuguese mercenaries in its service, and Chittagong had become the resort of a substantial European and Eurasian population, trading with nearby Bengal, indulging also in piracy and slave-raiding, profiting from the collapse of government there in face of the oncoming Moghuls. Now the leader of these *feringhi,* de Brito, was master of Syriam. He planned the conquest of Arakan, but his power was destroyed by a restored Toungoo dynasty early in the seventeenth century.

If 1600 may in some sense be a convenient dividing date in mainland history — to coincide with the arrival of the Dutch in the Archipelago — it seems to be on the whole only accidentally related to the activities of the Europeans. It saw the restoration of the Le, the temporary collapse of Toungoo, the victories of Naresuen. It is hard exactly to estimate the part the Portuguese played in the struggles among the various peoples to control the ricelands of the mainland and stabilise their kingdoms. What share should we rather leave for Bayinnaung and others whose ambitions expanded into megalomania among the uncertain frontiers within Southeast Asia? What part was borne by the peasants upon whom the burden of war, its fighting and its destruction, so heavily fell? Only perhaps in Arakan — seeking to maintain the insecure independence it owed to the weakness both of its Southeast Asian and its Indian neighbours by employing outside sources of power — did the Portuguese play an important political role. Certainly there was no external influence that might have contributed to the stability of the mainland in this most turbulent phase of its history. Even Chinese power — reduced by the weakness of the Ming — operated only in the exceptional area of Dai Viet.

The success of Ayuthia in its struggles with Toungoo led to attempts to establish control over the Shan states upon which Naresuen was engaged when he died in 1605. It was in this vigorous kingdom that first the Dutch, and then the English, established factories, at Ayuthia and at what had now become the vassal state of Patani on the Peninsula. The object of the Dutch Company in Ayuthia was to secure a link with the trade to China and also with that to Japan, since for some time Japanese traders had been coming to Siam. The Thai kings, on the other hand, hoped for the support of the Dutch against the Portuguese, and in 1609 sent an embassy to the Stadhouder Maurice at The Hague. The English, who arrived in 1612, could if necessary be played off against the Dutch. Their object was also commercial, but characteristically they were aiming less at a share in the intra-Asian trade than at the disposal of English manufactures, for which it was found there was little market. In the 1620s king Songt'am sought the aid of the Dutch and the English against the Cambodians, who had revolted during a renewal of the conflict with Burma, but in vain. Indeed the English left Patani and Ayuthia in 1623. The Dutch strengthened their position in the following decade, however, by promising help to a usurper, and in 1634 were permitted to build a small settlement on the river-bank at Ayuthia. On the other hand, the king, Prasat Thong, inaugurated royal commercial monopolies which first of all challenged the Chinese, but later employed them as factors and officials.

It was in keeping with the more forceful policy initiated by the Dutch in the Archipelago after about 1640 that, when in 1649 the court of Ayuthia failed to satisfy some claims made by the Company's agent van Vliet, he threatened to call on the Dutch fleet to attack the city. It was in keeping with the rather different situation on the mainland that this provoked a strong reaction, the Dutch factory was seized and all its inmates arrested and threatened with death. In 1654 a Dutch naval demonstration was staged in the Gulf of Siam. But the accession of king Narai in 1657 began a period in which the Thais called in the French with a view to limiting the power of the Dutch.

English Country Traders — looking to an area where the Company had little official interest — reopened the factory at Ayuthia in 1661 and were seen as a balance against the Dutch. Contact with the French began on the other hand through the missionaries of the *Société*. The favour Narai afforded them aroused the jealousy of the Dutch, who in 1664 secured a treaty granting them the monopoly of the trade in hides, which went to Japan, and a virtual monopoly of the trade between Ayuthia and China. This only made the king more anxious to overthrow them. English trade was fostered: the factory became official in 1675; and the Company's object was row not only to sell English manufactures, but also to participate in the Japan trade, which the Japanese could not do themselves.

The English supported Phaulkon, a Greek adventurer at the court of Ayuthia, but quarrelled with him, and he turned to the French. In 1680 Narai had sent an embassy to Versailles, but the French ship was lost off Madagascar, and new envoys were sent in 1684. In 1685 Louis XIV's return embassy reached Ayuthia in two men-of-war. The French hoped for a large-scale conversion to Christianity, but asked also for the right to place French troops in Bangkok and for a settlement at Mergui, vital for control of the Bay of Bengal, on the opposite shore of which Pondicherry had been founded in 1674. Phaulkon assented, though the French troops had to take the oath of Thai mercenaries. The English factory, beset by corruption, and without Phaulkon's favour, had been withdrawn in 1684, and now, in 1686, the Dutch factory was closed. This left the French predominant, and that was the ruin of Phaulkon. In July 1688 he was executed, and later in the year the French troops were evacuated, and the missionaries were treated for a while with great severity.

The Dutch recovered their position to some extent by an agreement of the same year and secured commercial concessions especially in regard to hides and tin. But they had lost the threatening position that had led Narai to look to the French and the Thais were careful not to allow them to regain it, even if they could have done so. In so far as there was any threat to Ayuthia from the Europeans in this period, the Thais had been able to turn it aside by utilising their divisions. Their

history perhaps made them peculiarly sensitive to the distribution of political power and the importance of diplomacy.

In the remaining phase of this period, 1700-60, the history
of Ayuthia is more taken up with local political problems, with
succession-disputes, with struggles against Cambodia and Burma.
In Cambodia in the seventeenth century the Europeans made
little impact. The Dutch factory there, withdrawn in 1622, re-
established in 1636, had an 'unfortunate history',[46] and an English factory in the early 1650s was unauthorised. The eighteenth
century saw a renewal of Thai attempts to control Cambodia,
which met local opposition and Vietnamese rivalry. In 1714
the king of Cambodia was driven out by his uncle with Vietnamese assistance. The Thais in 1715-7 vainly attempted to
restore him, but the uncle finally accepted Thai suzerainty.
This did not help him, however, to resist Vietnamese conquest
of Cambodian provinces. The period ends with an invasion of
Ayuthia by the Burmans under Alaungpaya in 1759, a renewal
of the old conflict with the Thais.

The kingdom of Arakan had risen in a period of Burman
weakness and Portuguese adventure, and Chittagong had become
a centre of piracy and slave-raiding and of *feringhi* power. De
Brito's plans, however, prompted the king of Arakan to turn
upon the Portuguese at Chittagong. The refugees took possession of Sandwip island, but their attack on Mrohaung failed
because the Dutch supported the Arakanese against the *feringhi*
(1615). The Dutch, indeed, were welcomed as a balance against
the Portuguese, and between 1610 and 1617 had a factory at
Mrohaung. Their military support, however, was very limited.
The result was a *modus vivendi* among the parties, and the
Dutch came to Mrohaung to buy the Bengali slaves of the
feringhi or the rice they cultivated. Their factories lasted from
1625 to 1627 and from 1630 to 1631. The threatening advance
of the Moghuls led the king to open negotiations with the
Dutch and the factory was re-established in 1635 for a few years.
Again there was a factory between 1653 and 1665, but it was
abandoned because the Dutch feared involvement in the growing struggle between the Great Moghul on the one hand and
the Arakanese and *feringhi* on the other. The result was the
Moghul defeat of Arakan, the annexation of Chittagong, and
the decline of Arakan. The establishment of a strong power on
the uncertain Bengal frontier left Arakan more at the mercy
of the Burmans who, moreover, were regaining their strength.

One aspect of Burman disintegration at the beginning of the
seventeenth century was the hold established by the Portuguese

adventurer, de Brito, upon Syriam: and he received assistance from the viceroy at Goa, anxious to maintain some influence in a period of Portuguese decline. The end of this venture was, however, certain, once Burman power was re-established. The Nyaungyan prince, a younger brother of Nanda Bayin, died in 1605 while trying to subject the rebellious Shan states, and his son and successor, Anaukpetlun, was for some years also engaged in the north. In 1608, however, Anaukpetlun took Prome, and in 1613 he captured Syriam. Next he invaded Tenasserim, driving out the Thais, but halting after he had re-taken Martaban. Then he captured Chiengmai, but on his murder in 1629 the Siamese project was abandoned, and in 1635 the Burman capital was moved back from Pegu to Ava. The policy of the new king, Thalun, was peaceful, and in his reign the Dutch established their first Burman factory, at Syriam in 1635, with the object of elbowing aside the Indian and Portuguese merchants. Thalun opposed the Dutch attempts to establish a monopoly, but they did succeed in easing out the English factory of 1647 ten years later.

More important to the Burmans were the Chinese, now about to make one of their spasmodic interventions in Burma's history. The change of dynasty in China led not only to secret society activities which spread among the overseas Chinese, and to Koxinga's flight to Formosa. The last of the Mings resisted in Yunnan till in 1658 he fled by the old Burma road to Bhamo, and upper Burma was ravaged by Ming supporters. These difficulties precipitated in the south a Mon revolt, a flight of Mons into Siam, an invasion of Siam, defeat and Ayuthia's recapture of Chiengmai. The Burman kingdom recovered in part because of a revolt against the Thais in Chiengmai and also because the Manchu dynasty established its authority in Yunnan. In all this chaos the Dutch had simply watched the decline of their trade. The restoration of order encouraged the idea of a factory at Bhamo, which attracted caravans from Yunnan, since it would enable the Company to open a trade with China. The Court of Ava forbade the project and in 1679 the Dutch closed their Burma factories.

This was the signal for a revival of English interest, and in 1680 the Governor of Madras sent an envoy to Ava. The influence of the French in Siam and in India was also a motive, and Burma was somewhat involved in the growing rivalry of the French and English from the late seventeenth century. The French plans for Mergui stimulated an English attempt to seize Negrais. An English dockyard was established at Syriam from the 1690s. The French had one there also by 1729. But both of these disappeared in the great Mon rebellion of 1740.

Incursions by Manipuri tribes from the north had given the Mons a new opportunity. They seized Syriam and Martaban, and established a king of their own, whose forces occupied Prome and Toungoo and began to threaten the capital itself. Finally in 1752 the Mons captured Ava and deposed the last king of the Toungoo dynasty. A new Burman leader, calling himself Alaungpaya, resisted. Late in 1753 the Mons abandoned Ava and early in 1755 Alaungpaya took Prome. He pushed southward and drove the Mons from Dagon, where he began to build a new city, Rangoon. Pegu was still independent and at Syriam the Mons were aided by a French agent, for the French led by Dupleix hoped to recoup some of the losses of the War of Austrian Succession in India by an adventure in lower Burma.

Rumours of substantial French aid to the Mons prompted a new English attempt to settle Negrais in 1753. In fact, after raiding Manipur and the Shan states, Alaungpaya took Syriam in 1756 and Pegu in 1757, and French influence was eliminated. The English failed to give Alaungpaya all the munitions he asked for, and they were accused of complicity in a desperate Mon revolt which took place while he was attacking Manipur again in 1758-9. The king decided to turn the English out of Negrais, and they were massacred by Burman troops in 1759. The marginal position that the Europeans had secured on the coast disappeared with the re-establishment of Burman power. That re-establishment was marked also by the new invasions of Siam, and Alaungpaya died in 1760 as his forces were encircling Ayuthia.

The struggles of the Thais and the Burmans on the one hand and the internecine strife in Dai Viet on the other contributed to the security of Laos, and it enjoyed prosperity under its great king Souligna Vongsa (1637-1694). In 1637 the Dutch had established their factory in Cambodia, and in 1641 a Dutchman went up from Phnom Penh to Laos to attempt to open trade in the 'land of gumlac and benzoin',[47] yet another illustration of the Company's activity in this phase from about 1640. Van Wuysthoff was the first European ever to visit Vienchang, but nothing came of his mission, partly owing to the impassibility of the Mekong. The period following the death of Souligna Vongsa was marked by a succession dispute. The Vietnamese intervened to uphold his nephew, and he recognised their supremacy in 1706. But in 1707 his cousin Kitsarath proclaimed himself king at Luang Prabang, and in 1713 the kingdom of the fragmented upper Mekong region was further divided when his brother Nokasat set up an independent principality at Champassak. This division invited intervention from the Menam valley and from Dai Viet. Under Alaungpaya, too, there was intervention in Laos as in Siam: the king of Vienchang — who was having trouble with his petty vassal, Tran Ninh (Chieng Khouang) — sided with the Burmans, who defeated the king of Luang Prabang. On the other hand, Dai Viet sought to levy tribute from Luang Prabang in 1750.

By 1600 the empire of Dai Viet was virtually divided under the fainéant Le dynasty between the Trinh in the north, and the Nguyen, south of Song Tranh. The Trinh were occupied pacifying Cao-bang, but after 1627 war developed between the two regions, and continued on and off for some fifty years. In that period both parties welcomed European merchants, especially as sources of munitions, but it was virtually impossible to carry on trade. The Portuguese had no factories in the region, but had gone to Tonkin to buy silk for the Japanese market, and traded to Fai-fo, the Nguyen port. The Nguyen invited the Dutch to trade, and their first factory was planted at Quinam in 1636. Their establishment of a factory in Tonkin, however, led to quarrels with the Nguyen, and the factory in the south was abandoned in 1641, reopened at Fai-fo in 1651, and finally closed in 1654.

The civil war also opened the way to missionaries, also welcomed by both sides lest the arms supplies should be cut off. The first mission was founded under Portuguese auspices in Tourane in 1615 as a result of exclusions from Japan by the Tokugawa, and the French Jesuit Alexander of Rhodes was sent to Cachao in 1627. He was expelled in 1630, returned in the 1640s, expelled again, and determined to work for French help. In 1658 two Frenchmen were appointed to lead the mission in face of Portuguese opposition. The Jesuits had also to give way, at least temporarily, to the Société des Missions Etrangères. But if Portuguese opposition was defeated in 1689, and the Jesuits accepted French patronage, the difficulties of the missionaries did not diminish. The end of the civil war enabled the rulers to give rein to their apprehensions of the subversive effect of the alien religion on a social order sanctioned by Confucianism. The persecutions became more regular, especially after the French venture in Siam. Catholic communities were never extinguished, however, and mission activity never ceased. After 1738 Pope Clement XII gave the north to the Jesuits who fled from China following the Rites Controversy, leaving the south to the *Société*. There were more Christians in the former than in the latter, but overall only some 30,000 at the end of the eighteenth century.

If the end of the civil war — and to some extent the lesson of Ayuthia — tended to reduce the scope for European missions in Dai Viet in the later seventeenth century, so also European trading factories disappeared. The Dutch finally left the factory in Tonkin in 1700. The English had established a factory in Tonkin in 1672, their eyes also on the Japan trade, in keeping with their new realisation of the importance of intra-Asian commerce. But the Tokugawa were obstructive, and the factory was kept on only till 1697, supplying silk for the European market. In any case the English were shifting their attention more to China, for which, as with the Dutch, Tonkin had been something of a substitute. In the 1670s they were looking to Amoy, then to Chusan and Canton, scene ultimately of their great commercial success. For a while (1702-5) — after the exclusion from Chusan — a rival English Company occupied Pulau Condore, an episode that ended with the Macassarese garrison's massacring the Europeans. Otherwise in the eighteenth century there were no European settlements in Vietnamese territory. To this the attitude of the rulers contributed.

The civil war had ended in stalemate. Above all the stalemate resulted from the fact that there were now two great centres of population and power in the empire. The Nguyen survived because of the wealth of the Mekong delta which Vietnamese colonisation tapped. They also had the benefit of Portuguese artillery which was superior. The Trinh, on the other hand, were hampered by the problem of the Mac in Cao-bang, who received the support of the new Manchu dynasty. The colonial south was bolstered by outside strength, the northern homeland restrained by apprehensions of its great neighbour. The country remained divided after the last campaign of 1672-3 at the Song Gianh, once the boundary of the Viet and Cham lands.

After the conclusion of a truce with the Nguyen, the Trinh were able to deal with the Mac. In 1677 their power was ended, and peace was secured with the Manchus. Otherwise the attention of the Trinh was given in part to the reduction of Laos, but more and more to internal reorganisation. This involved not only a struggle against alien sources of subversion, but an attempt once more to build up the central power. In the early Le days, the government had sought to guarantee the taxable masses against the great men: but in the subsequent disorders landed proprietors had grown strong. The civil wars and the heavy burdens on the peasants that they involved played into their hands. In 1711 Trinh Cuong sought to re-establish repartition every six years and to prohibit the growth of private property, but the decrees were a dead letter. On the other hand, *corvée* and taxes increased. The oppression of the peasants led to rebellion in the crowded delta area between 1739 and 1751. Some reforms followed between 1753 and 1756 but, despite its efforts, the régime remained weak, ripe for the Tayson invaders.

The Nguyen saw that their strength lay in their possession of and extension in the Mekong delta. The last remains of Champa were absorbed in 1697. The oppressed peasants of the seventeenth century settled in the new lands. The Nguyen also intervened in Cambodia in 1658, on the pretext of a border violation, and in Khmer dynastic struggles in 1674, in 1686 and in the 1690s. New provinces, including the Saigon area, were thus acquired and colonised. But the heavy burdens on the peasants of the south, deriving from the wars of extension and the oppression of the nobility, were to produce the rebellion of the Tayson.

The French, pursuing their rivalry with the English in India and China in the mid-eighteenth century, looked not only to the Mon regions in Burma but also to the Nguyen lands. A French East India Company mission under Pierre Poivre visited the Nguyen ruler Vo-vuong in 1748-50. Poivre failed to secure permission for a factory in Tourane Bay, but a modest one was established after 1753, and a limited repeal of the ban on missions secured.

In the seventeenth century the Europeans had profited from disturbed conditions in many parts of the mainland and had established numerous commercial factories. They did little to develop the commerce of the area, in any case a less attractive prospect than the spices of the Moluccas or, later, the coffee of Java. Only in Arakan and perhaps in Ayuthia did they achieve substantial political influence. In Arakan the influence of the *feringhi* was destroyed by the Moghuls – it had owed much to the power-vacuum in Bengal, peripheral to Southeast Asia – and the Dutch avoided real intervention. In Ayuthia the Europeans were successfully played off against one another, though the Phaulkon crisis may temporarily have limited Ayuthia's threat to Cambodia. Otherwise the influence of the Europeans was slight. If it had any importance, it was not because it changed the structure of mainland politics, but rather that it gave the mainland states new weapons to fight out long-standing struggles. The possession of Portuguese cannon perhaps helped to preserve the Nguyen. But this only contributed to the relative stability of Dai Viet in the early eighteenth century, in turn leading to a growing isolation and incidentally promoting the destruction of Laos, which had enjoyed a prosperity in the previous period that inaccessibility had prevented the Europeans sharing.

Both Ayuthia and Burma also enjoyed a relative stability in this period, until it was broken by the Mon revolt. The Portuguese were a spent force, the Dutch more concerned than ever with the Archipelago and with Java, the British with the new possibilities in India and China. It was only the French who in mid-century sought to counter the English by developing an influence in Burma and southern Dai Viet: but only with the most limited success. The mainland continued to contrast with the Archipelago in this period by witnessing on the whole a low and declining level of European activity. The activity of the Chinese — Ming rebels or Manchu dynasts — was perhaps more significant overall, but even that especially concerned Dai Viet and Burma, which had common frontiers with China, though of different degrees of accessibility.

11 The Philippines to 1760

THE EFFECT of the Portuguese incursion was to disperse many Malaccan merchants and Muslim state-builders to other parts of the Archipelago. The Sultanate of Mindanao appears to have been founded by such an adventurer, aided by the local sea-gypsy tribes, the Samals and Bajaus, though it remained only a stage beyond the loose tribal organisation of Luzon and the Visayas. The most important of the Sultanates in the region was Brunei in north-west Borneo, and the Muslim trader whom the Spaniards met at Cebu in 1565 was a factor of the Sultan of Brunei. These southern Sultanates, Sulu, as well as Brunei and Mindanao, were spreading their commerce, their political influence, and their religion, Islam, northwards into the Visayas and Luzon, and at Manila, convenient for the China trade, the Spaniards met Raja Suleiman, who insisted that he and his followers were not 'painted Indians'. Most of the people of the Visayas still were: Islam had no hold as yet. The Spaniards were to establish themselves not only where the Portuguese attempted to establish no influence, but also where the 'Moros' were weakest. In so doing, they were to add to the distinctiveness of this part of Southeast Asia.

The arrival of the Spaniards across the Pacific linked Southeast Asia in yet a new way with the outside world. Their objective had originally been the wealth of the East and their interest did not disappear with the discovery of America. Indeed this became the basis of a new empire in Southeast Asia. That empire — unlike the Portuguese and the Dutch — came to be confined to one region, islands that had been already colonised from the north and the south: now from the east.

In 1519 the objective of Magellan — in origin a Portuguese who had fought with Albuquerque at Malacca and gone with the subsequent expedition to the Moluccas — was the spice islands. He reached Samar and Cebu and was slain in Mactan. The remaining ships went on to Palawan, Brunei and Tidore, and the *Victoria* completed the circumnavigation of the globe. This and subsequent expeditions of 1525 and 1527 met Portuguese opposition in their attempts to penetrate the Moluccas, and in 1529 the Spanish king admitted Portuguese claims in the treaty of Saragosa. He did not, however, consider Spain excluded from the 'western islands', and a new expedition under Villa-Lobos, sent from Mexico in 1542, named them the Philippines after the Infante. As King Felipe II that prince ordered a new expedition 'to go to the said Philippine Islands and other islands contiguous thereto, . . . and to discover the return route to this New Spain with the greatest despatch possible, bringing or sending spices and other valuable articles of those regions'.[48] The expedition under Legazpi left New Spain in November 1564. The first settlement was made at Cebu the following April-May. Visits by Portuguese vessels, concerned over interference in the Moluccas, helped to induce Legazpi to move to Panay early in 1569. Thence in 1570 an expedition left for Manila, the centre of trade with China, and, after a clash with Raja Suleiman, took it. The following year, with aid from Mexico, permanent settlements were made at Manila and again at Cebu. Expeditions were despatched to establish Spanish control over neighbouring areas, meeting in tribal territory no organised resistance, and by the end of the century it extended over the coastal regions of Luzon and the Visayas.

To some Spaniards this activity was merely incidental. They hoped to evangelise the whole Far East. Their hopes were soon dashed. In Japan, indeed, the disputes with the Portuguese Jesuits, and the Tokugawa's apprehensions of the Spanish power in neighbouring Manila, to which Japanese had traded, contributed to the policy of seclusion. In 1596-99 there were semi-official and missionary-backed attempts to help the Cambodians drive out the Thais. But the main object of the Spaniards was to control the commerce between China, the Philippines, Borneo and the Moluccas. To the southward they met not only the opposition of the Portuguese, even after 1580, but more formidably, and nearer at hand, that of the Moro Sultanates, especially Brunei, who had marked out this field of commercial empire for themselves. In 1578 and 1581 there were expeditions to Brunei to intervene in a succession dispute. In the former year a capitulation was exacted from the Sultanate of Sulu, but an expedition of 1579 went to Sulu and Mindanao without achieving substantial results. Figueroa led an expedition to Mindanao in 1596, but he was killed thirty miles up the Cotabato river. Ronquillo took over, but achieved little, except to provoke further Moro retaliation. The Spaniards had evacuated the fort they had established at La Caldera (near Zamboanga), and this opened the way to Moro fleets, who could not round the east coast of Mindanao, to invade and plunder Cebu, Panay and Negros in 1599. In 1602 Gallinatos was sent to punish Sulu, but he was unable to reduce the forts of the town, and retired to Panay. By the end of the century Spain had secured a foothold in Ternate. But between that island and Manila there was still formidable opposition from the Sultanates — expressed also in retaliatory warfare on the Visayas which the Spaniards termed piracy — and the trade of Manila and China developed rather in association with Mexico than the Moluccas.

The Dutch wished both to dislodge the Spaniards in the Moluccas and to secure Manila as a means of access to the China trade. One of the Rotterdam fleets of 1598 anchored in Manila Bay in 1600 and plundered vessels there, but was driven off. The Company followed the example, and in 1614 Iloilo, the supply base for the Moluccas, was sacked. In 1616-17 van Spilbergen appeared before Manila. The Dutch were drubbed but kept up a blockade till the mid-1620s when the sphere of conflict moved to Formosa. Amid the Dutch emergency little could be done about other rivals to the south, indeed on occasion egged on by the Dutch. In 1616 Sulu Moros plundered as far as Camarines and Cavite. But the relative calm after the mid-1620s led to a Spanish attack on Sulu in 1630, and a retaliatory raid on Leyte and Samar in 1634 prompted the establishment of a fort at the Zamboanga bottleneck designed by a Jesuit. From this base the Spaniards attacked Sultan Kudrat of Mindanao in 1636 and 1637, and the following year Governor Corcuera mounted a great attack on Sulu. But the Sulus fled to the hills or to the Tawi-Tawi islands.

Furthermore the Dutch exerted greater pressure after 1640. Corcuera's relative neglect of Formosa led to Dutch triumph there (1642). Then, following an earthquake that in 1645 weakened Manila's defences, the Dutch threatened the capital that year and again in 1646. The result was withdrawal from the south. A treaty of friendship and alliance was made with Kudrat in 1645, another with the Sulus in 1646, and the garrisons were withdrawn from the Sulu Archipelago, though the Spaniards retained rights over certain islands, Tapul, Balanini, Siassi and Panguturan. A treaty with the Dutch in 1648 was based in theory on the principle of *uti possidetis*. But in 1662 the Spaniards were driven from the Moluccas. The following year they evacuated Zamboanga, though a Jesuit mission remained at Dapitan, populated by pagans and Visayan immigrants. The Dutch thus did not drive the Spaniards from Manila, but they did destroy their hold on the Moluccas and greatly weakened their efforts in Sulu and Mindanao. The Sultanates of Sulu and Mindanao were able to strengthen themselves, to become more centralised, while the Spaniards tried to handle the area by diplomatic means: in 1679 a treaty was made with Brunei, putting Palawan on the Spanish side of the 'boundary'.

In the eighteenth century it is perhaps significant of the modification of Dutch policies that the Spaniards were able to recover some ground vis-à-vis the Moros. In 1718-19 Zamboanga was rebuilt. But diplomacy was the order of the day even in the approach to Sulu. A peace treaty of 1725, which gave Basilan to Spain, was followed by more raids on the Visayas. But apparently it was hoped that the Sultan could control his *datus* and turn them from piracy to commerce if a new treaty was made, and this was done in 1737. The restiveness of the *datus*, however, was increased by the Sultan's admission of the Jesuits.

The Sultan went to Manila, was even baptised in 1750, but himself fell out with Spain. The conflict was renewed with bloody Sulu raids on the Visayas in 1753.

The explanation of this curious episode must surely be sought among the fundamentals of the Spanish-Moro conflict. Spain, impeded by the Dutch, had failed to subdue the Sultanates, and they had been able to strengthen their political structures. But the Spaniards had deprived them of the chances of building an empire and of attracting substantial international commerce. The restiveness of the *datus* was not surprising, nor was it likely that it could be relieved by developing a commerce with Manila. Even a strong Sultan could not contain it, and a Christian Sultan would make matters worse. The Sultanates remained: and they became increasingly the centres of wide-ranging piracy, directed not only against the Spaniards.

What perhaps requires explanation is less that the Spaniards failed to extend further in this period than that they retained their empire in Luzon and the Visayas in face of the Dutch and in particular of the Moros. It was hardly due to the vigour of Spanish commercial or agricultural enterprise, in which the Philippines remained rather peripheral. The initial failure to capture the trade between the Moluccas and China had been followed by the phenomenal success of the trade between Mexico and China for which Manila became the entrepot. Mexican silver provided a simple means for trading with a country that required nothing that Europe could produce and yet supplied silk, damask and porcelain. This was the origin of the famous Manila galleons. It provoked the jealousy of the Andalucian textile interests and of the Seville and Cadiz merchants who liked to see the silver passing through their hands and not those of the idolators. In turn this led to royal restrictions on the galleon trade. In 1591, for instance, a royal order prohibited direct trade between Manila and Peru, and in Mexico only Novidad, and after 1602 only Acapulco, were left open for the Manila trade. The number of galleons was limited and the value of their cargo restricted.

The metropolitan merchants did not secure the abandonment of the Philippines that they once sought. What they secured was a limitation that helped to prevent the realisation of the entrepot possibilities of Manila, and yet permitted sufficient enterprise to absorb the activities of the Spanish colonists. This meant that the Philippines avoided some of the oppression of Mexico. Crops were introduced from Central America: guava, pineapple, egg-plant, cacao, indigo, tobacco. But agriculture was relatively neglected: there were no vast slave-worked haciendas, there was no pastoralism. Little mining was undertaken. The Spanish entrepreneurs were monopoly-minded merchants in Manila looking to Mexico and to China. A further effect of this was that the Spaniards were concentrated in the capital. There was much less intermarriage than in Mexico or indeed in Portuguese India, where it formed a link when others had gone. And finally large numbers of Chinese came to Manila in the junks that met the galleons and found new opportunities in the Europeanised city, in retail trade and in internal credit activities. In many spheres the Spaniards indeed became dependent on them, but this by no means reduced their apprehension of another alien community, likewise, with its *mestizos,* concentrated in the capital — in the 'Parian' — and coming from a powerful and proximate country. In 1603 and in 1639 there were conflicts and again in 1662 when the Spaniards were apprehensive of Koxinga and took provoking precautionary measures.

The commercial ventures of Manila thus aroused opposition in Spain, did little to develop the Philippines (though thus sparing them some of the horrors then incident to development), concentrated the Spaniards in the capital, and brought in a Chinese community that did not add to their security though they may have viewed it with unjustified apprehension.

The conquest had been aided by ships from Mexico, and from 1606 Mexico subsidised the government of the Philippines, short of revenue for obvious reasons. But it was by no means the strength of its military forces — only a few hundred men at the end of the sixteenth century — nor the effectiveness of its administration that preserved the Philippines to the Spanish crown. In Spanish American style there were a Captain-General and an Audiencia checking the chief executive's power. Locally the conquered territory was first divided into *encomiendas,* some retained by the government, most parcelled out to deserving Spaniards who gained thereby the right to collect a poll-tax and levy statute labour, in return for protecting their wards (not unlike the Thai patrons). The private *encomiendas* were reduced during the seventeenth century and finally disappeared under a cedula of 1721. There remained the more regular provincial government organised from the late sixteenth century, headed by the *alcalde mayor* or governor, and below that the *pueblo* (later *municipio*), of which the *gobernadorcillo* was chief magistrate, and then the *visita* or *barrio,* generally containing one *barangay.* But the way this administration worked,

85

and even the nomenclature of some of its units, are incomprehensible without considering the significance of the missions and of the native ruling classes, the two groups upon which the Spanish empire really rested.

The Christian missionary endeavour had its greatest Southeast Asian success in Luzon and the Visayas, areas Islam had only been about to reach. Augustinians came with Legazpi in 1565, the Franciscans came in 1578, the Jesuits in 1581, the Dominicans in 1587, the Recollects in 1606. By 1594 there were 267 regulars in the Philippines. By 1655 there were 254 regulars and sixty seculars. Theoretically the secular clergy should of course have taken over settled Christian communities. In fact the growth of the secular clergy by no means kept pace with the rate of conversion. The regulars all along managed to hold on to the majority of benefices and to reduce the bishops' claim to visitation to nullity. They also opposed the training of Filipino seculars, of which there were 142 by 1750, mostly in subordinate positions. Furthermore the regulars were from the late seventeenth century entrenched in certain areas, as a result of a decision of the Council of the Indies of 1594. The bulk of the Tagalog provinces in southern Luzon, the citadel of Spanish power, went to the Augustinians and Franciscans; the Augustinians obtained Pampanga and Ilokos, the Franciscans Camarines, the Dominicans Pangasinan and Cagayan. The Visayas were divided between the Dominicans and Jesuits, and the Jesuits also settled in Mindanao. The Recollects came rather late and received little. The establishment of the different orders in particular areas might be thought disadvantageous to government control. But this would be to ignore some of the factors in the situation. And it was not simply that Spanish friars — and few *indios* or natives were admitted into the orders, none at all into the Society of Jesus, nor any *mestizos* or mixed-bloods, only European immigrants and *criollos* or local-born Spaniards — dominated local Christianised communities and ensured a measure of loyalty to His Catholic Majesty.

The Spanish conquest had been aided by the divisions among the inhabitants, not merely political, but linguistic. The missionary effort reduced the number of languages: some came to prevail, Tagalog, Ilokan, Pampangan, Bikol, and so forth, in particular areas. The parcelment of the islands among the various orders enabled them to concentrate on certain peoples, that is those using certain languages. The missionaries in fact generally used not Spanish, but native languages, and if these were reduced in number, there yet remained distinct 'peoples',

Even at the end of the nineteenth century less than 10% spoke Spanish. In the eighteenth century more emphasis had been laid on it in new community schools, but there were few teachers and few inducements. It opened the way to no career in the public service, or the church, and no other opportunity offered. The division among the *indios* meant that native troops of one province could be employed to deal with trouble in another: a native constabulary, mostly Pampangans, was much used.

There were only two periods of rebellion in the main regions of Luzon: the Pampangan revolt of 1660-1, resulting from the crushing burdens imposed by the Dutch war; and the Tagalog revolt of 1745-6 against the usurpation of communal lands by the religious orders. Some tension was, no doubt, worked off against the Chinese: Filipinos joined the Spaniards in the periodic massacres. In other ways the Spaniards' failures helped to secure them the loyalty of the coastal peoples. Only in the nineteenth century were missions and an administrative framework established, for instance, in the Ilokan cordillera. Beyond their limits were mountain peoples, not only as of old Negritos, but also the so-called Igorots, related to the coastal peoples, but divided from them by Christianisation and hispanisation. This division helped the Spaniards to assert control of the coastal peoples in Luzon. In the Visayas the missionaries sought to establish compact coastal settlements to facilitate their work. It also made them a prey for the unconverted Moro raiders. But in turn this helped to tie the Christian Visayans to the Spanish régime.

If the missions taught Spanish, it was generally to an élite class, the sons of the chieftains. While the friars were one pillar of government — and the less challenged because of the lack of Spanish settlers — the native élite was the other. It was an élite that, though somewhat mestizised, grew out of the pre-Spanish period and it was never to lose its influence. The *datus* and *maharlika* became headmen, or *cabezas de barangay,* and *gobernadorcillos,* or magistrates, in the *pueblos* or *municipios,* and with the other office-holders, such as the constables, the inspectors of palm trees and rice fields, the notary, the church officials like the fiscal or sacristan, formed the local élite, the *principalia,* a substantially hereditary oligarchy that gained local experience, to be later used, with accompanying corruption, in national government, after the power of the friars had been broken. Its position rested also on its economic power.

Besides the demands of the church — to cover the stipends

of priests and, except in the case of the Jesuits and Dominicans, fees for the sacraments — the peasants owed also the dues of the state. Rather in traditional Southeast Asian style, these consisted chiefly of the *polo* or government demand for labour (or *repartimiento*), and the *vandala* or forced sale of goods to the government: virtually this meant deliveries of rice or other products, since the government would not pay a fair price and so resorted to compulsion, which the Spaniards excused by referring to native indolence. The demands were especially heavy in the first half of the seventeenth century when the Spaniards were holding out against the Dutch threat and attempting to deal with the Moros: indeed an upward rise of population occurred only after the peace of 1648. The *alcaldes* were not well paid and were expected to repay themselves from their part in levying the tribute, a practice which conduced to oppression and peculation, and made the *alcaldes* rather like the *encomenderos* who were gradually displaced. But the *principalia* assisted both *encomendero* and *alcalde* in the collection of tribute and the requisitioning of labour and supplies. They also secured a percentage and the right to demand personal services from the people. This combination of economic and political power expressed itself in terms of the distribution of land.

Here again the pre-hispanic system continued with a difference. That system was built upon debt peonage and sharecropping. In the period of the Dutch war the power of the chiefs, augmented by their share of government power, enabled them to enrich themselves and to oppress others with *vandala* from which they were exempt. In the better conditions of the late seventeenth century the system became less oppressive, but share-cropping continued. Furthermore the land came more and more into private hands. The church's holdings represented only a small portion of the total land under cultivation. Much more came into the hands of local native landlords, exploiting their powers and their superior education to assume the ownership of lands ordinarily cultivated by their dependants. There was thus no continuity between the *encomiendas* and the nineteenth century *latifundia*, such as is sometimes assumed. More significant is this assumption of European-style property and displacement of communal ownership by an élite originating in the pre-Spanish period, but deriving increased influence from the conquest. It gives Philippines history an extraordinary continuity.

In the pre-1500 phase, the islands had been distinguished from the mainland and from the Archipelago in a rather negative way. The contacts to the north had not produced a political transformation. Towards the end of the phase, the islands began to be drawn into the commerce of the Archipelago, and new cultural, religious and political changes commenced in the south. The Sultanates, imposing themselves upon the tribal structures of substantially Nesiot peoples, were starting to stretch towards the north — stimulated by a reaction to the Portuguese incursion into the Archipelago — when the Spaniards intervened from across the Pacific. The Spaniards deprived the Sultanates of opportunity without effectively subjecting them, so that, affected also by the Dutch monopolies in the Moluccas, and then by the relative failure of Dutch marine control, during the eighteenth century they increasingly became pirate centres. In Luzon and the Visayas, on the other hand, the contrast with the mainland and the Archipelago was given a more positive content. The Spaniards, failing to create a commercial empire in the Archipelago, nurtured in these islands a population substantially Christianised and hispanised. They inaugurated a new connexion between Southeast Asia and the outside world, but its impact was largely confined to one part of Southeast Asia. Their unique régime there was paradoxically stronger inasmuch as amid the changes there was a potent continuity. The people passed from a relatively tribal to a relatively centralised government, but one that did not wish to eliminate all the old divisions. The effect was to place power not only with the missions but also with an élite of pre-Spanish origin. The islands retained their uniqueness, though the British ventures of the succeeding period began again to bring them into closer contact with the Archipelago.

12 New Guinea and Beyond

THE ACTIVITIES of the British were also to open up new possibilities on the most remote of Southeast Asian frontiers. Across them few contacts had so far been made. New Guinea — or at least the Vogelkop — had been brought into the commercial scheme of the Javanese towns and into the list of Majapahit's claims. The commerce and the claims were inherited by the Moluccan Sultanates, in particular by Tidore. The territory, on the other hand, was named New Guinea by a Spanish explorer of 1545. The Dutch, after eliminating the Spaniards from the Moluccas in the 1660s, assumed suzerainty over Tidore. The Papuans were stated to be under Tidore. The Company had no wish to become directly involved in so unattractive a territory — 'nothing but waste strands, lands and wholly barbarous, cruel and savage people', as an expedition of 1623 had reported[49] — and the Tidore claims might be sufficient to keep other powers away from the fringe of the Moluccas.

The Dutch interest in Australia was also directed in some degree towards ascertaining that it was not only unattractive, but sufficiently unattractive to act as a protective fence for the Moluccas. A yacht sent from Banda in 1606 touched the Cape York coast, but missed the Strait that the Spaniard Torres discovered later that same year while looking for *Terra Australis*. The expedition of 1623 went to Cape York and also to 'Arnhem Land', and Melville Island was 'discovered' in 1636. This was more or less the region visited by Bugis trepang fishers perhaps since the fifteenth century, but it did not attract the Dutch, nor seem likely to attract others. In the course of their Southeast Asian venture, the Dutch had also, of course, made contacts with western Australia, sometimes touched by vessels taking the 'roaring forties' route from the Cape to Batavia. Again no settlement was made. In the 1640s, a time of strenuous endeavour in the Archipelago, Governor-General van Diemen sent out the great explorer Tasman to renew the search for *Terra Australis*.

He circumnavigated Australia and discovered Van Diemen's Land. Before returning round the north of New Guinea, he discovered New Zealand. The Dutch never discovered the fertile and attractive east coast of New Holland, upon which the British were to inaugurate their Australasian settlements.

But were they also to inaugurate a phase of history that Australasia and Southeast Asia should share? This the Dutch had feared and avoided. Was a new connexion to be made between Southeast Asia and the outside world — as the Spaniards had linked it to America — now that the Dutch had lost their command of the seas? In most senses it would be a revolution, for the well-known north and the unknown south had little in common save for some related aboriginal tribes in Van Diemen's Land and the Andamans. And New Zealand's connexions were Pacific: it was thence that the Maoris had come, according to their legends at about the same time as the Thais had crowned their king in Ayuthia and Majapahit had set forth its claims over the Archipelago. The period from 1760 was, however, a revolutionary one.

PART TWO

Southeast Asia
1760–1942

Preface

IN THE PERIOD from 1760 to 1942, Southeast Asia was subject to major changes. One source of transformation was the industrial revolution that began in Europe and spread outside, involving all the world in economic and social innovation. The movement developed first in Great Britain. From the late seventeenth century onwards, the British had been trying by all means to expand their commerce, and this had stimulated technological improvement and invention, affected also by the scientific revolution of the period. From about the middle of the eighteenth century the population began at last to increase, and these factors, coupled with readily available coal and iron resources, promoted from about 1760 an industrial revolution of increasing rapidity. The expansion continued into the period of the French wars, though in an irregular way. Post-war the problem was to find countries able to absorb British goods and to carry on a reciprocal trade. The difficulty of the task was reflected in the recession of the 1820s, 1830s, and 1840s, the period of the Great Reform Bill, the Chartists, the repeal of the Corn Laws and of the Navigation Acts.

The period from about 1850, on the other hand, was one of rapid expansion, promoted by the gold-rushes, by the railway boom, by the industrial advance of other countries. In the last quarter of the century, indeed, Britain had to meet competition from Germany and the United States, able to overtake Britain especially in the newer sorts of industrial activity, electrical, chemical, and after the turn of the century automobile. The depression of the 1880s and 1890s was followed by general expansion and the first world war by prosperity and then by the great depression after 1929. This was a period in which the British economy, though expanding rapidly, was expanding less rapidly than its major competitors. Among those were now Japan and Russia. But the preeminence Great Britain enjoyed during the late eighteenth and most of the nineteenth century is an important clue to understanding the European impact on Southeast Asia in this period, as indeed is its relative decline in the first half of the twentieth century.

This does not mean that we should over-emphasise the direct impact of the industrial revolution in the early part of this period. So far no great market for European goods had existed in Asia: the Europeans had purchased Asian goods by disposing of American silver, by participating in intra-Asian trade, and by utilising in new ways traditional methods of compulsive exploitation. The industrial revolution was to effect a great change. It 'set a mass traffic of goods in motion; the lands of an ancient Asian culture were mobilised as consumers' markets for the large industries of the West and (under colonial capitalism) fitted into the trade system as areas for supplying the raw materials and plantation products of modern colonial mining and agriculture'.[50] But up to about the middle of the nineteenth century the impact of the revolution in Southeast Asia was largely indirect. Economically the principal effect was to assist Britain to command the trade within Asia and somewhat to expand and diversify it. British imports of textiles began to compete with Indian textiles, driving them from many markets, but domestic industry remained important throughout Southeast Asia.

After mid-century the industrial revolution was to bring a growing demand for tin for the expanding canning industry, a growing demand also for food products; and the ability of the West Indies to compete with the East in this sphere had been reduced by the abolition of slavery in the 1830s and 1840s. But the biggest changes came as a result of the improvements in transport and communications of the 1860s. These included the use of the compound engine in long-distance steamers, the opening of the Suez Canal in 1869, and the establishment of direct telegraph communication with Europe at about the same time. All brought Southeast Asia into cheaper and closer contact with world markets for sugar and coffee and tobacco, and after the turn of the century for rubber and oil. The demand for rubber began in the 1870s with the new electrical and bicycle industries, but in 1888 Dunlop invented the pneumatic tyre, and the boom came, as also for oil, with the creation of the automobile industry.

Naturally these influences of economic origin contributed to major social changes in Southeast Asia. Traditional village subsistence agriculture tended to be dislocated, traditional crafts and domestic industry abandoned, and the communal pattern of life was destroyed or distorted. Plantations with wage-labourers, or peasant farming for outside markets, shared the landscape. With these changes went also a rapid but unequal expansion of population, the result, in part, of widening economic opportunities, better transportation, health measures: death rates fell, the high birth rates of a society of agrarian cultivators dependent on labour persisted. Better communications and economic innovations also intensified European cultural influences, but facilitated other influences, Indian, Chinese, Japanese, Islamic, too. Furthermore, immigration, especially of Indians and Chinese, greatly expanded. In the midst of these changes, it was not surprising that, while some peoples, like the Bugis, survived by adaptation, the mass of the people were inclined to react negatively, by xenophobia, by harking back to an imagined golden age. And it was not surprising that the more educated leaders sought to turn new sources of power and new ideas to their own account. The related problems of nationalism and communalism were intensified by the economic stresses of the great depression which reacted so severely upon primary producing countries.

In some sense, therefore, in this period Southeast Asia enjoyed an unwonted community of experience. If in the previous phases, the history of the Archipelago, the mainland, and the Philippines tended to diverge, now all the countries were involved in world-enveloping changes of economic origin. But the tendency was for this common experience to produce a greater diversity. Firstly, this was due to the existing diversities, the product of historical processes already described and of geographical conditions. Thus within Southeast Asia the impact of economic change was diversified, and not only by obvious factors such as the distribution of raw materials. The great outlay required by any form of economic development in the region — in clearing jungle, making roads, putting down malaria — tended to concentrate it. Certain areas became the scene of intense response to the new demands. Others responded by concentration on supplying rice to these areas, and the deltas of the Irrawaddy and Mekong were opened up. Whole communities, indeed, became dependent on the position of one or two products in the world market.

The second source of diversity was the division of almost all Southeast Asia among different European empires between about 1760 and the first decade of the twentieth century. A new political structure was imported into this frontier region. *Strange notions of international law, of international relations,* of boundary, overlaid old patterns evolved in adaptation to the circumstances of Southeast Asia and imposed a new exactness even where territories and allegiances had already been more or less defined. Within the colonial boundaries there was again some common experience. Pacification by the colonial powers — as later their health measures — promoted the general growth of population and generally initiated social change. New systems of administration of whatever European variety had a dissolving or modifying effect upon existing society, working, for instance, against debt slavery and against personalised authority. In other fields policy often tended to facilitate the creation of 'colonial' economies, of unbalanced economies, and to inhibit any potential for industrialisation. New political ideas opened new horizons and new opportunities to the educated. Increased European settlement in the colonies, the result of administrative and economic developments, and the possibility of living a more European life, generally changed the attitude of Europeans to the culture around them.

Common policies were likely to have diverse effects in Southeast Asia. But the effects of imposing European rule were additionally diversifying because the process was a gradual one, extending through the period from 1760 to 1900, but especially fast after 1870; and because it was carried through by a number of different European powers, enjoying different relations with predominant Britain, establishing different constitutional and economic links between colony and metropolis, with different motives, different traditions, different backgrounds, different racial attitudes. And in one case a state sought to maintain an independence of all by borrowing something from each. It was under these various circumstances that economic forces played upon Southeast Asia. It was these circumstances that modified the changes they produced, anticipating some, restraining or re-shaping others. It was in this political and legal context that nationalism and communalism grew up.

In the establishment of these empires or fragments of empires there is perhaps a paradox. Thanks to Britain's early industrialisation, its command of the sea, thanks also to its conquest of India which added to its Asian resources of trade and manpower, this was a period of undoubted British predominance in southern and eastern Asia. Yet Southeast Asia was fragmented. The explanation of the paradox must clearly be sought primarily in the nature of British policy.

The distinguishing feature of earlier European empires — those of the Portuguese and the Dutch — had been their Asia-wide character. This was true of that of the British also, but in the period 1760-1900, their interests in India and China were predominant, and deeply influenced their policy in Southeast Asia.

At the opening of the eighteenth century the East India Company had possessed three principal factories in India, Madras, used as a centre for the Coromandel textile trade since 1641, Bombay, Catherine of Braganza's dowry of 1661, and Calcutta, acquired in the 1690s with the growing importance of the Bengal textile trade. The beginning of wider territorial control dates from the battle of Plassey in 1757. The decline of the Moghul empire conduced to anarchy in India and opened the way to political adventure by the Persian Nadir Shah, by princes of the empire and others, by the French East India Company, which hoped to destroy a British commercial supremacy it could not destroy otherwise, and by European extortionists and swashbucklers theoretically serving the East India Companies. The successful establishment of English dominion and the defeat of the French resulted not only from greater resources but also from the use of highly-trained native troops and from the command of the sea. The empire was expanded in the nineteenth century partly by reference to a Russian threat overland. The Indian Mutiny precipitated the complete assumption of Government control which had been increasing in each successive charter granted to the Company since its first acquired territorial power. The Mutiny also led to railway development, and the opening of the Suez Canal promoted greater economic and social changes. But above all the Government, under the impact of democratic changes at home, engaged in an educational and political programme that unleashed national and communal movements.

So far as Southeast Asia was concerned, the establishment of this dominion — especially the early struggles with the French — gave Britain a strategic interest in the further side of the Bay of Bengal. It also placed a strong state once more on the frontier of Burma. And it gave Britain extra resources for empire and trade eastwards. The expansion of the dominion gave Britain an interest in marcher territories, including those of the Southeast Asian mainland. And its development promoted the emigration of Indians and the export anew of Indian political examples.

The establishment of the Indian dominion had helped to give Britain a command of the China trade in the phase when opium had been made into its mainstay. China was important then as the major source of tea, and till opium was monopolised (the government secured a monopoly of its purchase in 1773, of its manufacture in 1797), the British had also paid for it by participation through the Country Trade in the traffic from the Archipelago to China, also facilitated by a command of opium. But if the Archipelago traffic lost its great importance in the early nineteenth century, and if in turn the importance of opium in China gave way to importations of manufactured goods from Britain, Southeast Asia still remained important because it commanded the routes to China from Europe and India.

Throughout the period, too, Britain generally aimed to uphold the integrity of China, and this reacted upon British policy towards countries in Southeast Asia that might be considered Chinese dependencies. In the early phase, the Company, driving a profitable trade at Canton, was opposed to any action that might prompt the emperor to turn it out. The pressure of the new manufacturing interests brought a change. In 1813 they secured the destruction of the Company's monopoly in regard to trade between Britain and the Indian ports. In the charter of 1833, they destroyed the China monopoly, and a period of pressure on China ensued, leading to the 'Opium War', the opening of five treaty ports and the annexation of Hong Kong; to be followed by a further war in the late 1850s and, in face of commercial disappointments, attempts to open overland routes to the Chinese interior. The partial revolution in policy towards China after the early 1840s suggested a revolution in policy towards Southeast Asian countries regarded as dependent upon it. But other factors came into play in Siam, and in Vietnam another power.

British policy in Southeast Asia was thus affected by British interests in India and China. In some ways those interests gave Britain a limited concern with Southeast Asia: in some ways they limited its concern with Southeast Asia. In yet others they helped the British to define their policies in Southeast Asian dependencies. But a third factor in defining Britain's policy in Southeast Asia in this frontier-making period was indeed its attitude to the European powers concerned.

The sources of British predominance generally in the late eighteenth and nineteenth centuries were the command of the seas, which ensured openings for British commerce and its superior competitive capacity, and the balance of power in Europe. If supremacy overseas became the means by which Britain defeated her major rival France by the early nineteenth century, that victory was the result not only of sea power, but also of that relative stalemate on the Continent which formed the background of 'Enlightened Despotism'. This stalemate British diplomacy promoted, in part by supporting the independence from France of lesser powers like Spain, like the Dutch Republic, also important in relation to the command of the Channel. The triumph over Napoleon ensured a British predominance that lasted throughout the century, guaranteed by Britain's command of the seas and by the balance in Europe. In Europe her predominance was used moderately, with the design of ensuring a concert of powers rather than a political supremacy in one power. Overseas the minor colonial powers, Spain and Holland, still retained empires, seen by the British still as a guarantee of the balance of power in Europe, and of the defence of the Channel. In fact Britain's predominance encouraged not only an avoidance of definite commitments on the Continent but an unwillingness to undertake colonial responsibility overseas. Such views were prominent among radical critics of the Government, but were influential within the Government also. The emphasis was not upon territorial acquisition, but upon strategic points, upon the protection of major routes, upon commercial opportunity.

Even the changes in Europe after the mid-nineteenth century did not greatly change the pattern of British interests or British attitudes. In Europe the Crimean war was followed by the creation of united Italy and of Bismarckian Germany. But this did not overthrow the balance of power. Overseas, indeed, the continued European stalemate was reflected in increased activity by almost all the powers, begun by the France of Louis Philippe and Napoleon III, facilitated by the opening of the Suez Canal, and encouraged by the depression of the 1880s and 1890s. The resulting rivalry produced a closer definition of colonial frontiers and allegiances, witnessed, for instance, in the increasingly widespread acceptance of the view, finally adopted by the Berlin conference of 1884-5, that effective occupation was the criterion of imperial possession. It produced new efforts by Britain to protect its major routes and its existing possessions. But it did not lead the British to abandon a conciliatory approach to the interests of other powers. All in all, through the nineteenth century, British supremacy was used relatively moderately in Europe and overseas.

These considerations helped to determine governmental attitudes towards British commercial interests in Southeast Asia. At certain times — for instance in the recession of the 1840s —

rather more was done for them than at others, but even then overall political decisions were not greatly modified. Particularly after spices had lost their importance — relegating the Moluccas once more to an obscurity they had suffered or enjoyed before the twelfth century — and after opium had solved the problem of remittance to China, and before the rise of the rubber interest in Malaya, British economic interests in Southeast Asia were not regarded as of primary importance. A limited exertion of diplomatic and naval activity was alone required to defend them. The imperial, Indian and Chinese, and European considerations thus prevailed. Local merchants, officials, and adventurers had the best chance of influencing policy when their interests could be made to coincide or to appear to coincide with one or more of these considerations. Not that their interests — those of merchants, officials, adventurers — were themselves identical.

These factors in British policy helped to determine the frontiers within Southeast Asia. The result was to establish the British stage by stage in Burma and in the Andaman and Nicobar islands, to establish them on the Malay Peninsula and in north-west Borneo; to leave the Dutch to build their domestic economy, and also ultimately an empire in the Archipelago, upon the resources of Java; to allow the Spaniards to remain in Luzon and the Visayas and to continue to extend from them and with their resources over Mindanao and the Sulu archipelago; to leave Laos and Cambodia and Vietnam almost alone till the French determined to step in and built an empire on Mekong and the Red River; and to preserve Thai independence, thanks to British restraint, the diplomacy of the Chakri dynasty and Siam's buffer position vis-à-vis the French in 'Indo-China' and the British in Burma and the Peninsula.

But these are not results simply of European policy: they are results also, as the Thai example not alone demonstrates, of Southeast Asian decision or circumstance. Circumstances in the Archipelago left little room for decisions, but in areas where European influence had been least there was resistance not merely of a piratical character. On the mainland, political attitudes could be developed. And they developed in the context of the relative isolation from European influences since about 1700, which contributed to a false understanding of current European power, and to a failure to modernise armaments and technology. In these circumstances the reaction to the advance of British power produced an aggressiveness in the Burmans that brought downfall at the hands of their new neighbours in Bengal. In Vietnam the reaction to knowledge of the

British conquests in India and the British victories in China was an isolationism that only further weakened the kingdom and a xenophobia that precipitated French intervention on behalf of Catholic missionaries. Only in Siam did the leaders attain some real understanding of the need to adapt to live. Elsewhere the catastrophe on the mainland was more abrupt than in the Archipelago because longer deferred.

The vast social changes of the period opened up new opportunities to the Christian missions: some would turn to them in conditions of bewildering transformation; some would seek through them access to European knowledge. Economic changes — for instance, the improvement of communications — aided them. Nor were they necessarily tied any longer to the fortunes of particular European powers: the work was shared by American Baptists and by German Lutherans as well as by Anglicans and French and Spanish Catholics. In this field, again, the European, or western, influences were diversifying, because of the diversification of western religious life, and the wealth and changed conditions that enabled it to make itself felt in Southeast Asia. Naturally the reception of it varied. In Vietnam there were limited toleration and then repression under the emperors, French intervention in favour of the missions, but much less influence for them thereafter. The Dutch remained cautious. One major reason was that some of the nineteenth century conditions — pacification, better communications, social change — worked in favour also of Islam and of Buddhism, and Christian missionary activity could often only strengthen opposition to Christianity. Religious motives intensified the Sulu opposition to the Spaniards, and even more the Achehnese opposition to the Dutch, aided as it was by a more general modernising movement in Islam, brought into closer touch with Southeast Asia by the use of the Suez route and the wealth that financed the Mekka pilgrimages. It was characteristic that the Thais should admit various missions and use them to learn European languages, techniques and medicine. But the European missions effected conversion mostly among peoples not absorbed by Islam or Buddhism, hill peoples like the Karens of Burma, Chinese immigrants in Borneo and the Straits Settlements, the Bataks. In this way they added yet further to the communal diversity of Southeast Asia.

To some extent the missionary cause was affected by the changes in European policy after the beginning of the twentieth century. The rise of democracy within the metropolitan countries contributed to an ideological element in their colonial policy and expanded the pressure for European education, for welfare measures, and for participation in colonial government by the native peoples. To this the American example after the annexation of the Philippines perhaps contributed. Certainly the model of British India affected British policies especially in Burma; the development of Dominion status suggested a goal, the Irish example an inspiration; while Lugard notions spread from Africa to North Borneo. In general the colonial powers — and their subjects — were affected by the ideological turn taken by the deadlocked European struggle after 1916 and the proclamation of the principles of self-determination and nationality.

The war also precipitated the triumph in Russia of the Bolsheviks, whose doctrines made an appeal to intellectuals in under-developed countries, and who, after failing to secure revolution in Europe, concentrated on attacking the European powers, above all Britain, through their colonial dependencies in Asia. This policy, which might be compared to eighteenth century Britain's strategy for securing its predominance, was endorsed by the Comintern congresses of 1920 and 1922. It involved an alliance with Asian nationalism, and the Communist parties of metropolitan countries were, in a novel sort of colonialism, to assist the movement in the dependencies. The crisis for the policy came in 1928, after which Russia concentrated upon internal transformation and the Comintern took an extremist line. With the rise of Hitler, Stalinist Russia attempted co-operation with the democracies, and the Comintern congress of 1935 adopted a popular front policy. This phase of co-existence produced some opportunities for, but some concern among Asian Communists. The *volte-face* of the 1939 Nazi-Soviet pact added to their confusion. But the significance of Communist, as of other European ideologies, can be appraised only in conjunction with the influences of the world of Islam, of India, of China, and of Japan, themselves taking in some sense a more Europeanised shape.

Lenin, for instance, opposed the contending influence of the pan-Islamic movement. Already Southeast Asia had been brought into closer touch with the Muslim holy lands, with the fundamentalism of the Wahhabites of late eighteenth century Mekka, with the reformism of late nineteenth century Egypt. The first war brought great changes in these lands. The Turkish empire collapsed and Ataturk brought the Caliphate to an end. The conquest of the Hejaz by the Wahhabi ruler Ibn Saud in 1924 raised great hopes of the pan-Islamic movement. But attempts to resurrect the Caliphate and rejuvenate the Islamic world came to an early end.

Closer connexions with the holy land affected Indian Islam, but also limited its special impact in Southeast Asia. The nature of Indian influence had, of course, changed in other ways also. Some of the older commercial connexions had persisted throughout the nineteenth century, such as the Coromandel trade to Acheh. But more important was the fact that in a sense the new British empire in Southeast Asia was an Indian empire. Indian wealth supported the Country Traders, Lascars manned their ships, Indian revenues helped to finance the British administrations. The administration in Burma remained closely tied to the Indian system till 1937; the Straits Settlements were administered from India till 1867 and after that their government was influenced by British Indian notions of administration; and the Raj of Sarawak was founded by a member of a British Indian family who had fought in Burma. Indian troops conquered Burma and garrisoned the Straits Settlements and Sikh police were imported to keep order in North Borneo. The political connexions also promoted other sorts of Indian migration. The Chinese had come as miners even in the eighteenth century and even to Malay states. Indian immigration on a substantial scale seems to have been more dependent upon the British connexion and to be most significant in Burma and the Peninsula.

In part the migration was, as in early Australia, compulsory: the Straits Settlements and the Andaman islands were convict stations, of which the Anglican Cathedral of Singapore and the cellular jail of Port Blair are the monuments. Otherwise the Indians at one level benefited from their superior knowledge of British legal, banking and administrative practice; and at another level as plantation workers they were welcome because of their amenability to discipline, and encouraged by the intervention of a government which mixed paternalism with its concern to ensure a cheap labour supply. In the war and post-war phase, the impact of Indian nationalism upon these fragmented, unstable and impermanent Indian communities in Southeast Asia was naturally limited and of slow growth. On the other hand the general example of Indian constitutional advance influenced nationalist intellectuals, especially in Burma. Their sentiments might, however, be complicated by a jealousy of the economic positions held by immigrant Indians.

Of more concern to Lenin and the Comintern were the changes in China, and these also affected Southeast Asia. The

105

old assertions of Chinese influence there had been long in disappearing. The last major intervention in Burma was in the Shan states in the 1770s. But elsewhere the British intervened much less — the Thais continued to acknowledge Chinese suzerainty till 1853 — and characteristically the Vietnamese case was exceptional. There China resisted the penetration of the French in the 1880s, at the same time as it attempted to hold on to Korea and turn its claims there into a European-style protectorate. But the failure successfully to resist the Europeans in Southeast Asia and elsewhere, or to turn their techniques to account against them, contributed to the downfall of the Manchu régime and to the revolution of 1911. (Sun Yat-sen had indeed become a revolutionary at the time of the Franco-Chinese war.)

But while Chinese political influence in Southeast Asia collapsed in face of the Europeans, the conditions they created fostered Chinese immigration on an unprecedented scale. The economic development of the nineteenth century and the establishment of European administration opened up new opportunities to the Chinese, above all those from Fukien, Kwangtung and Hainan, provinces remote and uninfluential, always unreconciled to the Manchu régime. The Hokkiens from Amoy dominated business and commerce in Southeast Asia; the Cantonese and Hakkas from Kwangtung mining; and the Hailams from Hainan catering, domestic and personal service. The fact that the immigrants were peasant in origin — though from provinces in touch with overseas commerce — makes their success in such fields (especially as compared with the relative failure of Southeast Asian peasants) surprising. The explanation may perhaps be found in the fact that a Chinese was bound to further his lineage — he had a place in a 'continuum of kin', past, present and future[51] — and he was committed to thrift and hard work. At the same time, the secret societies were especially strong among migrants, needing protection, and divided by trade and by tribe or speech, the more for being largely illiterate. But this nineteenth century pattern did not greatly differ from the earlier pattern. Equally, if in pre-colonial Southeast Asia, the Chinese had lived, other than economically, unto themselves, controlled if at all through Capitans China, in a large degree the colonial Europeans continued during the nineteenth century a system that bore some comparison to the extraterritoriality that at the same time they imposed on China. In some cases European administrators specifically opposed the integration of the Chinese with existing communities, adding to existing religious and cultural obstacles. But during the late nineteenth and early twentieth centuries changes were coming about, both quantitative and qualitative.

In one part of Southeast Asia, the Peninsula, more especially its west coast and the Straits Settlements, the Chinese became of real numerical significance, and their position there was quite special. There, and also in neighbouring countries, their status changed in other ways. In theory, of course, the Chinese had always regarded themselves as temporarily resident in the Nanyang, subsidising their people at home and intending to return to the lands of their ancestors. With improving communications from the late nineteenth century, this became rather less of a dream and more of a reality. In the early twentieth century some factors worked towards integration, including the more general spread of European culture among all communities and the adoption of more direct administrative methods. But the Nanyang communities were also brought into closer touch with the government in China.

The Europeans had forced the Manchu régime to relax its prohibition on emigration in 1860. Its last-minute reformers asserted the Chinese nationality of overseas Chinese in a law of 1909. This doctrine — once a Chinese, a Chinese till denationalised — was adopted by those who overturned the Manchu régime. The revolutionaries had gained much support in the Nanyang, as the Manchus had always feared. The communities remained a source of support and finance to the revolution, which could be tapped through the secret societies, the spread of Chinese education aided by teachers from China, and the increasing use of the national language. The general effect was to promote a Chinese consciousness among the Nanyang Chinese, which in turn stimulated a reaction among the colonial powers and among the colonial peoples, concerned at their economic position, their political separateness. The Nanyang communities were contacted, too, by the Chinese Nationalists, the K.M.T., and by the Communists, the C.C.P. Initially these parties worked together, encouraged by the Comintern in the early 1920s. Their falling-out lay at the root of the Comintern's change of policy in 1928. In Southeast Asia it weakened the influence of the C.C.P. among the local Communists, and upon this not only the K.M.T. sought to capitalise, but so did the Comintern, indicating an early source of Sino-Soviet rivalry.

This was to emerge fully, of course, only with the defeat of the K.M.T. In this the 'war' with Japan played a major role. But Japan impinged more directly on Southeast Asia. To some extent the influence of Japan had been felt in Southeast Asia before the Tokugawa isolation: Japanese traders were known in Dai Viet, in Ayuthia, and in the 'Philippine' islands in the sixteenth century. It was not surprising that the abandonment of the Tokugawa's isolationist policy in the later nineteenth century, coupled with growing industrialisation, should renew commercial connexions.

But what impressed Southeast Asian nationalists was the success the Japanese enjoyed (on a grander scale than the Thais) in beating the Europeans at their own game, a success demonstrated by the resounding defeat of China in 1895 and still more of Russia in 1905. Nor were Japanese nationalists dead to the possibilities of their position in relation to Southeast Asia: it was involved in the late nineteenth century pan-Asianism of Miyazaki Torazō, an associate of Sun Yat-sen, and of Oi Kentarō. The earliest nationalist movement in Southeast Asia, that in the Philippines, made early contacts with expansionists from nearby Japan and sought aid in a revolt against Spain in the 1890s. The success of the nationalist movements elsewhere in Southeast Asia, however, had to wait decisive Japanese military victories. In the last resort the overthrow of the colonial régimes depended upon the redistribution of power in Asia and the world at large.

The clue to these changes is to be found in the relative decline of the predominant power, Britain. The first signs of this in Asia were at the turn of the century. The building of the Trans-Siberian railway strengthened Russia in the Far East, and it was a problem hardly to be dealt with by means of the traditional supremacy at sea. Furthermore, the growing threat of Germany in European waters compelled the concentration of the fleet there. The result was a treaty with Japan and a settlement of colonial differences with France in 1904. Japan's victory in 1905 was, ironically in view of the widespread Asian enthusiasm for it, a product in part of British diplomacy. In the first world war Japan secured a greater command of East Asian waters. With Russia involved in revolution, the other power principally concerned was the United States.

In the nineteenth century the U.S. had been a minor maritime and commercial power in East and Southeast Asia. Though its initiative had precipitated the opening of Japan, generally it had followed in the wake of Britain in China and also, for instance, in Siam and Borneo; and though merchants in north Sumatra had received naval support in the 1830s and consuls had engaged in adventures in Brunei, this policy had not really changed. Even the acquisition of the Philippines in 1898 — regarded by Britain without disfavour and certainly as preferable to their acquisition by Germany — had marked a revolutionary assertion of the Pacific contacts of Southeast Asia, but not in power terms. In post-war East and Southeast Asia, the U.S. was indisposed to exert its strength beyond the naval base at Hawaii. The Washington conference of 1921-2 limited the navies of the major powers in the region and restricted the construction of naval bases in the China sea. The major powers also agreed to respect the territorial *status quo* in the region. This agreement replaced the Anglo-Japanese alliance, whose renewal the U.S. had opposed. In fact the British, and also the Australasians, had come to see this not only as a guarantee against Russia or, now, the spread of Communism, but also as a restraint upon Japan.

The Washington agreements created a power-vacuum in East Asian waters, which the aggressive Japan of the 1930s sought to fill. The depression, and the reaction of the colonial powers to a new economic competition, urged it forward. In 1937 it launched its 'war' on China. The Chinese Nationalists had drawn on Southeast Asian resources. For Japan also it became important even for its China conquest to seal off and itself tap the resources of the Nan-yo. The absorption of Russia in internal revolution, then in the German invasion, the failure to exert American power, the concentration of British resources in the European and the Middle East struggles, the divisions among Southeast Asian régimes and peoples, all these opened the way to the overthrow of the political structure created in Southeast Asia in the period of British predominance.

The British had determined to construct a naval base to protect their old empire in India and Australia and their new empire in the Middle East outside the limits of the Washington agreement at Singapore. The Peninsula had become, as it were, an outpost of empire. In another respect also, it had now become intrinsically important. Even in the 1890s the economic influence of the industrialising U.S. had made itself felt in Southeast Asia: the protective McKinley tariff had almost destroyed the state of North Borneo. With the first world war, the Malay states, like the Netherlands Indies, became, with their tin and rubber, the great dollar-arsenal of the metropolitan power. And it was yet a further paradox, perhaps — it was the strangest example of the change in the Chinese connexion with Southeast Asia — that Singapore, now the hub of British strategic and economic enterprise, was essentially a Chinese city, that Malaya itself was almost dominated by Chinese: a paradox that some have charged was played off against another paradox, the call for political advancement at the very time when economic and strategic interests had so deepened.

Australia and New Zealand had shared in the economic and political movement of the period from 1760, but its effect was not such as to bind them closer to Southeast Asia. Alexander Dalrymple, interested in a settlement in the Archipelago in the 1760s as a means of promoting trade with China, was interested also in *Terra Australis Incognita,* and indeed hoped to lead the voyage James Cook carried through in triumph. But, partly because of the Company's monopoly, no substantial trade developed between the Australasian settlements that ensued upon Cook's discoveries and — via Southeast Asia — the Chinese empire. The later attempts to create an entrepot for the acquisition of Archipelago produce on the northern Australian coast failed, above all because the Bugis who visited the area — one of whom Flinders met on his voyage of 1803 — were fishermen from Macassar and not enterprising traders. Port Essington was not a success. The trade of the Australasian colonies tied them much more to European markets, and there was little exchange between primary producing areas in Southeast Asia and Australasia.

In the 1840s and 1850s, Australia was an important market for Philippines sugar, but other sources of supply were later found, including Queensland itself. The early days of North Borneo saw an export of timber to Australia, and there was Australian enterprise in Malayan and Siamese mining. But economic links were not binding and political links were no stronger.

Australia and New Zealand relied on British supremacy at sea, and it was under that shelter, and also that of desert and jungle or distance and isolation, that the colonies were able to pursue 'white' immigration policies. It also shielded them from major European powers (perhaps the chief purpose of the north Australian settlements had been to ward them off the mainland) and later from industrial Japan, viewed with a mixture of fear and commercial hope. Where it was thought inadequate was in New Guinea. There the Dutch strengthened their claims following the British ventures in northern Australia. Beyond their limits the Australians themselves acted to ward off the Germans in the 1880s and then to keep out the Japanese by assuming, under special C-class terms, the post-war League of Nations mandate, giving themselves a colonial territory on the frontier of Southeast Asia. Otherwise the colonial régimes the British had permitted in Southeast Asia were simply seen as an additional barrier to the north.

It was perhaps significant that the Comintern — if no one else — saw Southeast Asia and Australasia as a unity. But while in the war the A.N.Z.A.C. powers had helped to defend the Middle East pivot of the British Empire, their fears post-war were mainly of Japan. Once he had seen that the U.S. would not exert its power in East Asia, the Australian prime minister Hughes had favoured the renewal of the Anglo-Japanese alliance. The overthrow of the Washington agreements compelled greater reliance upon Singapore — New Zealand had contributed £1m. to the building of the base in 1926 — and upon the Dominions' own defence effort. But there was no close liaison with the colonial régimes in Southeast Asia. The collapse of British power and the destruction of these régimes opened a new phase in Southeast Asian history and in the relationship between the Australasian Dominions and what was still for them substantially *Terra Septentrionalis Incognita*.

Section A: The Creation of the Colonial Framework

THIS SECTION deals with British policy and the establishment of colonial régimes in Southeast Asia in the period 1760-1900; the following section with the impact of economic and social change within that developing political framework. The latter covers also the subsequent phase 1900-40 when new influences played upon the area, a vast shift in the distribution of power was prepared and, in this context, nationalism and communalism emerged.

1 The Founding of the Straits Settlements

IN THE later eighteenth century the British had three major interests in the Peninsula and Archipelago, deriving from their involvement in India and China. The region, especially its western side, was important in relation to India because a naval base placed there could readily secure a command of the Bay of Bengal: by that means the French might be able to challenge British territorial dominion on the sub-continent. During the north-east monsoon, it was difficult for ships to remain in the Bay without a sheltered base: the only other base was in Ceylon, still in Dutch possession. Secondly, the region was important because through it ran the route to China, through the Straits of Malacca, and then up the China Sea or, in the adverse monsoon, via the Moluccas and east of the Philippines, a route discovered in 1758. Thirdly, the region was important because there the Country Traders could secure produce — tin, marine and jungle products — that would help build up the Company's investment in Canton where tea was procured. Britain's other interests in the Archipelago were much less significant. The settlements on the west coast of Sumatra failed to provide a competitive source of pepper and were inconveniently placed for more general trade. The desire to penetrate the nutmeg and clove monopolies in the Moluccas remained, but they were of decreasing importance.

Britain's policy in the Peninsula and Archipelago was not, however, determined by these interests alone. The independence of the Dutch Republic, and if possible its friendship, were cardinal points in Britain's European system. This restrained any pressure on the Dutch in the East, just as apprehensions about Spain or France had modified the policies of the Dutch towards the English Company in the days of their predominance. The British had, therefore, to hope that their strategic interests in Asia could be secured by relying on the Dutch to exclude France from areas to which they laid claim and by intervening in peripheral areas where the Dutch had no claim.

Commercially the position was extremely complicated. Already the Country Traders had found it possible to scoop away the tin of the Peninsular states and to open trade with the Bugis and thus indirectly to the eastern parts of the Archipelago. Dutch contracts were infringed, Dutch monopolies broken. Furthermore, the British conquest in India placed the Dutch at a new disadvantage: it impeded their sharing in the opium and textile trades to the Archipelago. But it is significant that the English Company — while never admitting the claim to an exclusive navigation in the Eastern Seas which the Dutch insisted upon perhaps all the more because of the challenge to their commerce — left the infringement of Dutch contracts to the Country Traders. As they became more important, more support was afforded them, but no very explicit denial of Dutch contracts occurred. A mission was sent to Bandjermasin in 1766, but the old Dutch relationships prevailed. Dutch pretensions in Keysers Bay on the Straits of Sunda were not challenged. And on the whole British interest was concentrated on more peripheral parts of the Archipelago, Acheh, Kedah, and Sulu, which, moreover, had some strategic importance in relation to India and China.

In the late 1770s, a dispute arose with the Dutch over neutral trade in the American war. The reforming party of the 'Patriots' in the United Provinces, oppressed by the relative economic decline of the Republic, was anxious to destroy the Stadhouder régime associated with the English connexion, and seized the chance of a break. The friendship of the Dutch lost, the British sought to eliminate by conquest the possibility of French occupation of their territories in the East. At the end of the war, the French remained predominant in the Republic. The English Cabinet therefore pressed for concessions that would

113

strengthen Britain's security in Asia and procure some gains to set against its apparently disastrous losses elsewhere. They tried for the Ceylon naval base of Trincomali, but failed. They did secure an explicit recognition of the right to navigate in the Eastern Seas. Furthermore the English were disposed to assert in the light of international law their right to trade to places not in effective Dutch possession. This was, of course, a severe threat to the Dutch. Rarely did their rights amount to possession: the basis of their empire was contractual.

The challenge the British presented was, however, a limited one. While France remained influential in the Republic, their position in Asia had to be strengthened. Suffren, the French admiral, had used Achehnese ports, and an English mission was sent to Acheh in 1782 and a residency established there in 1785. The hostility of the local chiefs led to its early abandonment. Suffren's bases in the Mergui Archipelago were also explored, and contact was made with the Bugis viceroy at Riau. The Bengal government felt that a settlement at Riau would protect the route to China and make the island an even greater entrepot for Archipelagic trade. But before action was taken the Dutch, concerned about their monopolies and about the approaches to Java, and then at war with the Bugis, defeated them and imposed the treaty of 1784. This recognised the suzerainty of the Dutch over Johore, and they established a fort at Riau. Two years later they enforced their authority over Selangor, and the defeat of the Bugis left the Menangkabau settlers free to strengthen their loose confederacy in Negri Sembilan. The English finally established a settlement at Penang also in 1786 by agreement with the Sultan of Kedah. It might be a 'commercial emporium', though rather far up the Straits. It would certainly be a naval station on the eastern side of the Bay of Bengal, especially needed in view of the Franco-Dutch alliance of 1785. But the challenge to the Dutch it involved was peripheral.

In 1787 the Patriots were overthrown by joint Anglo-Prussian intervention in the Dutch Republic and France, beset by economic problems that were shortly to precipitate revolution, did not intervene in their favour. The restoration of the Stadhouderian régime necessitated a redefinition of the relative positions of the British and the Dutch in Asia. In the following years the British sought to gain a new agreement from the Dutch, who might, it was thought, grant them Trincomali and Riau, in return gaining certain commercial concessions in India and an undertaking to prohibit British navigation east of

Sumatra. The Dutch, however, would not agree to such terms, and the failure to put Anglo-Dutch relations on a friendly footing no doubt assisted the overthrow of the régime at the hands of the victorious armies of the French revolution. In turn the British conquered Dutch possessions overseas, those in India and Ceylon, on the west coast of Sumatra, in the Moluccas, Menado in Celebes, and Malacca, and carried through the withdrawal of the settlement at Riau already planned by the Dutch. Heavy commitments in India, coupled with the menace of the French in Egypt, deferred any attempt on Java.

The treaty of Amiens of 1801 provided for the restoration of Dutch possessions, except for Ceylon, but Malacca and Padang were still in British hands when war was renewed. Concentration on the Mahrattas and on the French threat to India limited activity to the eastward. But, on the one hand, the victory at Trafalgar, and, on the other, growing French control of the Dutch Republic, encouraged a more vigorous policy. The Moluccas were re-taken in 1810 and Java at last occupied in 1811.

The approach of peace from 1813 onwards was marked by a resumption of traditional policies. The British believed they could secure what had eluded them after 1787, some provision for British interests without destroying the Dutch empire or the Dutch alliance. Ceylon and the Cape would be retained, the other conquests in Asia returned. Such was the basis of the convention of 1814. The strategic interests of Britain were more or less covered by the possession of Penang and Trincomali. The commercial interest in the Archipelago was no longer the same as pre-war. The spice monopoly had ceased altogether to be an object, since in the war the cultivation of clove and nutmeg had been spread outside the Moluccas. As for the investment in Canton, Indian opium now filled the bill. Unlike the proposals after 1787, the convention of 1814 thus said nothing about the Archipelago. The Dutch would consolidate their empire and keep other major powers out of the region of the China route. This consolidation would aid, and also be aided by their strength in Europe, supposedly increased by the annexation of the Belgian provinces of the Habsburgs.

Stamford Raffles, the Lt.-Governor of Java, had failed to persuade the Government to retain Java but, anticipating its return, he had sought to build a British empire outside Java which after the peace should remain in British hands. Many Dutch contracts he considered to have lapsed in the later eighteenth and early nineteenth centuries. The British should

115

conclude alliances with the Indonesian princes — a notion borrowed from the India of Richard Wellesley — and aid them in putting their territories to rights, suppressing piracy, and opening the way to commercial development.

The previous period had witnessed growing disorder within the native states and the broadening of piratical activities. The war only increased them: Dutch maritime police collapsed; and British naval officers were inexperienced and disinclined to involve themselves. The Country Traders had, if anything, a vested interest in disorder. The establishment of British entrepots did not necessarily reduce it: they sold arms and ammunition; they attracted vulnerable native vessels. The political process in the Archipelago had been dislocated by Dutch methods, but the establishment of English entrepots did not offer hope of political reconstitution along traditional lines. Raffles thus planned to exert British influence on the existing states, to maintain them *in statu quo,* and within their boundaries to regularise their political and commercial structures. He emphasised that his policy would effectively put down piracy in the hope that this would secure approval for it from his superiors in Calcutta and London. But it was disapproved in 1815. Even such schemes of indirect rule as Raffles was proposing were incompatible with British policy in the Archipelago.

This did not mean that Raffles abandoned his policy: he reshaped it. In 1818 he reappeared as Lt.-Governor of Benkulen, challenged the Dutch in Padang and Palembang, and attempted extension towards the Straits of Sunda. The authorities at Penang, concerned at the transfer of Bangka to the Dutch under the convention of 1814 and their return to Malacca, sought to conclude treaties by which various princes should bind themselves not to renew old contractual engagements likely to restrict British commerce. Such treaties were secured by William Farquhar at Siak and at Riau, but the Dutch, alive to the situation, anticipated him on the west coast of Borneo. The government in Calcutta were somewhat impressed by the argument that the Dutch, by rehabilitating their old treaties, would exclude British trade from most of the Archipelago. More impressive still was Raffles' argument that the route to China needed protection. He secured authority to go to Acheh, where he made a treaty of alliance with the Sultan, at that time engaged in a civil war with dependants who were abetted in Penang. Raffles also secured authority to found a settlement in the Johore empire. This he did at Singapore in January 1819, not indeed by agreement with the Bugis viceroy or the Sultan with whom Farquhar had treated, but with whom the Dutch had subsequently renewed the treaty of 1784; instead with a Malay prince of the empire, the Temenggong, who resided in mainland Johore, and the Sultan's brother, Hussein, who was recognised as Sultan for the occasion. Singapore, Raffles believed, would be a great entrepot, and also a fulcrum for the extension of British influence.

In London the Government had become conscious not only of the Country Trade interests, but also of other interests developed since the opening of the trade to India under the charter of 1813. These included the British houses established in Java during the British occupation to distribute British textiles and collect colonial produce such as coffee. In 1818, the Foreign Office proposed the appointment of a consul in Batavia. The Government was also impressed with the argument that the China route had been left insufficiently protected under the convention of 1814. Its object was, therefore, to provide fair opportunities for British commerce and new guarantees of the route to China. Initially it considered investigating the title-deeds of the Dutch empire. But this, it was now recognised, as perhaps it had not been pre-war, might invite other powers also to challenge the Dutch position and intervene along the route to China.

The Dutch, however, were sufficiently apprehensive of such an enquiry to offer commercial concessions both in Java and in states with which they were contractually connected. The British accepted the Moluccan monopolies, while in Java — and also in British India, where the Dutch gave up their old settlements — a system of double duties on the subjects and vessels of the alien nation was specified in what became article 2 of the treaty of March 1824. Article 3 provided against treaties made by either party with native princes in the Eastern Seas 'tending either expressly or by the imposition of unequal duties to exclude the trade of the other party from the ports of such native power' and for the modification of such clauses in existing treaties. New treaties with native princes were to be communicated by one party to the other: old treaties were 'understood' to have been communicated. The clauses were not very explicit: but too explicit a statement might only have provoked the intervention of other powers. The interests of British trade in the Archipelago were also covered by an agreement to cooperate against piracy (article 5), which seemed a necessary corollary to leaving the Dutch politically predominant, while giving the British commercial opportunity.

The conclusion of the treaty of 1824 had, however, been

delayed by the difficulty over Singapore. The Dutch declined to admit Raffles' challenge to their treaty relationships with Johore and recognition of an illegitimate Sultan: it was an area important to them since the eighteenth century above all as an outwork of Java. The British negotiators were not convinced that Raffles was in the right, but hesitated to yield till it could be satisfactorily shown that he was in the wrong. Important interests were involved: the route to China; a further guarantee of trade in the Archipelago in view of the precariousness of clause 3; and, while the negotiations hung fire during 1820-3, Singapore was increasingly used by British merchants who could evade the Company's China monopoly by trading to that settlement and transhipping there. The Dutch became perturbed over the effects of the delay on their influence in neighbouring native states, and in 1823 finally yielded over Singapore, determining, however, to retain Riau and the islands 'south of the Straits of Singapore'. They proposed also to leave Malacca and make no treaties on the Peninsula in the future, while the British should leave Benkulen, and make a similar undertaking in regard to Sumatra. A 'line' should be drawn down the Straits of Malacca and Singapore. In the actual treaty — again to avoid provoking others' jealousy of the 'exclusive Lords of the East'[52] — the line was replaced by articles effecting the division in so many words.

One difficulty was Raffles' treaty with Acheh: its abandonment so promptly seemed discreditable but the Dutch, if established there, would keep out other powers; the result was a note in which the Netherlands agreed to establish security for commerce in Acheh without infringing its independence. The destiny of Farquhar's Siak treaty is not clear, but presumably the British did not intend to maintain it. The 'line' and the articles that replaced it did not extend to Borneo. Probably the negotiators meant that also to be left to the Dutch, but did not say so, lest again the jealousy of others should be provoked.

What the treaty of 1824 clearly did do was, by eliminating the Dutch from one side of the Straits, to separate the destinies of the Peninsula and the Archipelago in an unprecedented way. The British had exercised their power in a limited manner because of their limited interests in the region and their concern for European relationships. They secured the Straits Settlements to ensure a command of the route to China and a share in the commerce of the Archipelago. Elsewhere the Dutch were to prevail, co-operating against piracy and providing fair opportunities for British commerce in Java and the other islands.

Those opportunities must rest in part upon the contractual system of the Dutch which was not otherwise challenged lest other maritime powers followed suit. But partly because of this the treaty was rather obscure in places, and in partially changed conditions a new, if still partial challenge was to follow. The Dutch hold remained fragile in many areas. And British officials, adventurers and merchants were restive. A modification of the Foreign Office attitude to the Dutch empire was to allow them some scope.

2 The Dutch Empire in the Archipelago

ONE RESULT of the British decisions of 1814 and 1824 was to leave the Archipelago in the hands of a power greatly weakened economically. It was natural that this should compel the Dutch to continue their eighteenth century concentration upon Java, as a means of keeping their kingdom afloat, of reviving their commerce, and of upholding a framework of empire in the outer islands. It was natural, too, that this should lead to protectionist measures that struck at British trade in Java.

Initially their objective was to ensure an outlet for the textile manufactures of the Belgian part of the Netherlands kingdom, which had during the war enjoyed the protected markets of Napoleon's Continental System. The high duty of February 1824 would, it was clear, limit the opportunities of the English houses, and by generally raising the prices of imported textiles tend to preserve native manufactures. The Dutch maintained that the treaty of March 1824 only regulated duties levied according to the nationality of 'subjects and vessels', and not those levied according to the actual 'origins' of the goods carried, which was the distinction they were using. The Dutch king's loss of the Belgian provinces after the revolution of 1830 seemed to offer new hope to the English merchants, and the Foreign Office took up their cause at a time of some commercial difficulty. It attempted to assert that the 'double duties' clause applied also to the goods of the other nation, though it was not

119

the system adopted in British India — but there rates were lower. The Dutch finally accepted this interpretation, but imposed a rather high rate; and, furthermore, they arranged rebates to the Nederlandsche Handel-Maatschappij (Netherlands Trading Company), the principal exporters, and subsidised a Dutch textile industry out of the profits of the 'cultivation-system'.

The N.H.M. had been established by Willem I in 1824 to foster trade between the Netherlands kingdom and its possessions. But, in their attempt to create 'Netherlands India' out of the defunct Company's miscellaneous collection of treaty relationships, the returning Dutch had met resistance, for instance from the Moluccan rebels of 1817 and from the Padris, Wahhabite fanatics who had extended their control in Menangkabau during the British occupation of the west coast of Sumatra; and the government's deficits were greatly increased by the Java war of 1825-30. This, with the financial drain of the struggle with the Belgian revolutionaries, suggested the need rapidly to expand and monopolise the produce of Java. The cultivation-system was the result, in essence the old system of forced deliveries writ large. The greater part of a greatly increased export produce was collected by the Indies government and consigned to the N.H.M. for sale in the Netherlands, and the N.H.M. advanced money to the needy home government. Upon the back of Java, therefore, the kingdom kept afloat; with Java's wealth Dutch commerce and industry were revived and Dutch railways were built.

A crisis in the unbalanced Javanese economy in 1839-40 led the Foreign Office's envoy in The Hague to hope for an agreement that would provide better opportunities for British merchants, whose imports were discriminated against by high duties, and who were virtually excluded from the export trade. He hoped at least to secure a larger opportunity for the importers. But the Dutch minister Baud had no intention of abandoning the nascent Dutch textile industry. Negotiations finally collapsed in November 1843.

The disappointments the Foreign Office faced in the commercial negotiations over Java — at a time, too, of general economic stress in Britain — reacted upon other parts of the settlement of 1824. It contributed to a distrust of Dutch extension and an anxiety to qualify the promised co-operation against piracy where the extension of Dutch territory might result. 'Such an extension of Dutch influence, or territorial possession, would, in all probability, be attended with consequences injurious to British interests', it was declared in 1838, 'and should be looked upon with jealousy by the Government of this country.'[53]

So far, indeed, the Dutch had not been disposed to extend in the outer islands: the state of their finances, the Java war, their reliance, perhaps, on the treaty of 1824, all tended to restrain them in areas where the prospect of applying the cultivation-system was slight. A substantial field, therefore, still lay open for the British entrepots in the Straits, even in Sumatra, where Acheh and the east coast states like Deli and Langkat proved important sources of pepper and betel-nut for Penang. There and elsewhere the Straits Settlements distributed opium, Indian and increasingly British textiles, as well as Chinese goods brought down by junks. New products were added to their trade, for instance with the discovery of Sarawak antimony in the 1820s, but in some ways it followed traditional patterns. A limited number of European-style vessels visited the native states. But essentially the Settlements were concerned to attract the visits of Bugis and other traders from the various islands of the Archipelago. Their prosperity might indeed be said to derive in part from the undeveloped character of the region: the expansion of its trade and consequent specialisation would involve the opening of other international ports and the establishment of more direct connexions with the outside world. Meanwhile they competed with existing entrepots for a relatively limited traffic. The Settlements were unlike earlier entrepots in relying less on compulsion. They were like them, however, in not relying merely on positional advantages: they attracted by their freedom from duties, easier to maintain because Indian revenues made up administrative deficits.

It is clear from this analysis why the Straits Settlements were opposed to Dutch extension, even if it were on liberal principles; though in any case their merchants and officials expected the Dutch to revert to compulsive methods. It is clear why the Straits merchants — heirs to the Country Traders — wanted to see the native states preserved. It is clear why they preferred this done without preserving the centralising and revenue-collecting activities of 'imperial' Sultans and aristocracies such as those of Acheh or Brunei — a preference shared by Governor Fullerton in the 1820s and distinct from the reforming notions of Raffles. If there was to be an exertion of European influence in the Archipelago, it should be that of the British, directed ostensibly at dealing with cases of outrage and piracy on British trade and trade coming to British entrepots. The special interests of the merchants gave outrage and piracy sometimes a rather special interpretation. The outrages might arise from attempts to carry through commercial agreements — sometimes monopolistic — with local rajas. And 'piracy' was applied to the attempts of the Sultan and rajas of Acheh to levy duties on traders going to or coming from their dependent rivers.

If, in occupying stations in the Straits, a focus of Archipelagic power, the British did not intend to create an empire of the Sri Vijaya type, nevertheless, in part because the actual structure of commerce had not yet greatly changed, the Straits Settlements did assume something of the character of old Palembang and did not entirely rely on position or freedom from duties. To their merchants the Foreign Office opposition to Dutch extension was welcome. But it did not derive from identical origins. To the Foreign Office, the extension of the Dutch seemed desirable on many counts — they would exclude other powers; they would deal with native outrages — if only it could be sure that the Dutch would prove liberal. The Straits Settlements, on the other hand, were interested in the maintenance of an entrepot system bolstered by the acquisition of an exclusive influence in the native states broken into their smallest components.

The decision of 1838 arose in reference to the pirates of the old imperial centre of Johore, *orang laut* serving the Malay chieftains of this broken-up empire. Some of the British had believed that the Dutch allowed the pirates to exist in the islands south of Singapore in order to injure that entrepot and promote the interests of the rival they had created at Riau. Hence the unilateral British action against the Galang pirate stronghold in 1836, to which the Dutch reacted by referring to the co-operation proposed in 1824. In turn the Foreign Office had qualified its attitude.

In Dutch hands Riau had in fact failed as an entrepot, particularly after the loss of Belgium and its textile industries. In order to assure their position in the outer islands despite this commercial failure, the Dutch, using some of the profits of the cultivation-system in Java, began in the 1830s to turn again to the extension of their authority. Their lack of marine force had prevented their putting their relations with Acheh on the footing contemplated in 1824. Their new policy was thus bound to take the form, so far as that old empire was concerned, of piecemeal encroachment, of inducing the petty states of east and west Sumatra to exchange a vestige of dependence on Acheh for a genuine dependence upon the residencies at Padang or Palembang. The success of the Dutch on the west coast was limited by the opposition of Achehnese 'pirates' and by the Padris, not dealt with till the Java war was over. But van den Bosch, creator of the cultivation-system, determined on Dutch extension ultimately to all Sumatra, including the east coast, where the Straits Settlements would be more affected; and there Jambi became a Dutch dependency in 1833 and Indragiri in 1838 and a post was established in 1839 at the confluence of the Panei and Bila rivers.

The treaty of 1824, to which the Foreign Office looked, did not of course offer very powerful weapons for resisting Dutch encroachments. It was hard to question old treaties if the Dutch produced them — they had been 'understood' to have been communicated in 1824 — and it was hard to insist that Farquhar's Siak treaty was still operative. The tendency of the 1824 treaty was indeed in the other direction: the fear of inviting others to question Dutch rights had limited the British questioning of them. No clause, for instance, seemed to cover the case of a Dutch conquest of a native state as distinct from a contractual relationship with it. Out of this gap arose the Foreign Office's unjustified doubt that the stipulations of article 3 could apply even to states in contract with the Dutch if the contract placed them under Dutch sovereignty: if you could not question sovereign rights acquired by conquest, could you question sovereign rights acquired by treaty? This doubt undermined the whole basis of the treaty even as a means not of resisting Dutch extension but of guaranteeing that it was carried out in a commercially liberal way.

The Dutch made the most of the gaps and the doubts, but ultimately decided that British opposition turned the balance against a policy that proved unrewardingly expensive. They determined to withdraw from most of the east coast beyond Jambi, retaining, they said, their sovereignty. The British half-heartedly maintained a right to object to this derived from the Farquhar treaty and from article 3 of the treaty of 1824. Early in 1844 the Straits merchants secured action by the British navy ostensibly directed against pirates in two Achehnese rivers. In fact it amounted to intervention in two commercial disputes that had led in one case to murder and in the other to the detention of a captain. On the west coast, French and American traders and naval vessels were also more and more taking matters into their own hands.

The Dutch became increasingly concerned at the risks to their position in the Archipelago following the conflict with the British over the treaty of 1824. In particular they feared

123

that British intervention would ensue upon the activities of British merchants. A demand for rice in China in the 1830s had brought traders from Singapore and elsewhere to Bali and Lombok. The Dutch sought to ensure their position by treaties with the Bali rajas, but ultimately three expeditions – in 1846, 1848 and 1849 – were required to reduce Balinese resistance. In Borneo the activities of Brooke, the Navy and the Foreign Office prompted new Dutch treaties with the Bugis-dominated states of the east coast, and in Celebes a bid was made for Bugis trade by declaring Macassar a free port in 1846 – a move that characteristically provoked apprehension in Singapore: 'if the Bugis are disposed to trade at Macassar, some vessels will proceed there direct from England, whilst the English firms established at Batavia will have branch houses at Macassar'.[54]

From about the middle of the century there was a shift in Dutch policy. The Government came increasingly into the hands of liberals, and the States General assumed a greater control over the Netherlands Indies. The cultivation-system was gradually abandoned in favour of the private interests it had itself largely built up, and this was preceded by inroads upon the consignment-system. The widening of markets for plantation produce placed Dutch emphasis upon its expansion and meant less protection for the textiles of Twente and Overijssel. But the liberalisation of the tariff also resulted from British pressure. The Dutch realised that it was a means of averting political intervention and of reconstituting the agreement of 1824, the more important because of the growing interest of other colonial powers in the area.

British pressure no longer derived from the general economic crisis of the 1840s, which had given way to the greater prosperity of the 1850s. The British houses in Batavia were content: indeed in 1868 they 'expressed their hope that no reduction may take place in the duties levied there, as at present they have a practical monopoly of the business, which notwithstanding the heavy taxes levied on it enables them to make very large profits'.[55] The cultivation- and consignment-systems had in fact prevented the development of Dutch rival houses. Thus, as those systems were gradually relaxed, the British houses that had held on during the 1830s and 1840s greatly benefited. Sudden changes would bring new competitors. More importantly, some motives in British policy always worked against any weakening of the Dutch position in the Archipelago, and they could be expected to emerge more strongly when the commercial crisis had passed and when other powers demonstrated interest in the area.

In 1860, Lord Wodehouse, then Under-Secretary at the Foreign Office — no doubt influenced by recent French exploits in Vietnam — praised the treaty of 1824: 'It seems to me in many respects very advantageous that the Dutch should possess this Archipelago. If it was not in the hands of the Dutch, it would fall under the sway of some other maritime power, presumably the French, unless we took it ourselves. The French might, if they possessed such an eastern empire, be really dangerous to India and Australia, but the Dutch are and must remain too weak to cause us any alarm.' The Dutch exclusive policy, he also noted, had been relaxed.[56]

There were thus not merely no serious reasons for opposing, but real reasons for accepting Dutch extension in the Archipelago. The reason for the fuss the Foreign Office made over accepting it in the 1850s and 1860s — in Bali and Lombok, in Acheh, Siak and the east coast of Sumatra — must therefore be that it wanted definite guarantees of liberal commercial treatment to replace those of 1824 and damp down the manifold complaints of the Straits merchants. Not that the Straits merchants would really be satisfied with Dutch extension even on liberal terms, for they were perenially anxious lest ruin should follow the narrowing scope of their entrepot traffic with the native states, where they hoped for naval backing. To the Foreign Office, the need to suppress piracy and disorder — the ostensible grounds for such intervention — was a further argument for Dutch control: it would save the Navy trouble and expense and avoid the intervention of other powers for the same purpose. The new arrangements with the Netherlands were represented by the liberal tariff of 1872 and by the Sumatra treaty of the preceding year, in which the British, in return for promises of liberal commercial treatment, abandoned their opposition to Dutch extension even in Acheh.

The treaty marked a further stage in the process by which the Dutch constructed an empire in the Archipelago under the generally benevolent, but at times threatening, aegis of the British. The treaty made the independence of Acheh plain to the world and the Dutch became apprehensive of the intervention of others, especially as their piecemeal advance in Sumatra had done nothing to gain them the friendship of the Sultan. From 1873 they were engaged in a long war with Acheh, the resistance strengthened by fanatical Islamic elements and ended only in 1904. The closing years of the century saw the building-up of Netherlands authority throughout the Archipelago. The Dutch, having begun by taking advantage of its disunity, ended by unifying it. The colonial conference of 1884-5 had emphasised that actual possession was required to exclude others, a principle the British had been reluctant to enforce. Only in Borneo were there serious wranglings with the British themselves. But Borneo had been a special case — or a series of special cases — since the crisis of the 1840s.

3 Borneo, Sulu and New Guinea

AT THE OPENING of this period the British had interested themselves in an area peripheral to Dutch power, in northern Borneo and Sulu, and to a lesser extent in New Guinea. The object was a share in the spice trade, the development of an entrepot for the trade of Archipelago produce to China, and a position on the eastern route thither. In 1762 Alexander Dalrymple, an emissary of the Madras Government, acquired the island of Balambangan from the reigning Sultan of Sulu, and from his son and successor in 1763 he obtained the grant of northern Borneo and southern Palawan as a means of ensuring control of the Sulu sea. Meanwhile, in the course of the Seven Years War, British forces had taken Manila and freed the legitimate, baptised, exiled Sultan from the restraints the Spaniards had imposed upon him. In 1764 he confirmed the earlier grants. The restoration of Manila raised the question of retaining these claims or acting upon them, for the Spaniards regarded the Sulu Sultanate as part of the Philippines in virtue of discovery and ancient treaties, despite their lack of effective occupation. The problem had to be seen in the context of European diplomacy: a British challenge to Spain in the East might help France to gain a hold upon Spain itself and its empire also. In 1773, however, a settlement was founded on Balambangan, only to

126

be abandoned two years later after a raid by jealous Sulu chiefs. So far British ventures had thus contributed little to closer links between the Philippines and the Archipelago.

During the short occupation of Balambangan the northern coast of west New Guinea had been reconnoitred in search of spices, and shortly before the French wars an attempt was made to establish a settlement in Dorey Bay, near present-day Manokwari. During the first wartime occupation of the Moluccas, the Company sought to acquire a foothold — in the Raja Ampat Islands, part of the Tidore lands — which might not revert on the return of peace. The restoration of the Moluccas under the treaty of Amiens, however, led to the dropping of this plan, and a decision to reoccupy Balambangan. Its isolation in the renewed war led promptly to its abandonment once more.

This peripheral area attracted the attention of Raffles, concerned also to establish connexions that would not revert to the Dutch at the end of the war. He sent a diplomatic and commercial mission to Sulu and Mindanao and advocated a settlement at Marudu in north Borneo. But this policy was disapproved, and there was no new Balambangan. The treaties of 1814 and 1824 left the Moluccas in Dutch hands. There, in fact, the Dutch maintained deliveries and a monopoly of purchase, without attempting the destruction of spice plants. The Moluccan ports remained closed, however, till 1853, the islands remained poverty-stricken. In New Guinea the Dutch showed even less interest. The establishment of the British settlements in northern Australia, however, prompted them to strengthen their position in the eastern parts of the Archipelago by despatching the *Dourga* on a voyage through the Banda Sea. Subsequently, in 1828, they set up Fort Du Bus in west New Guinea (abandoned in 1836), and assumed possession of the littoral between 141°E on the south coast and the Cape of Good Hope on the north.

The English adventurer James Brooke saw the founding of Port Essington, one of the north Australian settlements, as part of a challenge to the Dutch, to be taken up also by executing Raffles' suggestion of a settlement at Marudu. Arriving at Singapore in his yacht *Royalist* in 1839, Brooke learned, however, of the revolt in the Sarawak province of Brunei against the Brunei governor who was exploiting its antimony trade to Singapore. He went to Sarawak, helped a Brunei raja, Hassim, to put down the rebellion, and himself secured the grant of Sarawak government. His aim was now to support Hassim in the still somewhat Rafflesian policy of reforming all Brunei, of regularising its government and defining its exactions on the trade between the dependent rivers and the outside world. The policy involved striking blows at rajas who might be jealous of Hassim and anxious for their old sources of revenue. It also involved putting down the Mindanao or 'Ilanun' piratical communities settled north of Brunei, and punishing the neighbouring Saribas and Sekrang Dayaks who descended upon Sarawak. The latter Brooke also regarded as piratical. Yet the Brunei Malays had long ruled the tribes of the dependent rivers by playing off one against another and, indeed, in the days of Brunei's decline, the immigrant Ilanuns and other Bajau or sea-gypsy tribes, often led by adventuring Sharifs, had also become sources of power and influence for the rajas. Brooke's simplification of the issues, however, improved his chance of securing naval support.

The likelihood of unilateral action against pirates in areas where the Dutch had no claims had, moreover, been increased by the failure of the treaty of 1824 where they had claims. Brooke secured naval aid against the Saribas and Sekrang in 1843 and 1844. He sought further to interest the British Government by pointing to the coal measures near Brunei town and on its off-shore island of Labuan, of importance with the growing number of steamers in Asian waters. But what determined the Government to afford Brooke some support was the unsatisfactory situation with the Dutch, particularly after November 1843. In 1844 he was appointed agent to the Sultan of Brunei, a post designed 'to facilitate the suppression of piracy and the extension and protection of British trade'.[57] A naval station was to be acquired. The Dutch protested at British interference in Borneo, but the Foreign Office asserted that the treaty of 1824 did not prohibit British establishment there and declared that in any case it was not taking over Sarawak, but only a naval station off the coast. Balambangan was suggested, but Hassim ceded Labuan.

The crisis for Brooke's policy came in 1846, when a revolution in Brunei overthrew Hassim. The result was an attack on the capital by a British Admiral, the definite occupation of Labuan as a colony, and the treaty with Brunei of 1847. One clause of this provided against cessions of the Sultanate's territory without British consent: the Dutch claims over Borneo had been denied, other powers had to be kept out in other ways. Brooke became Commissioner and Consul-General and the first Governor of Labuan, while remaining Raja of Sarawak. His duty as Commissioner was 'to afford to British commerce that support and protection . . . peculiarly required in the Indian Seas, in consequence of the prevalence of piracy . . . and by reason of the encroachments of the Netherlands authorities in the Indian Archipelago'.[58] The Government had shifted away from the policy of 1824 and given some backing to an initially private enterprise. It had not taken over Sarawak, and its objectives were the suppression of piracy and the protection of commerce, objectives which the treaty of 1824 had apparently failed to realise. Brooke was indeed instructed to report any proposition that might lead to an arrangement with the Dutch.

A Dutch expedition to Sulu in 1848 prompted Brooke as Commissioner to draw that area into the scheme of British diplomacy in the Archipelago and to conclude a treaty with the Sultan on the lines of the Brunei treaty. But the result was a Spanish protest, backed up in 1851 by a new expedition to Sulu and a new treaty repeating the Sultan's submission to Spain. The Foreign Office in 1852 abandoned the effort to uphold the Brooke treaty. The most powerful argument the Spaniards used was that the French had respected their rights after attempting to occupy Basilan in 1845.

In other respects also support for Brooke's policy was being qualified. On the one hand commercial conditions were improving and so were relations with the Dutch. On the other hand, stimulated initially by Singaporeans jealous of Labuan and by Brooke's disappointed agent Henry Wise, the Radicals in England began to attack the inhumanity and inexpediency of the anti-piracy policy, more especially the massacre of the Sea-Dayaks at Batang Marau in 1849. The Foreign Office came to realise that it was being drawn further into Borneo affairs than it had intended. Furthermore the failure of his policy of indirectly ruling Brunei through Hassim had led Brooke to assert the independence of Sarawak and to aim at its extension at Brunei's expense; so that he now seemed to be using British power to advance private interest. But the final argument for the Commission of Inquiry of 1853 was political: it was a concession to the parliamentary Radicals by a coalition ministry.

The general result of the enquiry was to confirm the decision no longer to pursue an active policy in Borneo, and Brooke's successor lost the title of Commissioner. But the Raja was to be allowed to continue his efforts to 'civilise the natives and develop the resources and trade of Borneo'.[59] Actual recognition of his independence was, however, avoided, above all because the Government feared to recognise sovereignty in a subject of its sovereign. There was less naval activity than before. This contributed, with Brooke's change of policy after 1846 and the non-enforcement of the Sulu treaty, to the failure of Labuan as a commercial entrepot, and forced it to rely upon the inefficient efforts to raise its smoky coal: by the late 1850s there was talk of abandoning the colony. The position of the Raj in Sarawak was also weakened, about all by the Chinese rebellion of 1857. After this Brooke once again sought Government support, proposing a colony, a protectorate, a recognition of Sarawak independence, all in vain. Brooke turned to other powers, for instance France.

The Government's attitude began to shift somewhat. France was establishing herself on the far side of the China sea, and this made the retention of Labuan more important. It also made it more desirable to avoid Sarawak's falling into the hands of a major power. No doubt it might have been allowed to fall to the Dutch on Brooke's death: but meanwhile he might bestow it on the French. The result was the appointment of a consul to Sarawak, intended as a demonstration of interest rather than as an illustration of Sarawak's independence, which the Foreign Office still strove to avoid recognising. The fate of Sarawak could not be included among the topics discussed with the Dutch in the late 1860s. That might only precipitate a deal between the Raja and the French, especially to be avoided when some Americans were acquiring leases of Brunei claims in north Borneo. No intervention by the U.S. Government followed, but in 1868 the Foreign Office refused to allow the new Raja, Charles Brooke, to acquire the Baram river from the Sultan. The treaty of 1847 seemed a better safeguard against other powers than the uncertain disposition and tenure of the Brookes.

The early 1860s were marked by naval operations against the Ilanun pirates, significant because of the renewed interest in north-western Borneo they illustrated, significant also because of the renewed Anglo-Dutch co-operation they involved. Plans to attack the strongholds in the Sulu archipelago were, however, abandoned in view of Spanish claims. Spain had regained the Philippines after the Seven Years War and had retained them in the French wars. The loss of Mexico left the Philippines more dependent on their own resources, and the Spaniards allowed foreign merchants to develop them, though with some doubt as to whether it might rather increase the risk of losing this colony also. The increase in revenue that resulted facilitated the expansion of politico-military government and missionary activity in the mountain districts of Luzon from the 1840s and 1850s. It facilitated also the employment of steamers which opened the way to economic development in the Visayas by freeing them from piratical depredations.

The Spaniards, thanks to the prosperity of Luzon and the Visayas, were able to draw together an empire in the Philippines somewhat more compact than that the Dutch built with Javanese resources in the Archipelago. Not only piracy and the penetration of Islamic reformism conduced to further Spanish intervention in Sulu: so did the prospect of foreign intervention. It was desirable to suppress piracy lest others did it. It was also desirable to assert sovereign rights over the Sultanate of Sulu. The attempt to achieve this by a blockade in the early 1870s aroused the protests not only of Labuan but also of German traders (though both groups profited from gun-running). As yet, however, the German Government, though supporting its traders, did not appear to be aiming to secure territory. A protocol of 1877 established a *modus vivendi,* in which Spain agreed to refrain from any interference with British or German vessels, and to levy no duties upon their trade except where its authority was definitely established.

Growing apprehension that Germany might not continue to be so readily mollified contributed to the support the British Government afforded a group of capitalists who acquired the Brunei claims over north Borneo that the Americans had purchased in the 1860s and who acquired also the partially overlapping claims of the Sultan of Sulu. A company was formed which in 1881 received a royal charter as the British North Borneo Company. The territories it ruled did not thereby become British territory: the Sultans continued to be considered suzerains. But the British Government had secured through the charter a new means of preventing this territory falling into the hands of others, a more effective means than the treaty of 1847 afforded in changed international conditions. The charter precipitated a boundary argument with the Dutch, ultimately settled in 1891. It also precipitated an argument with the Spaniards, who considered they had a claim to 'Sabah' through the Sultan of Sulu, of whom they were the suzerains, not only by the treaty they had made in 1878, just after the concessions, but by earlier treaties. In a new protocol the Spaniards agreed to withdraw their claim on north Borneo in return for an explicit recognition of their sovereignty in the Sulu islands. The political boundary between the Philippines and the Archipelago had at last been defined.

To this definition the Germans assented with some reluctance. This was indeed the period of Bismarck's colonial ventures, also of the Berlin conference of 1884-5. A further shift ensued in British policy in Borneo. Already opposition to Brooke's acquisition of Baram had been withdrawn on condition that he promised to cede it to no others. The decay of Brunei led to further concessions to the Company and to Sarawak, the same condition being thereupon attached to all his territory. In 1888 the British Government definitely assumed a protectorate over the three diverse régimes its policy had allowed to develop in north-west Borneo. In the 1890s further encroachments on Brunei occurred. The Colonial Office, then reconstructing Malaya, had some plans for a possibly associated colony in Borneo also. But all that resulted was that the ruler of the remnants of the Sultanate was in 1905 given the assistance of a British Resident on the lines of those in the Peninsular states.

Bismarck's colonial policy had also launched Germany into New Guinea. Its demonstration of interest precipitated the Queensland annexation of the coast between the Dutch boundary at 141° and 159°E and late in 1884 the hoisting of the British flag at Port Moresby. A settlement with the Germans followed in 1885. Ten years later the British and the Dutch settled their boundary along 141°, with a bulge on the Fly river, and in 1910 the Germans also accepted the 141° line. The Dutch claim of 1828 had, of course, been concerned with the coast. In the late 1840s, however, as part of the definition of their claims to which the British activities of that decade provoked them, the Dutch had in a secret decree arrogated rights over the interior. In 1902 they established their post at Merauke, designed to restrain the raids of the Tugeri tribes into the British territory. With the Acheh settlement two years later, the empire stretched from Sabang to Merauke. Two years later again, newly federated Australia assumed full control over 'Papua'.

German interest in the region reappears at the time of the Spanish-American war, and no doubt afforded the British a reason for not opposing the U.S. acquisition of the Philippines, though they did not actively encourage it. To Manila the Americans had been brought by Roosevelt and a few expansionists. Dewey's success produced the paradox of American imperialism, renewing a contact across the Pacific initiated by Magellan and Legazpi, and giving the Philippines a new uniqueness in Southeast Asia. The islands were conquered and purchased from the Spaniards and conquered from the Filipinos. In the south there was diplomacy, too. In many parts of the Moro lands in 1898 Spanish power was still opposed. The Americans made a treaty with the Sultan of Sulu in 1899, but the resistance of local and island *datus* continued on and off till 1915. It was ended by diplomacy, by non-interference with Islam, by the hard-fought campaigns that made Pershing's reputation, by the Krag rifle and the Colt 45 and the Gatling gun and the slaughter they produced, as in the taking of Bud Dajo. After the end of organised resistance guerilla warriors carried on for a decade, as did the *juramentados,* combining *amok* and *jihad,* fanatical Muslim resistance such as the Dutch met in Acheh, another area never before under European authority. Under an agreement of 1915, the Sultan of Sulu abandoned any pretensions to sovereignty, and no successor was appointed to the Sultan who died in the 1930s. The British North Borneo Company continued, however, to pay the Sabah cession money to his heirs. The territorial re-definition in this area was completed in 1907 when the U.S. waived in favour of the Company its rights to administer two islands lying off Sandakan, though retaining possession of them.

4 British Malaya

WHEN it acquired Penang from the Sultan of Kedah in 1786, the Company promised him an annual payment, increased in 1800 after the acquisition of Wellesley on the other side of the harbour. It did not promise him what he sought, aid against his enemies, because it feared lest it should become involved with Siam, which had claims over the northern Malay states, and which was likely to enforce them after the Burmans had been decisively defeated and a new dynasty established at Bangkok. One of the more northerly of the states, Patani, had indeed asserted its independence in 1767 after the overthrow of Ayuthia. But the Thais put down 'revolts' in 1782 and 1790. Penang in fact had little commerce with the Peninsular states in its early decades, but the prospect of the return of the Dutch to Palembang and Bangka after the French wars suggested the need to open up the tin-mining states of Perak, Selangor, and — indirectly through Kedah — Patani. Such attempts met for a while the opposition of the Dutch in Malacca. They met also the opposition of the Thais, who entered Kedah in strength in 1821 and intervened in Perak. The Sultan of Kedah fled to Penang, but his appeals for help were vain, despite sympathy for him among local merchants and officials apprehensive of the establishment of Thai influence on the Peninsula and anxious to establish British influence.

The departure of the Dutch under the treaty of 1824 seemed to make action more urgent. For one thing, no one in the Settlements believed that they would abide by their promises in the Archipelago: it was all the more desirable to keep the Peninsula open to British trade. Secondly, the withdrawal of the Dutch left Perak and Selangor wide open to Thai penetration. The superior authorities in Calcutta had opposed any intervention that might invite conflict with the Thais. Warlike movements at Penang nevertheless restrained the Thai commander, the governor of Ligor (Nakorn Sithammarat), and in 1825 a British agent secured treaties with Perak and Selangor, settling their mutual frontier and providing for the protection of Penang traders. The Sultan of Perak offered also to cede the island of Pangkor (the Dindings).

Meanwhile the Supreme Government in Calcutta had determined to send an envoy to Bangkok, and chose Henry Burney (a nephew of Fanny). Initially it was planned to offer the Thais, in return for commercial concessions and the restoration of the Raja of Kedah, the conquests of Tavoy and Mergui which the Company expected to make in the first war with Burma begun in 1824. But this scheme was dropped. Thus Burney's treaty of 1826 by no means restored the Raja: indeed the British Government undertook to prevent his attacking the Thais in Kedah. Nor could Burney persuade the Thais to renounce their claims over Kelantan and Trengganu: they simply promised not to interrupt English commerce with those states, while the English promised not to attack them. The Thais consented not to interfere with Selangor, while it was agreed that the Sultan of Perak should send the symbolic tribute, the *bunga mas* or silver flowers, to Bangkok if he wished to do so. In this restrained way the new British power sought to deal with the oldstyle claims of the Thais on the Peninsula. Nothing was done for Patani, and there was a new revolt in the late 1820s.

Governor Fullerton, however, believed that more action was required in Perak. The state's central authority had declined, especially during the Thai invasion of Kedah which, more-over, had been preceded by a Kedah invasion of Perak on Thai behalf. The resulting disorder left the way open for Thai influence. Fullerton sent a mission to Perak to procure the Sultan's declaration of independence and refusal to send the *bunga mas,* and in a treaty of 1826 he definitely ceded Pangkor. The rebellious local chiefs built up their power by contacts with the pirates from Johore that raided the Straits, *orang laut* owing allegiance to various Johore Malay chiefs. In 1827 the Penang government, acting under a clause in the Perak treaty of 1826, attacked the chief in the Kurau river. It was a blow against piracy. But it was also designed to strengthen the central government in Perak.

In this state Fullerton was following a policy rather akin to Raffles', differing somewhat from his own policy towards Acheh. But in the Perak case there were no entrenched Country Trade interests to insist upon virtual independence for the dependent rivers, and apprehensions of the Thais were more pressing than apprehensions of the Dutch who had undertaken to respect the independence of Acheh. The policy resembled Raffles' in seeking to establish an indirect influence in areas where the superior authorities were opposed to direct rule and urging that the purpose of that influence was anti-piratical. It was a policy that, of course, bears some resemblance also to Brooke's. But in a despatch of 1827 the Supreme Government reproved Fullerton for proceedings that were likely to provoke the Thais and disapproved the Perak treaty of 1826. This limited the possibilities of intervention in Perak in the future and even of attacking piratical strongholds on the Peninsula. The scope of action was still further reduced by the Company's economising in preparation for the negotiations over the renewal of its charter in 1833, and, after that event, by its loss of interest in the Straits Settlements following its loss of the monopoly of the China trade.

Nevertheless — and even though the commercial interests of the Settlements remained as yet concerned with the Archipelago and beyond — the Governors did not altogether abandon the Peninsular policy of the 1820s. Naturally they sought still to put down Johore piracy, hampered as they were by the application of Common Law principles developed in different circumstances, by lack of naval forces, especially before the arrival of their first steamer in 1837, by the division of the Johore empire effected by the Dutch at Riau, and by injunctions against intervention on the Peninsula. Their frustration led to the attack on Galang in 1836 — Galang indeed was not on the Peninsula — and in turn this had two major results. On the one hand it stimulated the Dutch to renew proposals to co-operate against piracy, and when these were set aside, to intensify their own activity with a view to avoid further British unilateral action. On the other hand, it affected British relations with the Peninsular chiefs.

The suppression of piracy was bound to bring contacts with them and the use of the steamer to increase British influence over them. But the action at Galang more particularly convinced the Temenggong of Johore of his error, and that of his father who had ceded Singapore, in aiding and abetting the *orang laut* piracies. A resident of Singapore, he became closely associated with the Governors, now centred there, in their attempts to put down piracy, and afforded a much-needed additional aid to their exerting an influence on the Peninsula. The Temenggong, with Singaporean advice, promoted the development of Peninsular Johore, and secured and retained a special position in the complex of relations between the British and the Malay states which non-intervention had left in existence, but over which the local officials sought a civilising influence. Ibrahim's son, Abu-bakar, became in 1866 the first Peninsular prince to visit the English court.

In 1885 he was recognised as Sultan of Johore. In a treaty of that year his state came under British protection, and he undertook to grant no concessions without British consent. The British acquired the right to appoint a consul, but none was appointed. Only in 1909 did Johore accept a British agent who, under a new treaty of 1914, became General Adviser. The British thus strengthened their position in Johore. This is explained by their increased interest in the Peninsula and their increased concern about other European powers. But similar motives produced different policies towards the other Peninsular states. The ruler of Johore, in fact, still enjoyed a special position.

The Temenggong's success in the mid-nineteenth century had produced parties for and against him among Singapore merchants. Furthermore, while he was useful to the Governors, their support expanded his influence, and other Peninsular rulers became jealous. Hussein's son, Ali, allied with a merchant, W. H. Read, had to be bought off by a treaty of 1855. Omar, a prince disposed to piracy before he secured the throne of Trengganu, but thereafter disposed to reform and development, became apprehensive of the Temenggong's apparently exclusive influence with the Straits Government. Governor Blundell (1855-9) thus sought to cultivate friendship with him independently of the Temenggong. He was aided in the task by naval movements directed against the spread of Chinese piracy in the Gulf of Siam in the 1850s, an effect of disorder in the Celestial Empire during the Taiping rebellion, of naval operations on the China coast, and of the lack of controls at the free (and easy) port of Singapore. Blundell also invited Omar to send his sons to be educated in Singapore.

The problem was worsened by a civil war in the intervening state of Pahang, once part of the empire of Johore, and ruled by the heir of one of its officers, the Bendahara. Blundell tried to restrain both Ibrahim and Omar from intervening. His successor, Cavenagh, reverted to the policy of close association with the Temenggong. The Sultan of Trengganu then associated himself more closely with the Thais. This led to Cavenagh's bombardment of Trengganu in 1862, a lesson to Omar, a defiance of the Thais. Lack of regular authority had led to a violent irregularity.

The bombardment produced a reaction among the parties in Singapore, a protest from the Thais, and some disapproval in London and Calcutta. In turn this affected the attitude of the next Governor. Moreover, the end of the Company's rule after the Indian Mutiny of 1857 had led among Straits merchants to an agitation for transfer to Colonial Office rule. They believed that their special problems, including their treatment at the hands of the Dutch, might receive closer attention from Whitehall than from an over-burdened Indian Government that relied upon the Governor for advice; and they were led by a minority, including Read, who were anxious for more responsibility and made the most of Blundell's unpopularity. The transfer at last occurred in 1867. The views of the first Colonial Governor, Ord, and those of the Colonial Office, were formed very much under the influence of the 1862 bombardment. Thai claims over Kelantan and Tregganu were clearly recognised.

The activity of the local Governors since the 1820s had, however, in fact ensured that these states were not absorbed by the Thais in the way Patani was. The Sultan of Kelantan had acknowledged Thai supremacy in the 1830s, as a means of avoiding invasion during the suppression of further Patani revolts. It is worth noting that, at the suggestion of the Singapore authorities, a British vessel stood off the coast at the time, ostensibly operating against pirates, in fact, of course, warning the Thais against invasion. The Sultan retained considerable

137

political latitude. Omar of Trengganu had in part owed his installation to the Thais, but thereafter his independence of attitude helped to limit their authority, and his policy in the early 1860s had been only a passing phase. Even though it had culminated in the bombardment, and even though the British recognition of Thai claims was promoted by the fear of encouraging the French, established in 'Indo-China', to deny other Thai claims, the Sultanate retained substantial autonomy.

The virtual independence of the Sultanates — more especially of ill-governed Kelantan — was in fact to cause the British concern in the early years of the twentieth century, when the Peninsula was open to rapid economic development and other European powers were, it was thought, seeking to utilise or neutralise its strategic importance. The Governor, Sir Frank Swettenham, planned to assist Siam to secure written agreements from the Sultans, giving it *de jure* status, if it would employ British officers as Residents, and this resulted in the joint declaration of 1902. The negotiations illustrated the tripartite distribution of political power in the area. It was also significant that the agreement did not cover Patani, and that the Sultan of Trengganu would not accept a Thai-appointed Resident. Under a convention with Siam of 1909, the British took over the Thai claims, and they made agreements with the Sultans in 1910. That with the Sultan of Trengganu was on the lines of the Johore treaty of 1885, though another treaty was to follow in 1919.

The transfer of 1909 — establishing a new boundary between Peninsula and mainland — included also the states of Kedah and Perlis. In Kedah Thai rights had been recognised back in 1826. The local government assisted the Thais during the revolts and invasions of 1831 and 1838 (with which disorders in Patani coincided), going even further than their treaty obligations suggested, working with Thai authority since it could not be denied. But Governor Bonham aided in the negotiations that followed these revolts and that led to the restoration of the Raja of Kedah as a Thai vassal in 1842, though in 1839 Siam had carved out of his territory the small state of Perlis. The restoration established a situation more like that in the other northern states, and the receipt of a pension for the cession of Penang made the Raja somewhat amenable to the Straits Government. In 1888 the Siamese agreed to the appointment of a British consul in Kedah and Perlis. After 1909 Advisers appointed by the British took over from financial advisers appointed by the Thais.

In Perak the development of British influence had proved impossible after 1827. Furthermore, the decline in Johore piracy — the result of British and Dutch activities against the strongholds, the result also, as with piracy further afield, of the increasing commercial use of steamers and square-rigged vessels less open to attack and of the opening of additional entrepots which reduced the length and danger of voyages — meant that there was less chance of finding a reason for the deployment of naval forces in the absence of political instructions from the superior authorities. Yet Perak was becoming increasingly disorganised in the 1850s. Initially financed by Malay chiefs seeking to take advantage of the opening of the British market for tin with the end of protection for Cornish production, Chinese miners immigrated in increased numbers, and intensified and then through their secret societies took part in the struggle for power in the state. Cavenagh contrived to intervene under the treaty of 1825, but Ord's request for more regular authority was refused by the Colonial Office, and his plan to acquire Pangkor under the 'treaty' of 1826 was disapproved. He was thus reduced to attempts to mediate.

In Selangor, a loosely organised tin-bearing Bugis state, the local government also attempted indirect intervention. The 'piracy' of the incident of 1871 and its punishment were used to strengthen the vice-regal position of Tengku Zia u'd-din, a younger brother of the Sultan of Kedah. The ruler of Johore was persuaded to keep Mahdi, centre of Selangor opposition, in Johore, and arrangements clinched for the intervention of the Bendahara of Pahang on the Tengku's side.

An end came to these expedients with the appointment of Residents in the west coast states, including Sungei Ujong, one of the Menangkabau confederacy. This was the work of Ord's successor, Clarke, who, in the case of Perak, used the 'treaty' of 1826 and also occupied Pangkor. The main consideration behind the Colonial Office's change of policy was not concern to develop the tin trade or to make up supposed losses suffered in the Settlements by the opening of other entrepots: it was apprehension lest other European powers might intervene in an area flanking Singapore and the route to China. Against this there was no treaty provision covering these states, and no *de facto* provision in their stability. The motive for intervening was not, therefore, a revolutionary one. The method, the appointment of Residents to advise the existing rulers, seemed, furthermore, a logical outcome of the existing situation. The idea was presumably of British Indian origin. But the belief that it was

139

a matter of giving advice was of British Malay origin: it derived from local government experience with amenable rajas like those of Kedah and particularly of Johore. In fact, of course, the historical background of and the current situation in Perak and Selangor were very different. No basis had been laid for the acceptance of advice, even if offered more tactfully than that on debt-slavery given by the Resident in Perak, J. W. W. Birch. The murder of Birch and the punishment of the chiefs in the 'Perak War' of 1875-76 ensued. But paradoxically they only contributed to the tradition of advice and guidance. The Colonial Office blamed the crisis on Governor Jervois' talk of annexation and refused to abandon the Resident theory. But that the theory could be maintained subsequently was due to the punitive action which ensured that 'advice' would be heeded. The theory had developed from the practice forced upon a local government concerned to build up British influence on the Peninsula, restrained by its superiors' policy of non-intervention and concern for Thai claims, and so working indirectly and through existing chiefs and states for whose preservation and reform it struggled as best it could. But in the new period, while the theory remained, the practice changed, and with the growing development of the west coast states, British rule became more direct.

The divorce between theory and practice was probably already apparent when the Residential system was extended to Pahang. Governor Weld — once a New Zealand premier — had been concerned at the erratic granting of concessions there and the risks of foreign intervention, and in 1887 persuaded the Bendahara to accept a treaty on the Johore model. His successor, with the aid of the Sultan of Johore's diplomacy, managed to introduce the Residential system in 1888. Disturbances resulted in 1891-2. The difficulties of Pahang, and its revenue deficit — at a time, moreover, of declining tin prices — were an argument for the creation in 1895 of a federation with the more developed states of Perak, Selangor and Negri Sembilan. But the creation of a central government at Kuala Lumpur was to increase still further the disparity between the theory of advice and the practice of government. It was a factor that helped to determine British relations with the other Malay states. Significantly they received Advisers, not Residents.

The diversity of practice in, and likewise the common theory of British policy on the Peninsula arose from the peculiar circumstances of the establishment of British power there in the period between 1760 and the first world war, affected as it was by existing Malay, Dutch and Thai theories and practices. The Dutch were dealt with by severing the Peninsula from the Archipelago, even by dividing Johore. Thai claims were restricted but also restricted the British. And the Malay states were retained but somewhat updated, their Sultans ruling with British advice in varying degrees.

The British had come, with unusual European and also Indian resources, to occupy a commanding position in the Archipelago and on the major route connecting it with the outside world. They had not used those resources and that position to create a formal empire. The Dutch had been left with Java, the Spaniards with Luzon, as the bases for empires that ultimately spread, if somewhat insecurely, to areas, many of them peripheral, never yet under European control, Acheh, Sulu, west New Guinea. The British concerned themselves with northern Borneo, in part because of a temporary commercial dispute with the Dutch, in part as a result of private enterprise, in part as a means of defending the route to China. It was this, and their empire in India, that first interested them in the Peninsula. There, however, local interests could operate only indirectly and in face of an old mainland claimant with whom superior authorities did not wish to quarrel. From most of the Peninsula, the Thais were ultimately excluded. But it was only with the growth of the rubber industry, and the change in Britain's world economic position, that 'Malaya' came to have its own special importance in the British empire. And about the same time — in the second decade of the twentieth century — Britain's empire in Asia came to pivot less on India and China and more on the Middle East and India. Singapore became a vital outpost and gained, though in a different context, the vast strategic significance Raffles had attributed to it.

5 The Andaman and Nicobar Islands

THE ESTABLISHMENT of territorial dominion in India and the development of trade to China gave the Andaman and Nicobar islands their importance in British policy in the later eighteenth century. The search for sheltered bases on the east side of the Bay of Bengal led in 1789 to the formation of a settlement on the Great Andaman, moved in 1793, and finally abandoned in 1796. It was unhealthy, and by then the British had acquired not only Penang, but also Trincomali.

Suffren had used a base at Nancowry in the Nicobar islands as well as Acheh and Mergui and privateers in the revolutionary war followed his example. The Nicobar islands had been annexed by Denmark in 1756, and a colony supported by subventions from home and the missionary endeavour of the Moravians. The British removed the Danes in 1809, following the acquisition of the Danish factories in India, but no occupation followed. The object of the Danes had been the islands' trade in coconuts, betelnuts and birds' nests. It was a trade beyond the fringe of the Dutch empire, though not beyond the scope of the Sumatran Malays who appear to have had a longstanding commercial connexion with the islands.

The Danes, restored post-war to their continental factories, established a settlement on Kamorta in 1831. After its withdrawal in 1838, the number of outrages on foreign merchants increased, perhaps partly as a result of Malay commercial jealousy, certainly in part a result of the behaviour of visiting captains and crews; and the Country Traders based on Penang and Malacca, as well as on the British settlements in Arakan and Tenasserim, pressed for intervention. Still no settlement was made, and reference to alleged French intentions failed to drive the Government into an unrewarding commitment; but naval activity increased, sometimes involving injudicious violence. In the late 1840s the Danes, though selling their factories on the continent, sent a new expedition to the Nicobars. It led to no new settlement, but for a while restrained 'piracy'. In the early 1850s further 'horrid crimes' were reported, but the Indian Government was still indisposed to take decisive action.

The Andamans were of even less commercial value than the Nicobars and the Malays, though visiting them, were less influential. But they lay in the track of vessels crossing the Bay and in the track of mainland traders to the Nicobars. The indulgence in an Andaman slave-trade by vessels from Burmese and Siamese-Malay ports north of Penang did nothing to mitigate the savage treatment the tribal islanders meted out to crews who stopped for water or were wrecked. By 1855 the Indian Government was considering the notion of settlement on one of the Andaman islands, to be commenced cheaply as a convict station. It might be a step towards providing greater security for vessels visiting the Andamans and the Nicobars. A further argument advanced was that, with the conquest of Pegu, the Bay of Bengal became 'a British Sea'. Thus 'no foreign power could be allowed to establish herself in the Andamans or Nicobars'.[60] The Governor-General himself remained doubtful about assuming further responsibilities. What turned the balance was the Mutiny. A vastly increased number of convicts had to be disposed of, 'turbulent, refractory individuals'[61] not wanted in the Straits. Late in 1857, Port Blair, the original site of 1789, was reoccupied. The civilisation of the Andamans thus began with compulsory Indian colonisation and clashes with the natives. A more spectacular tragedy was the murder in 1872 of the visiting Viceroy, Lord Mayo, by a convict.

The Danes, despite their withdrawal, maintained their claims to the Nicobars. The continued complaints of 'piracy', however, made their position untenable, for they could do nothing, especially amid the Slesvig-Holstein crisis of the 1860s. They agreed to the assumption of British control in 1869, and in 1871 some convicts were transferred to Kamorta. The penal settlement in the Nicobars was withdrawn in 1888.

6 British Burma

THE BRITISH contacts with Burma played a role in British relations with the Andaman and Nicobar islands. Those contacts had been broken off by the massacre at Negrais, and Burma resumed its relative isolation from the European activities in India and the Archipelago. During these years Burman military confidence swelled in successful struggles with mainland neighbours. Alaungpaya and a successor, Hsinbiyushin, led the Burmans against their old enemies, the Thais, and, moving through Chiengmai and Vienchang, besieged Ayuthia in 1760 and again in 1767. The Burmans then turned back Chinese invasions of the subsidiary Shan state of Kengtung and of upper Burma, provoked by Shan raids across the Yunnan frontier, and they attacked Manipur.

The Thais were able meanwhile to regain their independence, and they maintained it despite the invasions Bodawpaya began in 1785. The Burmans succeeded, however, in conquering Arakan in 1784-5. The Arakan revolt of 1794 and its repression led to the flight of refugees to neighbouring Chittagong, and thus brought the Burmans again in touch with the English, now the possessors of Bengal and a great military power on the continent. A British mission was sent to Burma in connexion with the refugees and also with the fear that the French might find a base there. Fears about the French disappeared, but relations with the Burmans worsened. Busy elsewhere in India, the British had established no effective control of the Chittagong region, and this Southeast Asian frontier once more as in the later sixteenth century played an important part with the Arakanese. There for a number of years their leader Chin Byan organised refugees in raids upon the Burmans. The Burmans believed the British helped them, for they were well aware of British extension in India and apprehensive of it in mainland Southeast Asia. But their relative lack of contact with Europeans in the previous period and since 1760, coupled with their successes

against the Thais, gave them an unreal idea of their comparative strength which the British weakness in Chittagong only
encouraged. They counter-attacked, occupying Assam and Manipur, and preparing to assault Chittagong and Bengal itself. This

led to the first Burma war of 1824-6. The main British attack
came by sea and in the weakest part of the kingdom, and
indeed the Burmans' difficulty was increased by a Mon-Karen
rebellion. The result was the Company's victory, and its acqui-
tion of the border territories, Arakan, Assam and Manipur, and,

145

rather doubtfully, the Tenasserim provinces, Tavoy and Mergui, were also retained. The Burmans lost the conquests or re-conquests of the eighteenth century. They retained upper and central Burma, and also Pegu and the mouths of the Irrawaddy.

The chance of preserving independence for the remains of the kingdom depended in part on the ability of the Burman monarchy to adapt itself to the new situation. But the catastrophic losses were a catastrophe above all in their effect on the pride of the dynasty and only tended to promote resentment at the changing world and continued isolation. The last of the British Residents appointed under the peace treaty left the court of Ava in 1839. The court's attitude spread to the local officials who dealt with the British traders at Rangoon. The Governor-General Dalhousie appraised their activities in the context of a policy designed to uphold British prestige in India. The result was a second Burma war in 1852, the annexation of Pegu, and in 1853 of Toungoo, annexations the new Burman king refused to recognise, by which he lost all his coast-line and a province the Burmans had striven to absorb for centuries.

Mindon Min, however, settled in a new capital at Mandalay, and sought to develop better relations with the English. He adhered to this policy even during the Indian Mutiny of 1857. In 1862 and 1867 he signed commercial treaties facilitating trade up the Irrawaddy, in which British merchants were interested because of their hopes of expanding trade with China across the mountains to Yunnan. In the later years of the reign, how-ever, relations with Britain deteriorated: on the one hand, royal commercial monopolies interfered with the operations of the Rangoon merchants; and on the other hand the 'shoe question' prevented the reception of a British Resident in audience with the king. But above all relations with Britain deteriorated be-cause the king attempted to confirm his independence by de-veloping relations with other European powers. In the circum-stances this could only provoke the British, and Mindon Min's successor, Thibaw Min, moreover especially sought relations with France. A treaty with the Third Republic, then expanding in Laos and Vietnam, made in 1885, and believed to be not confined to its ostensibly commercial objects, seemed to threaten the security of British Burma and of India itself. It was perhaps the principal cause of the third Burma war.

The British annexed the rest of Burma. They also extended their control over the Shan states to the east, confirming the authority of *sawbwas* or chiefs who submitted, but dealing

146

separately with the state of Karenni east of Toungoo. The Chin tribes accepted British authority in 1895. The boundary with British India — with Chittagong, with Manipur, with Assam — was readily defined. That with China — in the Shan, Kachin, and Wa regions — less readily. In 1900 China agreed to a line between Myitkyina in the Kachin territory and the Salween river, and the Namwan tract was leased to Britain to facilitate communication between Bhamo and the Shan states. But on the rest of the line there was no agreement. China simply acquiesced in a unilateral declaration by the British. Their extension over the Shan states had also brought them into negotiations with the French and the Thais.

7 French Indo-China

A CRISIS in Dai Viet in the later eighteenth century had led to new European contacts. The heavy burdens wars of extension laid upon the peasants of the south were a factor in the rebellion of the Tayson brothers in the Nguyen lands in the early 1770s. The rebellion began in the less 'colonial' areas, in the old provinces of Quang-ngai and Binh-dinh. It was supported also by merchants anxious to limit feudalism and reunite the country, by Moi tribesmen, and by a descendant of the Cham kings. Amid the chaos the Trinh ruler marched to the south in 1774-5, but in 1778 one of the brothers was able to proclaim himself emperor. In 1786 the Tayson invaded the north in the name of the Le and destroyed the crumbling Trinh régime. The attempt of Le Chieu-thong to assert a real supremacy, and his appeal to the Chinese, who crossed the frontier in 1788, led only to the triumph of the Tayson brother who called himself emperor Quang-trung. But no stability ensued: Le legitimism was tenacious; commerce did not revive; the peasants found no social amelioration, only a change of master; and above all there was the threat of Nguyen Anh, a grandson of

147

Vo-vuong who had fled to Pulau Panjang and secured some European aid. Civil strife in Dai Viet had once more given the Europeans a foothold.

The French had continued to look to Dai Viet as a possible source of 'compensation' for the success of the British in India and China. Choiseul's plans of 1768 were ended by his fall and the subsequent dissolution of the French East India Company. Apprehensions of the French, however, played a part in the sending of an English mission in 1778, which followed the visit of two Nguyen mandarins to Calcutta, and which was also designed to amplify the trade through Dai Viet to China. But the disturbed state of the country prevented the establishment of a factory, and the French were in any case incapacitated by the loss of their Indian settlements in the American war. A new chance for them came when Nguyen Anh reluctantly sought their aid through the missionary Pigneau de Behaine.

In 1787 Pigneau and Nguyen Anh's son prince Canh arrived at Versailles, and a treaty was signed, providing, in return for aid, for the cession of Pulau Condore and of Hoi-nan (Callao) island in Tourane (Da-nang) harbour to the French. In fact neither France nor the French administration in India gave the Nguyen cause substantial aid. Pigneau did manage to raise some support in private quarters, however, for instance in Mauritius: he collected some military stores and he enrolled some adventurers. They arrived in time to consolidate the capture of Saigon the Nguyen had effected; they endowed Dai Viet with the star-shaped Vauban-type forts used by the colonial powers; and their artillery superiority helped Nguyen Anh to defeat the Tayson, rather as Portuguese artillery had helped his ancestors to maintain their independence of the Trinh. In 1792 he marched north, and at last in 1802 took the northern centre of Hanoi. Nguyen Anh, calling himself Gia-long, and his reunited country Vietnam, was recognised by China in 1804 and proclaimed emperor in 1806 in his capital at Hué.

It was not surprising, in view of the long connexion between civil war and foreign intervention, that, once established, Gia-long turned away from things European. Pigneau died in 1799, and by 1802 the reunifier of the Vietnamese lands had only four French mandarins in his service. The English, whose envoy to China had called in at Tourane in 1793, became more apprehensive of the French prospects after the Vietnamese empire had been re-united, and diplomatic missions were sent there in 1803 and 1804. There proved to be no cause for concern, and on the other hand there was no offer of a settlement. The Viet-

namese policy was now one of isolation, and no attempt was
made to play off one power by another.

Gia-long was no more open to the revival of French contacts
after the Bourbon restoration. A political mission of 1817-8 was
sent in vain, and under his successor, Minh-mang, the last
Frenchmen left the emperor's service. The weakness of French
influence was clear to John Crawfurd, a British envoy sent to
Bangkok and Hué in 1822. This, and the commercial unim-
portance of Vietnam now that opium supplied its investment
in China, seemed to relieve the Company of any need to break
down an isolation confirmed by news of English conquests in
India and illustrated by the emperor's refusal even to receive
Crawfurd on the ground that he was only the envoy of the
Governor-General and not of George IV. The fact that Vietnam
was a feudatory of China also made for a pacific policy on the
part of the Company, since it had no wish for any conflict that
might disturb the tea trade. The Crawfurd mission merely led
the emperor to rid himself of the remaining Frenchmen lest
their presence should invite the presence of Englishmen.

One effect of this isolation, however, was also to isolate Vietnam from modern weapons and technology, and a Confucianist
mandarinate dedicated to the maintenance of the *status quo*
was unlikely to encourage their development in Vietnam itself.
Yet, even though Minh-mang had achieved political isolation
by 1832, he went on to persecute the Christian missionaries and
thus make European intervention more likely. The reason for
this was again in part historical. The 1833 revolt in the south
or 'Cochin-China' led by Le Van Khoi involved Christians: Minh-
mang feared a new Pigneau working against the Nguyen. And
between 1833 and 1837 seven missionaries and some native
Christians were put to death. The policy was the more dangerous
in view of the religious revival in France under the restoration
which involved the vigorous ultramontane movement of Lamen-
nais and a reconstruction of the *Société des Missions Entrangères;*
and in view of the support that it might receive, as a gesture
to the Catholics, even from the post-1830 Orléans régime, and
that it was certain to receive from the French navy which, in
Asia, had in any case no other interests to protect.

The first Anglo-Chinese war, of course, represented a major
shift in power and policy in East Asia, and Minh-mang was
alive to some of the implications of the British struggle against
his suzerain. It produced a investigatory gesture on his part,
the embassy to France of 1840, which clerical pressure prevented
Louis Philippe from receiving. A new emperor, Thieu-tri,

149

reverted to the previous policy and renewed the persecutions, and French warships, more numerous in East Asia following the opening of China, visited Vietnamese ports to afford the missionaries protection. The object of Louis Philippe's minister, Guizot, was a treaty with China on the British model and a foothold for France in the vicinity, the alternatives considered including the Anambas and Natunas, P. Condore, Tourane and Basilan. Basilan was selected but the venture was a failure, and aroused Spanish protests which Guizot heeded (it was the time of his Spanish marriage proposals). No progress was made in Vietnam either. The missionaries suggested a sustained naval demonstration at Tourane which they believed would encourage partisans of the old Le dynasty in Tonkin who might, if successful, concede a base in Tonkin. The plan was vetoed. But there were naval actions, especially in Tourane harbour in 1847, designed to assist the missionaries. In fact they only added to Thieu-tri's not unjustified distrust and increased his persecutions.

That distrust also prevented his receiving the commercial mission of Sir John Davis. This mission represented a British recognition of a change in relations with the vassal Vietnam as well as the suzerain China. It did not succeed in leading Thieu-tri away from isolation. But the British did not react violently to their failure: they concentrated on the better commercial opportunities in China and did not abandon their moderation in Indo-China. The way was still open to the French if they should seek here 'compensation' for the Asian predominance of the British. And Vietnam had, as it were, taken out no insurance with the major maritime power in the region.

The new emperor Tu-duc's policy was influenced not only by the French naval action of 1847, but also by the rebellion of his brother Hong Bao, whose followers had referred to missionaries with a view to seeking European assistance. Hence the persecution edicts of 1848 and 1851. Further French action was deferred during the revolution of 1848, but Louis Napoleon interested himself in a plan of 1852 to secure a treaty from Vietnam containing guarantees for the missions and providing for the cession of Tourane according to the arrangement of 1787. The move would balance British gains in Pegu, contribute to Bonapartist prestige and gain Catholic support. But action was again deferred by the still more spectacular opportunities in the Near East and by the ensuing Crimean war.

Following his successful treaty at Bangkok in 1855, the British envoy John Bowring attempted in vain to open negotiations with

Vietnam. Defeated, he encouraged the French envoy Montigny to follow in his wake, equally in vain, though one of his vessels had destroyed the forts at Tourane. The Catholic missions were more desolate than ever, and late in 1857 Tu-duc decapitated a Spanish bishop, Diaz. As a result, the Spaniards agreed to send an army of Filipino Catholics to join a French expedition against Vietnam, a decision that represented a curious recurrence to the adventures of the late sixteenth century and was to delay the struggle against the Moros. Napoleon III had determined on the expedition late in 1857. Substantial forces were present in the East following the end of the Crimean war and the outbreak of the new troubles with China (the *Arrow* war). Under cover of co-operation with Britain in China — and during the crisis of the Indian Mutiny — the expedition might take steps to ensure the protection of Catholics and secure Tourane. The venture was delayed by a protracted negotiation in China that concluded with the treaty of Tientsin in June 1858. In the autumn the Franco-Spanish expedition took Tourane. But no Le revolt occurred in Tonkin, as the missionaries had promised, and the rains prevented an overland attack on Hué itself and spread sickness among the soldiers (especially the French). Against the protests of the Spaniards and the missions — whose interests were mostly in Tonkin — the French Admiral moved against Saigon early in 1859. The involvement of Napoleon in the Italian war, the new struggles in China over the ratification of the Tientsin treaty, the disappointment of the Spaniards, all weakened the expedition, which withdrew from Tourane in March.

The end of the China imbroglio, however, saw French control extended over three of the provinces that neighboured Saigon. These, and P. Condore, Tu-duc finally agreed to cede in 1862, also opening three ports and promising religious liberty. Tu-duc was influenced by the outbreak of the long-awaited Tonkin revolt. In this the French forces declined to intervene, despite the missionaries and the Spaniards: they preferred to use it to secure Saigon. In 1867 the naval authorities acquired in addition the three westernmost provinces of Cochin-China, without backing from a French Emperor concerned with Mexico and with the rise of Germany. The French had begun to create a colony in the territory that was also a colony to the Vietnamese.

The French also moved into Cambodia. The fortunes of that kingdom had continued to fluctuate with those of its more powerful neighbours. The revival of Siam after the Burman invasions of the 1760s led to attempts to assert its claims over Cambodia, thrown back by the Nguyen in 1773. The Tayson revolt gave the Thais a new opportunity in Cambodia, but Bodawpaya's invasions prevented their using it. In 1794, however, the Thais installed as king Neac Ang Eng, who in return recognised Siamese jurisdiction over Battambang and Angkor (Siemreap). His son deemed it wise also to placate reunified Vietnam, and in 1805 recognised the overlordship of Gia-long. This provoked the displeasure of the Thais, who occupied Lovek and Oudong, but not permanently. Gia-long finally reinstalled the king at Phnom Penh. In 1833, the Thais seized the opportunity afforded by the Le Van Khoi revolt, but their attack on Cambodia was defeated. Further conflicts led to the withdrawal of both Thai and Vietnamese forces, and king Ang Duong recognised himself as the vassal of both his neighbours. The midway position of Cambodia attracted the attention of Brooke after the failure of his commercial mission to Siam and Vietnam of 1850. It attracted Montigny, who also thought it opened the way to a brilliant coup. In fact the change in Cambodia's position followed the establishment of the French in Cochin-China. In 1863 the new king, Norodom, accepted the protectorate which the French Admiral believed the aftermath of the Trengganu bombardment provided a good opportunity for proposing. Furthermore in 1864 the French prevented Norodom's going to Bangkok to receive his investiture, and in 1867 they made a treaty with the Thais, who abandoned their protectorate in return for recognition of their claims over Battambang and Angkor.

The fall of Napoleon III and the disaster of the German invasion left the French in Cochin-China more on their own than ever: they continued to seize all their opportunities. An exploration of the Mekong in 1866 had confirmed earlier Dutch opinions of its inaccessibility. Attention turned to the Red River as an additional means of opening up China. In Tonkin Tu-duc had not succeeded in re-establishing order — hence no doubt his inactivity against the French in 1870 — and he had taken a group of Chinese bandits, remnants of the Taiping rebels called the Black Flags, into his pay. A French merchant found his trade up the Red River obstructed by them. After the news of the German evacuation of France, a small force was sent to Hanoi and it seized the citadel, only to lose its commander Garnier. The monarchist government at home refused to sanction a bigger expedition. Instead Tu-duc was required to recognise the Cochin-China annexations of 1867 and to declare the navigation of the Red River free.

The Republican governments from the late 1870s were concerned to uphold French prestige by overseas adventure, and they received some support from Bismarck who was anxious at once to divert them from the question of Alsace-Lorraine and to divide them from the British. Action in the Far East was delayed by adventures in Egypt and Tunisia. It came in the early 1880s, at the same time as the Bismarckian colonial challenge, in part indeed a gesture of solidarity with France. In 1882 a small expedition was sent to deal with the disorder obstructing Red River commerce. The French feared the British would open the Burma route to Yunnan first. An expedition of 1883 had much stronger backing in France and secured control of lower Tonkin. A bombardment of Hué compelled the emperor to accept a protectorate. The Chinese, to whom Tu-duc had sent missions in 1876 and 1880, challenged the French, but finally recognised their position in the treaty of Tientsin of 1885. A long resistance followed among the Vietnamese, suggesting a potential that the dynasty had never managed to exploit. It had not used the interval of the 1870s to promote reforms, despite proposals by mandarins like Nguyen Truong To and Dinh Van Dien. It had simply fallen back upon the Chinese, scarcely more capable of effective opposition. The new Emperor, Ham-nghi, for a while led the resistance. He was delivered up by Muong tribesmen.

The occupation of Tonkin brought the French into Laos. Here the Thais, recovering from the Burman invasions and profiting from the Tayson rebellion, had in 1778 occupied Vienchang, an ally of Burma, and carried off the superb Emerald Buddha to the Siamese capital. With the triumph of Gia-long, the king of Vienchang sent tribute to Vietnam, and at the time of the Burney negotiations at Bangkok tried to overthrow Thai supremacy, only to bring about a Thai invasion. The Thais were joined by the rival Lao states of Luang Prabang and Champassak, and Vienchang was crushed. But this stirred the Vietnamese, who acquired Vienchang's vassal Tran Ninh (Chieng Khouang), beyond Samneua. Luang Prabang itself sought to reduce Thai influence by offering homage to Hué in 1831 and 1833. But the offer was not taken up, and both Luang Prabang and Champassak remained virtually under Thai control. Bangkok was to profit from Hué's difficulties in 1884 to instal two commissioners at the court of Luang Prabang. French

153

protests — on the basis of Vietnamese claims — led the Thais in 1886 to accept a French vice-consulate at Luang Prabang. Then in 1893 the French announced their intention to extend to the Mekong. Following border incidents, troops moved in and warships attacked the Paknam fort off Bangkok. The crisis of Thai independence seemed to be at hand.

8 Siam

IN THE PRESERVATION of the independence of the Thai kingdom thus far, the restraint of Great Britain had played a part. That restraint derived initially from the indisposition to extend conquest from India to the Southeast Asian mainland, more especially since the states there were vassals of China, the source of the Company's tea. It had produced, for instance, a cautious policy in the Peninsula in regard to Thai claims over Kedah and the northern Malay states. The Supreme Government had even been doubtful about sending diplomatic missions to Bangkok: it was aware of Thai distrust of the conquering Company and feared not only that they would gain no commercial concessions, but that they might produce an incident that would lead to war, 'an evil of very serious magnitude'.[62] The Crawfurd mission of 1822, though it produced no incidents, gained nothing. It made the Thais more apprehensive, the Company more cautious, the Raja of Kedah more hopeless. The war with Burma, however, seemed to open new prospects. And, though Burney could not bully and had nothing to offer in Tenasserim, though his gains on the Peninsula did not satisfy Penang, he did secure from Rama III — prepared, unlike Minh-mang, to treat even with the emissary of a mere Governor-General — a treaty designed to facilitate British commerce with Bangkok.

The fact is that British restraint does not alone explain the preservation of Thai independence. In Burma and in Vietnam it was to confirm an isolationism that proved disastrous to the

154

independence of those states. The example of Burma, a neighbour of the British, indeed already lay before the Thais. Their reaction was, however, to attempt some sort of compromise, to go with the tide when they had to, a policy that had a long history behind it. Moreover, the position near the sea of their new capital at Bangkok perhaps made them more aware than their neighbours of trends in the outside world. And its immense command over the Menam, the core of the kingdom, removed the risk of rebellion and civil war, linked with foreign intervention, which their neighbours had to reckon with.

The commercial concessions that were made in the Burney treaty — more especially as the development of tax-farming virtually re-established the state commercial monopolies the British had tried to destroy — were hardly likely to prove satisfactory to British merchants in the changed conditions of the 1840s. Not only were new markets being sought in Southeast Asia. The end of the Company's monopoly of trade to China and the change of policy there suggested a change of policy towards its vassal.

Late in 1849 Sir James Brooke was instructed to negotiate a new commercial treaty. The old king had just turned away an American commercial mission then in Southeast Asia, and was set against any further concessions even to the British, which might 'change the fixed rules and customs of a great Country which has been established for many hundred years, and bring them all into confusion and ruin . . .'[63] Brooke proposed a decisive intervention in Siam, which would displace the king by the prince Mongkut — 'our king'[64] — secure British influence, and settle the question of the Malay states. These recommendations are important because the British Government did not accept them: it was still anxious for peace with Siam, whose frontiers marched with those of British India in Burma. Shortly after, Rama III died and Mongkut became king as Rama IV. With him and his ministers a new British emissary, Bowring, was in 1855 able to conclude a new commercial treaty, one that did away with tax-farming and established low customs duties, that introduced a British consul and a system of extraterritoriality, a treaty that, followed by treaties with France and other European powers, led to substantial commercial development by Europeans and helped to preserve political independence of them.

With the advance of British dominion in Burma, and that of the French in Vietnam and Cambodia, the independence of Siam became still more important to Britain. It was a buffer state, and Britain's policy in Malaya was restrained by the fear that any interference there would only encourage French interference with other dependencies of Siam (as the Trengganu bombardment had encouraged it in Cambodia). The acquisition of upper Burma led also to the acquisition of claims over the Shan states, some of which stretched even east of the Mekong. The plan to allow Siam to become a buffer here also met the obstacle of France's claims to extend up to the Mekong. The French naval demonstration of 1893 produced protests in London. The result of these was that the French promised to leave open an opportunity for constructing a buffer. The British then left Siam to make new territorial concessions to appease the French. By a treaty of 1893 king Chulalongkorn renounced his claim to the Laotian territories on the left bank of the Mekong, thus cutting them in half. The British now sought the creation of the promised buffer, but in vain. Instead in 1896 they surrendered their claims east of the Mekong, making that the frontier of Laos and Burma, and in return secured a guarantee of the independence of the Menam valley.

Sri Vijaya had controlled the isthmus and the Straits. The British controlled the Straits and were concerned at the revival of foreign interest in the isthmus in the 1880s. The success of the Suez Canal encouraged other projects elsewhere, and the French were particularly interested in a Kra canal that would improve the communications with their growing empire in Indo-China. British apprehensions were aroused by the 1893 crisis, yet the agreement of 1896 did not cover the Peninsula. As a result of this, and also of increasing concern about Germany, Britain made a secret agreement with Siam in 1897. Siam promised to cede no territory there without British consent, in return for a promise of British backing against aggression, and to make commercial concessions also subject to British approval. The latter clause proved exceedingly inconvenient to the Thais and, in order also to secure a railway loan and some reduction of extraterritorial rights, they agreed in 1909 on a new arrangement which included the transfer of their claims over the northern Malay states.

The acquisition of Siamese claims was made easier for Britain by the agreement with France made in 1904. That same year France acquired sections of Luang Prabang on the west bank of the Mekong. Three years later a new treaty was made. In this France agreed to return some of these gains and to reduce her extraterritorial rights. Siam, on the other hand, ceded the Cambodian provinces of Siemreap and Battambang.

'It is sufficient for us to keep ourselves within our house and home; it may be necessary for us to forego some of our former power and influence', Mongkut had said.[65] At least his dynasty had kept its house and home. The moderation of the British, and in the more competitive days of the late nineteenth century, their interest in preserving a buffer state, had contributed. But so had the readiness of the Thai kings to undertake a modernisation of their kingdom which anticipated if it did not rival that of the Japanese and in which they sought with characteristic sagacity to employ European advisers of differing nationalities. The other mainland kingdoms had already begun to fall under European sway. The long-maintained independence of the greatest of them, Burma and Vietnam, and the proud isolationism to which it, among other factors, contributed, made their fall the more catastrophic. The fate of the lesser states — those of the Shans and the Laos and the Khmers — had long been determined by the rivalries of their greater neighbours, and the latter's claims were taken up and thrashed out in European terms. Only Siam realised that even great states must in the new circumstances recognise their comparative smallness. It survived, with much of its 'former power and influence', through most of the nineteenth century. At the end of it there was still, as it were, territory to spare before 'house and home' were invaded.

With the treaty of 1907 the great monuments of the Khmer past returned to Cambodia, and the École Française d'Extrême Orient, founded at Hanoi in 1902, took over their investigation and preservation. The past in a sense was also to be colonised by Europe, by the Europeans and their archaeological and historiographical techniques. They were to reveal its greatness, a service to the world at large and to modern Southeast Asian nationalism. No doubt it was an easier task to avoid a 'colonialist' historiography on the mainland than in the Archipelago, for these two great areas had only latterly converged in the experience of European domination. But neither this experience, nor knowledge of the past, were to promote Southeast Asian unity.

Section B: Nationalism and Communalism

THE PERIOD between 1760 and the first world war saw Southeast Asia divided among European powers, except that one major state retained its independence in part by its measures of Europeanisation, in part by abandoning its old claims over neighbouring territories. This diverse and substantially novel political framework, gradually created, meant the pursuit of diverse as well as novel administrative policies. It also diversified the impact of economic and social change, and provided the context of the rise of nationalism and communalism, more especially in the period after the first world war.

1 Netherlands India

THE IMPACT of economic change in the Archipelago was profoundly affected by the return of the Dutch after the French wars and the policies they subsequently pursued. The eighteenth century had found the Company increasingly concentrating upon Java, using its political power and that of the native chiefs to secure colonial products, especially coffee, at a cheap rate in order to compete with other sources of supply. The collapse of the Company in 1799 animated a debate already begun as to the best means of increasing production in Java. The arguments in favour of free enterprise, coupled with private ownership of land — advocated for instance by the van Hogendorps — tended to give way to the assertion that compulsion was required, allegedly because of the natural indolence of the people, but really because the government, like its predecessor in the 1720s, was not disposed to give an encouraging price. The circumstances of the war made it difficult for Governor-General Daendels to dispose of the produce even of the forced cultures.

Initially Raffles intended to adhere to the system: he, too, was anxious to ensure a profit, as a means of convincing the superior authorities that Java was desirable as a permanent acquisition. But the war with America after 1812 made it even more difficult to dispose of coffee, since it cut off the neutral trade. It was this above all that led Raffles to abandon the forced cultures of the old system: it was shortage of revenue, coupled with his hope of securing the retention of Java, that led him to advocate instead a 'land-rent' system, influenced by the *ryotwari* system of British India. Outside the Preanger districts the forced cultivation of coffee was ended. Instead the government would exact from the village or *desa* a money rent based upon the productivity of the land. The expansion of the revenue would arise, Raffles believed, from the spread of free peasant cultivation of export products like cotton, or of rice. A major problem was assessment. In practice the tax settlement tended to be made with the headmen of the village — though not with the Regents, as under the Dutch Company's system — and this acted as a restraint upon the development of peasant enterprise, whatever impact the wartime price levels may have had.

Initially the restored Dutch retained the system, in so far as it had been effectively introduced. But it was certainly not a system calculated rapidly to restore the Netherlands economy, which had suffered since the eighteenth century from the erosion of its entrepotal position in Europe and from the decline of the industries that had supported, and to which the war had delivered conclusive blows. It was upon such a restoration that the new king, Willem I, was bent, and the colonies were directly under his control. The re-establishment of Dutch authority in the Archipelago was an expensive business, and the colonial treasury was depleted by the falling coffee prices of the 1820s. The real crisis began with the Java war of 1825-30, in part the result of Governor-General van der Capellen's cancellation of some leases in the princely territories that had conveyed seigniorial rights to European planters. This was a liberal measure that yet provoked oppression of the peasantry by the defrauded aristocratic lessors which, still more paradoxically, produced widespread support for a princely revolt against the Dutch. Van der Capellen was replaced by a special commissioner Du Bus. He recommended encouraging private European planters without giving them seigniorial rights. But Willem I determined upon the more radical scheme of van den Bosch and the financial drain of the Belgian secession crisis meant that the scheme, the cultivation-system, rapidly expanded in Java. The result in fact of the British decision to restore the Indies to the Dutch

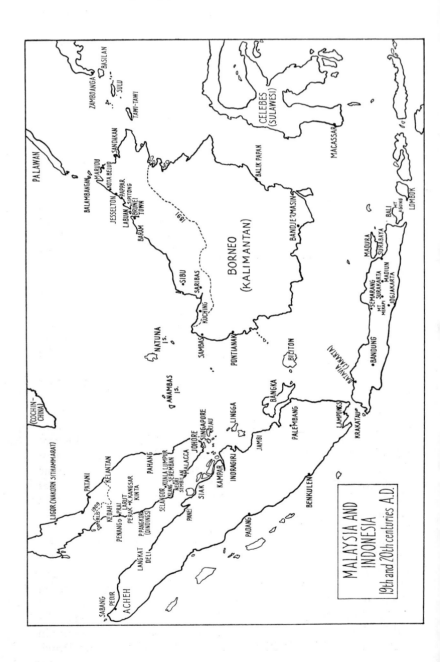

MALAYSIA AND
INDONESIA
19th and 20th centuries A.D.

was their recursion to the old Company system in a new and more extensive form that had a profound impact on Java and further differentiated it from the rest of the Archipelago.

Under the system the villagers were to be compelled to plant a certain area with an export product which was delivered to the government — in theory it was set off against the land-rent and in practice paid for at a low rate — and consigned by it for sale in the Netherlands to the N.H.M., which lent money to Willem I's needy administration. Many crops were tried, including indigo, tea, cochineal, tobacco, and silk, and some retained a footing in Java. But the major product continued to be coffee, with sugar, which required more machinery and thus more capital, coming as yet second. In this way, by the use of political power, the Dutch, as it were, anticipated the economic transformations that the industrial revolution was to effect elsewhere more especially after 1869. Yet, as Clifford Geertz has well said, Dutch policy consisted of 'one long attempt to bring Indonesia's crops into the modern world, but not her people'.[66] The Dutch laid great stress, even at this time, on the maintenance of custom or *adat*. Van den Bosch's disciple, Baud, thus issued instructions against 'all unnecessary interference with the social institutions and customs of the people . . .' 'The village government is in my opinion the palladium of peace in Java . . .'[67] At higher levels, Dutch power continued as under the Company to be associated with the *priyayi* élite. Van den Bosch, indeed, recognised the hereditary claims of the Regents, gave them a culture-percentage, a stake in the produce monopoly; and a native civil service developed parallel to the European. As Geertz again says, 'political control was pervasive enough . . . to prevent the expansion of peasant cane-growing . . .'[68] While sugar was grown on rice *sawahs,* to which it was well suited — and indeed it fostered irrigation and the expansion of *sawah* methods — coffee was grown on 'waste' or uncultivated lands: and over these the government assumed full control. The system thus helped to prevent the further development of individual commercial initiative among the Javanese peasants, insulating them from any connexion with profitable markets.

Not only political impulses, but also economic, tended, too, to stress the communal elements in village society. For some products, especially sugar, compact blocks of land were especially desirable; and hence there were pressures for the preservation of a village community with which officials could deal more conveniently than with individual landowners, which could provide land for those members whose lands were temporarily under

161

sugar, and ensure the distribution of forced labour among the households.

But the full impact of the system is not realised without emphasising the increase of population in Java. The system was, of course, made possible by the relatively dense population of Java from early times: that provided labour and the social and political structure to facilitate its utilisation. The cultivation-system in turn contributed to further expansion, as did the relative peace of Java after the war ended in 1830 — the 'Pax Neerlandica' — and the improvement in the transport system, again wrought largely by corvée and dictated by commercial motives, 'which prevented local crop failures from turning into famines'.[69] These were some of the effects in Java of the attempt to make up for the deficiency of Dutch capital by the availability of Javanese labour.

The changes after 1848 gave the States General a greater part in the government of the Netherlands Indies, and there were moves to give private capitalists, themselves the product of the success of the van den Bosch system in restoring the Dutch economy, a greater share in the exploitation of Java. There were thus inroads on the consignment-system in the 1850s, facilitated by the end of the Government's indebtedness to the N.H.M. The process was slow: the revenues were useful in promoting railway-building and public works programmes in the Netherlands. Gradually inroads were, however, made on the cultivation-system itself, though the coffee cultures lasted into the twentieth century. The major change had come in 1870, with laws that provided for the abandonment of the system in respect of sugar, and permitted private concerns to lease 'waste lands' on a regular long-term contractual basis and to lease village lands on a short-term basis while guaranteeing the non-alienation of the land by the peasants. The initial beneficiaries of the laws were the planters of the Indies, in turn the creation of the 'cultivation-system' the criticism of the abuses of which by 'Multatuli' and others they had turned to account. The depression of the mid-1880s was, however, to bring their plantations into the hands of large corporations in Europe.

The government's conservative policy on land tenures, reiterated in a law of 1875, indicated that it was continuing the administrative policy of the previous period in the new phase of Dutch enterprise. The villages remained a vast reservoir of labour for the private estates. Within them there was little room for the creation of a peasant proprietary. The dominance of the estates continued the work of the cultivation-system in insulating the peasant from the export market. This was particularly so because of the ascendancy sugar secured in these days of a greater supply of capital. The industry, as has been said, used *sawah* lands, negotiated for with the village, now on a temporary tenure, as well as the labour of the villagers. And it came to involve about 20% or 25% of the total rice field area of Java, much expanded by the combined inducement to irrigated cultivation provided by the sugar planters and the expanding population. In 1830 there were probably about 7m people in Java; in 1850 there were 9.6m; in 1870 16.2m; in 1900 28.4m. By this last date, possibly, the health measures of the Dutch were contributing to the rise. But their administrative policies were more important. Their objective had been to maintain the village communities, as a pillar of peace and order and a source of contract labour. Within those communities no individual ownership developed on a scale that might have led to the limiting of the growth of families from economic motives, as happened in post-revolutionary France, but not in the repartitional communes of contemporary Russia. There was no industry for labour to move into: the capital created had gone to build industry in the Netherlands. The Javanese village thus became in time overburdened, reaching the limit of even a rice-*sawah* to give a greater return for greater labour.

By the 1890s — a time of recession in any case — there were appeals to the Dutch conscience on the basis of 'diminishing welfare'. Java had early become a classic example of the impact of changes that expanded a peasant population without providing, or while obstructing the creation of an industrial structure that could absorb the increase, an example of the 'underdeveloped' area, its technological gaps, its over-population. But while there might be reasons in the far historical past for the comparative advance of Europeans over Asians in technological terms, and while the economic changes of the nineteenth century tended to turn the Asian territories into suppliers of raw material for European industry, the chance in the case of Java of absorbing an increasing population in a more advanced economic structure was immensely reduced by the long-continued policy of the Dutch, to whom the British had consigned the island, of making it pay while pretending to leave its customs and village system intact. Java was thus an early example of the problem and an extreme one. While the Dutch corporations developed a complex administrative structure and advanced methods, the Javanese simply worked their *sawahs* harder, and retreated into an inward-looking mode of life in which the peasant or *abangan* tradition prevailed.

This concentration upon Java — dictated to the Dutch by the nature of their policies — yet further deepened the historical and geographical contrast between it — and especially east and central Java, lands *par excellence* of the *sawah* — and the other islands. Throughout the greater part of the nineteenth century, the policy of the Dutch in relation to most of the outer islands was negative in character. In part that was again due to British policy, the British opposition to the occupation of east Sumatra in the 1840s for instance, and of Acheh till 1871. In other cases, however, British opposition stimulated Dutch advance, as in Borneo and Celebes in the 1840s, and this was followed, after about 1850, by an inclination once more to favour the spread of Dutch control. Yet in many areas Dutch control remained fragile, or was merely asserted to keep others out, and did not involve any real interference with the native states, relations with the rulers of which remained contractual. The essential reasons for this were that the Dutch were disinclined to spend the revenue drawn from Java, a traditional focus of empire in the Archipelago, on empire-building in the outer islands while the Netherlands economy required the capital its labour created; and that most of the islands, relatively infertile and scantily populated, under swidden cultivation, were not adapted to the cultivation-system. Only in regions of considerable population density, for instance the Menangkabau uplands of Sumatra and the Minahasa peninsula in Celebes, was a modified version of the system implemented, and there as elsewhere it inhibited the growth of native enterprise.

The success of the private plantation system in the outer islands after 1870 was again only exceptional: it was substantially confined to the relatively fertile east coast of Sumatra. There, too, it was not a case of growing ordinary colonial products, like sugar, in competition with producing areas in other parts of the world, but of growing 'a rare quality product with a monopoly position in the world market',[70] namely the Sumatra wrapper leaf for cigars. The venture began with the experiments of an obscure planter, Nienhuys, in 1863, but by the end of the century the region was the most intensively cultivated district outside Java. In the early twentieth century it still formed three-quarters of the total planted area in the outer islands. But the method of cultivation differed from that in Java. Tobacco was fitted into the *ladang* system of the east coast. The planter obtained concessions from the local sultans, using all the land conceded for tobacco on a system involving forest fallow for seven or eight years, and allowing the peasants use of a stipulated amount of land each year for the growing of rice. They became — as, in view of the pepper exports, it would seem they had not been earlier — subsistence cultivators. Moreover, 'in contrast to Java, the local population . . . was not drawn upon for estate work, both because it was quantitatively insufficient and, having enough land and freedom, psychologically disinclined'.[71] The plantations were cultivated by imported Chinese coolies, and later increasingly by Javanese, brought there by contract and held there by the 'penal sanction'. If there was a divorce between the plantations, their labour and management, and the swidden cultivators of the area, so there was a contrast between this area and the other islands.

Generally traditional leadership and local *adat* remained largely undisturbed by western economic or political influences, and both still bore the characteristics of the thinly populated scattered communities of earlier times. Trade with the Straits Settlements or other entrepots did not destroy the existing fabric — though the British weakened 'imperial' superstructures, as in Acheh — and the administrative intervention of the Dutch was limited. Indeed, their authority was not everywhere accepted, and in Acheh it was bitterly resisted. The resistance was strengthened by the influence of Islam, always intense in Acheh (Wahhabism had reached the Menangkabau Padris (Pediris) from the Achehnese port of Pedir). The presence of Islam helped to determine the changes of policy upon which the Dutch resolved around the turn of the century.

The 'Ethical Policy' was an attempt to remedy the defects in the economic and political system of the Indies, overlaid by moral and philanthropical considerations dictated by the advance of Netherlands democracy. The policy did not merely aim at improving the conditions for western investment, for instance in oil, at this time becoming important in south Sumatra and east Borneo, or in rubber, also important because of the advance of the automobile industry. The intensification of administration, the expansion of communications and public works, the spread of European education, might all contribute to this. But the aim was broader. It was to counter the overt and the latent opposition to Dutch rule by establishing such social and political conditions as would reconcile Indonesians to its continuance. And besides this there is a residue of philanthropy, of genuine liberalism, among the greatest re-

165

formers, men like Idenburg, Fock, Kielstra, van Deventer, and Snouck Hurgronje, the Adviser on Islamic Affairs. The policies of the Dutch thus again gave a special character to the impact of world economic change upon Indonesia; those in turn were given a special character because of the impress of Islam, as in the past, upon opposition to European rule. The Padri struggle in Menangkabau had been in part a struggle between Koranic law and matrilineal *adat*. The Dutch victory in the war had been followed by a virtual alliance with the *adat* chiefs, who had invited the Dutch in. In the early twentieth century Snouck helped to bring the Acheh war to an end by suggesting a settlement with the *adat* chiefs, dividing them from the Islamic leaders whose primacy the long-drawn-out struggle had effected.

In Java, Islam had long formed a rallying point of resistance to the Europeans and their works. This had been the case in the Bantam war of the mid-eighteenth century and, in the conflict with the Mataram principalities in 1825-30, popular support against the Dutch was enlisted by prince Dipo Negoro under the banner of Islam. Within Javanese society, however, there were divisions, as has been seen. The *kiyayi* and *ulama*, the Muslim teachers and scribes, sought to spread Koranic law and the Islamic way of life among the peasants: the *priyayi* sought to uphold the *adat* upon which their influence rested. Accordingly, too, the Dutch found another reason for linking their influence to that of the *priyayi*: 'Dutch support for the native aristocracy was in a large measure based on the existing rift between *priyayi* and *ulama*'.[72] The association of the *priyayi* with the oppressive policies of the nineteenth century, however, tended to undermine their traditional sources of power, and gave the *ulama* new opportunities to counter the influence of an aristocracy that appeared to have become an appendage of Dutch rule. The Pax Neerlandica and improved communications in Java aided Islamic evangelisation, and the burdensome life of the peasant no doubt induced him to turn more to the consolations of Islam, as well as to his own *abangan* culture — the inspiration of the Samin movement of the late nineteenth century — and its notions of a *ratu adil* or just prince. In the outer islands *adat* chiefs and expounders of Islamic law were also at odds.

Developments of the late nineteenth century had made Islamic life more intense both in Java and the outer islands. Improved sea communication after the opening of the Suez Canal brought a closer connexion with Mekka and the waning of the Indian

Sufi influence. Returning *hajis* and an influx of Hadramaut Arabs promoted Islamic orthodoxy, and Mekka-trained *kiyayi* founded new theological seminaries or *pesantren* that attracted students away from old village schools. These events, and the association of Islam with opposition to the Dutch, gave the westernisation of the Ethical period a special colouring.

Snouck realised that Islam did not yet dominate Indonesian life — that *adat,* like the customs of the Menangkabau, opposed its triumph — and that only a minority of its 'popes' were fanatics. But it would continue to oppose social institutions opposed to its tenets. He recommended toleration, which might reduce fanaticism, coupled with the encouragement of the *adat* chiefs of the outer islands and the *priyayi* élite of Java. But these elements did not alone hold the key to the social development of the Netherlands Indies. A modern Indonesia would have to be a westernised Indonesia. Clearly this was a response to the economic needs of Dutch policy, but it was also intended as a response to its political needs. For Snouck believed that the spread of western culture would provide a lasting basis for the connexion of the Netherlands and the Netherlands Indies. Essentially a policy of assimilation was his answer to the vast problems confronting the Dutch at the turn of the century. But the Ethical Policy had sincere philanthropical overtones.

This is particularly seen in the personal associations between some of the 'Ethici' and their *priyayi* protégés. Snouck himself helped Achmad Djajadiningrat, later Regent of Serang, through a European secondary school in Batavia, and Achmad's brother Hoessein followed his mentor to the University of Leiden. A coterie of young Indonesians met at the home of J. H. Abendanon, made Director of Education in 1900. Indeed it was, of course, the existing élite that was first of all to benefit from the programme of assimilation. But the aim, an economic, political and philanthropic aim, was to spread western education also at lower levels.

European education had hitherto been scanty. From the middle of the nineteenth century the government had allotted money to Regency schools for the education of native officials. In the closing decades of the century, there had been some development of primary education, both by the government and by missions operating especially in non-Islamic areas of the outer islands, for instance the Batak regions of Sumatra. Secondary education was available in Dutch schools which few could muster the cash or language to enter, and in a few missionary schools. Only 75,000 were at school in 1900. But from

167

1900 onwards facilities rapidly expanded, particularly after Governor-General van Heutsz devised a new type of village school to the cost of which the *desa* could contribute: by 1930 the number of pupils had risen to 1½ million in about 18,000 native elementary schools. Above these were the native primary schools, established on government or private initiative, with a course of seven years, and some 350,000 pupils by 1930. Parallel, however, were the Dutch-Native schools, which in 1927 had 66,000 scholars, providing native education on western lines with Dutch as a medium, leading via the post-primary schools and three-year secondary education to university training with a practical emphasis at the Engineering College at Bandung (1919), the Law College (1924) and the Medical College (1926), at the University of Batavia (1941), and, for fewer still, in the Netherlands.

Snouck had recognised that the success of his policy required that the western-educated Indonesians it produced must be given a greater share in administration in the Indies. The Ethical period saw some devolution of authority from The Hague to Batavia and from Batavia to the regional administrations. The object of the decentralisation plans was greater efficiency, but also increasing Indonesian participation in political life. A law of 1906 established village governments in Java, and under a law of 1903 municipal and Residency councils were set up in Java and later in the outer islands. Initially they were substantially nominated and European, later substantially elected and native. The ideological impact of the first world war pressed on this liberalisation and produced in 1918 a central advisory body, the *Volksraad* or People's Council, half nominated, half elected by members of the provincial councils. These were, however, then still substantially nominated and, moreover, since officials were eligible, the elected members were often village headmen. Further advance was limited by the profound reaction to these revolutionary changes in Dutch policy.

In Java the general tendency of the administrative changes was further to reduce the influence of the hereditary native administrators. They were affected by the establishment of Regency councils and by the development of specialist and welfare services staffed and run from the centre. In turn the peasantry 'found itself subjected to, and taxed for, a plethora of bewildering welfare measures whose importance and desirability it could not comprehend . . .'[73] But what contributed most to the popular *malaise* was the continued rise in the population, to which welfare measures contributed — by the 1930s the mortality rates in Bandung, even for natives, were no higher than the rates in Netherlands towns in 1900 — and which exceeded 40m by 1930. The *sawahs*, especially in east and central Java, became more and more overburdened with excess labour, the village 'a great sprawling community of desperately marginal agriculturists, petty traders and day laborers'.[74] In the circumstances the agricultural credit services made little impression. The introduction of annual food crops as staples alongside paddy — maize, cassava, sweet potatoes, peanuts — simply enabled the Javanese to cope with rising population without a major change of economic system. One possible outlet was settlement in other parts of the Indies, and this the government now sought to encourage, not merely in reference to plantation coolies for the east coast of Sumatra, but by establishing migrant villages in south Sumatra. But the Javanese were not great emigrants: the peasants preferred to devote even more painstaking labour to existing *sawahs* that represented a vast investment of labour and which they were loth to leave to start anew elsewhere. By 1920 there were no more than a total of 600,000 Javanese in the outer islands, while the population of Java increased by 300,000 p.a. Even the changes in Dutch policy in this period, therefore, did not permit the Javanese to escape from the effects of nineteenth century policies on their economic and social structure.

The changes, on the other hand, underlined the contrast of east and central Java with west Java, and still more with the outer islands. There the Ethical policies coincided with the determination to establish Dutch control more firmly in face of other European powers, especially after 1885, and the readiness to devote Indies revenues more to Indies purposes promoted the expansion of Dutch administration. Gradually a more unified realm was created, the contractual system being simplified after 1898 by the institution of the 'short contract'. The mere intensification of government activity had profound effects upon the traditional structure of society, undermining the old *adat* chiefs and the old economico-political structures by new administrative and judicial structures, new tax requirements, new police and education measures. Such changes opened the way more fully to the economic changes of the turn of the century and, combined, they led to a revolution. The building of roads opened many areas more fully to commerce with the outside world. And the outside world was coming to demand products that were readily adapted, as spices had been in an

169

earlier period, to the swidden lands of the outer islands, especially rubber, borrowed from the initial European plantations, and later copra and coffee, as well as pepper. The sparsity of labour and capital was not a major obstacle, and social and political conditions allowed much greater room for individual enterprise. The result was to produce in the outer islands what Java lacked — especially east and central Java — a class of individualistic smallholders and petty capitalists. The rubber growers were found in Palembang, Jambi and the east coast of Sumatra, as well as, to a lesser extent, in west Java; copra came mostly from the Minahasa, the western edge of Borneo and the Riau Archipelago, pepper from the Lampongs, peasant-grown tea from Priangan, smallholders' coffee from central and south central Sumatra, north Bali, central Celebes and Timor, peasant-grown tobacco from Lombok. The outer islands (and to a lesser extent west Java) were not simply divorced from Java (especially central and east Java) by becoming in this period the scene of important European extractive undertakings, but also by becoming the focus of a vast peasant production for outside markets. In 1894 native export agriculture was valued at 17m guilders, including 7m from Java and 10m from the outer islands; in 1925/7, striking an annual average, at 438m, including 83m from Java and 350m from the outer islands. The social accompaniment included 'greater class differentiation and conflict, intensified opposition between young and old, modern and conservative . . .'[75]

These changes had a profound effect upon the position of Islam in the Indies. The agrarian unrest in Java, with the exception of the Samin movement, crystallised around local Muslim leadership, and Islam focused peasant protest at apparently inexplicable change and disruption. But, more importantly, Islamic modernism penetrated to the Indies from the Islamic homelands, where great changes were taking place, from Mekka, from Cairo's al-Azhar University, and, to a lesser extent, from Lahore and Aligarh. The aim of the reformists was to preserve Islam by reformulating its doctrine in the light of modern western thought and freeing the Prophet's teaching itself from medieval glosses. The new movement appealed especially to the individualistic elements that were revolutionising life in the outer islands, and seeking an effective weapon against traditional *adat*. The most important reformist organisation in the Indies was the Muhammadiyah, founded in 1912, and its great success was in educational activities, its schools teaching a modern syllabus alongside religious instruction. Snouck had not

170

Netherlands India

reckoned with Islam's capacity to modernise itself, which was bound to affect the European régime.

The development of the western-oriented Indonesians upon whom he had relied to perpetuate the connexion with the Netherlands had also not followed Snouck's prognostications, but this was because his recommendations had not been implemented. The number of western-educated was not great, but the opportunities opened to them were smaller still. The Indonesianisation of the upper levels of the administration was never attempted, and the hereditary principle barred many from access to the post of Regent in the native hierarchy. At the lower levels, openings for Dutch-trained Indonesians even in the expanding service of the welfare state or the expanding western economic enterprises were insufficient to absorb even the limited number of school graduates, while the maintenance of *adat* tenures and the restrictions on professional advocacy in native courts reduced the openings for lawyers. The lack of opportunity at lower levels pressed competition on to higher levels, and those with the financial and mental capacity would proceed still higher up the educational ladder to avoid taking a lower job than seemed appropriate. Many became vociferous opponents of a régime that seemed to deny them their true position: their assimilation to Dutch culture made them hate as well as love it. 'The new intelligentsia, clamoring for political responsibility and co-determination, became the spokesmen for an anti-Western Indonesian nationalism.'[76]

But one of Snouck's prognostications was borne out: there was a gulf between this intelligentsia and the Islamic leaders, whether modernist or traditional. The former looked, without absolutely jettisoning Islam, to various western ideologies and to an idealised version of the past drawn from western historiography: the Islamic leaders aimed at a state ruled by Islamic law. The western-trained intelligentsia aspired to the national unity of the Indonesian Archipelago: its political unity was the creation of the Dutch, but they recalled the claims of Majapahit; and Islam had helped to destroy that empire.

The division of attitude among opponents of the Dutch régime was associated also with a division between Java and the outer islands. In the outer islands there was a middle-class community originating in economic change. In Java the instrument of change had been western education, and prestige was attached to it and to bureaucratic employment. Only in a few parts of the outer islands, such as the relatively densely populated Menangkabau region, was western education the road to

171

advancement. Those seeking it tended to go to Java, where the facilities were greater: and, since the bureaucratic opportunities were also greater, there they tended to stay, and to become assimilated with a Javanese intelligentsia initially at least substantially the offspring of the traditional élite. But while this process illustrated the differences between the élites in Java and the outer islands, to some extent it helped to mediate them. Menangkabau, for instance, became, after the end of forced coffee cultivation in 1908, the scene of capitalist development. Those of its inhabitants who sought careers in education and officialdom might be expected to have rather more sympathy with the individualism and Islamic modernism that thereafter spread in their communities than the Javanese, who were influenced against such developments both by their *priyayi* traditions and their western education. The Menangkabauers could, as it were, form a bridge between the élites, between the islands. But all the élite's differences were reduced for the time being by the common hostility to colonial rule.

There were indeed other diversities with which a nationalist movement had to reckon. Not merely with increasing development and expanded administration did the European community increase in numbers and with better communications and the presence of more females contrive to lead a more European life. There was also a substantial Eurasian group, more identified with Indonesia, but competing with educated natives for bureaucratic and clerical posts. And there were the more primitive peoples whom the improvement of communications and administration brought into closer contact with the outside world, and among whom Christian missions — which increased in the early phase of the Ethical period — had sometimes immense success. An example was that of the Bataks, already mentioned. The Rhenish missionary Nommensen had landed on the west coast of Sumatra in the same year that Nienhuys landed on the east coast. It was he who began their Christianisation and opened their way to educational advancement, the route, in a relatively crowded region, to participation in national life, where, like the Menangkabauers, the Bataks came to hold something of a mediatory position.

There were Catholic missionaries in Timor, Lutheran in Nias. But the other major centre of Christianisation was in the Moluccas and the Minahasa. It was from Ambon — and often through the agency of Ambonese — that Protestantism was disseminated in Halmahera and Buru and, after 1855, in West New Guinea. Within the Moluccas, indeed, there was little scope for capitalist enterprise. The European monopolies had been brought to an end only in 1864 (in the case of nutmeg in 1873), and among the Indonesians the Bugis retained their commercial dominance. Ambonese — and also Menadonese, restricted by the cultivation-system in Menado — sought their careers through education, and served not only in the missions, but in the lower echelon administration and in the colonial army.

The position of the Chinese community also changed under the Ethical policies. The Chinese in Java had long been important as revenue farmers and commercial middlemen, but they had been restricted from travelling in the interior and from acquiring land, and this helped to prevent their assimilation. In the outer islands, they had continued to form enclaves within the population whether on the west coast of Borneo, where the earlier mining communities came into conflict with the Dutch after the Java war and were ultimately broken up and impoverished; or in Bangka, where the government in the same period exploited the tin mines through them; or, later, on the east coast of Sumatra, where Chinese were imported to work on the tobacco plantations. In 1930 the Chinese community included about 750,000 born in Indonesia, and about 450,000 immigrants, small in numbers compared to the Indonesians, but important economically; and maintaining, even increasing its distinctness. This last was in part a result of better communications, which tied the overseas Chinese closer to China — more returned home — and facilitated the emigration of Chinese women, so that more peculiarly Chinese families would be created (the trend was like that among the Europeans). The disturbances in China, especially in the 1930s, were to increase female emigration, and also now to reduce the chance of returning thither. The more peculiarly Chinese families became more settled overseas.

A growing national consciousness also worked against assimilation, and the Chinese nationalists fostered it among overseas communities which they saw as a source of funds. Chinese schools were established and even locally born Chinese accepted their nationalist education. In the Ethical period the Dutch had moved in the direction of assimilation and in 1908 Dutch-Chinese schools had been set up. But the superfluity of clerks offered little inducement to attend them and the Chinese schools exerted a nationalist counter-attraction. Other measures of assimilation included the withdrawal in 1910 of the principal restrictions on travel in the interior of Java. This played a significant part in stimulating Indonesian nationalism.

Nationalist feeling had been excited by news of the Japanese victories over China and Russia, and the first response, among the *priyayi* élite, must have gratified the *Ethici*. In 1908 Wahidin Soedira Oesada, a retired Javanese medical subordinate, set up the first nationalist organisation in Java, the *Boedi Oetomo*, or Glorious Endeavour, a cultural movement aiming at the fusion of European and Javanese values, influenced by Tagore and Gandhi. The first political party, the *Indische Partij*, led by Eurasians including E. F. E. Douwes Dekker, great nephew of 'Multatuli', as well as Indonesians, was based explicitly on the principle of association, though more vehement than the government had anticipated. But *Sarekat Islam,* the Islamic League, definitely departed from the associationist path. The penetration of Chinese merchants into the interior threatened the Indonesian *batik* merchants, and this was the origin of the League in 1912. But it soon became a vast and generalised mass movement, with over 2m members by 1919. It gave expression to many elements in Javanese society affected by the changes it was undergoing. Its leaders included Islamic reformists like the Sumatran Agus Salim and Tjokroaminoto, a Surabaya businessman, and also secular nationalists, including young Marxists, like Semaun and Tan Malaka, seeking to steer the movement into revolutionary action. But mass support for the League came from the peasants, discovering in it some means of protest in a world changing for the worse, and following the lead both of the *kiyayi* and *ulama,* often still traditionalists but involved in the movement, and of the charismatic Tjokroaminoto. The League's aims were as vague as its size was vast. But the government's attempts to weaken it by in 1914 conferring legal status only on its branches in fact facilitated the penetration of the Marxists.

In Java there existed a Dutch lower-class which formed an avenue for the entry of European radicalism and of Marxism, carried by men like Sneevliet, and subsequently stimulated by the Bolshevik revolution and the activity of the Comintern. In 1920 the P.K.I. was founded. But in the following year it broke with the Islamic movement and in 1924 broke with mass support on a religious basis. Comintern directives on co-operation with 'bourgeois' nationalist movements indeed in this case conflicted with its opposition to pan-Islamic movements. The Communist party turned to building small cells of dedicated revolutionaries, the difficulty of controlling which precipitated the disastrous rebellions in west Java and west Sumatra of 1926-7. These areas were becoming centres of individual enterprise and theirs, in Sjahrir's phase, was 'a strange sort of Communism indeed'.[77] The revolts were the product of the transition: they were led by impoverished nobility, followed by the poorest peasants; some of the educated participated, those who had found opportunities in Java restricted by the 1921-3 recession, some religious leaders, despite the attitude of the top-echelon Communists. These areas were not the later strongholds of Indonesian Communism: rather the reverse. Meanwhile the revolts were easily suppressed. They helped to divide the Indonesian Communists: Tan Malaka had opposed the adventure, as against other leaders like Alimin and Musso; and when the Comintern adopted the Stalinist line of 1928, he broke with it and turned to 'national' Communism. The revolts also swelled the growing reactionary current in Dutch policy.

The inadequate implementation of the Ethical policy had already indicated the extent of the opposition to it among European settlers and companies and conservative-minded officials. The revolts gave its opponents additional ground for criticism and they blamed it for changes in Indonesian society that were in many respects the inevitable results of westernisation and in some respects perhaps the very result of its inadequate implementation. The policy, they said, had weakened central control, reduced *priyayi* prestige, upset village life, spread western education too fast, destroyed peace and order, undermined security for capitalist development. There was now a tendency to return to more traditional policies, designed to seal off the peasantry from outside agitation, and to remove the agitators to Boven Digul in West New Guinea. The research of the time was turned to account, that of van Vollenhoven and the *adat* scholars at Leiden, who advised gradual social evolution in the Indies and implicitly criticised over-hasty westernisation.

The ensuing depression also inhibited the Ethical policy. The fall of government revenues restricted expenditure on welfare measures. In some ways, however, the depression expanded the opportunity for individual enterprise in Java. The collapse of world prices struck a near catastrophic blow at the sugar industry. But the reaction was generally towards a subsistence agriculture, though some of the better quality rice was exported to purchase larger quantities of the poorer quality. In face of Japanese competition, the government abandoned the free trade policies of the 1870s and, behind a protective tariff, some minor Javanese industry appeared. But the tariff was directed against a competitor with the Europeans and the change was again a limited one. Javanese emigration increased, and the Eurasians, badly hit by the depression, vainly attempted a colonisation plan in West New Guinea. But the major features of the Javanese economy did not alter, while the impulse towards a conservative policy in regard to them was encouraged.

The clash with the Communists and the government weakened the more politically-oriented leaders of Islam and drew more attention to the Muhammadiyah. The Nahdatul Ulama, founded in east Java in 1926, was also non-political. Its object was to defend Islam against Wahhabist and reformist heresies; in a sense it was a conservative organisation, therefore, but one whose conservatism should not be exaggerated. And it tended to associate with the reformists of the Muhammadiyah in joint opposition to the colonial régime and to the secular nationalists. Another factor was that the overseas movements with which reformism was linked, and to which orthodoxy objected – in particular the Wahhabi movement that revived pan-Islam after Ibn Saud's conquest of Mekka in 1924 and the Indian Ahmadiyah organisation – ceased to be of influence in Indonesia: pan-Islam had collapsed. Sarekat Islam, no longer a mass movement, had shifted first in the pan-Islamic direction, and then towards open nationalism. The government had renewed the pre-Snouck controls on pilgrims undertaking the *haj* to Wahhabite Mekka, and tightened its controls over Muslim education, as well as over the nationalists' Taman Siswa schools. The government also strengthened the supervision the Regents exercised over the *penghulus* or Islamic law officers, and in 1937 sought to remove inheritance matters from their purview. This move in favour of *adat* tended to bring the reformists and the Nahdatul Ulama still closer together, and induced their final emergence into the political field with the formation of a new Islamic Federation or M.I.A.I. The following year, 1938, Agus Salim and others formed the Partai Islam Indonesia, and this sought representation in the Volksraad. There, indeed, the secular nationalists had accepted legislation that menaced Islam.

The collapse of Sarekat Islam and the P.K.I. after the revolts had opened up opportunities for the secular nationalists. In 1927 the Partai Nasional Indonesia had been founded at Bandung by a young engineer, Sukarno, a Javanese of the semi-*priyayi* élite, the son of a teacher, educated with the help of Tjokroaminoto. He was supported by some of those who had returned from the Netherlands, where – as an aspect of the modern colonial paradox – it had been easier to take up liberal attitudes. The party utilised the rural unrest in west Java that was a legacy of the ill-fated rebellion, but the government arrested the agitators, for instance Sukarno in 1929 and again in 1933, and in 1934 his colleagues Hatta and Sjahrir, men of Menangkabau origin, educated in the Netherlands, moderate Socialists. The nationalist movement was decapitated and deprived of a mass basis, but not destroyed, and in the 1930s it gained a political experience and sophistication which the Islamic leaders often lacked through its participation in the Volksraad and other councils that survived from the Ethical era. Islam, on the other hand, had the mass following.

The gulf between the two movements was illustrated in the last years before the Japanese invasion, as was the tenacity of the colonial régime that brought them together. After the outbreak of war in Europe, and especially after the German invasion of the Netherlands in May 1940, the majority of the nationalist leaders — including Sjarifuddin and Yamin, founders of the leftist Gerindo which had canalised some illegal-P.K.I. support in the popular front phase — declared their allegiance to the cause of the western democracies. No doubt it was partly a device to secure political concessions, in which it did not succeed; but it also showed that the secular nationalists saw the cause of Indonesian nationalism as allied to the defence of democracy. No such ties bound the Islamic leaders. The failure of the Dutch to offer the secular nationalists concessions, however, drew them closer to the Muslims, and in September 1941 the Council of the Indonesian People included both the M.I.A.I. and the Gapi, a federation of mostly secular nationalist parties. Only then did the Governor-General arrange a conference, only in January 1942. Only the Japanese threat was opening the way to power for the Indonesians. And the Partai Sarekat Islam Indonesia opposed co-operation with the Europeans, conscious of new possibilities for Islam in Indonesia.

2 Malaya

THE ESTABLISHMENT of the British settlements in the Straits and the treaty of 1824 divided the Peninsula from the Archipelago in an unprecedented way. For some decades the division was not a very positive one. The British, indeed, found mostly political reasons for non-intervention in the Peninsula, as the Dutch found mostly economic ones in Sumatra. The Straits Settlements, too, were primarily concerned with the trade of the Archipelago or even Southeast Asia as a whole, and Penang, after the foundation of Singapore, particularly with that of Sumatra. The Peninsula, like many parts of the outer islands, remained a thinly populated swidden area: perhaps in 1850 there were no more than ½m people; and some of these were Sumatran immigrants. They were ruled by loosely organised Islamic Sultanates traditionally based on the control of river communications, on veneration for the Sultan, and on a common faith that yet had not eroded local custom.

The Straits Settlements were the scene of a very contrasting development. Here there were European business houses, largely agents for firms in Britain or India. Here were also expanding communities of immigrant Chinese, who found opportunities as revenue farmers, merchants and middlemen, and as artisans. In a sense — certainly demographically — Penang and Singapore were Chinese cities. But over them was a framework of European financial activity and of European administration controlled and partly financed from India. The old tradition in Southeast Asian towns — of indirect rule through headmen — persisted. The Chinese were left to themselves and their loyalty was to their clan and tribal associations and to the secret societies. It was only when there were clashes among these — as with the Singapore riots of 1854 or the Penang riots of 1867 — that the administration came to have an inkling of the real nature of the Chinese communities.

The Settlements, however, were not without influence on the

Peninsula. In some ways their political influence was negative. Affected by one of the alarms that were periodically to arise about the future of the entrepots' trade, Fullerton attempted intervention in the 1820s, and then and even subsequently the Governors did much to exclude the Thais and to promote peace between the states. Such negative developments, like the exclusion of the Dutch, had their positive side. The preservation of peace, moreover, prepared the way for economic development, also encouraged by the advice and guidance some of the rajas received from officials and merchants. The ruler of Johore, for instance, promoted the exploitation of gutta-percha and the expansion of Chinese pepper and gambir plantations. If the Straits Settlements did not yet find major commercial opportunities in the neighbouring states — and indeed absorbed some of their entrepot traffic, as Penang had absorbed Kedah's — they did provide a route for Chinese migration into them. Malay chiefs in Perak and Selangor began in the 1840s to finance the more effective exploitation of their tin resources with Chinese labour, more thorough and psychologically more inclined than the Malays hitherto used (though there had been Chinese miners at Lukut in 1824). The reduction of duties in England in the 1850s and the development of the canning industry in the 1860s opened up much wider opportunities in the Larut and Kinta districts of Perak, round the new settlement of Kuala Lumpur in Selangor and Seremban in Sungei Ujong. Initially this economic development brought stability, subsequently instability. It produced an imbalance in the distribution of power among the Malay chiefs, and the resulting rivalries interleaved with the struggles between the two major secret societies into which the miners were organised to produce civil war.

The Straits Settlements were involved in these disturbances not simply as a result of their proximity, but also because the secret society struggles reacted upon their inhabitants (the Penang riots of 1867 were connected with the rivalry in Perak). The European and Chinese merchants pressed for more intervention than the local government had power to effect because the development of tin-mining was giving them a greater interest in the neighbouring states, and because Dutch extension in Sumatra and French in Indo-China were producing a new scare over the entrepot trade. The intervention that was finally authorised rather on strategic grounds adhered to previous traditions in its emphasis on advice to Malay rulers which was to be tendered in all fields save those of religion and custom.

The British intervention in Perak, Selangor, Sungei Ujong,

and later in Pahang, undoubtedly stimulated economic development, whatever its original motive. So did the continued rise
in the world demand for tin in the closing decades of the century. Both political and economic factors thus produced a rapid
expansion. New communication links were forged on the west
coast, and the railway was extended to Prai (in Province Wellesley) to link with the Penang ferry and to Singapore in 1909.
The development of this communication system — itself partly
determined by the pre-existence of the Straits Settlements, as
well as of the tin-mines — helped to locate the rubber plantations that rapidly expanded soon after the turn of the century
with the rise of the automobile industry, and in turn brought
about the creation of a fine road system. The rubber industry
overtook tin as the chief exporting industry in the course of
the first world war.

These enterprises demanded labour in a sparsely populated
country: the result was extensive immigration. Some was from
crowded Menangkabau. But it was Chinese who were imported
for working in the mines and clearing the ground for plantations, the latter a malarial task that could not have been carried
through without a continuous supply of immigrants to replace
those who went to an early death (the mosquito vector was not
known till 1898). Subsequently it was Indians who supplied
the plantation labour, while the Chinese remained miners or
became petty traders or artisans. Chinese immigration in Malaya
was novel only in its size, and there was still a minimum of
interference. A protectorate was established in 1877 to control
and later suppress the secret societies, and indentures — labour
contracts, made in return for the passage from China — ceased to
be legally enforceable after 1914. Indian — mostly southern
Indian — migrants came to the Peninsula initially under indentures, and also as free labourers, but the inadequate supply led
the planters — who favoured Indian labourers as easier to organise
and readier to accept low wages — to 'crimping', and the colonial
government stepped in to promote migration at a time of expansion, as well as to regulate it. It was able more readily to
negotiate with the British Indian authorities than with those
in China: but Indian immigration required more encouragement than Chinese. The new system of 1907-1910 aimed to do
away with indentures and finance all the services connected with
Indian migration by a special levy on users of Indian labour.
These changes were accompanied by the beginnings of a labour
code and of wage regulation and were thus not without a
humanitarian side. Other immigrants from India also came to

Malaya, clearly affected, though less directly than the labourers, by the British nature of both administrations, doctors, lawyers, teachers and clerks (some from Ceylon, too), Chettyar money-lenders familiar with the vagaries of British finance on the one hand and with the needs of peasants on the other, merchants closely tied to home firms.

The theoretical position of the British Residents was advisory: 'their special objects', the Colonial Office had declared in 1876, 'should be the maintenance of peace and law, the initiation of a sound system of taxation, with the consequent development of the resources of the country . . .'[78] After the Perak war, there was little resistance by the 'advised' rulers, while the great economic and social changes, and the administrative demands they made, put increasing power in the hands of the Residents and their District Officers. Then in 1895 the four states — Perak, Selangor, Pahang, and Negri Sembilan, a state composed of Sungei Ujong and its petty neighbours — were federated, and a Resident-General was established in Kuala Lumpur — under the High Commissioner, also Governor of the Straits Settlements, in Singapore — to co-ordinate the increasingly complex administration of the four states. Not only the Sultans but the Residents also saw their power restricted by a growing centralisation. In 1909, there were reforms. A Federal Council was set up to advise the Resident-General, now called Chief Secretary, and it included the rulers, the Residents, and four unofficials nominated by the High Commissioner. But the change did nothing to restore power to the states and the rulers were not powers on the Federal Council. The major impetus for it had come in fact from the planters, and from the High Commissioner's wish to limit the Resident-General rather than to restore the rulers' powers. Nothing much was done to remedy the Sultan of Perak's complaint of 1903: overcentralisation. New treaties were made with the rulers: the advisory tradition remained; but the real situation was still different.

This was underlined by the contrast with the other states of the Peninsula, much less affected by both the economic and political developments of the period. None of them was rich in tin, none of them attracted extensive Chinese immigration, and their somewhat stronger political structures were able to adapt themselves with a degree of outside pressure to conditions that changed somewhat more slowly. Even after the transfer of the Siamese claims in 1909, there was no call for complex administration. Not only did the relative lack of economic change tend to leave the unfederated Sultanates with more power than those in the Federation: the example of the F.M.S. affected both the British, concerned at the practical collapse of their tradition of advice, and the Sultans, who sought to retain the power their federated peers had demonstrably lost. In 1921 the High Commissioner Guillemard had to deny that the idea was entertained of a wider union, though it might have made for cheaper and more rational administration.

The world war brought considerable prosperity to Malaya, thanks to the increased demand for tin and, above all, rubber, and it became a major dollar-earner. Post-war there was a slump, and the rubber restriction scheme that was introduced in the 1920s, the Stevenson scheme, particularly affected Malaya because the Netherlands Indies did not join in and was able to secure a larger share of the world market. More efficiency was forced upon the Malayan producers again by the depression after 1929. This applied also to tin production, subjected to international restriction from 1931, and it led to the introduction of dredges, costly equipment that conferred advantages on the highly-capitalised European firms over the Chinese.

The depression reduced the flow of Indian labour to Malaya and the colonial government sponsored some repatriation in the early 1930s. In 1938 an increasingly nationalist Indian Government suspended the migration of unskilled Indian labour to Malaya as a result of the low wage rates there. The transitory nature of the Indian population, its low sex-ratio, the depression and the ban, all restricted the size of the community, which perhaps numbered $\frac{3}{4}$m at the time the Japanese invasion severed it from its homeland. Most of these factors also worked against the assimilation of the Indians with other elements of the population, and their political interest was in Indian nationalism. Of this there were three sources in Malaya: the Indian Government agency attached to the Labour Department after 1923; Indian journalism; and the Central Indian Association in Kuala Lumpur, founded in 1936 and stimulated by Nehru's first visit to Malaya in 1937, which promoted a solidarity hitherto lacking between the professional class and the labourers from whom it was not recruited.

If the depression reduced the Chinese share in tin-mining to 2/5, and the restriction scheme worked against the smaller Chinese mines, absolutely the volume of Chinese economic activities grew and their numbers continued to rise. Most Chinese coming to the Nanyang had remitted some of their earnings home and sought to return home if they became wealthy. The hostility of the Manchus and the relatively poor communications meant that few achieved this in the nineteenth century, and a non-transient 'Straits Chinese' community developed, the men taking local wives (rarely, of course, Muslim) in the absence of substantial female emigration. The changed attitude of the Chinese Government and improved communications of the twentieth century affected the Chinese community on the Peninsula as in the Archipelago. It at once became more transient and more Chinese. The depression, furthermore, meant that some Chinese left, but the administration sponsored the repatriation only of males. The Immigration Restriction Ordinance of 1928 and the Aliens Ordinance of 1933 — influenced by the depression — were also used chiefly to limit the number of males entering Malaya, and the Japanese attacks on China after 1936 increased the influx of females. The improved sex-ratio meant the setting-up of more peculiarly Chinese households. The war in China, and then the Japanese invasion of Malaya, tended to make these migrants permanent residents of the Peninsula, and the community numbered nearly 2m by 1941. Its numerical importance — vis-à-vis some 2m Malays, including some Sumatran or 'Malaysian' immigrants — made its position radically different from that in the Netherlands Indies. And yet Chinese nationalism was perhaps even more active within it.

The revolutionary Sun Yat-sen had organised branches of his organisation in Malaya in the first decade of the century. Its heir, the K.M.T., also saw the economic importance of the Malayan community. Teachers came from South China and the Chinese schools spread Chinese nationalism, even among Straits Chinese, using, moreover, the revolutionary national language that helped to counter linguistic divisions that the illiterate immigrants had brought with them. Politically the K.M.T. was prepared to use secret society techniques and also, and perhaps somewhat contradictorily, semi-western types of mass organisation that might attract the loyalty the Chinese traditionally focused on tribal and other associations, and involve them in political life. The K.M.T. was actually suppressed in 1925, and the immigration restrictions were partly political in motive. But the party remained well-established and continued to amass funds. After the opening of the China-Japan war of 1937, the K.M.T. made every attempt to encourage Chinese nationalism and collect money, and the government remained as lenient as possible although it was then at peace with Japan.

The Chinese Communists also used secret society techniques and mass techniques. Following the open split between Communists and K.M.T. in China, the Comintern tried to seize the initiative the C.C.P. had so far enjoyed in Malaya, and formed the Nanyang C.P. and then, in 1930, the Malayan C.P. It had little attraction for the Indians, concerned, if concerned with politics, only with their own independence movement. And among the Chinese, it concentrated in the depression on organising student political activity in the schools, through, for instance, the Singapore Students Federation; on developing a rudimentary western-style labour organisation, the Labour Unions, and using it for political purposes; and on creating mass front organisations like the Anti-Imperialist League and the Anti-Enemy Backing Up Society. Its major successes were among school teachers in Chinese schools, radicals who failed to secure jobs at home, and their pupils, and among some immigrant labourers. The war of 1937, however, gave their front organisations a new importance, though it led to a rift in the party, the extremists opposing the popular front anti-Fascist policy of the Comintern. Lai Teck was sent to deal with them, but the Nazi-Soviet pact hardly helped him.

For the British the first world war, and the ideological and constitutional changes it spurred on, raised more stringently than ever before the problem of the future of Malaya's social and political development. Nothing had been done so far to promote the assimilation of the various communities. Malaya's prosperity — it enjoyed the highest standard of living in Southeast Asia — helped to reduce any stress between the communities, and the British, unlike the Dutch, were not called upon to promote an assimilation policy. The Dutch tried to win over the Indonesian majority in this way, and tried to extend it to the Chinese minority. The British, on the other hand, were faced with no real opposition, and indeed the Malays and Chinese were fairly equally divided. The new urge towards political advancement post-war compelled the British to formulate a policy, and it might be thought that the policy they formulated indicated an intention to maintain their secure position in a country now increasingly important as a dollar-earner and as an outpost of empire. In 1887 Governor Weld had spoken of the Indians as a counterbalance to the Chinese and, though this was apparently an isolated remark, it was true that in the 1920s and 1930s little was done to reduce differences between communities that, as they became more integrated, were in fact drawing apart from one another. Was it *divide-et-impera*?

Certainly educational policy did little to overcome divisions, constitutional changes even increased them, and the measures

184

of the depression seemed to have a political bias against the Chinese. Even the loyal Straits Chinese appeared to be pushed aside, as a spokesman, Tan Cheng-lock, a legislative councillor in the Straits Settlements between 1923 and 1934, complained. By 1940 he was contemplating the formation of a Malayan Chinese Association. But the conservative Chinese, though they had much to lose from radicalism, had no tradition of political activity which, furthermore, might involve them with the secret society gangsters. Yet if the British did little to encourage a Malayan Chinese leadership, and if this may appear evidence of a policy of divide-and-rule, the facts must at the same time be considered, not only in the context of the depression, but also in that of the enduring tradition of the British connexion with the Peninsula, that it was based on advice and guidance of Malay rulers.

In the Malay states — though less perfectly in the Unfederated than the Federated — primary education in Malay was free for all Malay boys and girls and compulsory for all boys living within a mile and a half of a Malay vernacular school. But it was 'contained within a rural context',[79] and there was virtually no secondary education in Malay. Primary but not secondary education in Tamil was provided for the children of Indian labourers by estate proprietors. Secondary as well as primary education in English was provided in a limited number of government schools and in schools conducted by missionary bodies which received grants-in-aid from the government, but which usually charged fees. This led to employment as clerks or in government service, or to higher education, also in English, in the King Edward VII College of Medicine (1905) and the Raffles College of Arts (1928) in Singapore. But those — the majority — who had received primary education in Malay or Tamil found it difficult to jump the linguistic and economic barrier into secondary education.

As for Chinese education, the F.M.S. government assumed increasing control, initially in political matters (in 1920 it introduced regulations against the teaching of alien political doctrine), later in other matters also, and in return offered grants-in-aid. In the U.M.S. the Chinese schools continued to be privately sustained. But though secondary education was available, it was in Chinese, and its products did not find their qualifications accepted. Some, especially Straits Chinese, avoided this frustration by shifting to secondary education in English. But clearly education did little to draw the communities together: there was only a small group of English-educated who might be considered inter-communal. Governor Clementi (1929-34) proposed to give all races free education in Malay, which was to be made the common language of the country. This was unlikely to be acceptable to other communities. It was, however, connected with his political recommendations.

The Malay community was not yet outnumbered (at least not if immigrant Malays or 'Malaysians' were included), but its economic weakness was apparent. It is not true that it did not respond to the economic forces reaching Malaya. To these the peasants were exposed by the penetration of westernised administration, by which the village headman became a government servant rather than a traditional leader. The Malays did not become plantation workers or tin miners but, especially after about 1910, many smallholders, utilising facilities provided for the great estates, planted rubber Sumatra-style, and were often better able to withstand price-falls than the great estates. The increased demand for rice led to the commercialisation of the better rice areas, such as the plains of southern Kedah. But no Malay middle-class elements emerged Sumatra-style — immigrants were perhaps too dominant — and in the train of these changes came indebtedness to Indians and Chinese, and to this the F.M.S. government reacted by a policy of land reservations, begun in 1913 and reinforced in 1933, by the encouragement in the F.M.S. after 1922 of co-operative societies, and by the limitation of usury. The predominantly rural character of the Malay population — more especially the linear nature of their settlements, which made services expensive and health measures difficult, and reduced community spirit — did not increase the Malays' chances of betterment in other walks of life. And education, as has been seen, was not likely to create a Malay middle-class.

The economic and demographic situation of the Malays affected the political planning of Malaya in which successive Governors indulged. Sir Hugh Clifford had declared in 1927 that 'the adoption of any kind of government by majority would forthwith entail the complete submersion of the indigenous population', and that no mandate had been 'extended to us by rajas, chiefs, or people, to vary the system of government'. The objects came to be the restoration of the state governments by decentralisation and the opening of wider public service opportunities to the Malays in order to ensure that they were not submerged politically. The Under-Secretary at the Colonial Office, Ormsby-Gore, considered that the spirit and intention of British policy in Malaya had been carried out more simply and completely in the U.M.S. than in the F.M.S.: the point was to maintain the authority and position of the Malay rulers.[80] This attitude led to the gesture of returning the Dindings to Perak and spurred on measures of decentralisation in the F.M.S., already proposed in the 1920s by Governor Guillemard as a means of curbing expenditure at a time of falling rubber prices. Clementi — also at a time of declining revenue — planned that the Chief Secretary should become a Federal Secretary, that the State Councils should regain power, that the Residents should become more like Advisers in the U.M.S. Then the U.M.S. might become more inclined to join a Malayan union, and a conservative Chinese leadership might see the wider economic possibilities it held out and recognise the political advantage in coming to terms with the rulers. Co-operation and advance would thus be ensured.

One difficulty in the way of the programme was the difference of economic interest between the F.M.S. and the Colony of the Straits Settlements. The Colony had become more deeply involved with the rubber and tin of the Peninsula, in processing and exporting them, and with importing rice from other Southeast Asian countries to feed the increased population. But, despite the nationalistic economic policies adopted in neighbouring territories, especially after the depression, Singapore retained important entrepot interests, and the planters and miners feared its free trade influence. They believed that the weakening of the Kuala Lumpur government would subordinate the F.M.S. more to the High Commissioner, who was also Governor of the Settlements and advised by Executive and Legislative Councils there. Guillemard had withdrawn and Clementi compromised. But the Chief Secretary was replaced by a Federal Secretary in 1935 and the State Councils gained increased powers. These measures of decentralisation opened the way to greater Malay participation in government and administration.

It was under these circumstances that Malay nationalism began to stir. One of the earliest influences was Islamic reformism. It penetrated in the early years of the century to the relatively small group of urban middle-class Malays, some of whom were of Arab or Menangkabau origin, and all of whom had visited Egypt and Mekka. In particular it reacted against the extreme erastian character of Malayan Islam, which had been brought about by the concentration of the Sultans and their governments on the matters of religion and custom left to them by the British treaties. No political movement was built by the reformists: there was no individualistic Malay group to support it. Nor was one built by the orthodox hierarchy, so closely identified with the state administrations. The leaders of Malay nationalism were to come in the late 1920s and 1930s from other sources. On the one hand, there were the more radical products of the Sultan Idris Teachers Training College opened in 1922 at Tanjong Malim in Perak, the only institution to give secondary education in Malay; on the other, the products of the administrative college at Kuala Kangsar, founded in 1905, generally more aristocratic in origin. To the latter and to the Malay clerks who secured an English secondary education, decentralisation gave increased scope.

For all the groups within this intelligentsia, the main problem was the preservation of a Malay way of life over against wes-ternisation and the immigration of vast numbers of non-Malays. It was for this reason that Islam was more important to all of them than, for instance, to the Dutch-educated Javanese nationalists, and there were no middle-class Islamic modernists to polarise any differences with an *adat*-based élite. The groups differed — though without there being rigid dichotomies — in other respects. The more conservative — leaders of the Malay Unions of the 1930s — tended to favour a continuance of British rule as the best support against the Chinese. Others looked outside Malaya. Few of these looked to Communism, dominated by the Chinese: the latter were the only hope for Communism, Tan Malaka had decided, though he had made contact with graduates and students from Sultan Idris. The more extreme looked to the pan-Asianism of the Japanese or to Indonesian nationalism, to the power that was shortly to overthrow the British and their works, or to the élite of a country from which British decisions had divided the Malays, only to submerge them with Chinese. These extremists founded the K.M.M. or Young Malay Union in 1937, led by exiled Indonesians and by graduates of Sultan Idris and supported by students from Sultan Idris, the Agricultural College at Serdang, and the Trade School at Kuala Lumpur. 150 of the Union's members were arrested in December 1941 and were in jail in Singapore when the Japanese arrived.

3 British Borneo

NORTHERN BORNEO was a thinly-populated area with a fringe of Malay settlement and a number of other tribes on the coast and in the interior. It had no great agricultural resources, and it had till recently no important discovered minerals; and as a result, when rubber came to Southeast Asia, Malaya, with communications and services already developed, was more attractive. And northern Borneo attracted no vast immigration. So much the three régimes had in common, into which it was divided by the late nineteenth century, and into which it remained divided, despite some Colonial Office interest in unity in the Chamberlain period, up to the Japanese invasions, from which British protection failed to shelter it. All three régimes had been part of territory claimed by the old Sultanate of Brunei, though parts of North Borneo were claimed also by Sulu. All three — despite their commercial unattractiveness — came under British influence. But Sarawak and North Borneo were fragments of empire which were broken off piecemeal from Brunei. Different conditions prevailed, different sorts of influence were established, administrations that pursued different policies on economic, social and political development.

James Brooke's initial plan had been to establish a settlement at Marudu. From this he had shifted to scheming the reform and development of the empire of Brunei through indirect rule. After the revolution of 1846 and the death of Hassim, he changed again: the development and civilisation of northern Borneo was to take the form of the gradual advance of the Sarawak Raj over the rivers to the northward. The Brooke administration moved northwards from Kuching over a period of fifty years. It thus varied in longevity in different rivers, and characteristically was weaker up-river than down. It had certain broad features. It employed Malay administrative officers, but retained the first Raja's concern for the interior tribes that Brunei nobles had exploited or used against one another. But those in the south —

189

more exposed to European influences from the Raj and from the Anglican missions it admitted — were to some extent instruments of advance, commercial and political, in territories later acquired, and, in a more refined way than the Bruneis, the régime played off tribe against tribe.

The dynasty retained also the first Raja's apprehension about the Chinese — especially when organised in *kongsis,* like the early Sarawak Chinese who came from Sambas — and it was increased by the rebellion of 1857. In 1899 the second Raja established a colony of Foochows at Sibu and later another at Baram, hoping that they would spread more advanced farming practices among the population. He was still convinced, like his uncle, of the dangers of over-rapid development to the dynasty and to the native population. As the British consul wrote, 'it is because the ruler of the country regards his position as a trust held by him for the benefit of the inhabitants that this progress is necessarily slow, since sudden jumps from the methods of the past to the up-to-dateism of modern ideas, though advantageous to the pocket, and on paper attractive, are not always conducive to the happiness of the people . . . Improvements are made and commerce pushed wherever possible, without fuss or the elements of speculation . . .'[81]

The Borneo Company Limited of 1856 was the only important European firm, and it was engaged also in trade in other parts of Southeast Asia. Antimony, indirectly the cause of the foundation of Brooke rule, ceased to pay by the early twentieth century. Gold-mining at Bau, the original attraction for the Chinese, revived for a time (1898-1921), thanks to the introduction of the cyanide process. Some oil was exploited at Miri. The lack of agricultural and mineral resources, as well as dynastic policy, restrained development. And this meant that, though it spread civilisation and promulgated a constitution in 1941, the Raj did not create a modern state. The tribal divisions made for the security of Brooke rule and lessened the immediate problem of setting-up a political framework; but the immense task of creating a political structure that might ultimately replace the Brookes as they had replaced the only previous source of unity, Brunei rule, was not carried out. The dynasty stood in place of the sort of political structure that existed among the Malays on the Peninsula. Like the Peninsular government, it did not foster assimilation with the Chinese. Its disappearance was to leave little to set against their dominance, especially as the administration became more development-minded.

The rivers north of Brunei remained independent of European control before the establishment of the Chartered Company, and indeed its position was not fixed in some interdigital rivers till twenty years after the granting of the charter. Before this the colony at Labuan had sought to foster Chinese trade more particularly in nearby rivers, such as Padas and Mempakul, meeting the opposition of revenue-hungry Brunei rajas, uncontrolled by Brookean policies. Beyond this even Brunei control decreased, and on the east coast it lapsed in favour of the loose hegemony exercised by the Sultan of Sulu, more particularly in the Sandakan area. Like the Raj, the Company could utilise no structure of native rule: it had an even greater complex of tribes to deal with and it started later. Again its rule was peculiar: there were no dynastic interests, but there were shareholders, who wanted at least some dividend, and directors who had ideas and exerted a considerable control. But again there was no overall opposition to European rule within the territory, though the Mat Salleh rebellion of the late 1890s almost overthrew its fragile structure on the west coast. The Company subsequently sought native leaders of ability. The expatriate District Officers, like those in Sarawak, tried to use the chiefs and headmen, and in 1912 they were organised in three grades. In the 1930s greater efforts were made under Governor Jardine, who came from Tanganyika and experimented with indirect rule. He established in 1935 the Native Chiefs Advisory Council, and the following year set up a native administrative centre on the Keningau plain at Singkor, with twelve villages under a single chief, and permission to raise revenue locally. But there was no tradition of larger government; and it was feared that the structure of indirect rule would in fact produce the rule of the Chinese, to whom many of the chiefs were indebted.

On the other hand there was no economic transformation. The Company was restricted by its small capital and by the provisions of its charter. These must have been obstacles to Cowie's notion of a tobacco cultivation system in the 1890s. But so was the lack of population. The Company had begun with great hopes of mineral wealth which were disappointed. Its early days saw the development of timber exports, above all from the primary forest of the undeveloped east coast, to Australia and Hong Kong. But what saved the Company from early collapse was the tobacco boom of the 1880s, which attracted investors in particular from the Netherlands Indies. The fall in tobacco prices following the U.S. tariff of 1891 again put the Company in low water. The rescue came with the development of rubber in the early decades of the new century, first in plantations along the little railway that had been started on the west coast, and later in smallholdings, suiting the poor soil and the short labour-supply. For the plantations Javanese were recruited. But more important, more numerous, and more settled, was the Chinese community, numbering in 1931 48,000 out of a population of 270,000.

The government was apprehensive of its ultimate control. Yet the weakness of the existing political structure, and the lack of revenue, prevented a transformation of the native peoples. The Anglican Church, arriving later than in Sarawak, failed to evangelise as effectively in North Borneo as among the Dayaks. Most of its work and most of that of the Catholic mission took place in the towns and among the Chinese there. The government, too, relied very much on the missions for education, and subsidised them after 1905. On its part, it established vernacular schools: the first one, for sons of chiefs, opened at Jesselton in 1915, but it was never a success. Only in the 1930s did vernacular schools become more popular: there was no great incentive to attend them since, unlike some of the missions, they did not offer English, the key to advancement. As in Malaya and Sarawak, the Chinese maintained their own schools. Educational policy thus did little to promote an identity of interest among all the peoples of North Borneo. The Chinese, too, had come relatively late: there was no equivalent of the Straits Chinese; and it was hard to expect their assimilation, though there was some intermarriage with non-Islamic peoples like the Muruts. And, on the other hand, no native élite had been built up. Thus the Company, though initially enthusiastic for Chinese immigration — like the Governors of Labuan and unlike the Raja of Sarawak — became, with the penetration of the political ideas of the 1930s, apprehensive that even the minority Chinese would be able to dominate the weak native structures which alone had been developed. Behind British protection, and sheltered from vast political or even economic change, the régime had persisted into a new period to which it was hardly adapted. But it was only the Japanese invasion that compelled a transformation.

In the remnants of Brunei, on the other hand, remained a concentration of Malays and a Sultan, who did not receive a British Resident till 1905. In one sense Brunei — though once an imperial centre — then became like a Peninsular state, but it had less wealth as yet and fewer Chinese (3,000 out of a population of 30,000 in 1931) than those on the west coast. The discovery of its substantial oil resources occurred in 1929.

But their exploitation and its impact — the wealth it created, the ambitions it fostered, the religious revival it encouraged — belong to the post-war period.

4 The Philippines

THE neighbouring Sultanate of Mindanao had collapsed under Spanish pressure in the course of the nineteenth century, and the last recognised Sultan of Sulu died in the 1930s. But the infrastructure of the Sultanates persisted, even after the long American campaigns of the early twentieth century. As democracy advanced, the *datus'* followers became a band of voters, and new posts were filled by those with traditional sources of power. Indeed in some ways the infrastructure became more rigid: it was hard now to fight or pirate your way to *datu* status, and no longer legitimate. Ambitious recalcitrants turned to banditry. The American régime was socially conservative here as in the north and followed a Spanish régime that had never exerted an effective political control in an area never economically transformed. In the north there were economic transformation and political revolution, but even so the extent of social change could be exaggerated.

The British at the opening of the period had been interested not only in Sulu but also in the Philippines as a whole. Their conquest of Manila in 1762 did not establish their control much beyond its immediate vicinity: they had too few troops; and, under the peace of Paris, they evacuated in 1764. But the conquest had wider repercussions than its limited extent and brevity suggested, and may in some respects be compared with that of Java fifty years later. One effect was to provoke native revolt, provoked also by peasant opposition to monastic land-grabbing in central Luzon. In 1762-3 there was a revolt in Ilokos, headed by Silang, who had been appointed Governor by the English.

In Pangasinan Juan de la Cruz Palaris began a rebellion against the oppressive tribute system. These movements added to the apprehension of foreign invasion that the British exploit aroused. Throughout the remainder of their rule the Spaniards feared combined rebellion and invasion which indeed brought it to an end in 1898.

In yet another way the British conquest — not unlike that of Java — affected the future: the restored Spaniards attempted reforms, above all in the economic field, with the object of strengthening their régime. In addition the war had dealt a further blow at the Acapulco trade, and policy was also influenced by the post-war 'Enlightened Despotism' of Carlos III. In 1766 an attempt was made to establish a connexion with the Philippines round the Cape, but it was not followed up owing to the jealousy of Manilan merchants and officials. In the Philippines there were reforms by Anda (who had led resistance to the English) and by Basco. Basco sought to stir up the economy and in 1779 published a development plan. A royal decree of 1785 set up the Royal Philippine Company to promote Philippines commerce, and to assist Basco in face of opposition in Manila. But characteristically the great success of the period was a sort of minor cultivation-system which Basco set up, and it was his tobacco monopoly that ultimately balanced the budget. The attempts to enforce it, however, produced disaffection, especially in the most important region, Cagayan.

The Mexican subsidy became superfluous, but the breakaway of the Spanish colonies in America — including Mexico, always the second, or even the first, fatherland of the colony in the Philippines — faced the Spaniards with new problems. The galleon trade was abandoned, the subsidy disappeared. The Pacific link was weakened; was the Indo-European link to become stronger? The Philippine Company had not proved a success, and the chance of promoting Philippines development with Spanish capital seemed remote in the early nineteenth century. In fact, in search of revenue, and as a result of British pressure, the Spaniards abandoned many of their mercantilist restrictions on foreign enterprise, and foreign trade expanded, partly in American, but mostly — especially the import of manufactured goods — in English hands. Between the 1820s and the 1870s 'the Philippines was transformed from a subsistence economy to an agricultural export economy'.[82] Rice and hemp were the main exports at first, and later sugar, much of which went to Australia in the mid-century phase. Initially the economic changes were effective principally in the centre of the Spanish empire in Luzon. The more vigorous measures against the Moros from the 1840s enabled the Visayas to share in the economic transformation especially after the opening of the port of Iloilo in 1855 and of the Suez Canal in 1869. Even the mountain regions of Luzon, opened up admistratively by a régime which was at last finding revenue in the Philippines to finance expeditions and missions there as well as in Moroland, shared in the economic transformation. The 'Igorot' regions in Luzon now became the centre of terraced wet-rice cultivation.

Elsewhere in Southeast Asia in the nineteenth century export produce was often expanded either by forced peasant cultivation or, especially after 1869, by plantations drawing on reserves of village or alien labour. The Philippines were again exceptional, in that no real cultivation-system appeared in the early phase, which also set the tone of development in the later phase. In Luzon, population had been expanding since the end of the Dutch crisis in the late seventeenth century. What was lacking for a cultivation-system — which might make the tobacco monopoly no longer exceptional — was, it may be thought, Spanish enterprise and determination on the scale the Dutch produced after their restoration. But what seems most likely is that Philippines society was in a sense already too Europeanised. The rights of the ruling class, though derived from pre-Spanish origins, as also those of the orders, were already based on European notions of property, and both groups were bound into a system of more or less European-style administration which the Spaniards could disturb only at their peril.

Certainly economic change strengthened the existing system of monastic, native and *mestizo* landowning. The landowners secured new wealth and this increased the effectiveness of their old political powers. This was the period of the *caciques,* who secured control of the *barangays* and *pueblos,* deferring only to the local friar, and who are well described in the person of 'Capitan Tiago' in José Rizal's superb if Lytton-esque novel *Noli me Tangere* (1887). The increase of population, more especially in the central Luzon regions, and the penetration of a money economy, also helped to place more and more freeholders at the mercy of the *caciques* and to make more and more of them tenants on the *kasama* or share basis or, again especially in Luzon, on the *inquilinato* or cash system. In some sense, therefore, the economic transformation produced by foreign enterprise and its fertilisation of the Philippines economy by cash and credit was revolutionary only in making things more the same. In another way it contributed to a cultural revolution.

Anda had sought to limit Chinese participation in the economic life of the Philippines, not only because of the traditional Spanish apprehension of the Chinese, but also because he wished to open opportunities for more *criollos* and *mestizos*. The notion was that they would spread the Spanish language and culture and, in turn, Anda argued, rather like some of the later Dutch Ethici, this would guarantee allegiance to Spain. In 1850, however, the Spanish mestizo population still was only small. But it was not its smallness that was alarming, nor the penetration of Chinese mestization among the ruling groups. Their wealth, and the new connexions with the outside world, increased the spread of Spanish culture. Undoubtedly the structure of land-ownership and of local government was a conservative factor, except in so far as it intensified revolutionary trends among the peasants or *taos*. But what was alarming was that Spanish culture was helping to produce the *ilustrado,* new élite elements, substantially drawn from the old, but critical of the *status quo* in the Philippines. Its great attraction — the great inducement Spanish education now offered — was that it opened up new worlds of thought, new potentialities. It gave access to European liberal thinking, albeit mostly of the more dated and still eighteenth century-type Spanish variety. An élite acquiring such notions was bound to be restive in a country dominated by friars and *caciques* and Spanish officials (the latter only increased in number in the 1850s and 1860s by the loss of other Spanish colonies and by the spoils system adopted by the revolutionaries of 1868).

The crisis of opportunity was characteristically felt within the church first. The 'Enlightened' régime of Carlos III had seen the expulsion of the Jesuits, and another aspect of Anda's policy had been an attempt to assert government power by breaking that of the friars. The Archbishops had long sought to bring them under control, and Anda's contemporary, Sancho de Santa Justa y Rufina, tried to defeat them by employing Filipino seculars. But the weapon recoiled for the seculars had been inadequately trained, and the friars remained a pillar of Spanish rule. They continued to exclude Filipinos from the orders, too, and one rejected aspirant, Apollinario de la Cruz, a native of Tayabas, became in the early 1840s the leader of a movement that was regarded as heretical, became linked with *tao* discontent, and was put down only after a pitched battle in which a thousand Filipinos perished. Frustration among the seculars, where alone the Filipinos found a place, was increased by the return of the Jesuits in 1859. They went back to Mindanao. This meant that the Recollects shifted to the Manila-Cavite region, just where the seculars were strongest. Their resulting disappointment contributed to the unrest that found a more open outlet after the Spanish revolution of 1868 had brought liberal Spanish officials to the Philippines. But in the colony the reactionaries assumed power again even before they did in the metropolitan country, and this precipitated the Cavite Mutiny of 1872 and the subsequent garotting of three seculars allegedly implicated. In 1898 only one-seventh of the total Catholic population of 6.5m was in the hands of the seculars. Elsewhere the regulars, predominantly Spaniards, yet prevailed. Primo de Rivera had a rather different attitude to the spread of Spanish culture from his predecessor Anda more than a century before: 'the native priest, having the Christian spirit, educated in the seminary, enlightened by the friar ordinarily living with him, is probably the most hostile and most dangerous of those who confront us. And this is as it should be. When you instruct a man and give him a superior education; when you ordain him, train him in the gospels . . . that man can be no man's servant . . .'[83]

But there were other elements in the Cavite Mutiny also and other ways in which the actual effects of a policy like Anda's were unlike those he had anticipated. Spanish had been spread among a very small proportion of the population but among a significant portion of it. It overcame at that level some of the divisions that the preservation of dialects in the monastic system of education had helped to preserve. Initially in Luzon — the centre of European activity — but subsequently elsewhere an élite developed that was the first of Southeast Asian nationalist movements though utilising the resources of the most old-fashioned of European liberalisms. The *ilustrado* attended private schools or colleges under priestly direction in Manila, Iloilo or Cebu. Some went to Hong Kong or to Europe, and the opening of the Suez Canal made this easier. More Filipinos went to their Mekka, to Barcelona or Berlin ('If you can do no better, study in Spain, but preferably study in freer countries', Burgos, one of the martyrs of 1872, had recommended).[84] More books, more newspapers reached the Philippines and stirred the imagination of Filipinos. But perhaps it was an imperialist venture in Southeast Asia itself that inaugurated their closer connexion with the outside world: the expeditionary force sent to help the French in Cochin-China breached the colony's isolation.

It was characteristic of a national movement drawing inspiration from Spain that Masonry — long a form of protest against Catholic authoritarian régimes — should play such an important part in creating the initial organisations and in influencing the structure and ritual of later ones. It was characteristic of the sources of Filipino nationalism that it should initially be moderate in tone. Some Spaniards and Filipinos in Spain in 1888 founded the Asociacion Hispano-Filipino aiming at the compulsory teaching of Spanish, at reforms, at the improvement of communications. The following year one of its leaders, Marcelo H. del Pilar of Bulacan, bought *La Solidaridad,* a journal published in Spain, and it sought expulsion of the friars and representation in the Cortes which the Philippines had enjoyed only very spasmodically. The great José Rizal, scion of a well-to-do family of Laguna, educated in the Dominican Santo Tomas University and the General University of Madrid, was also a reformist, aiming at the reduction of abuses and the secularisation of parishes, and his Liga Filipina of 1892 did not aim at separation from Spain. But it was easier to be a liberal Filipino in Spain than it was in the Philippines: there he was a *filibustero.*

It is true that the régime introduced some reforms in the 1880s. Tribute was abolished in 1884 and compulsory labour much reduced, the provincial governments were reorganised, the legal codes revised. Governor-General Moriones did away with the Cagayan tobacco monopoly. But the reforms did not touch the real grievances of the *ilustrado,* and they were pushed in a more revolutionary direction. Furthermore, less moderate social elements were now involved. The law of 1863 had aimed to provide a secular system of elementary schools. In fact it was only partially carried through, and the schools remained much under friar influence and continued to use local dialects. But though statistics differ widely, undoubtedly the islands could claim by the 1890s a higher literacy rate than any other country in Southeast Asia, perhaps indeed than Spain itself. In the great towns, especially Manila, by far the greatest, a new and more radical class appeared — the product of economic change, of increased educational activities, of the opening of new horizons — of which Andres Bonifacio, the founder of the secret society Katipunan (1892), is an example. The discovery of the Katipunan was to precipitate the revolt of August 1896. But what gave the revolt its great impulse, above all in the Tagalog provinces round Manila, its great stronghold, was the support of the *taos,* who believed that independence must improve their lot. Monastic landowning was in fact concentrated in these old areas of Spanish settlement. The new system of land titles, introduced in the 1880s, had, moreover, been turned to account by the friars.

The revolution spread outside the Tagalog provinces, to Panay and to other islands, and there were mutinies among the native troops in Mindanao and Sulu, but it was most successful in Cavite province, the home of the Mutiny of 1872. Guerilla warfare continued there, even after the insurrectionary leader Emilio Aguinaldo, an ex-schoolmaster from Cavite who knew little Spanish, had been driven back into Bulacan. There the Filipino Republic was proclaimed at Biaknabato. But a truce between the hard-pressed rebels and the Spaniards, who were heavily involved in Cuba, was arranged through the conservative Manila lawyer, Pedro A. Paterno, and the leaders went in exile to Hong Kong.

Apollinario Mabini, the cripple who was the most advanced theorist of the Philippines revolution, and one of the few *ilustrados* of modest origin, believed that it was a model for the other Malay peoples. 'The Revolution has a final aim, to maintain alive and resplendent, the torch of liberty and civilization, in order to give light to the gloomy night in which the Malay race finds itself degraded, so that it may be led to the road of social emancipation . . .' Rizal, too, had thought of himself as the representative of the Malay race. The colonial powers, said Mabini, knew that the revolution was 'very contagious'.[85] In fact the early Philippines example of the potent combination of European nationalism and native élite seems to have found little echo in the Archipelago, let alone on the mainland. It was, perhaps, too early. The course of Philippines history remained rather separate.

In any case, Southeast Asian politics were then, as later when nationalism had developed elsewhere, power politics. If there was a breach in the colonial system in 1898, it was rapidly filled by a new power which, as it were, followed the Spaniards across the Pacific, and maintained the separateness of the Philippines by creating a new colony. The least developed imperialism came in contact with the most developed Southeast Asian nationalism. American officials met Filipino exiles in Hong Kong and Singapore and encouraged the renewal of operations in Cavite and elsewhere after the U.S. had declared war on Spain over Cuba and, half-imitating the earlier English example, blockaded Manila in early May 1898. The rebel leaders were not unaware of the realities of power politics. The Katipunan had sought to buy arms in Japan in 1895, but could not raise the cash. The Hong Kong Committee sent Mariano Ponce to Japan in June 1898, and pan-Asian idealists there, such as Miyazaki Torazō, an associate of Sun Yat-sen, were keen on helping: a grateful Filipino state would be a base for the liberation of China from western imperialism. The Japanese Government, despite frustration at the Triple Intervention that followed its victory over China of 1895, feared to intervene as American-Filipino relations deteriorated lest the U.S. should be antagonised. But a member of the General Staff, Kawakumi, thought Japan should foster friendship in the Philippines which might be useful, if not at once, in fifty or a hundred years. A number of men and arms were sent in mid-1899, but the ship sank, and the six officers who reached Luzon could do little to help the Filipino forces who were now struggling against the Americans. A new régime was to be established, and the Japanese had to bide their time. The Filipino movement was premature, not only in ideological terms, but in power terms also. If the Filipinos' example itself appeared to have little effect elsewhere, their connexion with the Japanese set a precedent. Even so it was not that which called attention to the Japanese as the hope of Asian nationalism, but the striking success the Japanese secured a few years later against the Russians. And this was just at the point when nationalism had begun to stir in Indonesia and elsewhere in Southeast Asia.

In May 1898 Aguinaldo had proclaimed a revolutionary government. In August Manila capitulated to Admiral Dewey. In December the U.S. purchased the islands at the peace of Paris. Aguinaldo believed — not entirely without justification — that the Americans had betrayed him, and the growing distrust conduced to the outbreak of hostilities between them and the rebels in February 1899. Guerilla warfare developed. The Americans procured the pacification of the Philippines, not merely by military means, but by effecting a compromise with the conservative landowning elements, many of whom, though jealous of friar landowners, had always been somewhat apprehensive of the revolutionaries, and especially of their military wing, generally, like Aguinaldo himself, of modest origin. There was no revolution in the social structure of the Philippines, far from it. The Americans brought the separation of church and state, religious freedom and a secular system of education. But they had difficulty in securing from the Vatican an arrangement for the purchase and resale of friar lands and for the withdrawal of the friars. The delay was to foster the Iglesia Filipina Independiente — founded with the aid of a well-to-do Ilokano journalist, Isabelo de los Reyes, and headed by a one-time rebel Gregorio Aglipay — and it flourished during 1903. But subsequently it lost influence, and upper-class participation diminished. In fact late in 1903 an agreement had at last been concluded for the buying-out of the friars' lands, and their actual number had already diminished to about 200. Much of the land indeed came into the hands of *caciques*. The change had only strengthened their position, removing rival landowners without relieving the *taos*.

The economic developments of the American period were indeed to intensify *cacique* hegemony. In the case of the Philippines conquest, the flag had not followed trade. The eyes of the Americans had been on wider opportunities in the Far East as a whole rather than on the Philippines where, indeed, the superior credit the English merchants could provide and the growing Spanish protectionism of the late nineteenth century had reduced the relative importance of American entrepreneurs, if not of the American market. The hoisting of the flag changed the pattern of trade, making the U.S. overwhelmingly the greatest market for Philippines exports, and also the greatest source of imports. The tariff of 1909 admitted American products free of duty into the Philippines. The Payne-Aldrich Act established freedom for Philippines exports entering the U.S., with quotas for sugar and tobacco, which were in turn eliminated in the tariff of 1913. The government discouraged the formation of large-scale estates by American corporations, above all because of the apprehensions of the American sugar-beet industry. The result was that the vast expansion of exports that took place under the free trade system with the U.S. took place within the framework of existing social and economic patterns. If the new imperialism aimed at fostering political independence, it was bound to be qualified by economic dependence. If its objective was democracy, it was bound to be compromised by social inequality. The Filipinos were the first again to face problems that have more recently beset other 'under-developed' countries.

The *taos* had hoped for liberation, but the reverse had resulted. Under the impact of economic forces, the old *kasama* and *inquilinato* systems became more oppressive than ever, and these two forms of tenancy spread both in rice and cash-crop areas. The small cultivator was squeezed out. In Nueva Ecija, generally regarded as a province of small landowners, by 1936

201

10% of the landowners owned half the cultivated land. The population increase, spurred by American public health and sanitation measures, tended in the same direction, and so did the impact of the depression. In Laguna there were 236 persons per square mile in 1901 and 639 in 1939, and in Bulacan 191 and 562. Nor did American education policy do much to relieve the *tao* from conditions of extreme dependence and ignorance, though it raised the literacy rate to 49% by 1939. Instruction was now in English, a foreign tongue, and poverty permitted only 48% of schoolchildren to go beyond third grade and 3% to high school.

The popular movements among the *taos*, especially of Luzon, indicate generally not so much the penetration of new ideas, such as Communism, as the persistence of old. A Communist, Jacinto Manahan, organised the Tenants Union in 1919, which in 1924 became the National Union of Peasants in the Philippines. But the Communist Party founded in 1930 by Crisanto Evangelista, was, though Manahan was involved, an urban movement. It was put down in 1931, so that it was Pedro Abad Santos' Socialists who capitalised on the depression. But more significant among the *taos* were, on the one hand, the old religious ideas, with the revival of 'Colorum' sects, the heirs of Apollinario de la Cruz, associated as in his day with agrarian protest and, as his followers had done, mixing Christian and primitive superstition. On the other hand, there was a continued belief — in different circumstances — that independence would bring relief from oppression, held for instance by the obscure Ilokan field-labourer Pedro Kabola who founded the Kapisunan Makabola Makasinag in 1923: its object was to drive out the Americans and the *caciques* and share the land equally.

The most famous of the popular movements aiming at independence was the Sakdal ('Accuse') movement of the 1930s, led by Ramos, a petty officeholder who had fallen out with the ruling groups and sought to rally popular support in the depression. In 1931 he was advocating non-co-operation, borrowed from Gandhi. In 1933 he formed a political party, which did quite well in the elections of 1934. But the only chance it had of securing power was to seize it, and this was chaotically attempted, after Ramos had tried to obtain arms in Japan, early in 1935. The constabulary suppressed the resulting disorder, the bloodiest affair being at Cabuyao in Laguna, where 50 Sakdalistas were killed and four constabularymen. The timing of the revolt was significant. It was a protest at the establishment of the Philippines Commonwealth. For Ramos that meant the success of the major parties. For the *taos,* a *cacique* semi-independence. The fact was that the political programme of the Americans had, like the economic, tended to hand over power to the existing ruling classes. In this, however, there had been some divergence between Democrats and Republicans.

Among the early allies of the Americans were a group of upper-class Filipinos, headed by T. H. Pardo de Tavera, who in 1900 formed a Federal Party aiming at making the Philippines a state of the Union, and who were much patronised by the American Commissioner W. H. Taft. But, under the organic act of 1902, the President ordered the setting-up of a Philippines Assembly, an election to be held in 1907, and for this the Federals organised themselves into the Progresistas. A Nacionalista party also appeared, aiming more openly at independence, led by Sergio Osmena, a Chinese *mestizo* from Cebu, and by Manuel L. Quezon. It triumphed, securing over a third of the approximately 100,000 votes cast by an electorate restricted by property and literacy in English or Spanish. In subsequent elections the Nacionalistas only improved their position.

The Democrat victory in the States in 1912 brought in an administration devoted to early independence. Somewhat ambiguously, however, the Jones law of 1916 provided for independence when a stable government had been set up. A Senate was created, the franchise extended, the legislature's powers increased. The self-determination ideas of Wilson led in 1919 to a mission from the Philippines aimed at persuading him to set a date for independence. Meanwhile the Filipinization of the public services proceeded rapidly under the Democrat Governor-General F. B. Harrison, who gave exceptional latitude to the legislature in this and other matters, and set up a Council of State giving Osmena great influence. This provoked Quezon to organise a new party which triumphed in the elections of 1922. But that brought Quezon up against the Governor-General, now, as a result of the Democrats' defeat, a Republican, Leonard Wood.

Taft had declared in 1908 that 'we wish to prepare the Filipinos for *popular* self-government'. It was not Congress' purpose 'that we were merely to await the organisation of a Philippine oligarchy or aristocracy competent to administer the government and then turn the Islands over to it . . .' Early independence for the Philippines would 'subject the great mass of their people to the dominance of an oligarchical and, probably, exploiting minority'.[86] Wood at once inherited these ideas and also hoped to encourage more foreign investment in the Philippines. He clashed with Quezon over both. The Filipino leaders — here again anticipating contemporary ex-colonial régimes — feared too much foreign investment, and under Harrison the government had launched into business itself. And Quezon opposed Wood's 'Presidential' notions. Wood, on the other hand, had evidence for the oligarchical nature of government, for its caciquism on a national scale, and for its refusal to remedy effectively the grievances of the *taos*. But the chief effect of his programme was only to tie the Filipino leaders closer together: Quezon and Osmena made it up in 1924, and both co-operated with the Democrata opposition of men like Claro M. Recto in 1926. Furthermore the whole trend of American policy was against intervention of the Wood type, and it was hard to recur to earlier attitudes after Harrison. Even Wood's Republican successor, Stimson, receded from his programme, and restored a 'Cabinet' system which secured the triumph of the Nacionalistas, such a triumph that the Democratas dissolved in 1932. Wood had thus weakened the opposition elements in Philippines politics; and when his programme was abandoned the Nacionalistas were all the stronger for it. Just at this point, too, the Democrats were returning to power in the U.S. But the new Nacionalista triumph left room once more for the jealousy of Osmena and Quezon.

In some sense there are here a number of paradoxes. Spanish policy was paradoxical: it opened the Philippines to foreign trade and influences, but sought to maintain their political dependence on Spain. On the other hand, American policy was early dedicated to self-government, while its tariff policy tied the economy closer to that of the United States. Within that self-government policy lay a further paradox. The trend of both Spanish and American rule was to preserve and enhance the power of a native landowning oligarchy. Under independence, therefore, the *caciques* might expect to rule uninhibited. Wood sought, as it were, to play off this paradox against the other: a delaying action would be accompanied by greater economic investment. The Democrats produced yet a further paradox that clinched the revulsion against this programme. Not all American interests saw the Philippines in the same way, and the depression strengthened apprehensions among the sugar-beet interests concerned at Philippines competition. Cadiz and Seville had once been jealous of Manila and urged the abandonment of the Philippines. And now in the U.S. economic and political interests seemed to coincide. The 72nd Congress, which had a Democrat House and equality in the Senate, passed the Hare-

Hawes-Cutting Act envisaging early independence. The Democrats' ideals were thus realised — paradoxically — because of a minor and probably misguided economic interest. Not to be outdone, the Filipinos produced a paradox. The Act had also resulted from a mission to Washington led by Osmena and his aide Roxas. Quezon thus opposed certain of its provisions and killed the proposals his rival brought back. He then headed a new mission, with his aide Quirino, and obtained the Tydings-McDuffie Act, which eliminated the provision for permanent American naval bases after independence, to follow in ten years. Fortified with this Quezon was able to win the 1934 election triumphantly. A convention drew up a constitution for the interim Commonwealth, and this was submitted to the people in 1935, in a referendum in which non-Christians voted for the first time. Later that year Quezon, Aglipay, and the indestructible Aguinaldo (he died, aged 94, in 1963) stood for the Presidency. Quezon triumphed. Osmena became Vice-President. About one million had voted out of a population of thirteen millions.

If some paradoxes were resolved, others remained. The economy continued thoroughly dependent, even if political independence was in prospect, and the rate at which the U.S. tariff on Philippines goods — hitherto protected and inefficiently produced — was under the Tydings-McDuffie Act to increase after independence was slowed down in a later law of 1939 as the depression receded from America. The existence of Filipino democracy was also qualified by the economic dependence of the masses and the cliquism of the *caciques*. The new Quezon administration attempted to tackle the agrarian problems lest they impeded the attainment of full independence. An act to regulate rice share tenancies of 1933 had been inoperative. A Social Justice Programme of 1935 achieved little more. In 1937 the government began to purchase large estates where tenant-landlord relations were bad. But it had little money at its disposal and so had the tenants. Another programme aimed at fostering migration to Mindanao: by 1941 some 16,000 families had arrived to meet the opposition of the *datus* and the malarial mosquitoes. All this did something to dampen disorder and preserve the *status quo*. So did the popular front policy of the Communists, pardoned by Quezon in 1938, and combining with the Socialists to form a new party. The Philippines were meeting various problems that other new nations were to meet — the problem of securing effective independence — the problem of creating popular government — the problem of maintaining security — and the problem of promoting economic development.

The Chinese community was regarded as another problem. The nationalists inherited something of the ambivalent attitude of the Spaniards on this topic, even though some of them were Chinese *mestizos* in origin. The Spaniards had welcomed the contribution of the Chinese to economic development, but were apprehensive lest they gained too great an influence. Nevertheless the nineteenth century had given them great opportunities in the Philippines, though they still numbered only 40,000 in 1900. The changes at the end of the century there as elsewhere checked the growth of assimilation, and Chinese nationalism found a fertile soil. On the other hand, the Filipino leaders became more apprehensive of them, and opposed the encouraging of Chinese immigration that some American interests sought. In fact the U.S. exclusion laws were applied, though in such a way that the Chinese in 1939 numbered over 117,000. They moreover dominated retail trade and agricultural credit. The question therefore was whether they would form a butt for political nationalism, or whether their enterprise and capital would be turned to account. Again the Philippines faced a problem that other ex-colonies were to face.

The comparison with neighbouring countries is perhaps more interesting to the historian than it was at the time. The early Philippine revolutionaries had sounded a wider appeal in vain. Since then, the Philippines had come under a new colonial system — if one with a difference — while the nationalist movements emerging in other countries had gone their various ways. The effects of colonial separateness were to last into the period of independence, but the Japanese invasion inaugurated a new phase of common experience. Here, again, the Filipinos had made early contacts. Ramos, too, had gone to Japan. There he had consulted Artemio Ricarte, a nationalist of the old vintage whom the Americans had deported and who had become a restaurateur in Yokohama. He was to come back with the Japanese invaders. And here was the final American paradox. The Philippines had been founded as an outpost in the Far East, but despite the increase of American power, they had ceased to be so. The outpost was Honolulu. The Philippines was virtually undefended. The way was open for the redistribution of power in the Far East, and independence was to come from the Japanese.

5 The Andaman and Nicobar Islands

In this period the course of development in the Andamans and Nicobars became even more divergent. The Andaman islanders had enjoyed less commercial contact with the Malay world, and the slave-raiders of Burma and the Peninsula contributed to a distrust of foreigners, in evidence whenever ships were wrecked on their coasts, illustrated again in the hostile relations with the convict settlement at Port Blair that culminated in the attack of May 1859. The subsequent attempts to improve relations with the islanders were successful except in the case of the Jarawa tribes, but contact with the outside world brought them vice and disease and hopelessness and the decimation of their numbers from about 4,800 in 1858 to a little over 600 in 1931. Nevertheless a contemporary writer thought the government had 'tended and petted' them in its attempt to avoid the extinction that the related Tasmanians had suffered.[87]

The development of the Andamans thus depended on the government and its convicts, and it took place mainly in the region of Port Blair. On the one hand, the government sought to exploit the timber resources of the islands, and a Forest Department was set up in 1883: it also established plantations of tea, coffee, coconuts, and later rubber. On the other hand, in order to reduce dependence on outside sources of foodstuffs, the convicts were given tickets-of-leave and encouraged to clear land. Often, however, they had no agricultural experience, and they had no security of tenure, and thus, while earlier hopes of mineral resources were apparently disappointed, agricultural development was restricted. In 1921 the Indian Government declared that its object was gradually to transform Port Blair from a convict settlement into a colony. Better tenancy conditions were granted and the ten years' probation as a labouring convict was abolished. Convicts were allowed to return to fetch their families. Most did not succeed in this, but the measures contributed to the creation of a homogeneous Andaman Indian community out of heterogeneous Indian antecedents. They did little, however, to promote agricultural development, since this community increasingly sought official employment, while some of the government plantations proved uneconomic. One of the last major groups of convicts to arrive — the Mapillas from the Malabar rebellion of 1921 — was more agriculturally oriented, though, like the Bhantus, a criminal tribe from central India, it kept apart from the main community. So did the Burman convicts, and also the Karen free settlers who came to the Middle Andaman from 1925. Overall the total population increased and the sex-ratio improved. In 1941 there were 14,872 males and 6,444 females.

By contrast to the Andamanese — save for the primitive people of the mountains of Great Nicobar — the indigenous Nicobarese increased in number, and their economy, substantially based on the coconut, flourished. In Chowra and Car Nicobar, most prosperous of the islands, and enjoying a large share of their exports, the population became relatively dense. And the role of the government was as slight as in the Andamans it was great. The Chief Commissioner of the Andamans and Nicobars simply sent two agents, usually Indians, to Car Nicobar and Nancowry, whose main duty was to keep the peace between the natives and visiting Burmese and Indian traders. The dichotomy between the Nicobars and Andamans was also to guide post-war policy. But the islands meanwhile had a part to play in the Japanese adventure.

6 Burma

IN BURMA, as elsewhere in Southeast Asia, the new economic forces of the nineteenth century made their impact in diverse political and administrative circumstances. On the one hand, the Burman kingdom had been re-created only after the middle of the eighteenth century, its control over Lower Burma and

Arakan was relatively recent, and in the hill regions and the Shan states there were peoples never assimilated by the Burmans. On the other hand, the British displaced the Burman kingdom piecemeal, and as an aspect of imperial expansion in India.

The traditional Burman administrative system had rested upon the *myothugyis* or hereditary township leaders. Even prior to 1825, however, they had in Lower Burma been largely supplanted by officials appointed by the re-established kings, the *taikthugyis,* who controlled 'circles' of villages. The British administration in Tenasserim, but still more than in Arakan, which was more under Bengal control, tended further to emphasise the appointive nature of the Burman officials they used. On the annexation of Pegu, many Burman *myothugyis* withdrew, while Mon *myothugyis* were few in number, and so the hereditary office virtually disappeared. The British Commissioners and Deputy Commissioners utilised *taikthugyis* and *gaungs* or police officers at the circle level and at the village level after 1876 the *kyedangyi,* or largest taxpayer, became a man of all work, undertaking a thankless task without enjoying traditional prestige.

It was after creating this administration in Lower Burma that the British annexed Upper Burma. There the *myothugyis* had been a much more genuine social force. Many, however, engaged in resistance or later were involved in rebellion. The British, too, had no understanding of the genuine *myothugyi* system. Commissioner Crosthwaite, drawing also on his Indian experience, argued that the *myothugyis* were usurpers of village power, and in 1888 it was decided that the Deputy Commissioners should designate a headman or *thugyi* for each of Burma's 17,000 or 18,000 villages. The *thugyis* should be influential citizens, vested with the powers of tax collectors, police officers, and petty magistrates, and responsible for roads, sanitation, and so forth. The system was consolidated by the Village Act of 1907. The new local administration was not built upon the old — as for instance, the Dutch pretended theirs was in Java — and so it had an especially dissolving effect upon the fabric of social life, even apart from the impact of new economic forces at work. The rapid development of bureaucratic agencies, especially about the turn of the century, partially in response to these forces, marked a further departure from personalised authority on the traditional pattern. It was hard for the mass of the people to comprehend or appreciate the government's activities even if of a philanthropic nature. This promoted social malaise, and the effect of economic change on agrarian

209

society was amplified by the introduction of a civil law which was adapted to deal with the more complex situation in India, and which became in Burma a source of bewilderment to the people, of opportunity to swindlers, and of employment to professional lawyers.

Before 1825 the economic development of Lower Burma was hampered by the prohibition of the export of rice favoured by the Konbaung kings. It was a thinly populated area that might be transformed by a more liberal policy, by the migration of skilled wet-rice cultivators from relatively crowded central Burma, by the building of bunds to prevent flooding, and by the opening-up of markets in Europe, in India and in Southeast Asia. All these factors were present, especially after 1852, and by 1900 rice, predominantly from Lower Burma, formed 85% of Burma's greatly increased exports, much of it going to India. The boom in the Irrawaddy delta produced there an untraditional society, with wage labour, a money economy, with individualism, without old social sanctions; a society also burdened by indebtedness, usury, foreclosure, which the Indian Cooperative Societies Act of 1904 could do little to remedy.

In Upper Burma change was slower and older patterns stronger. But improved communications brought it into ever closer touch with the outside world, better use of the traditional means, the rivers, introduction of new means, the railways, fostered by an Indian Government that had realised after the Mutiny their political as well as economic importance. By 1889 the permanent way had reached from Rangoon to Mandalay and by 1902 to Lashio. Upper Burma proved valuable by the turn of the century, not as anticipated as a route to China, or for its rubies, but on account of its oil, exploited by the Burmah Oil Company, and of other minerals like tungsten and silver-lead. World War I brought quicker change in Upper Burma, for the shipping shortage brought on a crisis for Lower Burma rice-growing, and induced a reverse migration to the north, and the oil-wells attracted a greater investment. The expansion of the population of Burma, promoted in part by better communications and economic development, was dramatic, though less dramatic than in Java, where special Dutch policies were so influential: the rise between 1872 and 1901 over the whole area was roughly from 7m to 10m.

Not all the expansion was indigenous. The Burmans could take ready advantage of new opportunities in traditional occupations like rice cultivation. In other fields they were ill-equipped or disinclined and there were, furthermore, others ready to seize the chance. Burma had come under British rule when British rule was well-established in India, and it was a rule exercised from India. These factors, as well as their proximity, gave the Indians advantages in Burma. Government departments and European firms found it preferable to employ as clerks and coolies Indian immigrants more accustomed to their ways, and the Oil Company was exceptional in using largely Burmese labour. Indian Chettyar moneylenders, accustomed to the methods of British banking, replaced the few, but rapacious, Burmese moneylenders in the delta after the 1870s. Indians came to predominate in retail trade and formed a large section of the urban population. In Rangoon they provided factory and wharf labour. By 1931, when the total population had reached nearly 15m, the Indians numbered just over 1m. Their numbers, their powerful economic position, their transitory character, the appearance of exploitation, their impact on all sections of the population, were to contribute to the problems of communalism that complicated the rise of Burmese nationalism.

In Burma, as elsewhere in Southeast Asia, there were Chinese, but the Indians had distance and other advantages in their favour. The Chinese, numbering some 194,000 in 1931, were mainly traders and artisans, with a few miners in the Tavoy region. On the one hand, there were those who came in from the south, mostly in this period, and fanned out from Rangoon along the railway and steamer lines; and, on the other, there were the Mountain Chinese, about 60,000 in 1931, living in the Shan and Wa states along the Chinese border. The Chinese attracted less attention than the Indians, though there were anti-Chinese riots in 1931. The community in Burma, too, was not overlooked in the promotion of overseas Chinese nationalism and education was regarded as an important instrument of nationalist policy. In 1935 there were 12,707 Chinese children between five and ten years old: 837 were in the four Anglo-Chinese schools and 2,965 in 65 unrecognised Chinese schools.

Lower Burma officials had from the late 1860s tried to integrate the better Buddhist monastic schools into a general programme of secular education. Because of the failure of many monks or *pongyis* to co-operate, more emphasis was later laid on lay schools, but the number of government schools remained few and they were poorly attended. Primary education was seen largely as a gateway to secondary education — where some of the best schools were operated by Christian missionaries — and thus to a job. The competition at that level — with the restricted number of posts available to Burmans, and the preference for

Indians or Europeans with technical, commercial or industrial qualifications — pressed those with the cash and the brains to go on to university training, provided at Rangoon after 1920. In law there was scope for trained Burmans, but most of the Burman undergraduates took arts courses. In these ways a new educated élite was created — sons of headmen, sons of prosperous individuals, sons of the enterprising like Nu's father, a small-town trader in the delta. They sought opportunity and increasingly found an outlet in leading a nationalist movement that united modern European ideas of various genres with traditions of a not distant Burman past.

The example of Indonesia suggests the significance of religion in relation to the rise of nationalism. Buddhism had indeed been one of the pillars of the old kingdom, and the king had his place as the protector of Buddhism. In the British period discipline within the monastic order or *Sangha* decayed, above all as a result of the government's unwillingness to appoint a primate or *thathanabaing*, and the resulting disorder added to the general social malaise. Buddhism at the same time remained the faith of the people and the *Sangha* continued to enjoy popular respect. Indeed attachment to it was a symbol of that popular protest against change, against the impact of alien forces, which was expressed in Indonesia by mass adhesion to Tjokroaminoto and the Sarekat Islam and in the Philippines by the mystique attached popularly to independence. Buddhism had provided a background for much of the resistance to British rule, for instance the rebellion in the Arakan and Tenasserim divisions in the 1830s and the disturbances after the victories of 1852 and 1886. 'The last important expression of the traditional type of Burmese nationalism was the attempt made by an ex-*pongyi* charlatan named Saya San in 1930-1 to throw out alien British rule and to re-establish a Buddhist-oriented court.'[88] In that movement there was a mixture of superstition and ideas of a golden past that may be common among 'primitive rebels'. But by this time a new nationalism was making contact with Buddhism, with the *Sangha*, and with the masses.

The new educated élite was divided from the old religious leadership by no such gulf as the Javanese élite faced as a result of its traditions and of Dutch policy, and no externally-inspired modernist movement competed with it. Instead the western-educated minority in Burma took the lead in attempts to re-vitalise and modernise Buddhism. In the late 1890s educated lay Burman leaders in the Moulmein region — long under British rule — thus began to sponsor non-clerical Buddhist schools which adopted a curriculum comparable to that of the mission schools. In 1906, stimulated perhaps by the excitement brought about by the success of the Japanese, educated Burmans founded the Young Men's Buddhist Association in imitation of the Y.M.C.A. There remained differences between the westernised intelligentsia — even if it was not divorced from Buddhism, and indeed often sought its reform — and the old-fashioned *Sangha*. And it was the *pongyis* who retained the allegiance of the masses.

Buddhism, an element of unity in the old kingdom, was in some sense an element of unity in the new nationalist movement. It had also a divisive force, and new religious dichotomies that had been created were thrown into relief by its revival. The Karens, never assimilated by Burmans or Buddhism, were liberated by British conquest from handicaps suffered under royal rule. The American Baptist Mission, established by Judson in 1813, enjoyed wider opportunities among them. The significance of these developments was illustrated, for instance, by the formation in 1881 of a Karen National Association in which the Christian Karens played an important part. Furthermore, the Karens now at last moved into the plains and they developed fairly extensive riceland holdings in the heart of the delta. Many of them were used in the military police and the army, and so, in British Indian style, were other hill peoples, for instance the Chins and Kachins. For the latter, who lived in the northern Shan states, a special political officer was appointed in November 1893. But the Chin tribesmen, west of the Chindwin river, were themselves not subdued till 1895. Such were the boundaries, such the peoples of British Burma: the notion of it as a nation-state was bound to provoke communal tension.

The complications of the communal issue were illustrated when the ideological ferment of the first world war spread to Burma as a result of the Secretary of State's announcement in August 1917 that the British aimed to develop self-government in India. Of India Burma was a part, and here were new opportunities for the Burman nationalists. In the following decades they were to shift between association with India in the struggle against the British and apprehensions of Indian social and economic domination, alternatives which different sections of the nationalists tended to weigh differently. The Congress movement was to provide a framework for the Burman challenge to British rule, and its methods of strike and boycott were to be imitated. But there was no close link with it. The initial moves were also significant. In December 1917 the Y.M.B.A. sent a delegation to Calcutta, pressing for separation from India, and then a separate settlement over the future of Burma. At the same time a Karen memorial pleaded for the continuance of British control.

As a result the Governor of Burma recommended increased self-government at the district level on the pattern of developments in India since 1882; and a majority of elected representatives on the Legislative Council, which had been predominantly a nominated and non-Burman body since its creation in 1897, despite the Morley-Minto reforms in India. But the Y.M.B.A. became alarmed lest separation should mean less advance than in India, and as a result of its pressure the Secretary of State agreed that he would include Burma in the 'dyarchy' proposals of India after an enquiry. During the delay the Y.M.B.A. organised a mass protest against the University Act of 1920: it seemed to envisage such high standards that it was suspected that the British object was so to restrict the number of the educated that Burma could never govern itself. Early in 1921 a boycott spread to government and some aided schools and national schools were founded. These developments imparted a new intensity to Burman nationalism, and the General Council of Burmese Associations, as the council of the Y.M.B.A. now called itself, boycotted the dyarchy enquiry of 1921. In 1923 dyarchy was introduced, though by now it was regarded by most nationalists as quite inadequate. It provided for a legislature of 103, with 79 members elected on a household suffrage, 58 of them Burman, and two Burmese ministers, responsible for 'transferred' activities, education, local government, public works, medicine, co-operation, forests. The system was indeed not likely to foster responsible parliamentary government. The ministers had no control of finance, and in order to carry a policy, they needed the support of almost all the Burman members, or else the support of other groups — business or communal representatives who might exploit their special position. Furthermore, the Shan states, federated the previous year, the Chin and Kachin areas, and the Wa and Naga hills, were all excluded from ministerial Burma.

In the struggle over education that thus created a new context for dyarchy, when at last it came, the *pongyis* had played an important part, stimulated by U Ottama, a mock monk who returned from India in 1921. He insisted that Buddhism was threatened by an alien government, combined this with non-co-operation, and so built a mass movement. His followers gained control over many of the local nationalist organisations or *athins* formed by the G.C.B.A. Indeed the influence of the *pongyis* at village level had been increased by the relative nullity of the non-traditional headmen. Thus those even of the westernised intelligentsia who wanted mass backing needed to co-operate with the less westernised *pongyis* — often like Ottama not true monks but frustrated men of ambition — and obtain it on the basis of extremist opposition to alien rule. In August 1924 Ottama precipitated a riot at Mandalay, and disaffection was widespread in 1924-5. But the turbulence of the period, unlike that in Indonesia, appears to have owed nothing to world Communism, perhaps because there was in Burma no local European working-class to transmit it, while the Comintern and the British Communist party concentrated on India.

The disturbances produced a split in the G.C.B.A., and some broke away to enter the Legislative Council through the 1925 election, including Ba Maw, a lawyer. But the scope for effectively dealing with grievances there was not such as to provide convincing arguments against those who regarded the whole alien constitutional structure with hostility. There was a cleavage between the representatives of European business and the Burman members, and between them and the communally-selected non-Burman group. Little constructive legislation was passed. The local boards and councils, established under the Rural Self-Government Act of 1921, were also viewed with apathy and became very corrupt. From them, by contrast to the councils in Java, the village headmen were initially excluded. This only further weakened their influence, and added to the unrest aroused by falling prices in the late 1920s and by the collapse of co-operatives during the depression.

The arrival of the Simon Commission in 1929 — its object being to review the working of dyarchy — produced meanwhile a new political orientation in Burma. A 'Burma for the Burmans League' advocated separation from India and curtailment of Indian immigration. This was above all a secular group, a Rangoon intelligentsia — vernacular editors, minor officials, and so on — aiming at freedom from *pongyi* domination. But mass backing lay with the *pongyis* and their associates, immediately less affected by Indian competition for official posts, and able to advocate non-separation and co-operation with the Congress in fighting for an autonomy which it was alleged the British wished to deny. The Commission was thus widely boycotted, and it reported in favour of early separation, with guarantees of the status of the new government.

The depression brought considerable violence in 1930, predominantly anti-foreign and mostly in Lower Burma. Late in the year the Saya San rebellion, organised by *pongyis*, broke out in the Tharrawaddy district, and early in 1931 it spread into other districts and up-river, though not into Upper Burma. British and Indian troops, aided by Karen volunteers, suppressed the largest rebel groups by early 1932. The effects on the westernised leadership were various. Ba Maw and U Saw made themselves prominent by undertaking the legal defence of the rebels. Another faction, that of U Chit Hlaing, on the other hand, was led to enter the Legislative Council, repeating a political trend that had ensued upon the disturbances of the mid-1920s. Most influential now were those among the elected councillors who stayed on good terms with the *pongyis*.

Meanwhile the Burma Round Table Conference had been held. At this the Burmans pressed for full self-government, the Karens for a federal Burma, with Karen, Shan, Kachin and Chin states. In a special report the Arakanese leaders also sought safeguards of their identity or a state of their own. Early in 1932 Ramsay Macdonald, the British premier, declared for an election on the issue of separation. In the ensuing campaign, an Anti-Separation League was formed out of the boycotting G.C.B.A. groups and the supporters of Ba Maw, and it made the most of popular suspicion of the British. The Separationists, on the other hand, tried to arouse popular hostility to Indian labourers and money-lenders. Not surprisingly, though, the Anti-Separationists triumphed. Once elected, however, some of them (though not Ba Maw) quailed before the prospect of participating in the proposed Indian Federation, and no clear decision emerged from the Legislative Council. The British Parliament thus introduced separation, and despite Burman apprehensions the new constitution, approved in 1935 and operative in 1937, discarded dyarchy, though not ministerial Burma, and provided more scope for real parliamentary government. In the new Council, in elections to which one-third of the male population and one-tenth of the female were qualified to vote, a Burman minister, depending on a Burman majority, now needed 67 out of 95 Burman seats. Minorities and other groups filled the remaining 37.

The 1936 elections gave three seats to a new faction, the Thakins. In 1931 the All Burma Youth League had been founded, aiming at reviving the national school organisation of the early 1920s and extending its contacts with non-national schools. Associated was an élite student group, who called themselves 'Thakins' (compare 'Sahibs') as an affirmation of their nationalism. Their inspiration was fluid, a compound of Sun Yat-sen, Sinn Fein, Nietzche, Upton Sinclair, and Palme Dutt; there were some Marxists among them, like Soe, Than Tun, and Thein Pe, drawing their Communism from Indian sources. The younger and more radical Thakins distrusted the old lawyer politicians and their reliance on xenophobic *pongyi*-led mass support. They found some support among the University-educated. At the University indeed the hopes and frustrations of the élite were at their tensest — particularly among those who might just not make the grade, and particularly at examination times. One effect of the resulting clash with the University authorities was the strike of February 1936, led by Nu, President of the Union, Aung San, editor of the student newspaper, and Kyaw Nyein. After it Nu and Aung San joined the Thakins. The Thakins also sought to work among labour groups, mostly in fact Indian. Their success in the 1936 elections was slight. Their opportunity was to come.

The new constitution meanwhile offered some possibility of carrying through constructive legislation that might at last alleviate popular distrust of the British constitutional experiments: Burma enjoyed more autonomy than any other Southeast Asian dependency, with the exception of the Philippines. But parliamentary life was harmed by factionalism and the lack of a dissolution system gave it great scope. Ba Maw managed to initiate legislation to benefit the agriculturist, such as the Tenancy Act. But his rival, U Saw, was able to use the anti-Indian riots of the previous year to embarrass him and finally bring about his fall. In the succeeding U Pu ministry U Saw was the strong man, enjoying mass support from the All-Burma Pongyis Council. With the opening of the war in Europe, his rivals Ba Maw and the Thakins urged a demand for early independence. Finally U Saw late in 1941 went to England to secure a promise of post-war Dominion status. No such promise was given, and on his way back he was found to be in touch with the Japanese. But some of the Thakins — such as Aung San and Ne Win — had already made contact with them, and late in 1941 a cadre for the Burma Independence Army which was to enter Burma with the Japanese in 1942 was formed in Bangkok.

The approach of the war and then of the Japanese thus dislocated constitutional development, and the invasion produced a situation of which Ba Maw and above all the Thakins were to take advantage. They secured a prominence and an opportunity for mobilising opinion that had hitherto eluded them. The earlier British experiments in constitutional government had taken place in a context of great social change: an élite largely not of traditional origin had sought to mobilise support on a popular basis; but that support was so xenophobic that participation in those experiments became contradictory. The young Thakins sought to break away from this paradox with little immediate success. But if the constitution of 1937 offered some scope for a new sort of politics, and for more effective popular integration into it, the long-term prospects were interrupted by changes in the world at large. The Thakins secured an unlooked-for opportunity. The question was whether they could secure popular support and whether their cohesion would survive the tensions involved in securing popular support in the future. And there was a new military element among them.

7 Siam

IN A NUMBER of the Southeast Asian countries most open to economic and political change in this period, social change had in some respects been peculiarly limited. These limits are still more apparent, perhaps, in Siam, which contrived to maintain political independence by admitting — in the Bowring treaty of 1855 and subsequent imitations — extraterritorial jurisdiction and restrictions on customs duties and by making territorial concessions in Cambodia, Laos, and the Peninsula. Siam did not undergo the changes elsewhere involved in the establishment of European administration. The continuance of indigenous government also affected the impact of economic forces.

It is true that one means of ensuring independence was found paradoxically in the Europeanisation of the administration. This began moderately with Mongkut, who employed some Europeans, but intensified with his successor Chulalongkorn, who began his reign with visits to Malaya, Java, Burma, and India, and subsequently took on some British Indian civil servants. The nobility, princes and innumerable royal children began to receive a modern education. In 1871 some were sent to Singapore, some to England, and subsequently an English School for the Offspring of Princes and Nobility was set up in the Royal Palace itself.

It was only, however, in the 1880s and 1890s, with the growing threat to Siam's independence, that really effective steps were taken to displace the old system of provincial administration, whereby power tended to be localised among particular families who became more or less hereditary in their office of tax-collectors and corvée-requisitioners. Prince Damrong visited Burma in 1889-90 and after 1894 as Minister of the Interior reorganised the provincial administration. The kingdom was divided into a number of circles or *monthon* each consisting of a number of provinces or *muang*, in turn broken into districts or *ampur* and then into villages or *tambol* where headmen were given a recognised position. The lords lieutenant were appointed by the Ministry, the governors of the provinces were salaried, the headmen exempted from tax. Corvée, as well as slavery, was discarded by the turn of the century, and the head tax of 1901 replaced it. The new officials required were to be trained in the Civil Servant School founded in 1899, which became the Chulalongkorn University in 1916. Chulalongkorn had written to Damrong: 'Foreign powers are attempting to claim our tributaries, and if we neglect to reorganise our administration in the provinces we might lose our independence. This is the mission for the Ministry of the Interior.'

Equally, as the setting-up of this Ministry suggests, the central government was reorganised. The aim again was greater efficiency, so as to ensure the preservation of independence. For this money was required. The policy was to avoid extensive foreign loans, lest this prejudiced independence: efficient collection of the revenue was extra necessary. A Revenue Office, set up in 1873, grew in 1887 into the Ministry of Finance. The old system of tax-farming disappeared and under the new local system taxes were to be collected directly. The attempt to increase the revenue was indeed obstructed by the restrictions prescribed in the treaties of the Bowring period. Most of these were finally lifted by 1928. In making concessions the Americans had taken a lead: they had less to lose than the British traders who had a dominant position, more to hope for, less to defend. And Francis B. Sayre, Wilson's son-in-law, had been a Foreign Affairs Adviser.

It was indeed characteristic -- and reminiscent of the days of Narai — that advisers, whose employment in major positions

219

became general from the 1890s, were now chosen from a number of different countries. Thus, in the Europeanisation of the judicial administration, undertaken with a view to negotiating the end of the extraterritorial system and its impediments to Thai autonomy, the services of the Belgian Rolin Jacquemins and other French and Belgian jurists were called upon. Certain concessions over extraterritoriality had been made by France and England in the treaties of 1907 and 1909, but again America took the post-war lead. Meanwhile various codes were issued in Siam — the first was the criminal code of 1908 — and by the late 1930s the end of the system had been negotiated.

In the creation of a Thai state sufficiently Europeanised to remain autonomous, the creation of an army played an important part. The Royal Guard of 1870 was its nucleus. Specialised military corps followed — placed in 1886 under a Military Affairs Department — and a military cadet school was opened. By the early twentieth century, these forces, with the navy, had been brought under a new Defence Ministry. In 1904 conscription was adopted.

The determination to maintain independence also promoted the construction of railways. The French advance of the 1890s, for instance, led to the beginning of a railway to Korat, part of the old Vienchang territories whose riverine connexions were rather with the Mekong than the Menam. Essentially, indeed, Bangkok's command over the Menam basin, the core of the Thai territories, was a guarantee of their independence. The reforms of the period strengthened that command. They also strengthened the traditional rulers of the country. The royal autocracy was now less limited in practice and its theory more perfectly realised. The princes and royal scions, educated in the palace schools, maintained their privileged position, and the supreme posts were filled by able princes like Damrong and Devawong.

There were, however, limited changes that may in some respects compare with those under colonial régimes. A number of officials emerged from other origins. They were often trained overseas — in various countries — at the expense of the state or of the princes, though there were never more than 300 abroad in any one year. Like those from colonial territories trained abroad, they were most radical when abroad, especially in this case those in France. But if this was the Thai equivalent of a revolutionary intelligentsia, it was a mild version of it. The revolution that overthrew the absolute monarchy in 1932 was in a sense a revolt within the bureacracy against princely predominance. And, as a further distinction, the military, with leaders educated in Germany and France, played and continued to play an important role, a factor that had not yet significantly emerged in the colonial areas of Southeast Asia.

Indeed the army was in a sense the spearhead of revolution. The autocracy first aroused discontent when Chulalongkorn's successor, Wachirawut, began to use in his own way its increased power. Thus he set up his own guards — the Wild Tiger Corps — and this provoked the army plot of 1912 and the demand for a constitution. A second conspiracy occurred in 1917, partly caused by resentment among the German-trained officers at the pro-Ally policy the government followed, with a view to avoiding the risk of an Anglo-French protectorate to exclude the Germans and to ensuring a better position for the revision of treaties (war was declared and 1,000 volunteers sent to France). Wachirawut's successor, Prachathipok, the 76th child of Chulalongkorn, rid himself of favourites, but swung back to greater reliance on the princes. This, and the retrenchments and extra taxes imposed after the onset of the depression, alienated both military and lesser civil servants. The king's talk of a constitution after his return from the United States in 1931 probably only fomented the discontent that culminated in the revolution — or coup — of June 1932. Prachathipok promptly conceded a constitutional monarchy, avoiding, as he said, the risk of foreign intervention. Resentment was indeed directed against the princes, not against the monarchy.

The nature of this coup, and the subsequent course of Thai history, cannot be understood without further reference to the economic movements of the previous period, refined in their impact by the nature of the régime. Their major effect in the later nineteenth century, coupled with that of the Bowring treaty, which put an end to the traditional embargo, was to stimulate the export of rice, and this was something the Thai peasant could produce without technological change by more extended cultivation of the land. Rice exports represented 60-70% of the total in the century after 1850: there was a slow erratic rise to the 1870s, and then a steady increase. Most of the rice came initially from the centre, then in the twentieth century more from the north-east. At the same time the population itself increased, from perhaps 5 or 6m in 1850 to 7.3m in 1900 and 17.3m by 1947. The relative emptiness of the country was a mediating factor, but so was the policy of the government. In making the foreign treaties it resisted abandoning all limits on alien enterprise. It was able also to pursue the basically traditional policy of maintaining a taxable peasantry.

221

The law was that a man could take such land as he could cultivate (limited to 50 *rai* in 1936). This prevented the growth of large landowners. There were fewer tenancy troubles than in delta Burma: absentee landlordism was significant only in parts of the centre and round Chiengmai.

All this contributed to the social and political stability of the régime: if there was no call for 'independence', nor was there a social crisis to give one popular backing. Even in the depression there was no social crisis. The economy had a wide subsistence basis and the peasants could still eat well. Furthermore, mild tariff protection, possible especially after treaty revision had been completed, had preserved some household industries, so that the inability to pay for imports was not a disaster. Bangkok, from its dominating position, was able in fact to regulate the impact of outside economic forces on Siam, just as it had earlier imposed commercial monopolies and put an embargo on rice. It was clear that the revolution could not be a popular revolt. Such, indeed, had never occurred in Siam.

The other side of the coin was that there was little stimulus to genuine economic or social advancement. Here again government policy played a part. It was financially conservative: if in colonial countries investment might be limited according to the purposes of the metropolitan power, in Siam it was limited as a guarantee of independence. But that weakened the economic and social bases of future progress. The monarchy, indeed, constructed a railway system, joined in 1921-2 to the Malayan system, but it was designed above all to promote political unification, and no roads were constructed that might compete with it. Many other public works, for instance irrigation projects, were also put off. Above all the conservative financial policy restricted the expansion of education. A Department of Public Instruction was organised in 1885 and a Ministry in 1891-2. But the construction of government schools was limited and many were set up in temple grounds — in fact assuring the continued influence of the Buddhist monks over the young, and in yet another way preserving a pillar of society.

This situation helped to characterise the revolution and to determine its course. The People's Party assumed power, but in the circumstances it did not in any way represent the people, nor was it a party. The revolution was a Bangkok coup, and it brought to power in that commanding capital, firstly, a new element in the bureaucracy, often highly educated overseas, though still embedded in the enduring traditions of patronage and deference to superiors; and, secondly, army officers, more powerful because the old traditions there coincided more exactly with the unequivocal hierarchy of a modern army, and because they had nothing else to do (the army was never in the event called on to defend the nation). And then there was the mass of the people, never politically enlivened by a struggle against colonialism, ill-fitted to take part in the measures of constitutional and democratic government now envisaged. In some ways Siam now compared more closely with other Southeast Asian countries. The comparison belongs still more to their post-colonial phase, when the élite, military and civilian, had to contend with demographic and developmental problems, and with its own divisions. But the Thai élite at least faced these problems with no post-colonial complex.

Among the leading revolutionaries or 'Promoters' were, on the civilian side, Nai Pridi Panomyong, who had been born into a family of some means, had studied law in France — where the princely Thai ambassador declared him a 'Red' — and had taught at Chulalongkorn, and, on the military side, Phya Bahol Balabayuha, who as an army cadet had been trained in Germany. The first premier, however, was Phya Manopakam, who had been Chief Judge of the Appeal Court. A conservative, he fell out with Pridi, who, during the depression in 1933, promulgated an economic plan, whereby the Bangkok government would turn the peasants into salaried workers and make itself chief dealer in rice and purveyor of goods. The plan, it may be thought, in some ways reflected Thai traditions, but it was characterised as 'Communist'. The resulting divisions among the civilians gave the military elements their chance, and the precedent of a successful coup was inviting. Thus in June 1933 Phya Bahol arrested Phya Mano and assumed the premiership. Possibly a royal revival of power was apprehended. In any case, the coup was followed by a military rebellion under prince Bavoradej. Its defeat, on the one hand, helped to bring about the abdication of the king, and, on the other, brought into prominence Luang Pibul Songgram, a French-trained soldier of quite humble origins, who was in turn to assume the premiership in 1938.

The growing military rule did not mean that the forms of democracy were neglected. In 1933 the Assembly, hitherto appointed by the Promoters, became half elected (partly indirectly, as in some colonial régimes), and a reorganisation of local government, including the abolition of the *monthon* system and the division of the kingdom into 70 *changwats,* was followed by provision for similar semi-elective provincial bodies. But in all this there were little democracy, much apathy, inefficiency and corruption, and plans to abolish the new system of local government were put off only by the entrenchment in it of prominent politicians. There was in fact no middle-class to enliven this system or develop it effectively. Power remained with the Promoters, especially the military element. In 1937, 53 of the 78 appointed members of the Assembly itself were military and 8 of the 78 elected. The government of the country had once reflected the cohesion of royal and princely families: now it reflected that of the army leaders and their followers. The new régime indeed aimed to expand education, and in 1935 a Primary Education Act was passed. But its effects were limited. The government was still inhibited by conservative financial policies. In addition, under the army-dominated régime, some 25% of the budget went on military expenditure. At the highest educational level, only 872 were enrolled at Chula in 1936/7 out of a population of $14\frac{1}{2}$m; overseas there were in 1937/8 some 80 students supported by the government, some 600 private students, mostly in Japan and the Philippines. For these numbers, in a non-colonial environment, there was sufficient bureaucratic employment. No discontented élite emerged. Siam remained a bureaucratic state, and patronage an important aspect of its society.

Political life was thus a matter of coup not revolt, of minority cohesion or otherwise rather than majority and minority. Even so some new sources of cohesion had been sought as social change had penetrated to Siam, especially after Chulalongkorn's reforms. In colonial countries that cohesion was often found at least temporarily in the struggle against the Europeans. In Siam, it rather took the form, as yet less common though not unknown in other Southeast Asian lands, of conflict with alien minorities. The Chinese were perhaps especially numerous in Siam because of the limits on European activity. The Thais were perhaps especially likely to absorb the anti-Chinese views of Europeans. In any case, it is not surprising that the plot of 1912, a symptom of social change, followed the Chinese revolution, or, on the other hand, that Wachirawut stressed that apprehension of the Chinese was an argument for supporting the régime. Certainly it was to be used as a political weapon by the Pibul administration.

Chinese nationalism indeed crystallised earlier than that of the Thais which it helped to crystallise. The Chinese had long predominated as traders and as tax-farmers, long employed by the king and the ruling aristocracy into which indeed some had penetrated. The Bowring treaty had displaced the great farmers, but in the economic changes that followed the Chinese secured new opportunities. With the development of rice production, they dominated middlemen and retail functions and rice-milling. Most of the tin mined in Peninsular Siam continued to be Chinese, though especially after the first world war European firms came in, as in Malaya, with the development of dredges (the first was Australian at Phuket in 1907). Rubber developed in the same region, much of it in smallholdings, but most of the larger holdings were owned by Chinese. By the 1940s there were probably over 2m ethnic Chinese in Thailand and, though the 'headman' system had been abolished by Chulalongkorn's reforms and most of these were regarded as Thai citizens, earlier tendencies towards assimilation had been reduced by factors operating here as elsewhere in Southeast Asia, the improvement in communications, the more frequent passing to and from China, the growth of the Chinese female population, the reduction of intermarriage, and the rise of nationalism. Sun Yat-sen visited Bangkok in 1908, and subsequently the Chinese Nationalist government, as Purcell says, fostered the existence of an 'enclave . . . partly for political reasons and partly for the sake of the remittances from overseas which were to be an important part of its financial strength. This enclave extended its membership from among the *Lukchin* [Chinese born in Siam], because many of them sent their children to schools where Chinese was the medium of instruction and they thus absorbed the nationalism taught therein, and because the increasing anti-Chinese feeling among the Siamese forced them more and more into the alien camp.'[89] The latter development was clearly linked with the emergence of new 'middle-class' elements in Thai society whose attitude differed from that of the old aristocracy.

The monarchy indeed responded also. One of the major impulses in its campaign against extraterritoriality was to ensure Siamese jurisdiction over the Asian protégés of the European powers; the campaign was spurred on by the emergence of the K.M.T. government in China; and no treaty was made with that country, allowing the entrance of a consul, till 1946. Prachathipok drew attention after a tour in 1928 to the Chinese in the southern provinces and their nationalism, and the measures of the revolution, while not going so far as Pridi, whose plan ostensibly aimed at the elimination of the Chinese middlemen, began with the stricter enforcement of existing legislation, such as that of 1918 requiring the teaching of Thai in Chinese schools.

Under the Pibul government, which made much of the penetration of Communism into the community, there were new economic measures against the China-born. Much of the government's interest in the economic sector was directed by it: it set up national trading concerns, reserved certain trades to Thais, increased immigration fees. It seemed that the share of the Chinese capitalists in the development of the Thai economy was to be restricted in favour of a Thai capitalism which the new Thai élite would create by political means. In some sense, like Pridi's plan, this programme represented a recurrence to an old tradition of government enterprise. Earlier, however, the régime had used Chinese acumen: could it now be thrown away? The risk of this was increased as the measures became more extreme, turning even — and somewhat contradictorily — against Chinese who were Thai citizens.

There were other aspects to the nationalism of the military régime. Relations with Japan were important. Indeed there had long been some consciousness of a similar destiny. Both were Buddhist nations that had emerged successfully into the modern world. The Japanese treaty of 1898 thrust the first major wedge into the system of extraterritoriality. The Thai élite reacted to the victory of 1905. The Thais were also alive to the shift in the distribution of power in eastern Asia in the inter-war period. In 1933 Siam abstained from the League of Nations censure over Manchukuo. The western powers began to fear a closer association between Bangkok and Tokyo and the possessor of Singapore was alarmed that it might lead to the construction of a Kra canal. The Thais, of course, were traditionally sensitive to shifts in the distribution of power. The rise of the Japanese, threatening as it did the whole structure of colonial Southeast Asia, raised, moreover, the prospect of Thailand's regaining her old empire, lost to France and England, in Cambodia, Laos and northern Malaya. It was a question whether the chauvinism that the military régime had unleashed would lead the Thais to misjudge the extent and implications of the redistribution that was taking place.

Siam may be said to anticipate developments in other Southeast Asian states in a number of ways. One of these was the adaptation and application of the conflicting European doctrines of self-determination and nationality. Siam itself contained minorities other than the Chinese, though hill peoples were fewer than elsewhere simply because relief was lower. Besides the Laos in the north-east, there were Karens near the Burma frontier, scattered Mon villages (unabsorbed remnants of migrations from Burma), Cambodians (descendants of prisoners), Vietnamese (descendants of Christians persecuted in their homeland), Malays, above all in Patani, where the Thais had retained their control despite local British pressure. But this did not prevent the emergence of the pan-Thai policy that coincided with the anti-Chinese measures and aimed not only at unifying the Thais but at Thai-ifying the minorities and re-creating the old empire in a new form. The policy of *Ratha Niyon* was proclaimed in 1939, the year when the country was officially named Thailand, and its apostle was Luang Vichitr Vadhakarn, a French-educated journalist who became Director of the 'Fine Arts Department'. The advance of the Japanese, the weakness of the French, the defeat of the British, created new opportunities for realising this programme. But was it to lead to too great a sacrifice of the traditional international standpoint? Siam had leaned to the predominant British but with moderation. Thailand turned to the Japanese, but sought reinsurance.

8 Cambodia, Laos and Vietnam

THE IMPACT of economic and social change in Cambodia, Laos and Vietnam, was in part determined by the late date at which French rule was established, and the fact that it was established piecemeal, at different times, under different circumstances, and under the impact of different policies. Paradoxically, the effective organisation of all these fragments into an Indo-Chinese Union in 1897 with a common budget, revenue and services, was also in some sense a divisory move, inasmuch as, while it maintained the fragmentation of Vietnam, it was in a way a Vietnamese empire, and of this Laos and Cambodia were aware.

The French protectorate over Cambodia was established half-way through the period, and its powers were substantial, especially after 1884. In fact, however, no vast transformations were effected: Cambodia was 'a backwater, a rear area, a stepchild . . .'[90] The economic life of the tribesmen and of the villages remained relatively undisturbed, and among the latter class differences remained minimal. Nor was there an educational revolution. The first senior high school was set up only in 1935, and attendance at higher institutions in France was discouraged. Some thirty médecins were trained at Hanoi University. Primary education was mostly left to the pagodas. Indeed popular Buddhism remained alive, ensuring a sense of identity among alien influences, 'a symbolic assurance of eventual liberation',[91] except, of course, to the unconverted Pnong tribes and the Muslim Chams. It was not surprising that the monarchy retained popular allegiance: the king, though confined to a religious role, found there a traditional source of strength that was given a new dimension by alien rule. Nor was it surprising that the nationalist, Son Ngoc Thanh, who in 1936 founded the first Khmer-language newspaper, *Nagaravatha* (Angkor Wat), should appeal not only to the younger members of the small semi-educated class, frustrated at its exclusion from power, but also to Buddhist monks who apprehended a decline of influence as a result of the introduction of western ways of life.

If this was one source of nationalism, there were others. Cambodia had preserved its identity before the imposition of the French protectorate by playing off its rival neighbours, Siam and Vietnam. The French, it has been said, 'kept Cambodia in being as a nation . . .'[92] In fact, they eliminated the Thai side of the balance, and while they did not make use of the Vietnam claims they had asserted to destroy the identity of Cambodia (though, while the western boundary was pushed back in 1907, many Cambodians remained in Cochin-China), nevertheless theirs was clearly a Vietnamese empire. It was not merely that the Cambodian economic outlet was Saigon. What economic change did take place introduced new Vietnamese elements, such as workers on the rubber estates. And the federal services used Vietnamese assistants. In a way — because of the past and because of the proximity of Vietnam — the Vietnamese were less tolerated than the more numerous Chinese who came in and controlled business activity, even though intermarriage decreased in the twentieth century.

In Laos, perhaps, this Vietnamese factor was less evident. Laos was indeed substantially cut off from Vietnam by the geographical barrier of the cordillera, except maybe in the Samneua region. The easier access was to Siam — which, after all, retained a large part of Vienchang — and in some sense the

French impact was negative. Nor did the French in a régime established only in 1893 make much attempt to exploit or even explore the resources of Laos: only tin was extracted on a commercial scale by a French company, and the revenue was subsidised by the Union. Laos was a buffer between Vietnam and Siam and Burma, and no attempt was made even to unify the fragments the French controlled, which included Chieng Khouang. The Resident was established at Vienchang, but the Luang Prabang king retained his title, and the princes of Champassak became hereditary governors. The population, of course, remained mixed, the Laos numbering about half the total, while there were a number of tribal groups like the Kha and the Tai and Meo: but at least government and missionary activity did not intensify their diversity as happened in Burma. Within the society of the predominant Laos, there was no great structural change. Agricultural life was only really affected near the major towns, Vienchang and Luang Prabang, where share-cropping developed. Education spread only slowly. The change that occurred occurred only at the highest level of Lao society. French rule was mostly direct. Under this administration, many of the lower-echelon mandarins of the old kingdom were displaced by Vietnamese civil servants. But the representatives of the princely families of Laos and Champassak and the heirs of the higher mandarins were wealthy enough to secure education at Hanoi and in France and to compose a 'new' western-educated élite.

If Cambodia was economically dependent on Saigon, Laos was cut off from its natural outlets in Siam. If the economic development of Cambodia saw an influx of Vietnamese, the lack of development in Laos necessitated budgetary aid from the Union. Economic and other conditions were unfavourable, but it is also true that no real attempt was made to create viable modern states in these two countries, and that their relations with Vietnam under the Union in some ways weakened that prospect. On the other hand, while in Vietnam itself there were substantial economic developments, the political structure bit by bit established by France, surviving, even preserved by, the Union, tended to diversify their impact upon admittedly already diverse situations, and to establish new divisions in a country indeed only recently recreated after centuries of simultaneous division and expansion.

Thus, after their frustration before Hué, the French first established themselves in 'Cochin-China', a region which had only recently been colonised by the Vietnamese as they pressed

through Southeast Asia. Moreover, the French made this frag-
ment of the Vietnamese empire they had broken off into a
colony of their own, ruled directly. The effective establishment
of a protectorate over the rest of the empire came a generation
later, and the mandarinate here was less completely displaced,
at least before the introduction of the Union. Again there were
distinctions, however. 'Tonkin' was ruled more directly than
'Annam', the central region of the realm where the emperor
remained established at Hué. It was within this diverse political
framework that economic and social change took place.

Where French policy had its unity, indeed, its impact was
diversified by the given social dichotomies. One feature common to all three regions was the expansion of the population
(to 23m in 1937), the result in part of the French establishment
of law and order, and the introduction of improved health
standards and mass vaccination. It was also the result of the
high birth rate characteristic of non-industrial societies. But
'Tonkin' remained the most thickly settled part of the country
as in pre-French times; here the reasserted monarchical policy
of maintaining a taxable peasantry had prevailed through most
of the nineteenth century and had aimed to preserve communal
land, to aid repartition, to avert great distinctions of wealth.

Another common French policy, the protective tariff of 1892,
aimed to ensure a market for the nascent industries of belatedly
industrialised France, and to procure them raw materials. This
helped to destroy the rural artisanate and limited the industrialisation for which Tonkin was in some respects ripe (the
total number of factory workers at the end of the period,
90,000, was no more than the total in Burma). It canalised
investment there — where there was no chance of agricultural
surpluses, and extension and flood prevention hardly kept up
with the population — into the extractive industries. Tonkin
was rich in zinc and tin and, unusually in Southeast Asia, in
coal, and Quang-yen coal became the chief mineral export of
the Union. But the villages in Tonkin, as in Java, became overburdened, marked by subdivision and the disappearance of
common lands, and the overall consumption per person of rice
in Indo-China fell between 1900 and 1937.

If this was partly because of the growth of population in Tonkin, unaccompanied by any industrialisation that might have
absorbed and restrained it, it was also due to the nature of
economic development in Cochin-China. There the old Vietnamese structure was less developed, still more in a frontier
stage, and, furthermore, the French conquest temporarily dis-

placed many of the inhabitants. The way was clear for the French to abandon the old Vietnamese policy of restraining the development of a substantial proprietary, and, having incurred a heavy outlay for canal construction, they allowed much of the land to come into the hands of large or middle-sized Vietnamese landowners, and to be worked for them by *ta dien* or leaseholders or by day labourers. A new bourgeoisie emerged, propertied and moderate, yet able to afford to educate sons who sought to change the colonial system. Its interests were mainly in rice, and the rice was mainly exported (in 1938 it formed 34% of exports, even after the depression had led to the opening of a corn market in France). In 1940 about 100,000 tons went to feed the hungry peasants of the Red River delta. Some of these indeed had migrated south when in the 1920s the 'Terres Rouges' were opened up to rubber companies which left the tribal Moi still using their *ray* methods in their reservations. But most of the 'Tonkinois' returned to their villages after their three-year contracts had expired: the villages, rather as in Java, subsidised the plantations, and vice-versa.

The employment of the Tonkinois in the south gives a clue also to the position of the Chinese in Vietnam, as it was affected by the different conditions in the different regions of the country. In crowded highly sinicised Tonkin, there were relatively few opportunities for them and, despite the proximity of southern China, there were only 35,000 there in 1936. By contrast there were 171,000 in Cochin-China, which was less sinicised, more Southeast Asian, as it were, and provided opportunities for them as well as for immigrant Tonkinois: they established themselves strongly in the rice trade and in rice-milling. Again the French pursued a common policy throughout the country, prohibiting land concessions and seeking, in the wake of the emperors, to control the immigrant communities through the headmen of their *bangs* or 'congrégations'. But economic circumstances meant again that this policy had a diverse impact. The communal problem was likely to bulk much more largely in the south than in the north. On the other hand, nationalists in the north, while they might hope for support from across the frontier against the western intruders, must also be apprehensive of a power which had in the past often asserted its claims over the lands of the Vietnamese people.

The first nationalist movement was indeed, not surprisingly in the protected lands, and predominantly a mandarin affair, stimulated no doubt by reaction to the establishment of the Union. Initially, however, it looked, as did other Southeast Asian nationalist movements, towards Japan. After 1902 Phan Boi Chau, who came from the province of Nghe-an (a home of revolutionaries), led a group of loyalists supporting prince Cuong De, a descendant of Gia-long. The idea of securing Japanese help for the overthrow of the French induced Phan Boi Chau to visit Japan in 1905, and others followed him. In 1908 he founded a League of East Asia, a pan-Asian movement, but two years later the Japanese, at the behest of the French, expelled Cuong De and Phan Boi Chau and dissolved the organisations among Vietnamese students. After the 1911 revolution some of those who had gone to China organised themselves on the model of the K.M.T. In the war Cuong De looked to Germany, while after 1917 Phan Boi Chau interested himself in Marxism. He was captured in 1925 and his career came to an end. Another wing of the mandarin movement, led by Phan Chau Trinh, sought rather for concessions from the protectorate on the basis of the principles of 1789, but evoked little response. The reformist manifestations that followed the deposition of emperor Thanh-thai in 1907 indeed met with repression, and the removal of troops from Vietnam in the war led to plans for an insurrection fostered by emperor Duy-tan. The result was the exile of the emperor to Réunion and the internment of Phan Chau Trinh. This marked virtually the end of the old mandarin movements, revolutionary and reformist. The ex-emperor was to die in 1945 as a French major and Companion of the French Liberation.

In the protectorate the nationalist movement had an early start, in part simply because it derived so immediately from the traditional mandarin class, which reacted against the French, but secured access through its wealth and education to new ideas and new overseas contacts. In the colony social change was more profound, and it was only after the war, and in part as a result of its ideological stimulus, that a new nationalist movement appeared there, marked for instance by the founding of the Parti Constitutionaliste at Saigon in 1923. The Governor-General appointed by the Radical-Socialist Cartel of 1924 was disposed to make concessions in response to the wishes of this party, but little came of Varenne's plans, and his successor Pasquier merely superimposed a 'Grand Conseil des intérêts économiques et financiers de l'Indochine', with 28 French and 23 Indo-Chinese members, over the consultative assemblies in Tonkin and Annam and the Colonial Council in Cochin-China.

In the north there were also changes. The preceding years had seen the opening in 1907, the prompt closure after the Thanh-thai disturbances, and the reopening in 1918 of the University at Hanoi. In these years new contacts were made with the outside world by soldiers and war workers sent to France — some 100,000 in all (they included some Cambodians: Khim Tit, Cambodian premier in 1956, was a French corporal in 1918). Bismarck had tried to foster French interest in Vietnam: Vietnamese soldiers returned to help regain Alsace-Lorraine; but they imbibed nationalist ideas and looked to the overthrow of the French in Vietnam. New echelons of the administration had been opened to Vietnamese: but there were still too few openings even for the few who had the opportunity of secondary education. In Indo-China there were more European public servants than in all British India. Frustrated intellectuals, teachers, soldiers, minor officials, these supported the Parti National or V.N.Q.D.D. founded at Hanoi in 1927 on the K.M.T. model. The crisis of the depression tempted it into action, and the counter-action of the police precipitated the desperate throw that began — and more or less ended — with the occupation of Yen-bay by the town garrison. Repression followed, and by 1933 the party had ceased to exist in Vietnam, though, with the aid of the K.M.T., it remained alive in Yunnan and Canton.

The repression of all the nationalist movements helped to bring about the supremacy of the Communists, who were moreover better organised. The dominating figure here was Nguyen Ai Quoc, later known as Ho Chi Minh. He was born in 1890 of a mandarin family in Nghe-an. He was educated probably at the Lycée Quoc-hoc at Hué, a nationalist school founded by Ngo Dinh Kha, once a minister to Thanh-thai and father of Ngo Dinh Diem, who was also a pupil, as were Vo Nguyen Giap and Pham Van Dong, himself the son of a mandarin involved in the Duy-tan affair. Nguyen Ai Quoc left Vietnam in 1912 as a ship's cabin-boy, was cook's help to the great Escoffier at the Carlton Hotel during the war, joined an Overseas Workers Association which supported Ireland's struggle for independence, hopefully haunted Versailles after the proclamation of the 14 points, went to Moscow in 1924, and finally joined the Comintern mission in Canton. Here he founded the Thanh-nien, or League of Revolutionary Youth, whose activities were allowed to continue for a short while even after the K.M.T. coup of 1927, and whose trainees increasingly penetrated into Vietnam. At Hong Kong in 1930 Nguyen Ai Quoc organised the Indo-Chinese Communist Party, affiliated to the Third International. Its members sought to turn to account the discontent of the depression in Vietnam. This only provoked French reaction and the arrest of Nguyen Ai Quoc in the British colony in 1931. The movement was dislocated.

With the checking of the extremists, there seemed some renewed hope for the moderates, more especially as the young emperor, Bao-dai, freshly returned from France, called to his service a mandarin from a family converted to Catholicism in the seventeenth century, renowned for his integrity and competence as governor of Phan-thiet province. But the opposition of the French led to Ngo Dinh Diem's resignation. With this nationalism turned to abstention, or to extremism. The French had never made a gesture to the moderates. Perhaps the major obstacle was not so much the vested interests in Indo-China as the lack of a consistent policy in Paris: no ministry was ever in a strong enough position to hammer out a forward-looking programme. From late 1932, there was some revival of the Communist party, spurred on by the inauguration of the popular front policy in 1935. More open action was possible in Cochin-China than in the protectorate, though cells were organised especially near the Chinese frontier. In Cochin-China also the religious sects became increasingly political. The north was the stronghold of the Catholics. In the colony, the penetration of alien culture had led to the creation of the Cao Dai movement, a curious blend of Catholicism and other religions, and the Hoa Hao, a Buddhist sect. In both there was pro-Japanese sympathy. For the Japanese, on the other hand, Indo-China was of importance both in the encirclement of Chiang Kai-shek and in the penetration of Southeast Asia, and the war in Europe was to give them new opportunities.

PART THREE

Southeast Asia Since 1942

Preface

IT WAS ONLY with the removal of the old distribution of power in Southeast Asia that the nationalist and communal forces secured their opportunity. That removal, however, was effected not only by the withdrawal of the Europeans to engage in the European war. It was also effected by the incursion of yet another outside power into Southeast Asia, aided by its political fragmentation and by the lack of co-operation even among the so-called A.B.C.D. régimes. This power was Japan, and it was under the aegis of Japanese policies that political change took place.

Japan's major objective through the previous decades — indeed in a sense ever since the first world war — had been to establish its hegemony in China. The war of 1937 had not achieved this. Japan looked to Southeast Asia, in part in order to defeat China by excluding western influence from its confines, in part as an alternative, for its own sake. The signature of the Nazi-Soviet pact of 1939 was discouraging, for the occupation of Manchukuo at the beginning of the decade had by no means removed the Russian threat which had been present in Japanese minds at least since the 1890s. The pact did, however, make Britain and France more ready to acquiesce in closing overland routes to China. Germany's early victories in Europe opened up new possibilities for Japan and, the Germans being obliging, it was able to establish a hold on Indo-China through the Vichy French, and to force them to make concessions to the Thais. The Dutch in Indonesia did not give way, and the British had not been defeated by the Germans.

The Japanese awaited Soviet involvement in the war before acting. In April 1941 they were able to secure a neutrality pact with Russia. In June Russia was invaded. Hoping for a quick German victory, the Japanese yet waited, believing that opposition in Southeast Asia might yet crumble. As Hitler's army came to a halt, they resolved not to miss their opportunity. Pearl

Harbour, the distant American base, was put out of action. The other major objective was, of course, Singapore. The British lacked air support, and the *Repulse* and the *Prince of Wales* were sunk. But the Japanese in any case approached overland. Initially Burma and Thailand were important to them in relation to their major objectives in Malaya and the oil-rich Netherlands Indies. It was only later — when the Germans had clearly failed to defeat the British — that the conquest of India was introduced into Japanese plans and Burma gained a new importance. The Philippines — though earlier regarded by Japanese extremists as a possible base for liberating China — was, of course, drawn in because it flanked the southward advance.

Within its Southeast Asian conquests, Japan's aims were presented in the form of the Co-Prosperity Sphere, but the essential objective was to mobilise the resources of these countries for the war effort and latterly, as the Japanese military position deteriorated from 1943 onwards, to establish political barriers against the returning colonial powers. On the one hand, therefore, there were major economic changes, not merely the result of wartime destruction, but also of the severance from world markets, and of the sometimes catastrophic effects of attempts to tie the Southeast Asian economies to the Japanese industrial system. The complete inadequacy of Japanese shipping, especially as the U.S. gained air superiority, promoted railway-building: in their attempts to overcome land-barriers in Southeast Asia, the Japanese resorted to harsh versions of traditional Southeast Asian forms of compulsion, the enslavement of prisoners-of-war, the impressment of *romusha*. Though its effects were somewhat mitigated by the wide subsistence basis of the economy of many regions (and the collapse of the sugar plantations was by no means a great loss to the Javanese peasants), the economic upset, as also the labour demands and the neglect of health measures, all contributed to popular unrest.

At the same time in ex-colonial countries the prospect of independence aroused the hopes of social improvement, even revolution, or of the recapture of a glorious past, that were popularly associated with the overthrow of the old system. In Thailand, on the other hand, the régime enlisted popular support by the territorial gains it made — in Cambodia, in the Shan states, in Malaya — through Japan's cavalier treatment of the nineteenth century frontiers of Southeast Asia. The Japanese thus ensured their influence. In the ex-colonial territories they attempted to ensure it through the manipulation of communal divisions and of existing élites, complicating their interrelationships, intensifying their contacts with the masses, often adding a new military leadership to the generally civilian leadership of the colonial period. That leadership had also to reckon with the underground movements — often Communist-inclined — that both the oppressive policies of the Japanese and the millennial hopes of the future did much to foster.

In the two decades following the defeat of the Japanese, the leadership produced in the colonial and Japanese periods sought to create and rule states that would enjoy the independence that only Thailand had retained in the previous phase. In these tasks it faced a sea of troubles. The very complexity of the problems facing it tended to divide it as to the use of the various specifics for social and political ills it had drawn from diverse European and Asian medicine-chests. The relative small-ness of the leadership did nothing to ensure cohesion, rather the reverse, and feelings of personal insecurity and maladjust-ment — in which clashes of culture were individualised — added to the difficulties of rational decision-making and stressed sub-jective motivation in politics. The appalling problems these conditions created within the leadership were intensified once the unifying factor of a struggle for independence against a colonial power — where it existed — had disappeared. Further-more, this vastly increased the leadership's difficulty in retaining mass allegiance, a difficulty that only added to the tension within it.

Great hopes had been popularly attached to the idea of independence, of the end of alien dominance, and it had been assumed, as by the Sakdalistas, that the political revolution would mean a social or economic revolution also. But success in the struggle for independence often only consolidated the position of the leadership, and no further revolution followed. That prospect had already been apparent in the Philippines. The exception to prove the rule was, as usual, north Vietnam: and there indeed agrarian revolution was imposed from above to guarantee the independence of the state and the position of its leadership. Generally, with the end of the independence struggle, the leadership had still to face the problem of ensuring mass allegiance to the new political structures, in the absence of extensive education, in the absence of extensive political experience, in the absence of an organisational substructure that might integrate the people into the new sort of politics that the western-educated intelligentsia were generally disposed to adopt.

The obvious means was a programme of economic advance

and social amelioration. But in face of this again there lay many obstacles, aside from the difficulties facing the leaders themselves, obstacles that were in some sense of the very essence of the 'colonial' economies that even politically independent states had to cope with; and the attempt to raise living standards was obstructed everywhere by the continuing rapid rise in population characteristic of such economies which the weakness of the medical services (there were only 6,000 doctors in all Southeast Asia in 1956/7) did not restrain. By 1958 the total population was 172m; by 2000 it is expected to be 415m. Over 40% of the population was under 15, demanding a vast investment of effort and capital.

Attempts to introduce industrialisation were impeded by a deficiency of technological skills and by lack of capital, even though government might, on old Southeast Asian and colonial patterns, seek to shoulder a large share of the entrepreneurial burden, as the Philippines government had to the delight of Harrison and the despair of Wood. In many cases, indeed, geographical conditions did not favour industrialisation, and attempts to diversify rather than industrialise would have produced greater rewards. Impressed by the vastness of the gulf now separating Asian and European states, the vast gulf between underdeveloped and developed, the leadership tended to give industrialisation a special importance. Yet further difficulties in the way of it were presented by the distrust of western influences, of western capital and technicians, the legacy of the colonial past; and by the communal divisions, obstructing the use of what skills and capital the countries did possess, the legacy of the distant as well as the colonial past. In varying degrees the countries also suffered from wartime destruction and post-war civil strife.

The immensity of these problems made it harder to take rational decisions. There was, in addition, a temptation for politicians, unsure of the continuance of power, to turn the legacy of distrust and division to account, rather than utilise. for instance, Chinese skill and capital. Indeed the notion of the nation-state, applied in the context of post-colonial Southeast Asia, could be a peculiarly disruptive one; attempts to insist upon such a basis of unity might only produce the reverse and provoke the disruptive claim to self-determination. Even in states based on other principles than the nation-state principle, like the Federation of Malaysia, the chances of rational economic development were greatly reduced by the obstacles presented by constitutional clauses inserted as a result of communal and political pressures. Equally the chances of international co-operation are small. On the one hand, substantially colonial economies are similar rather than complementary, as became apparent to the members of the Association of South Asian States (A.S.A.) founded in 1961 by Malaya, the Philippines and Thailand. And on the other hand, the states are divided not only within themselves but among themselves by the presence of minorities and by the presence of historical claims upon one another's territory deriving from the pre-colonial or even the colonial period, and likely to dissolve a pattern already dislocated by the Japanese.

If all these factors work against successful economic and social policies, failure here in turn tends to stress distrust and divisions and to conduce to a politics made up of charismatic allegiances, of xenophobic gestures, of recurrence to old imperial traditions, of assumptions of power by military wings of the leadership — as the most effectively organised, as the most potent combination of the old and the new — of apprehensions of Communist influence among the masses, of piratical warfare, of guerilla war-fare. In some sense all these features illustrate the extent to which both the colonial and post-colonial phases had failed to transform the basic conditions in which Southeast Asian politics operated. It was still a matter of seeking the allegiance of the peasant masses, of the mountain peoples, of the alien communities. Now the means were more complex, more diversified, and the leadership more divided about them.

Thailand both resembled and differed from the ex-colonial territories. In some ways — in the resort to pan-Thai or anti-Chinese programmes, in the emergence of military dominance — it anticipated developments among them. But if Thailand's economy was also undeveloped and undiversified, there was less distrust of western aid; and if the Thais were poorly educated, their traditional system had been less dislocated, and the notion of independence had not been present to arouse millennial hopes. The other countries also differed by reason of different conditions, different pre-colonial and colonial experience. In some ways, for instance, the pre-war Philippines was already exhibiting features of post-war ex-dependencies. But yet a further source of differentiation among these countries was the impact of outside economic and political forces.

Post-war, the technological gap between the developed and underdeveloped countries continued to widen. How were the non-industrialised countries to share in the prosperity of the industrialised parts of the world? To some extent this has been brought about by the operation of economic forces, though their impact in Southeast Asia would of course depend on its diversity. The Korean war induced a temporary prosperity above all for the rubber and rice-producing countries. After 1953 raw material prices, however, tended to fall, and in the case of rubber there was competition from the synthetic product. International restriction on tin production was revived in 1957. Another means of sharing prosperity was the giving of aid by more advanced countries. In some sense this was a result of the workings of conscience among the wealthy. Much more it was the result of political motivation, and it was all the more diversifying in its effect. It was subject to political fluctuations, conditioned by political objectives. By no means was it adjusted to the economic needs of the various countries: Laos and South Vietnam received more per head than depressed Burma or Indonesia. Very often aid was military in character, or simply bolstered an existing régime. And in other ways it was rather misconceived.

The problem of poverty in Southeast Asia was not overwhelming in the sense that it was in India and China, yet it was these countries that Britain and the U.S. had in mind when considering aid to the intervening region. This again tended to divert attention from some of the most valid economic programmes in Southeast Asia, from the diversification of production, from the stabilisation of prices on world markets. But these remarks serve to emphasise the impact in Southeast Asia of world political forces.

Again their impact was multifarious in character, varied by the time-factor. The initial political phase was in itself a diversifying one. The advance of the Allies had dictated various Japanese moves in various areas, and the success of the Allies directly affected the outlying areas of New Guinea, Burma, and the Philippines first of all, though they contacted underground movements elsewhere also. Then the war was abruptly ended in August 1945 by the dropping of the atomic bombs on Japan. In some countries this meant an interregnum, followed by a phase, such as had occurred in Burma and the Philippines, when great discretion was allowed the local military commanders. The Americans naturally now had an effective influence on policy. In the Philippines they — or MacArthur — stressed early independence, and in Thailand they opposed extensive intervention. The Nationalist Chinese were brought into Southeast Asia by being made responsible for the occupation of part of Vietnam. On the other hand, the Americans' opposition to the return of the French was neutralised by the British, especially by their local commander, and in the Archipelago the British and Australian soldiers prepared the way for the Dutch, as yet delayed. That same year saw the opening battles between Dutch and Indonesians, however, and the following year saw conflict in Vietnam. Some countries were fought over in the world war, others were now to suffer the destruction of colonial wars. There were other factors of timing. In some countries the re-established colonial régime was able to restore some of the pre-war economic stability. In others independence came too soon for this sort of aid. And it came at a time when yet other forces had begun to play upon Southeast Asia from outside.

1947-8 may perhaps mark a new phase in the impact of out-side political forces in Southeast Asia. India had provided 70-80% of the British forces in Asia in the war. The post-war period brought the British Indian empire to an end. Following hard upon the independence of India and Pakistan came that of Burma, though the Andaman and Nicobar islands were made over to India. Britain retained dollar-rich Malaya, strategically important Singapore, and politically backward Borneo, where Sarawak and North Borneo had indeed been turned into colonies with a view to ultimate decolonisation. The old colonial struc-ture had lost its major sanction, and new policies could be expected. These years nevertheless saw the continuance of the struggle of the French and the Dutch — though in new ways — to retain their empire, their own political systems making diffi-cult any major readjustments of policy. But the whole area — diverse as its political conditions were — was increasingly drawn into the 'Cold War' struggle. No one could, indeed, expect so fragmented an area to remain a vacuum once the British and Japanese structures had been destroyed.

The Cold War, like the struggle following the first world war, emerged from the European situation. The old Comintern had been buried in 1943 in the heyday of co-operation against Hitler. Its heir, the Cominform, was born in October 1947. Post-war the Soviet Union had pinned its hopes on revolution in Europe, on the French and Italian Communist parties. The Marshall Aid programme of June 1947 was among a number of indications that these hopes would not be realised. The new Zhdanov line represented the world as divided into two hostile camps: a new period of struggle was envisaged. Again action shifted to Asia. In Southeast Asia the Communist parties were generally in confusion as a result of the Soviet Union's con-centration upon Europe. In most countries they were unable to secure the lead in nationalist movements. The exception was Vietnam, where the party had struck out a line of its own. The Zhdanov line was put over at the Calcutta Youth Conference of early 1948. The result was increasing violence, in some cases directed against colonial authorities. But if India provided a channel for these instructions, China was soon to bulk much larger upon the scene.

From February 1947 the C.C.P. and the K.M.T. were openly at war in China. By late 1949 the C.C.P. was in sight of complete triumph. This was bound to boost the struggle in Southeast Asia and to orient the Communist parties there more to China. In November 1949 at the Australasian Trade Union Conference Liu Shao-chi called for an armed struggle for liberation. Training was offered in the military and political techniques that had brought the C.C.P. to victory in the rather different circumstances of China. And the C.C.P. had still more particularly Chinese weapons in its armoury. The Chinese revolution had been born in humiliation and defeat, and the Communists were no less nationalist than the Nationalists. They sought to reassert in new forms the pre-colonial claims to suzerainty China had maintained in Southeast Asia. They could attempt to utilise the long-standing sympathy for the revolution of the Nanyang communities which the pre-colonial and colonial periods had created. They could marry the traditional policy of fragmentation to the modern ideas of self-determination and nationality and create in the mountain confines of Southeast Asia Kachin and Thai autonomous states. And they could readily produce border conflicts in regions where old and new allegiances had never been reconciled.

In reaction to these changes, the Americans in turn became more committed in Southeast Asia. The Chinese content of the changes influenced their attitude. For the victory of the C.C.P. marked a traumatic setback, and coloured their view of the situation both political and economic in all East and Southeast Asia. The Korean conflict of 1950 produced a new definition in their policies. It committed the U.S. to the revival and even rearming of Japan and to the preservation and exclusive recognition of the Nationalist régime in Formosa. These policies had their bearing on Southeast Asia. Industrialised Japan might aid in the economic development of the area, and the Nationalists might focus the loyalty of the Nanyang Chinese. This, to some extent, conflicted with the Wilsonian notion of alliance with nationalism in Southeast Asia.

There indeed American policy caught the various countries

at different stages of development. In some countries it was possible to play Wilsonian idealism — as its author had intended — against the Communists. The Americans could press the Dutch to make the final concessions to the Indonesian nationalists who put down a P.K.I.-led rebellion. In Vietnam, on the other hand, the struggle against the colonial power was still far from complete. This, the geographical position of Vietnam, the Communist influence in its nationalist movement, led the Americans to aid the French and the Chinese to increase their aid to the Vietnamese. In the course of the struggle, however, a rival notion of the Vietnamese state emerged. Still more, Laos and Cambodia profited from opportunities to perfect their political independence. Colonial Malaya, colonial Borneo, were a problem for the British. Among the independent régimes, on the other hand, the Philippines now became — as had been briefly envisaged at the end of the nineteenth century — an outpost of U.S. power in the Far East. It was easier for an independent state to accept this status — more especially one that contained a Chinese minority and was near the mainland — than it was for a struggling nationalist movement. That illustrated the reverse of the colonial paradox between promoting political advance and maintaining important interests. It was possible here to put U.S. policy at least ostensibly on the basis of treaty relationship between sovereign states. In the case of Thailand, again, the U.S. did not rely on a colonial power or on idealistic sympathies. Its change of policy had coincided with a return to militarist rule in Bangkok. The Thais were indeed sensitive to shifts in the distribution of power. Uncolonised, but most concerned about its Chinese community, Thailand found it easiest to come to terms with external powers. Some Thais indeed suspected that the military had — as in the Japanese phase — committed themselves too deeply to one side in the power struggle. In independent Burma — which, of course, had only a small Chinese community, but a long border with China — the Americans were faced with idealism of a rather different source that came to affect other régimes as their independence was perfected. And if economic aid of some sort always formed part of American policy and part of the calculations of the Southeast Asian leaders who were influenced by that policy, the same was the case with the policy of the British and the Indians.

Southeast Asia was a traditional field of Indian as well as Chinese influence. Independent India was thus especially aware of the importance of the area, of its exposure to China. Early on Nehru sought to foster the independence of Indonesia and to aid Burma. Undoubtedly he believed that nationalism would be the best defence against Communism, that fully independent states would be better able to deal with subversion than those tainted with colonialism. He played down the claims of Indians in Burma, and in his policy there was little place for the indigenous minorities that the colonial powers had brought forward and in the latter days protected (Burma and India co-operated in handling the Nagas). The India of Nehru opposed pacts with the West and watered down the communiqué of the conference convened by President Quirino of the Philippines at Baguio in 1950. China had been the focus of American interest in Asia: this had helped to determine American policy in Southeast Asia. For Britain, India had consistently been the pillar of Asian empire, and it still played a major role in British policy in Southeast Asia. Britain thus gave some weight to Indian-conceived policies and to Indian criticism of more power-conscious American policies. India, too, was, like Japan, ex-pected to make an economic contribution to Southeast Asia. Undoubtedly the Colombo Plan of 1950 was initially conceived in this context.

New shifts in the policies of international Communism made the mid-1950s the heyday of Indian influence in Southeast Asia. In the early 1950s the stalemate between the two world powers — a nuclear, but not merely a nuclear stalemate — became apparent to the Soviet leadership. With the 19th Congress of 1952, Stalin's death in March 1953, and the Korean armistice, policy began to shift towards one of peaceful co-existence and of economic competition with the West in underdeveloped countries. China's adoption of this policy produced a *détente* in her relations with India, and Chou En-lai and Nehru endorsed the five principles of 1954, respect for territorial in-tegrity and sovereignty, non-aggression, non-intervention in internal affairs, equality and mutual benefit, co-existence. These Nehru regarded as guarantees against the support of subversive movements in Southeast Asia. The Chinese also accepted the principle that Chinese abroad should become citizens of their countries of domicile or dissociate themselves from political activities. The climax of Nehru's policy came at the Bandung conference of 1955. Meanwhile the new policy of the Communist bloc found the Southeast Asian Communist parties at different stages. The P.K.I., defeated before, was able to emerge afresh. Others had difficulty in adjusting: out of power, they found Russia and China courting the governments in power. In Indo-

China the war was brought to an end. The Geneva agreements envisaged the reunification and independence of Vietnam. For the Viet Minh it seemed like triumph. For the Indians it was a major step in bringing stability to Southeast Asia through the setting-up of independent national régimes.

Whatever success this policy might have enjoyed, it was defeated at once by two factors, by the continued presence of two world powers in Southeast Asia. One was the U.S. Its creation of the S.E.A.T.O. alliance soon after the Geneva agreements was bitterly criticised in India. In Southeast Asia itself the Manila pact — under which the parties agreed that in the case of an armed attack on any of the signatories or their forces they would act to meet the common danger in accordance with constitutional processes (the U.S. limiting its commitment to cases of Communist aggression) — was indeed signed only by Thailand and the Philippines. Since Britain was a signatory, Malaya and the other British territories still not independent were covered. To the annoyance of the Indians, Laos, Cambodia and 'free' Vietnam were 'designated', though no action to defend them would be undertaken by the parties without their government's consent. To the Indians this treaty, and subsequent American actions in South Vietnam (where, too, a dictatorial government was allowed to take measures against the Chinese minority) and in Laos, seemed to destroy the effectiveness of the five principles.

In some ways, however, the American presence indicated a realistic recognition of the threat that China still presented in Southeast Asia. There was no real chance that China would regard co-existence as an end in itself. The exclusion of the West from Southeast Asia was simply a means to an end. But China's relations with Russia played a part in the ultimate reversion to the policy of struggle. The revival and deepening of the Sino-Soviet rift indeed had its origins in the recognition by the Chinese that their success would be limited in a policy dependent upon economic competition. Russia was far more industrialised, far more likely to capture the allegiance of the underdeveloped countries. The shift in Chinese policy was evident after 1957, still more after 1959. With the revival of border disputes with India, the influence of India's 'neutralism' declined. Furthermore, Indian trade with Southeast Asia had actually fallen off. In this the competition of the Chinese had played a part, though the Japanese industrialists had, of course, been far more successful.

The reaction to these developments varied among the governments and Communist parties of Southeast Asia — in different geographical situations, at different stages of development. Burma and Cambodia emphasised their neutralism. In divided Laos conflict was intensified until, with Russian aid, a queasy neutrality was attained. In Vietnam the Sino-Soviet rift coincided with the determination in the north to achieve by force the peaceful unification that the Americans and the south had prevented: its leadership recognised the risk that in the process they might finally fall under the domination of the great neighbour the Vietnamese had for centuries sought to avoid. And there were new opportunities for China in the Malay world.

While the Americans escalated their activities in Vietnam, and sought to maintain Thailand's participation in the S.E.A.T.O. pact, the British recognised the weakness of their India-based strategy. This perhaps contributed to the construction of the Malaysian Federation. In Malaya the effect of co-existence policies and the great efforts of the British and others had brought the 1948 'Emergency' to an end, but the Malay community had become more ready to compromise with the Chinese. In Malaya the Chinese were too numerous, too powerful, to form a butt for nationalist groups, as in other countries. Their presence, however, was an argument for compromise with the British, who were able to put their interests on a new footing. Malaya, partially self-governing from 1955, independent from 1957, did not join S.E.A.T.O., but concluded a defence agreement with Britain, allowing for the maintenance of a strategic reserve to assist in defence and to fulfil international obligations, but to some extent limiting the use of bases in Malaya. These restrictions were even vaguer in the 1963 agreement with Malaysia. The new Federation seemed to offer a means for the decolonisation of the Borneo territories. It also aimed to reconcile the paradox in Singapore's position. Singapore, politically separated from Malaya since 1946, was predominantly Chinese in population: its politics seemed to move left. Yet the base had certainly not lost its importance. Malaysia, it was believed, would make a major contribution to the stability of the region.

In fact the scheme was to lead the Filipinos — anxious to demonstrate an independence of the West they could not demonstrate otherwise — to claim North Borneo (Sabah). And Indonesia had been virtually ignored. That country, independent from 1949, had enjoyed not only the benefit of Communist aid in the co-existence phase: it continued to enjoy the endorsement of American idealism. Even when its nationalism became more aggressive, both power blocs continued to support it. Successful in the West New Guinea campaign — on the basis of prescriptive right — and impressed by the revolt in Brunei in late 1962, Indonesia 'confronted' the new 'colonialist' creation in the name of self-determination. The intensity — and initial frustration — of its campaign led Indonesia to leave the United Nations. Despite renewed differences over the position of the Chinese community, Indonesia was drawn to closer political association with China, still excluded from the U.N. But did this mean that the oldest Communist party in Asia — orientating itself towards China — was at last to triumph? How would the Russians react? and how would the Americans reconcile their idealism vis-à-vis Indonesia with their strategy for Southeast Asia as a whole?

With the answers to such questions, Australia and New Zealand were deeply concerned. The war had made them conscious of the importance of sea-power; the reoccupation had brought Australian troops into Southeast Asia. The disappearance of British predominance at sea and of the colonial régimes in Southeast Asia — leaving ultimately only the Portuguese remnants and the protected state of Brunei — raised above all questions of security. If the Australians were not simply to rely on the jungle and desert that had once deterred the Dutch, if the New Zealanders were not to rely on the distance and isolation that had so long preserved their country from major powers, they needed the alliance of the major power in the Pacific, the U.S.A. The onset of the Cold War made this more apparent but also gave them their opportunity. The U.S. readjusted its policy towards Japan. For a peace treaty, Australasian consent was desirable, but not essential, and it was apparently the prompt aid afforded them in the Korean war that influenced the Americans in favour of the A.N.Z.U.S. pact. Under this each party recognised that an armed attack in the Pacific on the possessions or forces of either of the other powers would endanger its own peace and security and undertook to meet the common danger in accordance with its constitutional processes. In 1954 the A.N.Z.A.C. powers participated in the formation of the S.E.A.T.O. alliance. The then Mr R. G. Casey, for instance, had recognised that the mainland countries of Southeast Asia were important to the security of Australia. The disappearance of the old Southeast Asian framework led to the participation in building a new. The despatch of Australian air squadrons and of New Zealand paratroopers to Thailand in the Laos crisis of mid-1962 and the gestures of aid to the U.S. in Vietnam in

1965 indicated an anxiety to maintain the relationship with the U.S. The effect that prompt action in Korea had had on the Americans was kept in mind.

As Casey argued, the importance of the mainland partly turned on its relationship to the Peninsula, the lynchpin of Southeast Asia: it was indeed from the mainland that the Japanese had approached the Peninsula. The importance of Singapore had long been recognised. With the approach of Malayan independence — and the prospect of the removal thereby of the S.E.A.T.O. guarantee of the Peninsula — the A.N.Z.A.C. powers recognised their interest in maintaining what had been a pivot of British strategy in the Indian Ocean and contributed greatly (though in 1941 inadequately) to their security. Early in 1955 Australia determined to place troops in Malaya and proposed the formation of the Commonwealth Strategic Reserve to Britain and New Zealand. The A.N.Z.A.C. powers were associated with the defence agreements of 1957 and 1963. With 'confrontation', they were increasingly committed against the Indonesians. Barwick's diplomacy was undoubtedly exerted during 1963 in attempts to bridge the rift with the Malaysians. Indeed confrontation meant (to borrow a phrase of F. L. W. Wood's) a new 'A.N.Z.A.C. dilemma'.[93]

Undoubtedly there were other strands in Australasian policy. In part these paralleled other strands in British and American policy. The participation in the Colombo Plan indicated, for instance, a belief that India might make an economic contribution to Southeast Asian stability. It indicated also a belief that the A.N.Z.A.C. powers could make their own contribution. No doubt a reciprocal traffic — between substantially primary producing economies, between tropical and subtropical or temperate agricultural regions — could not develop overnight. No doubt trade with Japan offered more potential. Even the supply of oil from Indonesia was in the hands of world-wide British and American companies who regarded their installations there as a relatively minor, even expendable enterprise. No doubt the A.N.Z.A.C. powers could not undertake vast investment programmes in Southeast Asia. They could, however, give educational and technological aid. In yet other ways, there was a parallel to Indian policy. This was particularly apparent in the case of Indonesia. At the end of the war, the activities of the waterside workers in Australia — affected by left-wing Indonesian nationalists, for instance in Brisbane — had made it difficult for Chifley government to take the side of the Dutch. In any case it was felt that a stable and friendly independent nation-state might be the best hope of security to the north, and Australia took part in the U.N.'s mediatory activities during the subsequent Indonesian struggles. The belief in an idealistic solution in Southeast Asia declined with the change of government in Australia; it declined above all, however, because of the deterioration in the international situation. Yet while Australia thus came to oppose the claim for West Irian and to co-operate with the Dutch there, it sought to remain on friendly terms with Indonesia. Even the determination to aid Malaysia, and the apprehension about east New Guinea, did not lead to the severance of all Australian aid to Indonesia.

Within the Dominions, indeed, many believed that their foreign policy associated them too closely with the British and the Americans. Participation in S.E.A.T.O. had been criticised as dividing Australasia from India and from most of the Southeast Asian countries. China's abandonment of co-existence struck a blow at India-based policies. Action in Thailand and Vietnam was still criticised. Australasians still wished to believe that Wilsonian idealism offered the solution. Perhaps the feeling was stronger in New Zealand than in Australia, simply because New Zealand was more isolated. It was an idealism after all that had originated in American isolationism.

If this idealism, and the belief that it really provided the solution to the problems of the new situation in which the Dominions found themselves, did not determine foreign policy, it did produce gestures of friendship towards the countries of the 'Near North'. Such, for instance, was the Volunteer Graduate Scheme, created in Australia in the early 1950s with strong backing from the Student Christian Movement. A similar scheme in New Zealand also anticipated the American Peace Corps, and over the years a number of graduates have served in the educational and medical services of Indonesia. Immigration reform was a tougher proposition. In 1958 the Australian government made the issuance of entry permits more discretionary, and between 1957 and 1961 some 2,800 non-Europeans were naturalised. But this seemed only an argument that the Government should make its policy more open, and enjoy the credit of it. Practically, of course, even the most large-scale programme would not solve the problems of Asia. But a shift, for instance, to an American-style quota system might serve idealistic objectives. One difficulty was that a quota would probably involve taking just the trained people that Asian countries themselves so much needed to utilise. The best contribution the A.N.Z.A.C. powers could make appeared to be the training of Asians.

251

Idealists might become concerned that, apart trom this, there was little they could do to guarantee the survival of the Dominions. They could still work to guarantee that, if they did not survive, it was not because of ignorance. Educational and other media have been used in Australia to ensure that the Near North did not remain the Unknown North. In New Zealand, too, they now counter a trend towards isolation. While there are many rifts to bridge, in some sense Australia and New Zealand are now seen and see themselves as Austral-Asia.

1 Vietnam

INDO-CHINA was important to Japan, both in relation to its war in China and to its plans for Southeast Asia, and, with their capitulation to the Germans in Europe in mid-1940, the weakness of the French became very obvious. Late in August the Japanese undertook to respect French sovereignty and the territorial integrity of Indo-China, in return for a recognition of their preponderant economic and political interests. In September a Japanese naval demonstration secured military facilities in Tonkin, designed to facilitate the war on Chiang Kai-shek. The weakness of the French encouraged the Thai nationalists, and early in 1941 Japan imposed its mediation on the two parties in a developing border war. In a treaty of May 1941 Indo-China retroceded to Thailand the provinces of Battambang and Siemreap in Cambodia, and parts of Champassak and Luang Prabang on the right bank of the Mekong lost in 1904.

The German invasion of Russia opened the way for a fuller overthrow of the colonial frontiers, but in Indo-China the Japanese sought accord with the Vichy régime. Late in July they secured military, naval and air facilities in southern Vietnam, and indeed the Saigon air-base — within bombing range of Singapore — was used in the southern offensive at the end of the year. For the moment the presence of the French was rather convenient to Japan than otherwise, but it tied up a large body of Japanese troops. The Vichy Governor-General, Decoux, moreover, sought to counter the appeal of pan-Asian propaganda by developing a 'mystique Indochine', fostering loyalist youth movements, expanding education, while repressing even moderate political activities. The Japanese, however, protected movements like the Cao Dai and the Hoa Hao.

With the Allied offensive of 1943, the Japanese position deteriorated, and in March 1945 they took over direct control in Indo-China. Fearing a Badoglio, they displaced Decoux, who had in fact opened relations with De Gaulle and the forces of

French liberation. The independence of the states of Indo-China was announced, though Cuong De was not brought from Japan, and it was Bao-dai who denounced the protectorate treaties and renamed the country Vietnam. But the conservative nationalist government he formed under Tran Trong Kim was allowed little effective power and had little hope of winning popular support amid conditions of famine and chaos. Only at a late date did it gain control over the 'colony' of Cochin-China. The policy of the Japanese thus followed that of the French in weakening the more moderate nationalist elements.

Furthermore the Indo-Chinese Communists had equipped themselves to attract nationalist support. In 1941 the Central Committee retired over the Chinese frontier, and set up the League for the Independence of Vietnam, or Viet Minh, in order to group nationalists together in a struggle against France and Japan and for independence and agrarian reform. The Chinese were distrustful, even though Nguyen Ai Quoc changed his name to Ho Chi Minh, but their attempts to set up a competing organisation were in vain. The Chinese believed that the French would not return — and President Roosevelt was opposed to their recolonisation — and hoped a Vietnamese state would develop in their orbit. But it was difficult to contain the Viet Minh, who alone could effectively utilise the popular discontent with the paddy-exactions and repressions of the Franco-Japanese régime. From 1944 Vo Nguyen Giap indeed built up an army for the Viet Minh, with some American aid, and the movement was well placed to dominate northern Tonkin in the Tran Trong Kim phase. The capitulation of the Japanese led in early September to Bao-dai's abdication and Ho Chi Minh's proclamation of independence.

The proposals of the French provisional government, dating from March, were very different. It envisaged a federal Indo-China within a French Union, with foreign affairs and defence in French hands, and Cochin-China, Tonkin, and Annam as separate units in the federation with Laos and Cambodia. Much depended on the occupation forces. The High Command divided the country at the 16th parallel. South of this British and British Indian troops came in to disarm the Japanese. In fact General Gracey aimed to restore the French, and his measures led to the flight of the Viet Minh's Committee of the South and the re-establishment of French civil administration. In Cochin-China, too, the new High Commissioner, d'Argenlieu, could find separatist collaborators among the Gallicised landowners, officials, business and professional men of the old colony. But was Cochin-China, now the granary of Vietnam, to be the basis for outside conquest, as in the late nineteenth century? or was the strength of their position there to lead the French to compromise? In Tonkin and Annam, the Vietnamese homeland, the Viet Minh was much stronger and Chinese influence much greater. Indeed north of the 16th parallel the occupation forces were those of the Nationalist Chinese, anxious, like the Chinese in the late nineteenth century, to oppose conquest by the French. Ho Chi Minh sought to conciliate them by widening the bases of his nationalist appeal and nominally dissolving the Communist party; though it seems that, even while the Chinese were still present, his movement continued beneath the surface to destroy its opponents, including provincial mandarins like Ngo Dinh Khoi (a brother of Ngo Dinh Diem). In February 1946 the Chinese agreed to withdraw in return for the surrender of the French concessions in China itself. This seemed to mean that a compromise was at hand. Ho Chi Minh made a preliminary agreement with the French agent Sainteny in March, by which France recognised the state of Vietnam as a member of the federation and the Union, while the uniting of the three areas — Tonkin, Annam, and Cochin-China — was to be the subject of a referendum. French troops then entered Hanoi.

Even before the anticipated conference had opened at Fontainebleau, however, the High Commissioner — enjoying a traditional autonomy which the instability of the governments of the Fourth Republic did nothing to reduce — had recognised the Moi plateaux as an autonomous region and, still more significantly, had recognised an autonomous republic of Cochin-China. D'Argenlieu dealt the conference the *coup de grâce* by calling a conference at Dalat in August, with delegates from Cambodia, Laos, Cochin-China, and the Populations Montagnardes. The opening of outright conflict came late in November when, following a number of incidents, the French attacked Hai-phong. The struggle, already joined in the south in Gracey's day, spread over all Vietnam. The French lacked the men and supplies for a quick victory, even if shipping had been available. They secured control of the cities and communications but not of the countryside. And they lacked the men and supplies for the guerilla warfare that ensued. The Viet Minh were better able to organise resistance than the old dynasty.

It was in this context that during 1947 the French began to shift away from the policy of Cochin-Chinese separatism and attempt to attract nationalist support for a new Bao-dai régime.

In December the ex-emperor signed an accord with D'Argenlieu's successor, Bollaert. The régime, set up early in 1948, won
some concessions, including the union of the three regions.
Furthermore, though Bollaert in a speech of September 1947
had still declared that France was the protector of minorities,
the 'Thai federation' that was created was brought to swear
allegiance to Bao-dai. But his régime did not enjoy sufficient
autonomy to attract nationalist support. In June it secured the
recognition of the independence of Vietnam as an associated
state within the French Union, but that independence was
hedged about with restrictions. A definitive agreement, that of
the Elysée (March 1949), still left the French in diplomatic
and military control and, according to the Pau agreements of
1950, Vietnam was in a customs and monetary union with Laos
and Cambodia that seemed too much to resemble the old
Union. Few were attracted to the régime: intellectuals looked
to the Viet Minh or remained aloof from politics. Treaties of
'independence and association' were negotiated only in 1953-4.

The French concessions to the nationalists in Vietnam — be-
lated and sapped by the difficulty of decision-making in the
Fourth Republic — had been pressed on by the advance of the
Communists in China, and by the necessity of establishing a
counter-régime before the Communist-led Viet Minh could thence
receive an accession of strength. So far it had not been helped
by Moscow, which was hoping in 1946 and early 1947 that
France itself would become Communist. (In March 1947 the
French Communist leader, Thorez, as Vice-Premier, counter-
signed the order for military action against the Republic.) The
shift towards violence in Asia, following the check in Europe,
opened up wider prospects for the Vietnamese. Still more did
the victory of the C.C.P. and the setting up of the People's
Republic in October 1949. Once more China would oppose a
French conquest. Yet in some sense the prospects were narrower.
They induced further outside interference. The U.S., shifting
towards a policy of 'Communist containment', saw the Viet Minh
as an aspect of international Communism, and aided the opposing forces. The Communists increased their aid to the Viet
Minh. Furthermore, the Chinese offered training in Maoist
guerilla tactics. Once more the adoption of Chinese methods
was to promote a southward movement. But, though the Viet
Minh became more rigidly Communist, even the Vietnamese
Communists were anxious to preserve Vietnam from Chinese
domination. Chinese methods, indeed, had earlier provided a
defence against China. Even — or perhaps most of all — in the

Vietnamese case, there was a core of truth in the Nehru analysis.

The tactics of the Viet Minh amounted in fact to building a political structure to rival that of the French and Bao-dai. It was based, of course, upon the villages and upon the tribes (the fact that the Chinese community in the north was rela· tively small perhaps only aided the Viet Minh). The Bao-dai régime, on the other hand, refused to come to life. It did not receive the support that would enable it to build contacts with the villages. The methods to which the French were driven — including the use of napalm — did not aid their cause. And the activities of the Viet Minh in mountain regions led them to disperse their forces. It was the determination to defend the approach across the Plain of Jarres to Vienchang — part of the Associated State of Laos — that provoked the most disastrous dispersal. The defeat at Dien Bien Phu underlined the impos- sibility of military victory in the *sale guerre* that was withering the flower of St. Cyr. Though the end of the Korean war had left the Chinese more free to help the Viet Minh, new currents in Communist policy were to enable Mendès-France to secure an armistice. The Soviet Union, too, hoped to ensure the French rejection of the European Defence Community — again it was putting European objectives first. Impressed by the prospect of Communist victory, and believing that the rest of Southeast Asia would rapidly collapse, the U.S. Government, on the other hand, had considered a Guernica-type strike at its opponents. Its actual unwillingness to risk war, however, was concealed by the un· willingness of its allies. The British, affected by recent evidence of nuclear destructiveness, worked for a compromise. Under the Geneva agreements of July Vietnam was, pending national elec- tions in July 1956, to be 'partitioned' at the 17th parallel, close to the early seventeenth century division between the Trinh and the Nguyen lands. Neither zone was to participate in military alliances. The U.S. agreed to abide by the agreements without actually signing them, but immediately moved to create the S.E.A.T.O. structure. The Bao-dai régime — nationalist but inef- fective to the last — would not accept the agreements. Later in the year the Pau arrangements came to an end, and with them the remnants of the old Indo-China structure. Any economic ad- vantages they offered were sacrificed to political exigencies.

Northern Vietnam, as so often exceptional in Southeast Asian history, had come under Chinese influence. Exceptionally, too, it now underwent an agrarian revolution. In fact, there was no real land reform problem and the initial motives were mainly

political – to put land into the hands of those who would owe
it to the régime – and the economic results disastrous. More
consolidated efforts followed in 1958-60, but the objects were
still political, namely large-scale collectivisation, expansion of
production and industrialisation. With Russian and Chinese
aid and technicians, and heavy pressure on peasant living
standards, some industrialisation was achieved in an area where
some had existed pre-war. Communications were poor, and the
only obvious asset was coal. But the major problem was that
the food supply remained totally inadequate, while the population rose rapidly; and collectivisation was not the answer, as
it seemed to be in the Russia of the late 1920s. One observer
indeed suggests that rice is 'bourgeois', 'reactionary', inasmuch
as it requires the patient labour of many devoted hands, and
collectivisation, borrowed from wheat areas, does not guarantee
this.[94] Yet it might be argued that the whole economic programme – which borrowed much from the Chinese example,
though not the 'communes' of 1958 – was in fact designed to
avert satellite status, to be some guarantee of independence, to
avoid a full-scale popular revolt – paralleling the upset of
earlier régimes – that might bring in the Chinese to 'save Communism'.

The failure of this paradoxical policy involved the North
Vietnam leaders in yet a further paradox. Reunion with southern
Vietnam – the rice-bowl – became the more essential, and a
powerful motive for the Viet Cong war. But if the seventeenth
century apprehension of the Chinese had restrained the Trinh
in its struggle against the Nguyen, so now a war to the south
tended to increase Chinese influence, even though the object
might be to secure the rice that may facilitate industrialisation
and so avert satellite status. Within the leadership there were
divisions, above all between Truong Chinh and others who
looked to the Chinese, and Vo Nguyen Giap and the army
leaders who were much more lukewarm or hostile. The growth
of the Sino-Soviet split was naturally reflected in this leadership.
Ho Chi Minh, at the head of the government – an old man –
required all his skill at once to balance his colleagues and to
maintain as a guarantee of independence as close ties with
Russia as possible without antagonising the Chinese. In the war
to the south Russia favoured negotiating reunification and
China favoured campaigning to the finish. The continuance
of the campaign and its escalation made the position of the
Russians and of the Russian party increasingly untenable. Yet

it was still perhaps possible that unification — even achieved in the Chinese style — would rather limit than increase Chinese penetration.

In part this situation was, of course, the result of the policy pursued in southern Vietnam. Initially this prevented the north putting its development on a pan-Vietnamese footing and turned it more into the Chinese than the Southeast Asian sphere. A new outside power had stepped into the colonial south. The U.S. President, Eisenhower, assured Bao-dai's minister, Ngo Dinh Diem, of his support. A Republic of Vietnam was set up after a fraudulent plebiscite in October 1955. The frontier was sealed and the national elections evaded. The régime was strengthened by a reaction to news of the agrarian terror in the north and the peasant revolts there following the Hungarian uprising.

In the subsequent years the growing dictatorship of President Ngo more than dissipated this reaction. In some ways it resulted — perhaps paradoxically — from the very intensity of his nationalism and from the fact that he came from the Vietnamese homeland. He saw himself not simply as a Nguyen ruler, preserving the independence of the south against the north with outside aid, but as a new Gia-long using that aid to reunify Vietnam after a long period of division. To this end, he must establish his power in the south first. Thus he crushed the sects which, alienated by the Viet Minh in the late 1940s, had become more Francophile. His régime became increasingly authoritarian, bolstered by the French totalitarian doctrine of 'Personalism' or *Nhan Vi,* by the concentration of power in his family, by the removal of moderates and reformers, by fraudulent elections based on refugee constituencies. Some 850,000 refugees had, indeed, come from the north, and it was upon them in particular that the régime rested. Again, the north had been the stronghold of Catholics: some 600,000 of the refugees were Catholic, as was the President himself. The south resented dictatorial rule, rule in the hands of northerners, rule in the hands of one mandarin family, rule in the hands of Catholics. After all it had a tradition of relative independence of the north and its Confucianist mandarins; it had been most affected by French liberal traditions; its religion was Buddhist, Taoist, spiritualist — it was not where the missionaries had concentrated. The régime was to end in bloody violence late in 1963. But even before then it had been subjected to the attempted paratrooper putsch of 1960 and the palace had been attacked early in 1962. Its measures against the Chinese — assimilation for all those born in Vietnam, exclusion of aliens from certain professions — carried through even in face of K.M.T. protests, merely kicked away one pillar of the political structure. The régime had alienated beyond hope of redemption by such means the all-important elements that might have linked it with Vietnamese village life.

At the same time, the régime hesitated to win the villagers by effective attempts at agrarian reform. The region — especially Cochin-China — was one of large landowners and tenant farmers. An ordinance of 1955 aimed to give tenants written contracts, to fix rents at 15-25% of the principal crop, to limit interest on loans. In fact enforcement was difficult: probably most tenants paid 33⅓% or more and their tenure was insecure. Another ordinance of 1956 provided that no person was to own over 100 hectares of rice land: the excess was to be sold to the government for resale to the tenants or to others. The process lagged badly, and generally land policy did little to attract support. The peasants indeed remembered the days when the Viet Minh had controlled the countryside and the landlords had fled to Saigon. They were wide open to the revival of Viet Minh tactics of mingled persuasion and violence. The government's reaction — its raids, its counter-violence — only promoted further opposition. It imported from Malaya the notion of 'strategic hamlets'. In Malaya, however, it had been a matter of moving Chinese squatters; in Vietnam it was a matter of uprooting Vietnamese villagers. The growing violence of the battle in the countryside — especially in the delta region — included, too, the self-defeating use of napalm that the French had essayed. The scope of insurgent operations grew larger. The Americans had trained an army with a new Korea in mind and not for counterinsurgency. The deterioration of the situation led to their growing participation and that of their allies.

In part this deterioration resulted from the policy of the Ngo régime towards the mountain peoples, the third pillar of Vietnamese society. It made the autonomous areas of northern Vietnam appear more attractive, though in fact the tribes there were more advanced, and there, too, there were revolt and repression. Tribal resentment at the influx of lowland Vietnamese into the highlands — sometimes northern refugees seeking new homes — added to the Viet Minh's opportunities. Through the border territories aid could penetrate to the insurgents from the north via southern Laos. And any attention the Americans and South Vietnamese gave to them would tie them up as similar operations had tied up the French.

The disappearance of the Ngo régime produced a vacuum

at the centre without solving the problems it had created in the countryside. A number of military leaders contended for power, but few respectable civilian leaders were available. Amid apprehensions that the resistance would collapse, the Americans began in 1964 to bomb the Laos supply-routes and in 1965 first military and communications targets and then other installations in North Vietnam itself. This was hardly likely to bring success in the south. It might, however, reduce infiltration from the north. The escalation of the war was accompanied by offers to negotiate, together with offers of economic aid. But the U.S. was not prepared to accept a complete unification even if accompanied by an ostensible neutralisation — now advocated by the French of all people. At the most the Americans seemed to envisage the re-establishment of economic links between north and south. Was this enough for the North Vietnamese? or had the escalation of the war committed the decision to the Chinese? To the latter continued struggle was perhaps preferable to any sort of reunification.

2 Laos

THE SITUATION in Laos had as ever been affected by the situation in the neighbouring territories of Thailand and Vietnam. The Japanese permitted the Thais to acquire those parts of Luang Prabang and Champassak ceded to France in 1904 and not regained in 1907. On the other hand, the Vichy régime sought to strengthen the prestige of the Indo-Chinese rulers as part of the 'mystique Indochine'. A treaty of 1941 incorporated Vienchang into Luang Prabang, while Charles Rochet stimulated the Decouxist National Renovation Movement led by Katay Don Sasorith. In turn the overthrow of Vichy by the Japanese led to a proclamation of independence in April 1945, and the surrender of the Japanese enabled the prime minister, Petsarath, a member of a younger branch of the royal house, to announce in Vienchang independence for all Laos and to form a committee of Free Laos (Lao Issara) including members of his family and most of the small élite. The Nationalist Chinese occupation forces acted as a delaying action on the return of the French forces, and only by April 1946 had the Issara been quelled or driven over the Mekong. The Free Laotian government was established in exile in Bangkok where it was welcomed as an opponent of an always unwelcome French rule in lands that capital had once controlled. In a *modus vivendi* of August 1946, however, the French recognised the unification of Laos — that is, of those parts of Luang Prabang, Vienchang and Champassak under their influence — and a constitution was promulgated in 1947. The changes in French Indo-China policy dictated by events in Vietnam led to Laos' becoming an Associated State of the Union in 1948, and to the 1949 agreement that gave it greater autonomy. This left the exiles with little in the way of issues and their movement — to which the new military régime in Bangkok was in any case opposed — dissolved in 1949: most returned to Laos, including Souvanna Phouma, but not his half-brothers Petsarath and Souvanna Vong. Petsarath faded out of politics, but Souvanna Vong had already broken with the other emigrés — especially Katay Don Sasorith — and favoured armed resistance in concert with the Viet Minh.

During 1951 and 1952 Laos enjoyed relative security under governments led by Souvanna Phouma and by Phoui Sananikone, a member of an important Vienchang family who had led resistance to the Japanese. But in March 1951 Souvanna Vong had appeared as head of the Laotian dissidents in northern Vietnam and formed the Pathet Lao, and when in 1953 Viet Minh volunteers began to move into northern Laos — through the region most open to Vietnamese penetration — with them came the Pathet Lao to set up a government in the province of Samneua. Spurred by this and by events in Vietnam, the French granted Laos full autonomy within the French Union.

The French had been able to avoid in Laos identification of Communism and nationalism, as in Vietnam. Indeed the fact of identification in Vietnam was an argument against it in Laos. But their new gesture had a number of untoward results. Firstly, it meant the departure of French officials from the tribal areas. The Pathet Lao, who might be hampered by the Buddhist Lao peasants' opposition to the Vietnamese, could utilise the Khas' opposition to the Laos. Secondly, the departure of the French administration from Laos removed an element of cohesion in a kingdom long divided, only recently reconstituted under the rule of one of its royal lines, a kingdom the prey of guerilla warfare in the 1940s; and now power tended to come into the hands of feudal families in the centre and the south. Thirdly, Laos' emergence as a full Associated State committed Navarre to its defence and led to the defeat of Dien Bien Phu.

In 1954, however, Laos was in a stronger position than Vietnam, and not simply because the division of Vietnam was welcome in Laos. The Communists were not liberators in Laos. But, despite the pressure of the Indians, the French retained two air bases and a military mission, and Phong Saly and Samneua provinces — which commanded the approaches to Luang Prabang and Vienchang respectively — were awarded to the Pathet Lao pending the regrouping of Laotian forces and the holding of elections in 1955. A new source of disunity had been added to the old. Furthermore, Laos, always dependent financially on the other Indo-Chinese countries, was in a precarious position economically.

Agreement between the Pathet Lao and Souvanna Phouma's government was reached only in 1957 — it had been opposed in 1956 by Katay Don Sasorith's Nationalists — and under it Souvanna Vong entered the cabinet and there were Pathet Lao members in the National Assembly from May 1958. The delay prejudiced the attainment of unity. For, meanwhile, a new conservative group had appeared. Among the 'Young Ones' — students returned from abroad, soldiers, junior officials, formed into a Committee for the Defence of the National Interests — there was discontent with Souvanna Phouma's concessions to the Communists. Furthermore, Laos' economic situation had invited American aid in the form of a commodity import programme. But this tainted the régime with corruption. A new government came in under Phoui Sananikone which introduced a tough policy towards the Pathet Lao. New fighting followed in Samneua and Phong Saly in 1959, in the course of which the royal army, poorly trained by the French, fared badly, and spread alarmist rumours of a Viet Minh invasion (September).

This induced Phoui to return to neutralism. But again circumstances had changed. Laos had not been able to profit from the co-existence phase. And now late in 1959 there followed an American-inspired coup by the Defence Secretary Phoumi Nosavan, and the C.D.I.N. triumphed in the elections of April 1960. A new neutralist coup by Kong Le, a parachutist captain, followed in Vienchang in August, while the cabinet was away in Luang Prabang, and Souvanna Phouma was called upon to attempt a coalition with Phoumi. The failure of this led to civil war, with the U.S. backing Souvanna Phouma's opponents, Phoumi and Prince Boun Oum of Champassak, who advanced from Savannakhet on Vienchang in December. In turn Souvanna Phouma secured aid from the Russians. They also joined the British — co-chairmen in 1954 — in supporting a new conference in Geneva advocated by Sihanouk of Cambodia. Late in 1961 this agreed on basic terms for guaranteeing Laotian neutrality under a coalition government. Presumably the Russians wished to avoid Chinese intervention and so supplied arms to the neutral régime, but also wanted and for the same reason an early settlement. The coalition was installed in June 1962, and in July fourteen nations at Geneva agreed to respect Laos neutrality, thus furling the S.E.A.T.O. umbrella.

In some sense — and because Russia and the U.S. had been able to come together — Laos had managed to return to 1954, but in very different circumstances. The conservative swing in Laos politics had in fact weakened its security, strengthened the Pathet Lao, and ensured the Viet Minh a command of the 'Ho Chi Minh trail' to the south, on which Tchepone was a main base. Undoubtedly U.S. policy was much influenced by concern over Thailand. Naturally — and by railway — Laos was a gateway into Thailand, especially into its Laotian provinces in the northeast. But to sponsor Thai policies in Laos was unlikely to reduce Lao distrust of the Thais, and in fact it did much more. Early in 1962 Phoumi was to conduct a rearguard action, and his rout produced a panic over the invasion of Thailand. Early in 1965 he was in vain to attempt a coup. His influence, it seemed, was ended, and a precarious neutrality was ensured in Laos. But his activities — and those of the U.S. — had helped to leave Thailand open to infiltration, if not to invasion.

3 Cambodia

INITIALLY in this phase events in Cambodia followed a pattern somewhat similar to those in Laos. The early years of the war saw a demonstration by Buddhist monks organised by Son Ngoc Thanh, stimulated by resentment at the loss of the western provinces to the Thais. The end of the Decoux régime saw king Sihanouk proclaim independence, following Bao-dai, and the Japanese installed Son Ngoc Thanh first as foreign, then as prime minister. But if he had earlier made use of Cambodian fears of Thai irredentism, now he made himself unpopular by seeking the support of local Vietnamese. Once more the mid-way position of Cambodia aided the establishment of European authority. The British occupying forces arrested Son Ngoc Thanh, and king Sihanouk proclaimed loyalty to France and accepted the *modus vivendi* of January 1946. By the end of the year the lost provinces were regained. This weakened the Free Cambodians or Khmer Issarak, partly centred there, and many surrendered under amnesty in 1947, becoming Democrats in the Assembly. Others looked to the Viet Minh from 1948. Distrustful of the Viet Minh, and obtaining no support from the new Thai régime, some were won back in 1949, when Cambodia became an Associated State. But opposition from the Democrats and the Issarak, allied with the Viet Minh, subsequently grew, and in 1951 Son Ngoc Thanh returned from France. Finally in 1953 the king did away with the Assembly and determined to outbid the opposition by winning full independence from the French. The Viet Minh entered Laos in March 1953, and after a prolonged crisis and much demonstrative diplomacy, the king of Cambodia secured the independence he sought. In November 1953 he re-entered Phnom Penh in triumph.

By 1954 Cambodia was in some ways in a stronger position than Laos. Under the agreements of that year, the Issarak did not secure the privileged position of the Pathet Lao, though Cambodia did pledge itself not to enter military alliances or take part in any aggressive policy. Less exposed to the north, Cambodia had suffered less infiltration, and the national cause had outbid the Communist cause. In part this was due to the greater authority of the king. Then, again, Cambodia was economically in a stronger position. The predominantly subsistence economy had suffered little damage, and rice exports could be built up. And if Cambodia was technologically backward, it enjoyed the stability guaranteed by a peasant proprietary and by the absence of a population problem. Much of this was illustrated in Sihanouk's apple-cart triumph of 1955. He had resigned the throne to his father and built up a new party, the People's Socialist Community or Sangkum Reastr Niyum. Benefiting both from traditional authority and from success in the struggle for independence, it won all the seats in the Assembly.

Another problem Laos and Cambodia shared, though in different ways: the problem of security involved in the dissolution of French Indo-China and the situation of the two countries between Thailand and Vietnam. In Laos the delayed creation of unity had been further put off by intervention from the Communist north and from pro-western Thailand, and an uneasy neutralism was only gradually attained. In Cambodia Sihanouk was in a better position to decide policy. To some extent Cambodia had been looking towards Thailand. Saigon had been its economic outlet, but that region was in Vietnamese hands (though it still had a substantial Khmer population). The through railway to Bangkok appeared rather more attractive. In 1954-5, it seems, Sihanouk sought a territorial guarantee from the U.S. He secured a military agreement in 1955, but no more. Even this military agreement was limited because India believed Cambodia ideally suited to its Southeast Asian policy and accordingly used its position on the International Control Commission of 1954. Sihanouk came to endorse the five principles. But this did not result merely from Indian pressure, or even from the desire to draw on a wide circle of countries for economic aid to his backward, if contented country, in support of plans that would reduce reliance upon Chinese and Vietnamese skills and open a Cambodian overseas port at Sihanoukville. It resulted from his position in relation to Thailand and to southern Vietnam and from his recognition that America was committed, especially after 1955, to both of them.

In view of Cambodia's history, it was not surprising that its present ruler took the neutralist line and sought the support of Indian influence. But India's support proved inadequate: its policy did not work because it was not applied among Cam-

bodia's neighbours. After one of several border incidents with
his neighbours, Sihanouk recognised Communist China *de jure*
in July 1958. In 1960 he declared that 'if Cambodia is surrounded by countries aligned on the Western bloc, it is not for
that matter an isolated country'; 'neutral Cambodia has many
friends, and friends that count'.[95] Even Cambodia's reaction to
the Viet Cong war and to the prospects of Viet Cong triumph
must be seen in this context. If, then, Cambodia would no
longer be 'surrounded by countries aligned on the Western bloc',
it would still face Vietnam and Thailand. Reassurance from the
major power in the region would be essential. And this meant
China (which in the past had been prepared to contemplate
fragmentation of the region), even if, paradoxically, Cambodia
had excluded the local Chinese from certain professions; even
if it is conceivable that it was pressed to provide a channel for
aid to the Viet Cong. In the event of the neutralisation of the
whole region, Cambodia would still require a guarantee. Would
India's policy ever work? Cambodia's position between Thailand
and Vietnam had long been a standing invitation to outside
powers.

4 Thailand

THE Thais had taken advantage of Japanese pressure on French
Indo-China to operate some of the pan-Thai policies of the
military régime and regain the cessions to Laos and Cambodia
of 1904 and 1907. But their policy was not merely dictated by
irredentism. When, after the ultimatum of 8th December 1941,
they agreed to the passage of Japanese troops, it was because
this was the only means of preserving the remnants of Thai
independence. And Pibul Songgram was obsessed by doubts until
he was reassured by the early defeats of the Allies to the south.
Thus convinced that Thailand had seen which way the wind
was blowing, in January he declared war on Britain and the

U.S. In the wake of the Japanese, it was true, the Thais made war on the Shan states and in July 1943 acquired Kengtung and Mongpan. The Japanese, moreover, ceded to them the four northern states of Malaya, thus realising another part of the imperialist programme. With 1943, however, came the prospect of probable defeat for the Japanese, and Pibul prepared for an ultimate attack upon them that might put him right with the Allies when the wind blew the other way. In the event he resigned in 1944. Thailand's credit with the Allies was saved by the 'Free Thai' movement — some volunteers had been trained by the Americans and sent to south China to infiltrate in 1943 — with which Pridi, who had resigned from Pibul's government on his capitulation to the Japanese, had established a connexion.

At the end of the war the Thais made concessions to the Nationalist Chinese government, signing a treaty of amity in 1946, and admitting for the first time an ambassador and consuls. The Thais sought also to conciliate Britain by returning its territories — thus re-establishing the Patani frontier — much more promptly than those of France. But Britain had been piqued by the Thai declaration of war, by the use of Thailand by the Japanese invaders, and by the damage done to its large interests in Thailand, and wanted some change in the political structure in that country. The Americans were anti-imperialist and, as in the earlier negotiations over extraterritoriality, had no great commercial interests to serve. So the Thais sought to play off the U.S. — which had not recognised the declaration of war, and saw Thailand as liberated territory — against the British, who were able to impose compulsory rice deliveries and repeat the prohibition on a Kra canal, but not to effect any major political change nor, in particular, any reduction in the armed forces.

Seni Pramoj, the ambassador in Washington, a descendant of Rama II's 61st child, became premier. Only after the agreement with the British was signed early in 1946 were elections held and then Pridi became premier. A party system emerged, but it was in fact a matter of factions or cliques, amalgams of personal followings in which patronage and corruption were still important. The Democrat opposition contrived to connect Pridi with the shooting of king Ananda in June, and in August he resigned, to be succeeded by another Promoter. Late in 1947 the military leader Pibul carried out a coup and Khuang, the Democrat leader, was installed as a window-dressing measure, and in order to ensure foreign recognition for the coup. Then

Pibul assumed power himself. An attempted coup by Pridi was defeated early in 1949 by army and police action, and another in 1951, and increasingly the appallingly corrupt Phao Sriyanaond, the Deputy Chief of Police, Pibul's aide in the Japanese phase, and the commander of the First Army, Sarit, a participant in the 1947 coup, became the strong men of Thailand. In 1957 Sarit triumphed, exiling Phao and Pibul. After another temporary legitimising régime, Sarit assumed the premiership. In October 1958 he scrapped the constitution and in 1959 summoned a Constitutional Assembly. On his death in 1963 his associate, General Thanom, succeeded him.

The nature of Thai politics had not changed. There had been no western intervention to change it. There was no pressure from within. No invasion, no struggle against colonialism stimulated popular participation in politics. Economically, too, most areas remained stably based on subsistence agriculture (though decreasing productivity gave some cause for concern), while rice and rubber guaranteed export earnings. Politics remained a matter of coups by the Promoters and military leaders, legitimised by temporary administrations and some democratic trappings. Indeed the period witnessed the completion of the military predominance of the 1930s over the civilian faction. The gulf in policy was not, however, as wide as might be suspected. Such issues as had enlivened politics pre-war reappeared in new forms under both the civilian and the military régimes. These issues were, of course, 'non-colonial' issues, the questions of Thai irredentism and of the Chinese.

In relation to the former, it is true that, while Pridi had restored the pre-1938 privileges for Muslims in Patani, apprehensions of the new military régime produced a revolt there early in 1948. In Cambodia and Laos the pre-Pibul and post-Pridi policies were, however, closely connected. Pridi had fostered the Issarak movements of Laos and Cambodia and created a 'Southeast Asia League' after the Dutch police action in Indonesia. In a sense, however, this was simply an alternative to the earlier policy of regaining the lost provinces which the French had reacquired. In 1948 Pibul and his followers were denouncing Pridi's ideas as 'Communism'. But the 1953 notion of a 'Buddhist Bloc', and the promotion of transport connexions, indicated a hope of association with the newly independent states of Laos and Cambodia. It was, too, a means of dealing with growing discontent in the Lao areas of north-east Thailand, beset by tenancy problems and penetrated by the Viet Minh, penetrated also by a Lao nationalism designing to recreate the old kingdom of Lan Chang. The failure of the Bloc policy was perhaps inevitable. Thailand was soon engaged in violent border disputes with Cambodia. And Sarit — whose secretary was Luang Vichitr — supported his cousin Phoumi in Laos and was disgusted at the settlement of 1961-2, though American and allied forces had been rushed into Thailand on Phoumi's rout.

The Buddhist Bloc proposal had been influenced also by Peking's recognition of a Thai Nationality Autonomous People's Government, centred in Yunnan, in January 1953. In this move Pridi, who had fled to China, was thought to be influential. But there had been some continuity between his attitude to the Chinese community when in power and that of his successors. Pridi had been relatively favourable, of course, after the treaty of 1946. But his economic policy — involving an export monopoly of rice which, though installed because of Thailand's commitment to deliver rice to foreign countries under the peace treaties, bore some resemblance to his plan of the 1930s — was widely defended as helping to break the stranglehold of the Chinese. It was continued till 1954 by Pridi's successors. They also sought to Thai-ify the economy by limiting alien business activities and by creating government corporations as pre-war. In practice the government, police and army officers who ran these corporations compromised with the Chinese entrepreneurs. The former secured wealth and expertise, the latter protection: it was a pattern that had recurred in the history of Thai government activities in the commercial sphere and their relationship with the Chinese community.

The Peking government accused the military régime of oppressing the Chinese in 1950. Certainly there had been anti-Chinese police raids — increasingly under Phao they were called anti-Communist raids — and there were even, as pre-war, measures against ethnic, not merely alien Chinese. The Peking government could not make its claim to protection felt. The fact was that the Thai régime felt secure behind the American protection that, as a non-colonial country, it was able to accept and, as a country near the Chinese border and with a large Chinese minority, it was keen to accept. Pibul had supported the U.N. in Korea. And Bangkok flourished as the S.E.A.T.O. centre.

It was a question, however, whether the military régime had not over-committed the country. By its alliance with the U.S. it could pursue an anti-Chinese policy, even obtain support in its Laos policies. But these policies, if resembling Pridi's, were certainly more extreme. And the army, of course, had a vested interest in the U.S. alliance. The shift in American policy in the late 1940s had occurred just as Pibul's régime was seeking respectability. The increase in American aid enabled it to maintain a large army. It could be argued that, as pre-war, the military had allowed its extremist policies and its interests to lead the country too far away from its traditionally supple policy towards shifts in the distribution of power in East Asia. Undoubtedly much of the U.S. commitment in Vietnam, the assurances given by Dean Rusk in March 1962 that individual S.E.A.T.O. members could aid Thailand without unanimous S.E.A.T.O. assent, and the rapidity of American reaction to Phoumi's rout, these were determined by apprehension about future Thai policies. Thailand was in a sense the core of mainland Southeast Asia, as the British and the French had seen, as the Japanese had seen. That had helped it to maintain its independence. In turn it was important to the Americans, and its legacy of independence made them especially sensitive to its importance.

5 Burma

THE Japanese victory in Burma was quickly complete by late May 1942, and about 400,000 Indians fled before the invaders. The Burma Independence Army followed in the invaders' wake, concentrating on establishing political control through local committees under the Thakins' leadership, though the Japanese excluded them from the Shan states, and there was strife with the Karens. The Japanese, too, looked to Ba Maw for an administration, and it included only two Thakins, though, with the exception of Communists like Thein Pe, who fled to India, and Soe, a guerilla in the delta, most of them collaborated. 1943 brought independence, covering also the Shan states, except, of course, Kengtung and Mongpan. The new constitution was Fascist in character, with Ba Maw as Adipadi, and various

Thakin Ministers, including Nu, foreign policy, Aung San, defence, Than Tun, agriculture. The Thakins used their opportunity to build organisations and political followings. Mya, the Deputy Prime Minister, Than Tun, and Tin, for instance, led the All-Burma Cultivators League, dating from 1938, Ba Swe and others were associated with the All-Burma T.U.C., dating from 1940. Aung San and Ne Win led what was now called the Burma National Army. But several Thakins, including Kyaw Nyein, were also associated with the underground.

In 1944 the Japanese vainly attempted an invasion of India, and the 14th Army began to reoccupy Burma. In Burma, therefore, there was no interregnum on the Japanese collapse. With B.N.A. support, the Thakins had, however, constructed late in 1944 an organisation that would help to overthrow the Japanese and also render Burma independent of British control, the Anti-Fascist People's Freedom League. In this, too, Thein Pe and Soe were involved. The Supreme Commander, Mountbatten, was anxious to use Burma as a base for further operations and accepted A.F.P.F.L. co-operation. At the end of the Japanese occupation it was thus in a powerful position.

The plans of the Churchill government envisaged the gradual re-establishment of pre-war government and ultimate Dominion status for ministerial Burma, the tribal areas being kept apart till their inhabitants showed a wish for amalgamation. The Labour government spoke of early advance towards self-government in the Commonwealth, with special arrangements for the hill peoples. The A.F.P.F.L. demanded independence. The constitutional contrivance by which India secured independence within the Commonwealth was not yet available as an example to neighbouring Burma. Moreover, the difficulty of securing popular support for anything short of independence, clear enough pre-war, was now emphasised by the breakaway of the two Communist factions, Soe's Red Flags, the revolutionary Communists, and Than Tun's and Thein Pe's White Flags, the orthodox Communists. Aung San thus sought a constituent assembly and independence by early 1948, and to this Attlee assented. The Shans, Kachins, and Chins had agreed to take part in the assembly, though the major Karen organisation, the National Union, boycotted it, and formed a paramilitary National Defence Organisation to parallel the A.F.P.F.L.'s private army, heir of the B.N.A., now called the People's Volunteer Organisation. One dramatic interlude was the assassination of Aung San, Mya and other cabinet members by an embitteredly powerless U Saw. Independence was nevertheless inaugurated by a new government headed by Nu at an astrologically-chosen but otherwise inconvenient moment, 4.20 a.m. on 4th January 1948. Burma was constituted a Union, with separate states for the hill peoples. These had limited powers. The Shan state (which included retroceded Kengtung and Mongpan) and the Kayah state (pre-war Karenni) had the right to secede, the Kachin and Karen states no such right, and the latter no clear boundaries. The Chins accepted a closer connexion still, and their territory was called the Chin Special Division. Separatist unrest in Arakan in 1946-7 led to the setting-up of a commission on Arakan statehood, but it never completed its report.

The whole future of the first state to break away from the Empire-Commonwealth since 1775 (except, perhaps, Ireland) was immediately jeopardised by a series of political catastrophes. Firstly, influenced by the changed attitudes of international Communism, which did not even try to win over the A.F.P.F.L. Socialists, and by the frustrating success the A.F.P.F.L. had enjoyed in the struggle for independence, the White Flags took to open rebellion; and the P.V.O., largely left-wing, but opposed to more westernised socialists like Kyaw Nyein and Ba Swe, failed to afford the government full support, despite concessions like the nationalisation of water transport, a land redistribution act, which hit the remaining Indians, and the continuance of the post-war British rice monopoly. Secondly, the K.N.D.O., seeking a large Karen-Mon state in the south, took advantage of the government's difficulties. It seized Mandalay early in 1949, and virtually besieged the government in Rangoon. That gateway to Burma the government held. But only gradually did it recover its authority elsewhere, even in the lowland regions, during 1950 and 1951. Then came a new peril. From late 1949 fleeing Chinese Nationalists had been moving into Kengtung, and from 1952 they moved across the Salween, just as Ming remnants had moved into upper Burma in the 17th century. The Union government feared that the Chinese Communists might pursue them. A Burmese counter-offensive — significantly called 'Operation Bayinnaung' — found apparent evidence of American support for the K.M.T.

Already Burma had espoused a 'neutralist' foreign policy. Like its withdrawal from the Commonwealth, this was dictated not merely by its colonial experience, but by the presence of the Communist factions and the apprehension that any other policy would provoke outside support of subversion. The disturbances after independence and the rise of Communist power on Burma's

frontier — the new government in Peking was promptly recognised by Rangoon — only gave Burma further arguments for
neutralism. Thus the alarm of 1953 — the same year that China
recognised a Kachin state — led Burma to suspend U.S. aid.
This was followed by a fall in rice prices, and Nu's endorsement of the five principles was accompanied by barter agreements for the sale of rice to the Soviet Union and Communist
states. The chief advantage of co-existence, however, was the hope
that the local Communist parties would be jettisoned. On a
visit to the U.S. in 1955, Nu insisted that Burma could not
'abandon her neutrality without increasing the risk of losing
her independence through subversion'.[96] Indeed the acceptance
of U.S. aid in 1956 precipitated a visit from Bulganin and
Khrushchev. Moreover, the Chinese may have sought to underline
the danger by provoking a border dispute in a region where
boundaries had never really been defined even in colonial days.
Late in 1956 Burma made concessions in order to settle it without its becoming a Cold War issue: three Kachin villages and
the Namwan tract were to go to China. But the agreement was
not definitive. Following the shift in Chinese policy, marked
by the dispute with India, Ne Win's first government concluded a new agreement, exchanging an area in the Wa territory for the Namwan tract. Moreover, it agreed to enter into
no military alliance directed against China. Late in 1960 Nu,
back in power, signed the treaty.

Wartime destruction and the short tenure of the reconstructing colonial power had vastly increased Burma's economic problems. So did the subsequent disturbances, among which must
also be included Muslim terrorism in Arakan. Post-war the
number of Chittagong Muslim Indians in Arakan had increased:
the newcomers were called Mujahids and looked across the
border for support — to Jinnah's movement, to Pakistan — as
had earlier Arakan rebels. These and other political problems
interfered with the development programme that Burma's
leadership sought to implement in order to win the people's
support now that independence had been gained. Nu was identified by many as the Sedja Min, the ideal ruler of folklore, creator
of social utopia. There was thus a popular Burman as well as
a European context for the welfare state plans that aimed at
creating Pyidawtha (Happy Land). Associated were the left-
wing land reforms, involved in the act of 1948 and another
of 1952, directed at redistribution, at the formation of co-
operatives, and ultimately, it is said, at collectivisation: if this

appeared to be a Chinese programme, it had, of course, been designed from the start to outbid the Communists and ensure Burma's independence.

The plans also envisaged substantial industrialisation — an indication of the desire to escape colonialism and secure independence in another way. For the period 1953-60 the plans involved big educational schemes and substantial investment, in part by the government, in other spheres. This would expand agricultural output in order to feed the increased population and (since Burma was not overpopulated) to provide, by the export of rice, the foreign exchange needed for industrialisation. Mineral production was hard to restore, and indeed the gross national product was less in 1957 than in 1939. But up to 1955 substantial capital was available, above all as a result of the Korean boom and the resultant earnings from Burma's agricultural exports, over which a Rangoon government had substantial control. The lack of skills among the Burmese and their indisposition to employ foreigners impeded advance, however, and from 1955 capital itself was in shorter supply, despite barter with the Communist bloc. Adjustments in the development plan in 1956 and 1957 laid more emphasis on agriculture than on industry, and generally slowed down the rate of investment.

In turn this produced political tensions. The Thakin leadership — after the exclusion of the Communists — had held together during the struggle for independence and the struggle to preserve the independent state. The development programme laid a greater strain on their unity, for from it arose the problems of allocating investment in the various fields in which individual Thakins had special interests and secured political support. The chief division was between those who emphasised industry and those who emphasised agriculture. To some extent this division also reflected different levels of westernisation among the élite and the popular elements to which it appealed. The Socialist core of the A.F.P.F.L. was divided by 1953, Thakin Tin and Kyaw Tun — not graduates — concerning themselves above all with the agricultural programme, as distinct from the 'college' set, led by Kyaw Nyein and Ba Swe. Moreover, Nu — without an organisation of his own — was jealous of Ba Swe and Kyaw Nyein, and somewhat contradictorily sought support both among the minorities and among the Buddhists. (His initiative lay behind the Sixth Theravada Synod held in Burma in 1954-6.) When the development programme had to be curbed, the tensions within the élite were strained to breaking-point. The crisis came in 1958.

The elections of 1951 had witnessed a complete triumph for the A.F.P.F.L. (except in Arakan). Those of 1956 saw the growth of an opposition group, the National Unity Front, more left-wing, reflecting popular disappointment with the achievements of the welfare state programme, as well perhaps as the new orientation of international Communism. In the mid-1958 split Nu and the Tin faction turned to the Front for support, and to the Shan and Arakanese minorities (Nu came out openly for an Arakanese state). In face of their opponents, Kyaw Nyein and Ba Swe, they survived a no-confidence motion in the Chamber of Deputies. Nu's faction, the 'Clean A.F.P.F.L.', prepared for elections by seeking support from the minorities (Nu now held out the prospect of a Mon state) and from the left, offering generous amnesty terms to surrendering Communists, P.V.O.s and other rebels, hoping thus to defeat the other faction, the 'Stable A.F.P.F.L.'. In September, however, the army stepped in, prompted, it is said, by younger pro-'Stable' officers, concerned at the advance in Communist influence, the decline of security, and the threat to the Union itself involved in the promises to the minorities. Ne Win assumed the premiership on a caretaker basis. His tenure was prolonged — despite the original provisions of the constitution — till February 1960 when elections were held which — despite the army's anti-Nu measures — produced a great victory for Nu and Tin and a great defeat for Ba Swe and Kyaw Nyein. Nu owed much not merely to left-wing and minority support, but also to his charisma, to his association with Buddhism which had a wide and traditional appeal, as well as to popular detestation of the authoritarian rule of the army.

Nu's new government faced the problems it was bound to face because of the way it came to power. In a constitutional amendment of 1961, he carried out a pledge to make Buddhism the state religion. But this produced opposition from a National Religious Minorities Alliance, representing 3m non-Buddhists; there was a Kachin revolt, and Karen resistance continued. Furthermore even Buddhist minorities were disturbed, because Nu had promised them more than he could give. The Shans' hopes had been raised before 1960 (probably the K.M.T., falling out with the Union, had fostered separatism), and the attitude of the Ne Win caretaker régime had produced open rebellion. But Nu could not satisfy them. Again, the Union (ex-'Clean') Party was beset by the same rivalry that had broken the A.F.P.F.L., rivalry between Thakins like Tin and the more educated, between ex-resistance and professional politicians.

The army leaders were opposed to Nu's religious and federalist policies, and in March 1962 brought off a new coup. This time their government was not simply a caretaker affair. It abandoned Nu's religious and minority policies. But, yielding to the old left-wing P.V.O. element in the army, it adopted the Tin agricultural policy. It wooed the N.U.F. and proclaimed its attachment to socialism. Burma was to try a new combination of fragments of the old A.F.P.F.L. programme. But the trend of all the governments of the late 1950s and early 1960s was away from industrialisation, away from the programmes of the more western-educated, of Socialists like Ba Swe and Kyaw Nyein. If the trend was not towards Buddhism, as with Nu, it was towards the Burman agrarian revolution of Tin. Undoubtedly this programme, like the industrialisation programme, reflected a desire not only for the welfare state and for political influence: it reflected also a desire to guarantee independence by economic success. The fact that it was chosen indicated not only Burma's technological deficiencies and the difficulties faced in world markets. It indicated, as did Nu's programme, the pull of popular participation in politics against the West and its economic and social attitudes. This was the striking feature of post-war as of pre-war Burma.

6 The Andaman and Nicobar Islands

THE JAPANESE arrived in the Andaman and Nicobar islands in March 1942. They brought an end to the penal settlement on the Andamans, freeing the prisoners and burning the records, and there Subhas Bose temporarily set up his government of Indian liberation at the end of 1943. But suspicion of British contacts produced a Japanese reign of terror, especially among the English-speaking Car Nicobarese, while the Jarawa areas in the jungles of the west of South Andaman were apparently bombed. The naval blockade fell heavily on the Andamans and induced greater attempts at self-sufficiency.

From 1947 the Andamans and Nicobars formed the only D-class state in independent India, governed by a Chief Commissioner appointed by the President, with a local nominated advisory council, and represented in the Indian Parliament (Lok Sabha) by a member also nominated by the President. In the Andamans the major emphasis has been on overall economic development, including the chief exports, timber and coconuts, but stressing also the need for greater self-sufficiency. The period since 1949 has in fact seen the substantial realisation of plans for the settlement of agricultural colonists, above all refugees from East Bengal, and by 1960 some 3,000 families had arrived (many Burmese had left). The Nicobars did not share in this plan. There the coconut economy remained, and government agents sought to develop co-operative trading societies in the southern islands on the lines of that in Car Nicobar with a view to eliminating the control of Malayan Chinese.

The island-groups continued greatly to contrast with the rest of Southeast Asia. In fact, the post-war period saw the fuller realisation of the 'colonial' plans for the Andamans of the 1920s, in some sense in turn the result of the convict settlement and the decline of the negritos, as well as of changes within India. The Nicobars, tied to the Andamans by the British, remained so tied, despite their different character and development, and their somewhat closer connexion with the rest of Southeast Asia.

7 The Philippines

THE POST-WAR PHASE in the Philippines was marked as was the pre-war by paradox. The nationalist leaders had extensively collaborated with the Japanese, but MacArthur insisted that Osmena, who came back from exile, should recall the Congress, and released Roxas, who had served in the puppet Laurel government. The transition to independence in 1946 — with Roxas as President — was thus effected with the minimum of social and political change. Paradoxically, too, the economic tie remained close. Upon this the Visayan sugar-barons insisted. The Philippines trade or Bell Act of 1946 provided for free trade till 1954, with absolute quotas for the principal Philippines imports into the U.S.: after 1954 all commodities would be subject to a 5% increase in tariff per annum. The U.S. arrogated the power to allocate the quotas despite the grant of independence, the peso was chained to the dollar, and Americans secured equal rights with the Filipinos in the exploitation of Philippines resources. There was indeed great opposition to the act and to the constitutional amendment involved in the last clause. But the Americans had made payment of war damage compensation dependent on its acceptance. The following year an agreement provided for the establishment of naval and army bases outside Manila. 'It is somewhat anomalous but true that the Philippines remained tied to the U.S. by economic and military bonds almost as closely as before political connexions had been severed.'[97] Philippines history was displaying its continuity, born in some sense of the continuity of its social structure.

The war had, however, produced at least a temporary dislocation, more especially in the rice areas of central Luzon, where Quezon's pre-war measures had done little to improve the tenancy situation. Many landlords fled to Manila, Socialist and Communist and peasant union leaders gained control in the barrios, and the hope was raised of a disruption of social as well as political patterns. Agrarian discontent lay also behind the Communist-formed Huk movement, which began as an anti-Japanese resistance on the Tarlac plain. After the war, Luis Taruc and other Huk leaders, according to united front policy, uneasily co-operated with Osmena, but Roxas and the Liberals triumphed. The few Democratic Alliance deputies elected were excluded from the House of Representatives (for which, it may be noted, the electorate was restricted still to literates: the Philippines still contrasted with other Southeast Asian countries). The situation in central Luzon deteriorated. But full armed struggle — dictated also by the new international Communist line — was delayed by the attempts of Quirino, Roxas' successor, to negotiate with Taruc. The Communist party participated in the 1949 elections. But the failure to secure any agrarian reform and the violence of the army and the constabulary were to complete the alienation of the peasantry.

If the trend in international Communism after 1949 stimulated the Huk movement, the U.S., on the other hand, began once more — as at the turn of the century — to see the Philippines as a bastion of its policy in the Far East. To this the Philippines — with their particular social climate, their unoppressive experience of colonialism, their proximity to China — found it easy to adjust. A new mutual security treaty of 1951 reframed the 1947 pact on military bases. The U.S. had also promptly responded to Quirino's request for an economic mission. The object of the Bell mission of 1950 was indeed 'to see what could be done to make of the Philippines a reliable ally and a secure base in the Pacific'.[98] It urged the fostering of new industries, the development of communications, the encouragement of sound trade unions, a tax on imports to divert dollar exchange to the acquisition of capital goods, increased and more equitable taxes, and financial aid conditioned on carrying out these and other reforms. It also recommended breaking-up large estates, ensuring tenants an equitable share of the crop, extension of credit, technical improvement and diversification of production. In 1952 the American expert Robert S. Hardie reported in favour of vast reforms that would virtually end tenancy. American influence thus paradoxically came to be associated with internal reform in the Philippines after Americans had ceased to rule there. But it was not effective. Indeed the association perhaps inhibited change.

Agrarian reform became a major issue in the 1953 presidential campaign. Magsaysay, Secretary of Defense under Quirino, and as such responsible for an effective campaign against the

Huks (Taruc was to surrender in 1954, though Jesus Lava sought to negotiate and emerge into the politics of co-existence), now opposed the Liberal Quirino as the candidate of the Nacionalistas. They were joined by the Democrats who represented the sugar barons of the western Visayas, alienated by Quirino's turning to reform. Magsaysay's trump card, however, was his charisma, the support he enjoyed from the *taos,* whom he had freed from oppression by reforms in the army and constabulary and helped by a programme of legal assistance; and it was this that brought him victory. But as for agrarian reform the peasant demands were amorphous; many Nacionalista leaders like Laurel and Recto were not committed; and, while the sugar barons felt fairly secure — they were however contradictorily entrenched in the administration, they were protected by the Bell trade act which continued the quotas, they ran necessarily large-scale mechanised operations — the owners of rice lands, especially in central Luzon, could bring much pressure to bear on Congress, particularly as many were middle-class professionals in Manila in informal contact with members of the lower house. There were indeed economic arguments to be used against reform in the sense of redistribution — it was doubtful if it would increase production; it might provide only a temporary stop to the process of fragmentation and recumulation; it might not be the best method of freeing capital for industrialisation — and as for resettlement in the Moro lands, the government would find it impossible to carry through on a sufficiently large scale to make any impact.

It was only in 1955 that Magsaysay pushed through a land tenure bill, setting up a Land Tenure Administration under the President, and then it was not an act likely to achieve any major social change. Yet another powerful argument used in favour of the *status quo* was that the bill was an American device to ensure the continuance of a colonial economy, as Recto put it. It was an argument that gained some support from Filipino intellectuals, who wanted a more independent course in foreign affairs. Again, when the Americans were most reforming they seemed — as in Wood's day — most colonialist. The interests that benefited most from the American market could profit from anti-American sentiment that fed upon the ties those interests had established with the U.S.

The continued conservatism of the régime showed itself in other ways also. If it had any wish to transform the economy, it had no wish to utilise Chinese skill and capital. Indeed the Magsaysay régime promoted a law to exclude aliens (above all, of course, Chinese) from the retail trades. A traditional distrust had, perhaps, been promoted by the Communist victory in China. But it was significant that by a régime under the American aegis such nationalist gestures were made (even if American advice sought to restrain them).

With the death of Magsaysay in an air-crash in 1957, the régime lost even its charisma. Under his successor Garcia, there was little implementation of the tenancy laws, and this, and perhaps the new shifts in international Communism, produced a recurrence of Huk activities. The emphasis was on emotional nationalism and attacks on alien vested interests. The Liberal Vice-President, Macapagal, had little to do, and built up support in the barrios by appearing, Magsaysay-like, as the defender of the small man against money and power. He triumphed in the election of 1961.

The new régime, advised by the banker and oilman Sixto Roxas, struck at the exchange controls and the corruption they involved, at the corruption of the (conveniently Nacionalista) sugar interests. Its Five-year Integrated Socio-Economic Program, designed to increase productivity and establish new consumer industries, enjoyed some success. But again there were nationalist gestures against the Chinese community; and again both vested interests and nationalist appeals were involved in Macapagal's foreign policy. The continued paradox of Filipino-American relations made the contacts the Philippines at last established with island Southeast Asia paradoxical also.

In foreign policy the Magsaysay régime had intensified the ties with the U.S. The Philippines joined the S.E.A.T.O. alliance. If Quirino's plan for a Pacific pact had failed, and India had ensured that the communiqué of the Baguio conference was more or less non-political, at Bandung Carlos Romulo opposed Nehru and the five principles and defended participation in the Manila pact. In subsequent years the Philippines government established closer relations with some Southeast Asian countries and in 1958 joined Malaya and Thailand in setting up A.S.A. But this organisation had little substance. In any case two of its members were also S.E.A.T.O. members. It was with the third that the paradox developed. Clearly it, too, was an important element in the defence system to which the Philippines was committed, even if it was not an actual member of S.E.A.T.O. But when the Malaysia project emerged, the Philippines at once claimed that it was weak, 'Chinese' in character, a threat to the western defence system, and weakened it further by demanding Sabah.

For the inhabitants of the southern Philippines, North Borneo, as also Celebes, was the source of a lucrative if largely illicit trade that, along with growing educational opportunities, promoted social mobility and stimulated an Islamic revival among the Moro communities, as witnessed, for instance, by the first Muslim Filipino Conference held in June 1955 at Cotabato. But, in demanding Sabah, the Manila government was concerned rather with motives at once broader and narrower, with the assertion of independence of the U.S. that adhesion to S.E.A.T.O. paradoxically required, and with private interests financially involved in the claims of the heirs of the Sultan of Sulu which were being pressed. The matter had been a political football since 1946 when, twelve days after Philippines independence, as ex-Governor-General Harrison pointed out to Quirino, North Borneo had become a Crown Colony. Consequently, in 1947, the administration of the offshore islands had been relinquished by the British. The heirs of the Sultan might indeed have some ground for arguing that the status of the territory granted in 1878 (not all North Borneo) had been changed, since the Company had been operating theoretically under the sovereignty of the two Sultans, though also under British protection. The disappearance of the Sultanate in the 1930s and the acquisition of claims by the Philippines government, however, produced further anomalies, more especially if that government was to be regarded as bound by the territorial agreement of the convention of 1885. Macapagal might have been content with a gesture and perhaps some compensation for the private interests that believed North Borneo possessed oil. His policy, however, became embarrassing as Malaysia was confronted by a larger neighbour, a power that avowedly had no interest in the maintenance of the western defence structure and that might go so far as to sponsor Muslim irredenta in the southern Philippines (despite — or because of — a clash of economic interests).

8 British Borneo

BECAUSE of its strategic importance, North Borneo had suffered great destruction in the war. Partly because of this, a Crown Colony was established. A restoration of the old Company régime could hardly have been expected. The post-war world was too insecure: and, furthermore, this last piece of colonialism was intended to hasten political advance. But the economic resources of North Borneo offered no basis for a rapid transformation: it exported rubber, copra, timber, but remained a net importer of food. Some progress was made in education, though by 1956 only 35% of the children were at school. Two-thirds of these were Chinese and, though immigration was banned in 1949, the Chinese community was increasing faster than the others. These factors delayed political advance. Some progress was made with local government under an ordinance of 1951, and local authorities were established at Kota Belud in 1952, with chiefs and headmen and later Chinese as members, at Sipitong in 1955, and at Pappar in 1956. In a number of places town boards were set up under an ordinance of 1953. The Legislative Council dated from 1950: it remained predominantly official and entirely nominated. The first elections in North Borneo, held in 1962, were purely local. It was one of the least advanced of Britain's dependent territories.

In Sarawak the old régime disappeared for the same reasons as that in North Borneo, but not with the same lack of violence. The 1941 constitution was continued, but the Malays feared the loss of the position they had enjoyed under the Brookes. A Malay movement against the cession led to the murder of Governor Stewart late in 1949. Certainly the colonial phase witnessed the expansion of the Chinese community — which had favoured the cession — and it amounted to some 30% of the population. In their political plans, however — which culminated in a new constitution in 1956, providing for elections to the Council Negri indirectly on the basis of elected local authorities, and for the introduction of the 'member' system (or dyarchy) — the British, like the Brookes, sought to leave a place for the indigenous people, particularly the Sea-Dayaks. The Chinese shared the relative prosperity of Sarawak — based on rubber and pepper exports — but the younger among them, discontented with the authority of tribal and clan associations, turned to left-wing politics.

The establishment of colonial authority naturally revived the schemes for association between the Borneo territories and between them and Malaya that the Colonial Office had toyed with in the 1890s. They might now provide the means at once to economic development, security, and political advance which it was hard for the Borneo territories to attain on their own. At the end of the war some sort of Dominion of Southeast Asia appears to have been envisaged. The transfer of the North Borneo capital from the east coast to the west coast perhaps indicated an intention of focusing the colony's future more on the Peninsula and Singapore. The Colonial Office had indeed appointed a Governor-General in Southeast Asia in 1946, and the Foreign Office had appointed a Special Commissioner. With the achievement of the post-war settlement, the two posts were combined as a Commissioner-Generalship. The three Borneo territories came to co-operate in the spheres of judiciary, aviation, and survey, and in 1953 the Commissioner-General convened an inter-territorial conference which became a standing conference. Possibly the approach of Malaya's independence induced more definite attempts to promote unity. In July 1957 Governor Abell of Sarawak urged the need for closer co-operation, and in February the following year the Governor of North Borneo urged the consideration of a constitutional arrangement. In Sarawak and North Borneo interracial apprehension worked against any change in the relationship with Great Britain. And Brunei had also to be reckoned with.

Brunei was exceptional in British Borneo in being predominantly Malay and in being wealthy. Post-war the Brunei oil measures had been exploited and brought vast revenues for the little protectorate. The social improvements that resulted contributed to a growth of political and religious awareness and of unrest at European predominance. These factors assisted the rise of the Party Rakyat, which was organised by A. M. Azahari — born in Labuan of an Arab father and educated by the Japanese in Indonesia — and which was affiliated with Malaya's left-wing Rakyat Party. In the first elections to the Legislative Council in 1962, it secured all the seats, but it was

285

still outnumbered by non-elective members. To some extent Malay restlessness contributed to a nostalgia for the old Brunei empire, and there was some hope of Malay support at least in Sarawak. This the Rakyat sought to organise. On the other hand, Brunei's revenue would then be tapped for less wealthy neighbours, and in 1958 the Sultan had been said to prefer a simple tie with Malaya and others autonomy in the Commonwealth.

The development of the Malaysia proposals precipitated in December 1962 a revolt led by Azahari and supported by Brunei Malays and Kedayans (an Islamised tribe, long treated as second-class citizens). Denied political power so far, the Rakyat took the last chance to seize it. The British quickly suppressed the revolt, but it had a number of results. It helped to prevent the inclusion of Brunei in the Federation. And if Azahari had established links with the agent of the Sulu claimants (a son of Osmena called Nicasio), much more importantly he had aroused the interest of the Indonesians. Their confrontation of the Federation did not cease with Brunei's failure to join. They could claim that the peoples of Sarawak and North Borneo — of the rest of 'Kalimantan Utara' — had not been properly consulted, either by the Cobbold Commission in 1962 or by the U.N. survey in 1963. They could point out that the Borneo delegates to the Malaysia parliament of 1964 were appointed by the Sabah and Sarawak legislatures, not elected. In the name of self-determination, they could denounce 'neo-colonialism'.

9 Malaysia

IN MALAYA the Japanese utilised the communal divisions in order to establish their political control. They looked to the Malays, turned to account their apprehension of other races, and seemed to afford them a means of maintaining their supremacy. Furthermore the Japanese appeared to envisage

286

closer association with Indonesia, a goal of extremer nationalists who saw in it the solution to the problem of preserving Malay culture. The nationalists rejoiced when Sumatra and Malaya were treated as one unit by the Japanese army administration and the old contacts across the Straits were strengthened. In 1944 they tried to celebrate Koiso's promise of independence for Indonesia. The loss of the northern states — ceded to Thailand in October 1943 — had indeed been a disappointment and reduced their strength. But from mid-1945, in association with the moves towards 'Quick Independence for Indonesia', the Japanese fostered the K.R.I.S. (All-out Effort of the People) movement under Ibrahim bin Yaacob, a past president of K.M.M. and Lt.-Colonel in the Malay Volunteer Force of the Japanese army. The K.R.I.S. movement broke down because of the capitulation.

Japanese policy towards the Chinese presented a contrast. It contrasted, too, with Japanese policy towards the Indians. Some 60,000 estate labourers were taken to the death railway in Thailand, and some 40,000 of them died. But in other ways the occupation gave the Indian community a feeling of consequence, because it seemed to be in the forefront of the move to liberate India. By contrast the occupation began for the Chinese with a considerable massacre of K.M.T. supporters, Communists, and volunteers who had fought in the jungle. It remained a period of uncertainty for the mass of the Chinese, as well as of economic hardship, and squatting in the jungle, begun in the depression, greatly increased. A Communist minority turned to guerilla warfare, and organised the Malayan People's Anti-Japanese Army, from 1944 secretly supplied by Force 136 in Ceylon.

The war ended suddenly, without the reconquest that must have involved carnage and destruction, and also co-operation with the Chinese guerillas with whom the British were already in touch. Nevertheless the post-war political proposals envisaged a new position for the immigrant communities. They were proposals drawn up, it has been argued, when the war of reconquest was still expected, and aimed at doing the best that could be done for the Malays in the anticipated circumstances, and they were eventually implemented, even though circumstances were not as anticipated, because the full significance of the lack of a campaign was not realised. In support of this argument is the fact that predominantly Chinese Singapore was excluded from the proposed Union, which was to be formed by bringing the states under Crown jurisdiction. By making it a separate Colony, its entrepot interests would be protected, and so would Malay predominance in the Union. In the new Union, citizenship was to be open to all born or to be born in the Union or the Colony, or resident there for 10 of the preceding 15 years disregarding the occupation period. The rulers accepted the revision of the protection agreements undertaken by the mission of Sir H. MacMichael, whose task was arguably facilitated in several states by the fact that another of his duties included the regulation or confirmation of the successions during the wartime period. The constitution came into being in April 1946.

The extent of the Malay reaction came as a surprise to those unfamiliar with the events of the occupation. One of its leaders was Dato Onn, an English-educated District Officer in Johore, grandson and son of prime ministers of Johore. He had supported K.R.I.S., but now looked to the rulers as guarantors of Malay status. In Johore in January Onn founded the Malay Peninsula Movement to oppose the Union proposals, on the ground that they would lead to the political as well as economic dominance of the Chinese. In March a conference of similar organisations met in Kuala Lumpur and founded the United Malay National Organisation with Onn as president. The Malays believed they had powerful friends in Britain, and took courage from the long-standing sympathy for them. Indeed the authorities early agreed to negotiate for the revision of the constitution. The result was the creation of an elaborate federal structure, which replaced the Union, and the introduction of more restricted citizenship proposals.

The Chinese community had not come forward to defend the Union scheme in 1946. No doubt the events of the war and the disorder of the post-war period discouraged leaders from assuming public prominence that might mark them down for extortion or blackmail. More generally, the community had never been oriented, or even encouraged to become oriented, towards participation in political life. Apart from the K.M.T. and the Communists, the only predominantly Chinese party was the Malayan Democratic Union, founded by English-educated intellectuals in December 1945, non-communal and extreme left-wing in programme. It had little influence on the Union negotiations.

Later in 1946 and in 1947 there were attempts to organise those opposed to the Federation plans into a Pan-Malayan Council of Joint Action, with Tan Cheng-lock as President. It represented the Chinese, the Indian, even the extremist Malay opposition of the Putera and the M.N.P., led by men like Burhanuddin and Ahmad Boestamam. The Malay Nationalist Party, founded in October 1945, strongly represented the old K.R.I.S. leaders, and had broken with U.M.N.O. in June 1946. Its support of 'Indonesia Raya' was dampened by news of the Dutch police action against the Republic. It was dampened, too, by Tan Cheng-lock, while, on the other hand, Malays, opposing its apparent co-operation with the immigrants, gave their support to U.M.N.O. In October 1947 the P.M.C.J.A. organised a hartal or stoppage of work, and in November it issued a People's Constitution, mostly the work of a Singapore lawyer, Eber, former president of the M.D.U. But the Federation nevertheless came into operation in 1948.

The M.C.P., and its M.P.A.J.A., had meanwhile benefited from the interregnum caused by the sudden end of the war, and by the shortages and disruption of the reoccupation phase. Late in 1945 most of the Army was paid off, and the M.C.P. shifted to other tactics. Conditions favoured insurrection, but international Communism as yet did not. The M.C.P. turned to labour organisation. In the Chinese community, hitherto transient, organised by clan and society, there was no trade union tradition, and the Communists sought to organise a T.U. structure on a political basis. Attempts at a general strike and a demonstration on the anniversary of the fall of Singapore early in 1946 came to little. The Communists turned to participation in the radical popular movements formed to protest on behalf of the immigrant communities against the Federation proposals. Only in 1948 did the M.C.P. shift to open violence. This was no doubt connected with the shift in policy of international Communism, but it was also the result of internal pressures. Almost entirely a Chinese movement, the M.C.P. was joined by those traditionally accustomed to join clan and tribal associations to help them on in life, and who had correspondingly high expectations from the M.C.P. For both reasons, the wartime leader, Lai Teck, was displaced by his wartime aide, Chin Peng (who had been given the O.B.E. in 1945), and a new Maoist strategy was adopted. The resulting terrorism precipitated the 'Emergency' after June 1948.

In these circumstances the left-wing groups, including the M.N.P., vanished from politics. There remained the U.M.N.O. on the one hand and the M.C.P. on the other. But this did not precipitate the triumph of the Malays. It made them feel strong enough to compromise, as Clementi had once hoped. And it brought forward at last a moderate Chinese leadership which recognised the advantage in making terms with the more conservative Malay movement associated with the rulers. The

British Commissioner-General, so far from sponsoring divide-and-rule, played a part in organising a Communities Liaison Committee, begun at Onn's house late in 1948, and including Tan Cheng-lock. From this emerged a proposal he had once before envisaged, to create a Malay Chinese Association. This would parallel the U.M.N.O., win organised support from the Chinese community, and co-operate with U.M.N.O. It was set up in February 1949. It agreed to discrimination in favour of the Malays in education, economic aid and, temporarily, in political status, but sought also a more adequate position in Malaya's political life for the Chinese. The Chinese leaders had seen the need of some organisation to win community support for moderate politics, and their success would depend on the concessions of the Malays. The Malay leaders, on the other hand, had come to see that some sort of deal with the immigrant communities was the only guarantee of their political future. Indisposed to join Indonesia Raya, the Malay aristocrats could not forever rely on the British, whereas advance towards independence would guarantee their position within their own community and their compromise with the immigrants.

In 1951 Onn founded the Independence of Malaya Party to crystallise the co-operation of the C.L.C. But most Malay support remained with the U.M.N.O., which he left to Abdul Rahman, a member of the Kedah ruling family who had read history and law at Cambridge, and most Chinese politicians remained with the M.C.A. The two communal groups co-operated, however, in various municipal elections after 1952, each group placing candidates where its community had the most voters, and enjoying thereby triumphant success. At the centre a sort of dyarchy was created. But in the first elections for the Federal Legislative Council, held in 1955, there were no communal seats, and the Alliance secured 51 out of 52 constituencies, thus dominating a Council of 98. A different principle of co-operation had been followed from that in the municipal elections. The scope of Federation citizenship had been expanded in 1952, but many Chinese had so far failed to register, and the delineation of constituencies throughout the country (as distinct from the municipal areas) had produced fifty seats with a Malay majority, only two with a Chinese, none with an Indian. But fifteen Chinese and two Indians were elected on the Alliance ticket, the Tengku having with an eye to the future insisted on a substantial number of immigrant nominations, and the electorate having voted for them, on the platform of *merdeka* or independence. Onn's new Party Negara fought on communal lines. So did Dr Burhannudin's new creation, the Pan-Malayan Islamic Party, which secured the odd seat in Krian. That party represented both the abiding discontent of religious leaders at the success of the aristocrats, and that of the more extreme nationalists who, for instance, regarded Patani as Malay irrendenta and still looked towards Indonesia Raya. Burhanuddin had indeed turned up at Bandung.

Merdeka was secured in 1957. The new constitution, drafted by a commission including an Australian representative, was, of course, federal. A monarch was to be chosen for five years by a conference of rulers. He was to act in accordance with the advice of his cabinet, responsible to a legislature consisting of a partly-appointed Senate and a House of Representatives comprised of 104 elected members. The states remained under their hereditary rulers or, in the case of Penang and Malacca, under governors. Other safeguards for the special position of the Malays were written into the constitution, and Islam was the state religion. It remained to be seen whether, once the enthusiasm *merdeka* aroused had passed, the Malays could still contemplate concessions to the Chinese. The related question was whether the M.C.A. could win the support of the Chinese masses as more of them became voters (and under the constitution of 1957 the citizenship regulations were further expanded). Was the conservative alliance envisaged by Clementi and Onn to continue? or were the Malays to swing to the P.M.I.P.? or was it possible that the communities could co-operate at lower social levels? The Socialist Front did not suggest that the last was likely. Its Malay element, the Party Rakyat, led by Ahmad Boestamam, another ex-M.N.P. leader, had no real Malay support. In the state elections of 1959 the P.M.I.P. was successful in the more purely Malay states of Kelantan and Trengganu. The parliamentary elections later that year again testified to their strength in that area (they secured 14 seats all on the east coast), but the Alliance secured 74 seats. 52 of its 69 Malay candidates, 19 of its 31 Chinese, three out of four of its Indians were successful. It won 24 of the 40 constituencies in which the Chinese now predominated. 13 seats went to a combination of the S.F. and the P.P.P., a left-wing Ipoh-centred group critical of Malay rights. The stage was set for further co-operation along existing lines.

The M.C.P. meanwhile had been defeated, in part by testimonies of political advance and community co-operation, in part by the Briggs plan for relocating the squatters, in part by Templer's drive, in part by the inadequacy of its own programme, which attempted to follow Maoist specifications in the quite different rural context of Malaya. The M.C.P.'s campaign never became more than terrorism, and it was impossible for it to adapt to shifts in international Communist policy after 1951. In 1955, indeed, Chin Peng sought to emerge into the political field, advocating the most minimum of minimum programmes, but in vain. After 1957 most areas were declared free of terrorism, and the Emergency was finally ended in 1960. The M.C.P., still unable to appear openly, concentrated, for instance, on attempts to arouse Chinese opposition to the national education programme. This programme sought to create a common curriculum — with a Malay content — in all schools. It also sought to emphasise Malay and English at the secondary level. About three-quarters of the Chinese schools assented to this as a condition of aid.

Community co-operation in the Federation was no doubt stimulated by the generally buoyant economy of the country and the relatively high standard of living. In the Japanese war, the economy had been upset: the major exports, tin and rubber, fell off, the major import, rice, was restricted by the collapse of Japanese shipping, and the food shortage helped to create the Chinese squatter community which was a factor in the Emergency. The colonial power returned for long enough to rehabilitate the economy, and its departure was peaceful. Tin recovered slowly after the war, despite the extensive destruction of expensive dredges (the smaller Chinese firms recovered more quickly than the European). Rubber production was more rapidly restored, and the Korean war led to a great boom. Replanting grants after 1955 stimulated efficient production of a natural product that had to face the competition of a synthetic rival. The government, recognising Malaya's dependence on a few exports, concerned itself with diversification of the economy. It also stressed rural development and tried to promote cash crops — for instance, oil palm — among Malay small-holders. The five-year plan of 1956 had, however, to be stretched out in 1958, and meanwhile population continued to rise at the rapid rate of 32 per 1,000. The problem was far greater for neighbouring Singapore. There the population rose at 39 per 1,000, one of the highest rates in the world.

In both countries, the Chinese population increased especially rapidly, with the setting-up of Chinese households, a trend begun pre-war; and in Singapore the population was about 80% Chinese. The rapid increase of population underlined the fears for Singapore's economic future. Throughout its history there had been concern lest it should cease to be able to rely on entrepot traffic. In the post-war period of growing economic nationalism in neighbouring countries, the concern was intensified, though in fact Singapore benefited from the collapse of central economic control in Indonesia in the 1950s. But its leaders were increasingly doubtful of its ability to keep afloat — and raise the living standards of its rising population — without closer economic association with Malaya from which it had been politically severed in 1946. Yet the Tengku in Malaya — which had its own industrial programme — looked askance at a city populated by Chinese and increasingly, it seemed, moving left.

The colonial government in Singapore had been substantially democratised in 1955 and in 1959, and a bill had passed the Legislative Assembly in 1958 providing that aliens resident for eight years and taking the oath of loyalty could have the vote. These developments envisaged large-scale participation by the Chinese in western-style politics. The traditional loyalties were to clan and tribal associations, and participation in politics in the western style was bound to involve methods that would generate a countervailing mass enthusiasm. The youthful character of the population also gave a special intensity to the politics of anti-colonialism in Singapore. These factors — and also national pride, stimulated in particular among those who attended Chinese schools and were frustrated at the inadequate recognition in the Colony of their qualifications — put leftism and even Communism at a premium. Something of a pattern thus resulted. The 1955 elections were won on a platform of independence and a welfare state by the Labour Front socialists of David Marshall and Lim Yew-hock. As Marshall put it, '*merdeka* will rally the majority of the people against Communism'.[99] And first Marshall and then Lim secured major concessions from the British Government that led to self-government in 1959. But in the election of 1959 the more left-wing People's Action Party triumphed. In power the Labour Front had sought to break the Communist hold upon the Chinese secondary schools and trade unions, and so had won an unpopularity of which their opponents had made use. Now the P.A.P. and more especially the English-educated social democrats in it like the Cambridge-bred lawyer Lee Kuan-yew faced the future; they faced, too, a reckoning with their past allies. Their programme was one of independence through merger with Malaya. They succeeded — and consolidated their position against the left-wing which broke away to form the Barisan Socialis in July 1961 — because the Tengku had broken the Singapore pattern

293

of events by changing his attitude to Singapore and abandoning his uncompromising opposition to merger in May 1961. In part this may have been due to the changes in the international situation and to the crisis in Laos. It was also due to the result of the Hong Lim by-election the previous month, in which the P.A.P. candidate was decisively defeated by a breakaway left-wing opponent campaigning for complete independence, Ong Eng-guan, one-time student in Melbourne and Mayor of Singapore. The U.M.N.O. leader came to feel that the P.A.P. under Lee's leadership was a guarantee against something worse, which might come about when the 1959 constitution was revised in 1963.

The idea appeared to be made more palatable by the notion of offsetting predominantly Chinese Singapore in a federation of Malaysia to include also the Borneo territories and their indigenous though mixed majorities, territories whose future the independence of Malaya had again brought in question in 1957, but which had remained yet undecided in face of mutual jealousies and intercommunal apprehensions. In the Malaysian Federation Sarawak and Sabah were given more parliamentary seats than their population suggested; they were given control of immigration; and their indigenes were to enjoy similar rights to the Malays' on the Peninsula. Singapore received autonomy in education and in civil service matters and remained a free port. But its internal security was under federal control, and only fifteen members were sent to the federal parliament. Some of these conditions, of course, limited the pursuit of rational economic policies within the Federation. In other ways, they put the existing political structure in all the territories, but especially the Alliance in Malaya, under great stress. But economic and political developments were profoundly affected by the development of Indonesian confrontation. It strained the economy. In Malaya it appeared to rivet Alliance control more strongly, if perhaps in a more brittle way. The elections of 1964 were a triumph. And S.F. leaders and extreme Malay nationalists — looking still to 'Indonesia Raya' — found themselves behind bars early in 1965 (Ibrahim bin Yaacob was in Jakarta). But there was concern at P.A.P. activities on the Peninsula, and amid growing communal tension Singapore seceded in August.

In a campaign against the Federation, Indonesia could play up the claims to self-determination of the various peoples. It also claimed that the Federation was 'neo-colonialist'. With independent Malaya, indeed, the British had found it relatively easy to put their interests on a new footing. The Malay leaders were anxious for foreign investment as a counter to Chinese dominance. They were prepared, too, to remain in the Commonwealth (unlike Burma) and to enter into a defence agreement, though, in deference to the Chinese, not to enter S.E.A.T.O. The creation of the Malaysian Federation — including the Peninsula and the Borneo territories, all of them considered important in the nineteenth century in relation to China — was seen by the British as strengthening western defence in the region. The use of Singapore — Chinese in population, but a bastion still in the defence of the Indian Ocean and Australasia — was important to them. A communiqué of November 1961 was vague enough to satisfy the Alliance and the British, and internal security — a major issue with Marshall and Lim — was left to the Federation. The negotiations had, however, reckoned without the Indonesians, whose opposition intensified after the Brunei revolt. Attempts to compromise by giving the Indonesians the alternative satisfaction of a 'Maphilindo' association failed. Attempts to appease Indonesia by a last minute re-investigation of the wishes of the Sabah and Sarawak peoples — indicated already in elections of December 1962 and June 1963 — were, perhaps, pursued too unconvincingly (the inauguration of Malaysia was deferred for a fortnight, but Malaysia day, 16th September 1963, was announced before the U.N. officials had presented their report). But it could be argued that appeasement would have made little impact on Indonesia, whose policy was dictated by domestic considerations. There was indeed no reason to suppose that the secession of Singapore would suffice to bring confrontation to an end.

10 Indonesia

IN JAVA the Japanese sought to achieve the maximum of effect by reversing Dutch policy and allying with the Islamic elements in society. The climax came in November 1943 with the organisation of the Masjumi, designed to 'strengthen the unity of all Islamic organisations' and aid Japan 'in the interests of Greater East Asia',[100] and deepening the popular roots which the Islamic movements already possessed. The secular nationalists were allowed far less scope until late in 1944, and only then could they begin to create the mass following they had not enjoyed pre-war. They were faced also with dissident underground groups, fostered by the harsh economic effects of the occupation, one led by the Socialist Sjahrir and by Roeslan Abdulgani; another, ex-Gerindo, led by Sjarifuddin, the illegal-P.K.I. leader of the 1930s, until his arrest in 1943; a third by Sukarni, an associate of the non-Stalinist national Communist Tan Malaka, and by the Sumatran Chaireul Saleh. The occupation had also brought into existence a new military élite. Only when Koiso promised independence late in 1944 did their political experience enable the secular nationalists to seize administrative control and build a mass following.

In mid-1945 the Japanese set up a committee to investigate Indonesian independence. At its first session Sukarno expounded Pantja Sila, the political doctrine of the secular Javanese nationalists. At a second session, in July, the territorial limits of independent Indonesia were discussed. Yamin saw the problem in historical terms and referred to Sri Vijaya and Majapahit. Sukarno emphasised the importance of controlling both sides of the Straits. The new Indonesia was to include British Borneo, Brunei, Timor, Malaya and New Guinea. In the event, the Japanese decided not at once to include Malaya, but to push ahead with independence for the old Dutch territories. Additionally, the Japanese naval leaders fostered an anti-western resistance movement led by Subardjo, and drawing on the national communism of Tan Malaka.

Before independence had been proclaimed, however, the Japanese had capitulated. But the hands of Sukarno and Hatta were forced by underground groups and independence was proclaimed in Batavia on August 17th. A Republic was set up, with power in the hands of the President, Sukarno, and a Central National Committee or K.N.I.P. An elected assembly was to be created in the future. The pressure of the underground groups, which were apprehensive of a monolithic political structure created by collaborationists (in A.F.P.F.L. style), led to the adoption of a multi-party system. The major organisations that appeared were the Partai Nasional Indonesia, essentially led by the old secular nationalists, and the Masjumi. The resistance leader Sjahrir headed a Socialist party which, unlike these, did not have a mass following, but he became the first premier. The Republic, established in Java, struggled to establish its control in Sumatra also. In Acheh the revolution had taken the form of a reassertion of the religious leaders, the *ulama,* affiliated with the Masjumi, against the *adat* chiefs. On the east coast, on the other hand, the collapse of the plantations had seen their occupation by the local labour force, and early in 1946 there was a violent outbreak against the aristocrats associated with western economic developments that had left the peasants land-hungry. The leaders of the outbreak, as also those on the west coast, associated themselves with a mass movement against the Sjahrir government led by Tan Malaka (apparently back in Java after late 1944) and by disappointed ex-collaborationists.

Meanwhile the Allied troops met considerable opposition, especially the Dutch, as indeed they had after the earlier restoration of 1816. By early 1947 they were confined to the main towns in Java and Sumatra. It was this, and British pressure, that induced them to negotiate. In Borneo, Celebes, the Moluccas and Lesser Sundas, however, where the Japanese had allowed less political activity than in Java, and where there was no social revolution as in Sumatra, the Allied troops, Australians, had been able to take over, and subsequently the Dutch asserted their control, in parts of Celebes, nevertheless, only by the notorious methods of Westerling and his firing squads.

Under the Linggadjati agreement of November 1946, the Netherlands was to recognise the Republic as the *de facto* authority in Java and Sumatra, and the two governments were to co-operate in setting up a sovereign democratic federal state, the United States of Indonesia, to include the Republic and

Southeast Asia Since 1942

states centred on Borneo and the Moluccas. The Dutch — the Netherlands Communist party supported the Government's policy — clearly hoped to play off areas which they controlled against those which they did not — rather like the French in Indo-China. Furthermore, falling back on the old aristocracies and securing the co-operation of political opportunists, the Lt. Governor-General van Mook unilaterally set up the state of East Indonesia in December. This made it difficult for Sjahrir to secure the ratification of the Linggadjati agreement by the K.N.I.P. in face of nationalist opposition played upon by Tan Malaka and others. Furthermore the Dutch claimed that the Linggadjati agreement envisaged an interim government over all Indonesia which should control a joint gendarmerie with powers in the Republic as well as outside it. The resultant dispute led to the Dutch premier's order on July 20th for an all-out attack on the Republic, and the army fanned out.

At the United Nations, to which the matter was brought by Australia and India, the U.S., concerned — like the Communist bloc — for its European policies and so, like Britain in the nineteenth century, restrained in its attitude towards the Dutch, produced a compromise. The Security Council tendered its good offices to assist a settlement, and a committee was set up, including Belgium, Australia and the U.S. An agreement was finally secured aboard U.S.S. *Renville* in January 1948. This provided for the setting-up of the U.S.I. after the holding of a plebiscite to determine whether the population of Java and Sumatra wished to form part of the Republic or of another state within the U.S.I. But differences remained as to the powers of the joint interim federal government, and meanwhile no plebiscites were held. Indeed the Dutch, allegedly on a provisional basis, began to set up other units in the territory whose control they had by now acquired. In January van Mook recognised a state of Madura, in February West Java or Pasundan was inaugurated, and later in the year East and South Sumatra.

The Republic was now substantially confined to east and central Java, though they, of course, were historically centres of Archipelagic empire. Discontent at these reverses was increased by food shortage and inflation. The new Hatta cabinet had to face popular opposition led by Sjarifuddin who, after the arrival of Musso, a leading figure in 1926, from Moscow, took a stronger stance. The Stalinist P.K.I. had (partly because of the international line) been quiescent in the early years of the revolution: it had supported Linggadjati, and a Sjarifuddin cabinet had signed the *Renville* agreement. Now it became more

298

bellicose. The plan was for a P.K.I.-led revolution later in 1948, but — as in 1926 — it was begun prematurely — by a revolt in Madiun in September — and the government was able to repress it. But Tan Malaka's new national-Communist Partai Murba benefited.

The defeat of the P.K.I. was, in the context of the world struggle now being joined, greatly to influence U.S. attitudes in the next crisis in the relations between the Dutch and the Republic. The failure of Vice-President Hatta's negotiations over the *Renville* agreement led in December to a second Dutch 'police action'. The cabinet was captured, but the military operations did not secure the countryside. The U.S. was alarmed lest the nationalist movement should be driven into Communist hands, and indeed Tan Malaka sought to control it till his execution in April 1949, and a follower, Chaireul Saleh, continued disturbances till early 1950. Meanwhile the U.S. had induced the Dutch to make some concessions, and in August a Round Table Conference had met at The Hague. An agreement was hammered out whereby by the end of the year sovereignty over the Netherlands Indies was to be transferred to the U.S.I., a federal government formed of the Republic, with post-*Renville* boundaries, and the federal units created by the Dutch. The exception was West New Guinea, retained by the Dutch partly as a Eurasian homeland, partly as a potential source of oil. But above all it was a gesture indicating that the Dutch were still an Asian power. Such a gesture facilitated the passage of the agreement through a States General where as in France a multi-party system produced great rigidities on major issues of policy. The Netherlands-Indonesia Union also set up in 1949 hardly filled the bill.

The federal system, tarred with the Dutch brush, did not last. 1950 saw its rapid disappearance, and Indonesia recurred to a unitary centralism even more Dutch. Indeed the Javanese, who had argued for strong central government in 1945, were the most numerous of the peoples of Indonesia, and held the one traditional centre of Archipelagic empire that independent Indonesia — despite the wishes of 1945 — possessed. Yet to some extent the federal system was a response to the wide regional variations throughout the islands that the Dutch had brought together, and there was a danger that a non-colonial and merely unitary government would pay them too little attention. But Javanese leadership in Indonesian nationalism was still moderated as pre-war by the presence of other elements especially of Sumatran origin. This was true of the appointed K.N.I.P. and of the army in particular. The rebellions of the first few years came from extremists. Some of the Ambonese Christians — once important in the colonial administration and in the colonial army, in the absence of opportunity in the undeveloped Moluccas — proclaimed a South Moluccas Republic in April 1950. The revolt was quelled, and there was an exodus to the Netherlands, but guerilla activity continued. On the other hand, there were revolts by movements seeking to create Islamic states as distinct from the syncretic state of Pantja Sila. These included the Darul Islam movement in West Java, the movements in South Sulawesi (Celebes) led by Kahar Muzakar (killed in February 1965) and in South Kalimantan (Borneo) by Ibnu Hajar. In Acheh, a partial restoration of the *adat* chiefs produced the Daud Beureuh revolt in 1953. But that was perhaps also the symptom of a new trend in Indonesia.

The war and the struggle for independence had wrought great destruction, and these disorders impeded reconstruction. But prosperity might have alleviated conflict and maintained a general acceptance of unified rule. Wide differences among the élite, given expression by the multi-party system and by Presidential disputes with cabinets, prevented effective decisions by the various governments of the early 1950s in the social and economic field, where divisions of opinion manifested themselves more openly than in the period of the struggle against the Dutch. Only in 1956 was a five-year plan produced; even then it was on a relatively small scale, insufficient to give the economy any real lift; and in any case it was never implemented and ultimately superseded. The main consensus of agreement was again negative: that foreign enterprise should be regulated lest it amount to economic colonialism; but how it should be regulated was another matter. Yet it was the best earner of foreign exchange, and the Indonesians lacked trained personnel (the old princely territories of Java were the best source of officials, since they had maintained a large staff pre-war; the well-educated Christian Bataks were useful, too). And development pressed. The population was increasing at the rate of 2% per annum, and in Java the pressure on subsistence was stringent. The area under rice had expanded in the depression of the 1930s and in the Japanese occupation, but it was insufficient; and attempts were made to increase production, and to develop other foodstuffs like fish and cassava. Migration held out limited prospects. The solution had to lie in the direction of industrialisation in Java. For this export earnings must be used. But the restrictions on foreign enterprise, and the promotion of foodstuff production, meant that they must come from the outer islands. There, too, they must come above all from the oil companies, which survived without being able to expand, and from smallholder production of rubber and copra in Sumatra, Kalimantan and Sulawesi. But the requisite large-scale decisions were not made. The only major achievements were in education. The collapse of the Korean boom after 1952 made decisions more essential, but no easier to take. The export earnings of the outer islands came to be merely keeping the Javanese economy afloat. Economically Java now depended on the Archipelago in an unprecedented way; but that only made the assertion of its political advantages — its population, its position, its experience — more important.

The principal Javanese party, the P.N.I., thus sought to entrench itself by unproductive expenditures, such as the creation of an immense bureaucracy. At the same time, the 1953-5 administration of the P.N.I. leader, Ali Sastroamidjojo, whose appointment had precipitated the Acheh revolt, sought to maintain a conviction of revolutionary *élan* and unity by a more vigorous foreign policy. It took steps to bring the abortive Union to an end. It promoted the Bandung conference. And it intensified the demand for West New Guinea (West Irian), now taken to the U.N. This the Dutch had never transferred. Their presence — in conjunction with the Ambonese revolt — could be considered a threat to Indonesian security. But that was only one element in the Indonesian struggle to secure a territory that had proved as intrinsically worthless as the Dutch had originally thought.

Thirdly, as the first national elections approached, the P.N.I. and the President, apprehensive of a Masjumi victory, sought some sort of alliance with the P.K.I. in order to ensure the support of rural Java to which the government had failed to bring prosperity. The basis of co-operation was again a nationalist foreign policy. Under the leadership of D. N. Aidit, an East Sumatran, educated at Batavia, and associated with the pre-war Gerindo, and under the impulse of changing attitudes in international Communism, the P.K.I. had begun to recover from the discrediting revolt of 1948 by presenting itself as an Indonesian patriot organisation. It was easier for the P.K.I. than, say, for the M.C.P. or the Burma Communists to adjust its policies because its earlier revolt had, unlike theirs, so decisively and immediately failed. The new line was approved at the Fifth Congress in 1954, and on these terms the P.N.I. facilitated the P.K.I.'s acquisition of posts that put it in closer touch with the

Javanese masses. The oldest Communist party in Asia was on the way to a new period of expansion.

The first general elections — held in 1955 — were indeed the critical turning-point in post-independence Indonesia. A few seats went to the Protestant Parkindo, a few to Sjahrir's P.S.I., a few to the Murba which Tan Malaka's heirs had carried on. The Communists polled some 18% of the votes, giving them 39 out of 260 members. But the significant feature of the election was the way the all-important vote of populous east and central Java was distributed. It went to the P.N.I., the P.K.I., and the Nahdatul Ulama, a more conservative, less reformist Islamic grouping than the main body of the Masjumi, from which it had broken in 1952. The former three were thus primarily Javanese parties, the last, the Masjumi, primarily an outer island party. The elections, from which much had been hoped, did not prove a panacea. On the contrary, by polarising the differences between Java and the outer islands, by putting power predominantly into Javanese hands, and by decreasing the mediating influence of western-educated outer islanders who had been important in the appointed K.N.I.P., they inaugurated a crisis.

The outer islands had already become restive over the utilisation of their export earnings by the unitary government, more especially as it came to be directed to non-productive ends. Most was spent in Java, and the peasant proprietors and small traders in the outer islands found that little was done to aid them. The roads, for instance, had hardly been touched since 1942. The toleration of Communism in Java added to the growing stress between the central government and the middle-class and Islamic reformists of the outer islands: in the latter it seemed now a far more alien growth than in an island long habituated to bureaucratic and authoritarian concepts of society. Even *adat* elements in the outer islands, resentful of Javanese centralism, sank their differences with social groups with which they had once clashed. The elections intensified the stress by reducing the *de facto* influence the outer islands had enjoyed in government and making the dominance of the Javanese plainer. The resignation of Hatta in December 1956 dramatised it. There followed the moves to establish 'autonomous areas' in the outer islands which so alarmed Jakarta in late 1956 and early 1957. Reliance on their export earnings was a matter of life and death in Java and, in the absence of a degree of industrialisation that might have put relations with the outer islands on a new economic basis, political control over them was essential. It became all the more necessary to play up the West Irian

Indonesia

campaign, not only to encourage the Javanese to tighten their
belt, but to attempt to maintain an Indonesian unity that was
essential to them however tight they pulled it.

Late in 1597 the campaign reached a new pitch of intensity,
which seemed to indicate growing Communist initiative. The
extreme anti-Dutch and anti-Eurasian measures with which it
was accompanied, which amounted to wholesale expulsion and
expropriation, and which included the destruction of the
K.P.M., the major steamship line among the islands, were likely,
too, to worsen the economic situation. There was a reaction,
therefore, in the outer islands, and a revolutionary government
was proclaimed at Padang in February 1958. It was led by
members of the P.S.I., by men like the Sundanese Sjafruddin,
by Masjumi-men like Harahap, Sumitro and Natsir, and supported in Menangkabau and Menado. But it did not link up
with the remnants of previous extremist revolts, nor even with
that in Acheh, for it represented the less extreme mediating
elements that had played a part in the Republic before 1955-6.
And it did not attract mass support, much more involved in
the straight-out xenophobia of the Jakarta leaders. These factors helped the army to put down the revolt.

The crisis discredited constitutional democracy and introduced
the more recent phase of 'guided democracy'. This was a more
authoritarian régime, but it was not monolithic. It was marked
by a return to the 1945 constitution, by the banning of the
P.S.I. and the Masjumi, and by the creation of a Presidential
cabinet. This was headed by Djuanda, a non-party Javanese,
and included Saleh, a Sumatran survivor of the Tan Malaka
movement, and Yamin. After Djuanda's death late in 1963,
there were three vice-first ministers, Leimena, a pro-revolution
Ambonese Christian, Saleh, and Subandrio, a non-party Javanese
sympathetic to the P.N.I., and Yamin's successor as maker of
ideology was Sastroamidjojo. The Javanese thus afforded the
outer islands a marginal political influence. In the army it was
less restricted.

The army had gained a new prominence with its success in
1958: it predominated in regional government, especially outside central and eastern Java, where the old bureaucracy had
been and was strongest; it predominated in the running of
former Dutch enterprises; and it secured a recognised position
among the ramshackle political structures of guided democracy.
But it did not secure for itself an exclusive dominance over the
government, and it did not attempt a coup. Above all, this
resulted from the divided nature of the army élite itself — 'a

303

pattern of cleavage between a more strongly Islamic group of officers, mainly non-Javanese, who are determined anti-Communists . . . , and a less strongly Moslem group, mainly Javanese, who have trust in the President and are willing to tolerate the Communists'[101]: any assumption of supreme power would reveal these divisions and break up the army. The army thus contained within itself many of the basic élite divisions of Indonesia. It was this that had made it a matter of diplomacy to organise the operations of 1958 — headed indeed by a Batak ex-member of the colonial army, Nasution — and made it easier to accept during 1961 the surrender of the errant officers of 1956-7. But it also meant that the army avoided overthrowing Sukarno, who enjoyed a sort of general legitimacy as a revolutionary and as head of state and who sought to expand it — in the absence of any definite organisational support — by formulating ideologies and by refashioning state symbols drawn from the past.

In the field of foreign policy, again, Sukarno and the army could agree. First, the campaign for West Irian, and then the campaign to crush Malaysia provided areas of accord between them. The first was secured at last in 1962-3, subject to a U.N. plebiscite in 1969. The second began almost at once with the Brunei revolt. For the army, these campaigns helped to justify its position in the Republic and to build Indonesia up into at least a second-class military power. For Sukarno, they not only echoed his programme of 1945: they were a field for charisma, for slogan-making oratory, for revolutionary *élan,* on which his political position depended. And for both they were a source of unity in support of the régime. Indeed, as with West Irian, so over Malaysia the government could argue a security threat. Might not Sumatra look to Malaya and create a new Sri Vijaya? had not Singapore fostered economic independence in the outer islands? and were not western bases in this context a threat like those of the Dutch in West New Guinea?

The Communists formed a third feature of the post-1958 political structure. To the army, more especially its Islamic elements, they were objectionable. To the President, with a different ideological background, they were desirable with a view to offsetting the dominance of the army. Something of the pre-1958 conflict thus found different expression. Ostensibly the P.K.I. seemed strong as a result: it had 2-3m members, it ran the T.U. Federation or S.O.B.S.I. and the Peasant Front. But in order to gain the President's protection against the pressure of the army, the P.K.I. had to campaign for his state ideology, and to use such slogans as 'National Interests above Class Interests'. A possible switch to a more militant strategy was, in view of army control, difficult, and Aidit simply made gestures towards Peking and Tirana. The government, indeed, was supported by the Soviet Union, which supplied military and economic aid especially after 1960, including up-to-date bombers. And on the other hand, the U.S. continued to vie with the U.S.S.R. in support of the régime. It promoted the transfer of West Irian in 1962, though it had opposed it (or failed to support it) when a Masjumi government was in power in 1956. And its aid was even greater, aid that went in practice to shoring up the régime, and not to effective development, since the capitalist-minded section of the élite was emasculated and the economy under bureaucratic and military control. Here, indeed, the U.S. attached its cause in Southeast Asia to nationalism, even its extremest form.

If, however, the foundation of Malaysia threatened the political balances in Malaysian countries, the opposition to it threatened those in Indonesia. In the course of 1964 and early 1965, it seemed that the P.K.I. could begin to adopt a more radical line and to look to China. The régime had gained no satisfaction from a 1955 treaty with China over the nationality question, and (so far from making use of Chinese skills or capital) in 1959-60 had taken measures to repatriate some 40,000 Chinese. Now, by leaving the U.N. when Malaysia was admitted to the Security Council, it seemed to be moving more into the Chinese orbit. But this very fact meant that the P.K.I. was still operating within a national context. Even if all western aid were cut off, Indonesia would not remain simply dependent on China, unless Russian aid were also cut off, and the American forces miraculously disappeared from mainland Southeast Asia, and the British from the Peninsula. In a sense the Indonesian leaders were safely making gestures of friendship to China. And the amount of help they could expect to receive in crushing countries with by far the largest Chinese population in Southeast Asia seemed limited. On the other hand, the 'fraternal' nature of confrontation tended to restrict extremities on both sides, if not to bring them together. Even if a more extreme policy had ensued, and a more real Chinese alliance, the P.K.I. would still not have won the battle within the country. And any attempt to seize power would, it seemed clear, be defeated.

The P.K.I. had built its popular support in the days of parliamentary democracy largely from a peasantry still village-oriented, traditional in outlook. That support was thus massive but nonmilitant. The P.K.I. was in turn dependent on Sukarno in the days of guided democracy, and it never gained access to positions of decisive government power. When later in 1965 it apparently associated itself with the 'September 30th Movement' in an attempted coup, it only demonstrated its ultimate weakness and the unwillingness of the masses to follow a revolutionary line. This was, perhaps, another miscalculation following those of 1926-7 and 1948. It was likely severely to reduce P.K.I. influence and to increase the army's but not to conclude confrontation.

Postscript

IN THE INTRODUCTION to this book, it was suggested that Australasian students might have some contribution to make to the writing of Southeast Asian history in part because of the very separateness of Australasian history. In the preface to its concluding part, dealing with a period when those histories at last come more together, some references were included to the contributions Australasian governments have made to Southeast Asian countries and to those their critics thought they should make. In turn it would seem from the ensuing discussions that Southeast Asia has presented Australasians with nothing but an 'A.N.Z.A.C. dilemma', with political problems they can do little to solve and economic problems they can do little to alleviate. This book has been able to do scant justice to the variety of experiences and the diversity of cultures with which Australia and New Zealand have been brought into contact. But that contact might modify their own uniformities and rigidities and stimulate a deficient self-criticism. The political dilemmas, the economic intractabilities in the relationship with Southeast Asia may remain. But those are not all the Unknown North has to offer to those who came to *Terra Australis Incognita* to seek freedom and mine gold.

Notes

1   W. G. East and O. H. K. Spate, *The Changing Map of Asia*, Fourth Edition (London and New York, 1961), p. 217.
2   Quoted in J. C. van Leur, *Indonesian Trade and Society* (The Hague, Bandung, 1955), p. 161.
3   *Ibid.*, p. 261.
4   Sir S. Runciman, *The White Rajahs* (Cambridge, 1960), p. 52.
5   J. C. Templer, ed., *The Private Letters of Sir James Brooke* (London, 1853), ii, p. 304.
6   C. P. FitzGerald, 'Overseas Chinese in Southeast Asia', *The Australian Journal of Politics and History*, VIII, No. 1 (May 1962), p. 71.
7   C. A. Fisher, *Southeast Asia, a Social, Economic and Political Geography* (London and New York, 1964), p. 208.
8   D. G. E. Hall, *A History of Southeast Asia*, Second Edition (London, 1964), p. 5.
9   Fisher, *op. cit.*, p. 67.
10 P. Wheatley, *The Golden Khersonese* (Kuala Lumpur, 1961), p. 298.
11 G. Coedès, *Les États Hindouisés d'Indochine et d'Indonésie* (Paris, 1948), p. 221.
12 B. Schrieke, *Indonesian Sociological Studies*, Part One (The Hague, Bandung, 1955), p. 15.
13 *Op. cit.*, p. 66.
14 Quoted in van Leur, *op. cit.*, pp. 343-4.
15 Max Weber, quoted in *ibid.*, p. 97.
16 Hall, *op. cit.*, p. 119.
17 Schrieke, *op. cit.*, p. 11.
18 *Op. cit.*, p. 170.
19 G. Sansom, *The Western World and Japan* (London, 1950), p. 56.
20 Van Leur, *op. cit.*, p. 164.
21 *Ibid.*, p. 195.
22 H. J. Benda, *The Crescent and the Rising Sun* (The Hague, Bandung, 1958), p. 11.
23 B. Schrieke, *Indonesian Sociological Studies*, Part Two (The Hague, Bandung, 1957), p. 235.
24 *Ibid.*, p. 248.

Notes

25 Benda, *op. cit.*, p. 12.
26 Schrieke, *op. cit.*, Part One, p. 45.
27 K. Glamann, *Dutch-Asiatic Trade 1620-1740* (Copenhagen, The Hague, 1958), p. 6.
28 Van Leur, *op. cit.*, pp. 181-2.
29 Hall, *op. cit.*, p. 287.
30 Van Leur, *op. cit.*, pp. 263, 245.
31 Schrieke, *op. cit.*, Part One, p. 62.
32 Hall, *op. cit.*, p. 327.
33 Schrieke, *op. cit.*, Part One, p. 66.
34 *Ibid.*, p. 73; Glamann, *op. cit.*, p. 93.
35 Schrieke, *op. cit.*, Part One, p. 79.
36 Glamann, *op. cit.*, p. 212.
37 *Ibid.*, p. 243.
38 Van Leur, *op. cit.*, p. 281.
39 Benda, *op. cit.*, p. 13.
40 Hall, *op. cit.*, p. 304.
41 Glamann, *op. cit.*, p. 166.
42 Hall, *op. cit.*, p. 311.
43 *Ibid.*, p. 155.
44 *Ibid.*, p. 241.
45 *Ibid.*, p. 243.
46 D. K. Bassett, 'The Trade of the English East India Company in the Far East 1623-84', *Journal of the Royal Asiatic Society* (1960), p. 36.
47 Hall, *op. cit.*, p. 415.
48 Quoted in E. J. McCarthy, *Spanish Beginnings in the Philippines, 1564-1572* (Washington, 1943), pp. 27-8.
49 A. Sharp, *The Discovery of Australia* (Oxford, 1963), p. 46.
50 Van Leur, *op. cit.*, p. 5.
51 G. W. Skinner, *The Chinese in Thailand* (Ithaca, 1957), pp. 92-3.
52 A phrase George Canning used in 1824. See N. Tarling, *Anglo-Dutch Rivalry in the Malay World, 1780-1824* (Brisbane, London, New York, 1962), p. 155.
53 Quoted in N. Tarling, *Piracy and Politics in the Malay World* (Melbourne and Singapore, 1963), p. 106.
54 Governor Butterworth in 1846, quoted in N. Tarling, 'British Policy in the Malay Peninsula and Archipelago, 1824-71', *Journal of the Malayan Branch Royal Asiatic Society*, XXX, Part 3 (October 1957), p. 149.
55 Governor Ord, quoted in *ibid.*, p. 153.
56 Quoted in *ibid.*, p. 164.
57 Quoted in *ibid.*, p. 193.
58 Quoted in *ibid.*, p. 196.
59 Quoted in *ibid.*, p. 205.

Notes

60 J. P. Grant, quoted in N. Tarling, 'Pirates and convicts: British interest in the Andaman and Nicobar islands in the mid-nineteenth century', *Journal of Indian History*, XXXVIII, Part 3 (December 1960), p. 523.

61 F. J. Mouat, quoted in *ibid*, p. 525.

62 The Supreme Government in 1824, quoted in Tarling, *J.M.B.R.A.S.*, XXX, Part 3, p. 30.

63 The Senabodi of Siam, 1850, quoted in N. Tarling, 'Siam and Sir James Brooke', *The Journal of the Siam Society*, XLVIII, Part 2 (November 1960), p. 55.

64 As note 5.

65 In a letter of 1867, quoted in A. L. Moffat, *Mongkut, the King of Siam* (Ithaca, 1961), p. 124.

66 C. Geertz, *Agricultural Involution* (Berkeley and Los Angeles, 1963), p. 48.

67 Quoted in J. S. Furnivall, *Netherlands India* (Cambridge, 1939), p. 140.

68 Geertz, *op. cit.*, p. 58.

69 *Ibid.*, p. 80.

70 J. van Gelderen, in B. Schrieke, ed., *The Effect of Western Influence on Native Civilisations in the Malay Archipelago* (Batavia, 1929), p. 92.

71 Geertz, *op. cit.*, p. 110.

72 Benda, *op. cit.*, p. 16.

73 *Ibid.*, p. 39.

74 Geertz, *op. cit.*, p. 90.

75 *Ibid.*, p. 120.

76 Benda, *op. cit.*, p. 39.

77 Quoted in B. Grant, *Indonesia* (Melbourne, 1964), p. 21.

78 Quoted in C. N. Parkinson, *British Intervention in Malaya 1867-1877* (Singapore, 1960), p. 316.

79 J. M. Gullick, *Malaya* (New York, 1963), p. 203.

80 See R. Emerson, *Malaysia* (New York, 1937; Kuala Lumpur, 1964), pp. 174-5, 326.

81 Quoted in S. Baring-Gould and C. A. Bampfylde, *A History of Sarawak under its Two White Rajahs* (London, 1909), p. 417.

82 B. Legarda, Jr., 'American Entrepreneurs in the nineteenth-century Philippines', *Explorations in Entrepreneurial History*, IX, No. 1 (1956), p. 142.

83 Quoted in C. A. Majul, *The Political and Constitutional Ideas of the Philippine Revolution* (Quezon City, 1957), p. 115.

84 Quoted in L. Yabes, ed., *José Rizal: on his Centenary* (Quezon City, 1963), p. 221n.

85 Quoted in Majul, *op. cit.*, pp. 80-1.

86 Quoted in C. A. Grunder and W. E. Livezey, *The Philippines and the United States* (Norman, 1951), pp. 85, 101.

87 M. V. Portman, *A History of our Relations with the Andamanese* (Calcutta, 1899), i, pp. 209-10.

88 J. F. Cady, *A History of Modern Burma* (Ithaca, 1958), p. 9.

89 V. Purcell, *The Chinese in Southeast Asia* (Oxford, 1951), p. 157.

90 M. F. Herz, *A Short History of Cambodia* (New York, 1958), p. 66.

91 D. J. Steinberg, *et al., Cambodia* (New Haven, 1959), p. 95.

92 Herz, *op. cit.,* p. 62.

93 F. L. W. Wood, 'The Anzac Dilemma', *International Affairs,* XXIX (1953), pp. 184-192.

94 Hoang Van Chi in P. J. Honey, ed., *North Vietnam Today* (New York, 1962), p. 117.

95 Quoted in Ton That Thien, *India and Southeast Asia 1947-1960* (Geneva, 1963), p. 210.

96 Quoted in W. C. Johnstone, *Burma's Foreign Policy* (Cambridge, Mass., 1963), p. 102.

97 Grunder and Livezey, *op. cit.,* p. 275.

98 *Ibid.,* p. 284.

99 Quoted in L. A. Mills, *Malaya: a political and economic appraisal* (Minneapolis, 1958), p. 137.

100 Quoted in Benda, *op. cit.,* p. 150.

101 H. Feith in R. McVey, ed., *Indonesia* (New Haven, 1963), p. 328.

Bibliographical Note

AMONG the general histories of the region, D. G. E. Hall, *A History of Southeast Asia* (London, 1964), holds pride of place, and the present author, like many others, is much indebted to it. J. F. Cady, *Southeast Asia: its Historical Development* (New York, 1964), covers the period up to 1945. B. Harrison, *Southeast Asia: A Short History* (London, 1963), is briefer, but useful.

The major geographical texts include E. H. G. Dobby, *Southeast Asia* (London, 1950), and C. A. Fisher, *Southeast Asia, a Social, Economic and Political Geography* (London and New York, 1964).

Other general books are the late Victor Purcell's *The Revolution in Southeast Asia* (London, 1962), and *The Chinese in Southeast Asia* (London, 1951; new edition, 1965). Works concentrating more on the contemporary period include J. H. Brimmell, *Communism in Southeast Asia* (London, 1959); O. E. Clubb, *The U.S. and the Sino-Soviet Bloc in Southeast Asia* (Washington, 1962); W. H. Elsbree, *Japan's Role in Southeast Asian Nationalist Movements* (Cambridge, Mass., 1953); K. T. Louka, *The Role of Population in the Development of Southeast Asia* (Washington, 1960); F. von der Mehden, *Religion and Nationalism in Southeast Asia* (Madison, 1963); Ton That Thien, *India and Southeast Asia* (Geneva, 1963); and V. Thompson and R. Adloff, *Minority Problems in Southeast Asia* (Stanford, 1955). R. Emerson, *Malaysia* (New York, 1937), a classic discussion of inter-war Indonesia and Malaya, has lately been republished (Kuala Lumpur, 1964).

Some material on Australasian interests in Southeast Asia before the second world war may be found in Eugene H. Miller, *Strategy at Singapore* (New York, 1942); I. F. G. Milner, *New Zealand's Interests and Policies in the Far East* (New York, 1940); and J. Shepherd, *Australia's Interests and Policies in the Far East* (New York, 1940). Essential for the post-war period are the two volumes, edited by G. Greenwood and N. Harper, *Australia in World Affairs, 1950-1955* and *1956-1960* (Melbourne, 1957 and 1963). I. Southall, *Indonesia Face to Face* (Melbourne, 1964) gives a somewhat sentimentalised account of the Volunteer Graduate Scheme.

In the first part of the present work, the author has relied substantially on the general histories and upon G. Coedès, *Les États Hindouisés d'Indochine et d'Indonésie* (Paris, 1948; new ed., 1964); G. Coedès, *Les Peuples de la Péninsule Indochinoise* (Paris, 1962);

312

Bibliographical Note

K. Glamann, *Dutch-Asiatic Trade, 1620-1740* (Copenhagen and The Hague, 1958); J. C. van Leur, *Indonesian Trade and Society* (The Hague and Bandung, 1955); M. A. P. Meilink-Roelofsz, *Asian Trade and European Influence in the Indonesian Archipelago between 1500 and about 1630* (The Hague, 1962); B. Schrieke, *Indonesian Sociological Studies* (The Hague, Bandung, 1955, 1957); and P. Wheatley, *The Golden Khersonese* (Kuala Lumpur, 1961).

Some other material for this period occurs in the following lists which, however, mainly cover the period since 1760.

The present author's own works deal mostly with the political division of the Malay world in the late eighteenth and nineteenth centuries. They are *British Policy in the Malay Peninsula and Archipelago, 1824-71*, published as a whole number of the *Journal of the Malayan Branch Royal Asiatic Society*, XXX, Part 3 (October 1957); *Anglo-Dutch Rivalry in the Malay World, 1780-1824* (Brisbane, London and New York, 1962); and *Piracy and Politics in the Malay World* (Melbourne and Singapore, 1963).

There is a growing literature on Malaya and Malaysia, though, partly because the Colonial Office records are not yet open to inspection, little has been published on the inter-war period. Useful are: Chai Hon-chan, *The Development of British Malaya, 1896-1909* (Kuala Lumpur, 1964); C. D. Cowan, *Nineteenth-century Malaya. The Origins of British Political Control* (London, 1961); J. M. Gullick, *Malaya* (London and New York, 1963); G. Z. Hanrahan, *The Communist Struggle in Malaya* (New York, 1954); S. W. Jones, *Public Administration in Malaya* (London, 1953); L. A. Mills, *Malaya: a political and economic appraisal* (Minneapolis, 1958); C. N. Parkinson, *British Intervention in Malaya* (Singapore, 1960); N. Parmer, *Colonial Labor Policy and Administration* (New York, 1960); V. Purcell, *Malaya: Communist or Free?* (London, 1954); L. W. Pye, *Guerilla Communism in Malaya* (Princeton, 1956); T. H. Silcock and Ungku Abdul Aziz, *Nationalism in Malaya* (New York, 1950); Wang Gung-wu, ed., *Malaysia* (London and New York, 1964); R. Winstedt, *Malaya and its History* (London, 1948): Wong Lin Ken, *The Malayan Tin Industry to 1914* (Tucson, 1965); and Wong Lin Ken, 'The Trade of Singapore, 1819-69', *J.M.B.R.A.S.*, XXXIII, Part 4 (December 1960). A stimulating article on the elections of 1955 is I. Tinker, 'Malayan Elections: electoral pattern for plural societies?', *Western Political Quarterly*, IX (1956), pp. 258-82. K. G. Tregonning, ed., *Papers on Malayan History* (Singapore, 1962), contains important contributions on Malay politics from W. Roff and Y. Itagaki. Valuable, but as yet unpublished, are E. Thio, *British Policy in the Malay Peninsula, 1880-1909* (University of London, Ph.D. thesis, 1956), and C. M. Turnbull, *The Movement to remove the Straits Settlements from the Control of India, culminating in the transfer to the Colonial Office in 1867* (University of London, Ph.D. thesis, 1962).

Dealing more especially with Borneo are M. H. Baker, *North Borneo. The First Ten Years, 1946-56* (Singapore, 1962); S. Baring-

313

Bibliographical Note

Gould and C. A. Bampfylde, *A History of Sarawak under its Two White Rajahs* (London, 1909) ; G. Irwin, *Nineteenth-century Borneo; a study in diplomatic rivalry* (The Hague, 1955) ; S. Runciman, *The White Rajahs* (Cambridge, 1960) ; K. G. Tregonning, *Under Chartered Company Rule. North Borneo, 1881-1946* (Singapore, 1958) ; and J. Willi of Gais, *The Early Relations of England with Borneo to 1805* (Langensalza, 1922).

Published material on Indonesia is immense, and the following is merely an indication of some of that in English: J. Bastin, *Raffles' Ideas on the Land-Rent System* (The Hague, 1954) ; J. Bastin, *The Native Policies of Sir Stamford Raffles in Java and Sumatra* (Oxford, 1957) ; H. J. Benda, *The Crescent and the Rising Sun* (The Hague, Bandung, 1958) ; R. J. Bone, *The Dynamics of the West New Guinea Problem* (Ithaca, 1958) ; H. Feith, *The Decline of Constitutional Democracy in Indonesia* (Ithaca, 1962) ; J. S. Furnivall, *Netherlands India* (Cambridge, 1939) ; C. Geertz, *Agricultural Involution: the processes of ecological change in Indonesia* (Berkeley and Los Angeles, 1963) ; B. Grant, *Indonesia* (Melbourne, 1964) ; B. Higgins, *Indonesia's Stabilisation and Development* (New York, 1957) ; D. Hindley, *The Communist Party of Indonesia, 1951-1963* (Berkeley and Los Angeles, 1964) ; G. McT. Kahin, *Nationalism and Revolution in Indonesia* (Ithaca, 1952) ; E. S. de Klerck, *History of the Netherlands East Indies* (Rotterdam, 1938) ; J. M. van der Kroef, 'Two Forerunners of modern Indonesian Independence: Imam Bondjol and Thomas Matulesia', *Australian Journal of Politics and History*, VIII, No. 2 (November 1962), pp. 148-163; R. T. McVey, ed., *Indonesia* (New Haven, 1963) ; R. van Niel, *The Emergence of the Modern Indonesian Elite* (The Hague and Bandung, 1960) ; L. Palmier, *Indonesia and the Dutch* (London, 1962) ; B. Schrieke, ed., *The Effect of Western Influence on Native Civilisations in the Malay Archipelago* (Batavia, 1929) ; W. F. Wertheim, *Indonesian Society in Transition* (The Hague and Bandung, 1956) ; H. R. C. Wright, *East Indian Economic Problems in the Age of Raffles and Cornwallis* (London, 1961) ; and C. E. Wurtzburg, *Raffles of the Eastern Isles* (London, 1954). Anonymously edited is *The Indonesian Town. Studies in Urban Sociology* (The Hague and Bandung, 1958).

Historical material on the Andaman and Nicobar islands appears to be rather scanty. Some may be gleaned from P. K. Sen, *Land and People of the Andamans* (Calcutta, 1962). Among a number of accounts by officials employed there are F. J. Mouat, *Adventures and Researches among the Andaman Islanders* (London, 1863), and M. V. Portman, *A History of our Relations with the Andamanese* (Calcutta, 1899).

The historiography of the Philippines is substantial even in the English tongue, but the Spanish period, especially the greater part of the nineteenth century, has been neglected. Works covering it include E. Alzona, *A History of Education in the Philippines, 1565-1930* (Manila, 1932); M. C. Católico, *Liberalism in the Philippines during the Spanish Régime* (University of California, Berkeley, unpublished M.A. thesis, 1937); H. de la Costa, *The Jesuits in the Philippines 1581-1768* (Cambridge, Mass., 1961); M. L. Diaz-Trechuelo, 'The Economic Development of the Philippines in the Second Half of the Eighteenth Century', *Philippine Studies*, XI, No. 2 (April 1963), pp. 195-231; E. A. Julian, *British Projects and Activities in the Philippines 1759-1805* (University of London, unpublished Ph.D. thesis, 1963); F. M. Keesing, *The Ethnohistory of Northern Luzon* (Stanford, 1962); B. Legarda, Jnr., 'Two and a Half Centuries of the Galleon Trade', *Philippine Studies*, III, No. 4 (December 1955), pp. 345-72; K. C. Leebrick, *The English Expedition to Manila in 1762* (University of California, unpublished Ph.D. thesis, 1915); D. D. Parker, *Church and State in the Philippines, 1565-1896* (University of Chicago, unpublished B.D. dissertation, 1936); and J. L. Phelan, *The Hispanisation of the Philippines* (Madison, 1959), a superb book.

José Rizal's *Noli me Tangere*, recently translated by L. M. Guerrero (London, 1961), aside from being an exciting novel, gives us an insight into late nineteenth-century Philippines society. Books on the revolution include T. Agoncillo's controversial *The Revolt of the Masses* (Quezon City, 1956) and his *Malolos* (Quezon City, 1960); C. A. Majul's excellent *The Political and Constitutional Ideas of the Philippine Revolution* (Quezon City, 1957) and his prize-winning *Apollinario Mabini, Revolutionary* (Manila, 1964); and D. D. Parker's unpublished *Church and State in the Philippines, 1896-1906* (University of Chicago, Ph.D. thesis, 1936). M. B. Jansen, *The Japanese and Sun Yat-sen* (Cambridge, Mass., 1954) gives some information about the revolutionaries' contacts with Japanese nationalists. So does J. M. Saniel, *Japan and the Philippines* (Quezon City, 1962).

Published material on the American and contemporary phases is large. It includes, *inter alia,* valuable books, such as G. A. Grunder and W. E. Livezey, *The Philippines and the U.S.* (Norman, 1951); G. L. Kirk, *Philippine Independence* (New York, 1936); Dapen Liang, *The Development of Philippine Political Parties* (Hong Kong, 1939); and F. L. Starner, *Magsaysay and the Philippine Peasantry* (Berkeley and Los Angeles, 1961). The present author is indebted to R. M. Stubbs, *Philippine Radicalism: the Central Luzon Uprisings, 1925-1935* (University of California, Berkeley, unpublished Ph.D. thesis, 1951).

Books on the 'Moro' lands include V. Hurley's swashbuckling *The Swish of the Kris* (New York, 1936); S. Y. Orosa's *The Sulu Archipelago and its People* (London and Yonkers, 1923); and N. M. Saleeby's recently republished *The History of Sulu* (Manila, 1908). P. A. Ortiz gives an account of Philippines claims in 'Legal Aspects of the North Borneo Question', *Philippine Studies*, XI, No. 1 (January 1963), pp. 18-64.

One of the most informative books on the early British connexions with Burma is D. G. E. Hall, ed., *Michael Symes: Journal of his Second Embassy to the Court of Ava in 1802* (London, 1955). Among other works the present author has laid under tribute are R. Butwell, *U Nu of Burma* (Stanford, 1963); J. F. Cady, *A History of Modern Burma* (Ithaca, 1958); J. L. Christian, *Burma and the Japanese Invader* (Bombay, 1945); J. S. Furnivall, *Colonial Policy and Practice* (Cambridge, 1948); D. G. Hinners, *British Policy and the Development of Self-Government in Burma, 1935-1948* (University of Chicago, unpublished Ph.D. thesis, 1951); W. C. Johnstone, *Burma's Foreign Policy* (Cambridge, Mass., 1963); D. P. Singhal, *The Annexation of Upper Burma* (Singapore, 1960); H. Tinker, *The Union of Burma* (London, 1957); and F. N. Trager, *Building a Welfare State in Burma* (New York, 1958).

The Human Relations Area Files volumes on *Cambodia*, by D. J. Steinberg, *et al.* (New Haven, 1959), and *Laos*, edited by F. M. Le Bar and A. Suddard (New Haven, 1960) are compendious. Less so is M. F. Herz, *A Short History of Cambodia* (New York, 1958). Sisouk na Champassak, *Storm over Laos* (New York, 1961), is a piece of contemporary history by one not uninvolved. The best general history of Vietnam is Le Thanh Khoi, *Le Vietnam, Histoire et Civilisation* (Paris, 1955). J. Buttinger, *The Smaller Dragon* (New York, 1958), is less useful, especially on the French period. Other books include J. F. Cady, *The Roots of French Imperialism in Eastern Asia* (Ithaca, 1954); J. Chesneaux, *Contribution à l'histoire de la nation Vietnamienne* (Paris, 1955); B. B. Fall, *The Two Vietnams* (London and New York, 1963); E. Hammer, *The Struggle for Indo-China* (Stanford, 1954); P. J. Honey, ed., *North Vietnam Today* (New York, 1962); P. J. Honey, *Communism in North Vietnam* (Cambridge, Mass., 1963); A. Lamb, 'British Missions to Cochin-China, 1778-1822', *J.M.B.R.A.S.*, XXXIV, Parts 3 and 4 (1961); D. Lancaster, *The Emancipation of French Indo-China;* R. W. Lindholm, ed., *Vietnam. The First Five Years* (East Lansing, 1959); C. Robequain, *The Economic Development of French Indo-China* (London, 1944); G. Taboulet, *La Geste Française en Indochine* (Paris, 1955, 1956); V. Thompson, *French Indo-China* (London, 1937); and D. Warner, *The Last Confucian* (London, 1964).

Some works on Thailand are Chula Chakrabongse, *Lords of Life* (London, 1960); J. Coast, *Some Aspects of Siamese Politics* (New York, 1953); K. P. Landon, *Siam in Transition* (Shanghai, 1939); J. C. Ingram, *Economic Change in Thailand* (Stanford, 1955); W. D. Reeve, *Public Administration in Siam* (London, 1951); G. W. Skinner, *The Chinese in Thailand* (Ithaca, 1957); V. Thompson, *Thailand, The New Siam* (New York, 1941); W. F. Vella, *The Impact of the West on Government in Thailand* (Berkeley and Los Angeles, 1955); W. F. Vella, *Siam under Rama III* (New York, 1957); H. G. Quaritch Wales, *Siamese State Ceremonies. Their history and function* (London, 1931); and D. A. Wilson, *Politics in Thailand* (Ithaca, 1962). Unpublished is Detchard Vongkomolshet, *The Administrative, Judicial and Financial Reforms of King Chulalongkorn* (Cornell University, M.A. thesis, 1958).

Index

Index

Index

A

abangan 164, 166
Abdul Rahman, Tengku 290, 293
Abell 285
Abendanon 167
Abu-bakar (of Johore) 136
ACAPULCO 84, 194
ACHEH, Achehnese 11, 13, 41-5, 49-51, 53, 55-7, 64, 103, 105, 113, 114, 116, 118, 121-3, 125, 132, 133, 135, 141, 142, 164-6, 297, 300, 303
Achmad Djajadiningrat 167
adat 65, 161, 165-7, 169-71, 175, 176, 188, 297, 300, 302
Aeta 9
AFRICA ix, 27, 36, 46, 55, 104, 191
Aglipay 201, 205
Aguinaldo 199, 200, 205
Agung 49, 50
Agus Salim 174, 176
Ahmad Boestamam 288, 291
Aidit 301, 305
Airlangga 13, 26, 28
Akbar 43
Alaungpaya 74, 76, 77, 144
Al-Azhar University 170
Albuquerque 36, 81
alcalde 85, 88
Alexander of Rhodes 77
Alfurs 9
Ali (of Johore) 136
Ali Sastroamidjojo 301, 303
ALIGARH 170
Alimin 175
Alliance (U.M.N.O./M.C.A.) 290, 294, 295
ALSACE-LORRAINE 153, 233
Amangkurat I 58
Amangkurat II 58
Amangkurat III 60
AMBON, Ambonese 40, 41, 45, 49, 52, 53, 66, 172, 173, 300, 301, 303

AMERICA 3, 35, 38, 47, 54, 81, 91, 96. See also UNITED STATES OF AMERICA
AMIENS treaty 115, 127
AMOY 49, 78, 106
AMSTERDAM 48, 49
Anahwrahta 14, 26, 29
ANAMBA ISLANDS 150
Ananda, indexed under Rama VIII
Anaukpetlun 75
Anda 194, 196, 197
ANDAMAN ISLANDS, islanders xi, 3, 9, 91, 102, 142-4, 207, 208, 243, 277, 278
Ang Chan 70
Ang Duong 152
ANGKOR xiv, 12, 18, 26, 152, 156, 253
ANNAM 15, 230, 232, 254, 255
Anti-Enemy Backing-Up Society 184
Anti-Fascist People's Freedom League (A.F.P.F.L.) 272, 273, 275-7, 297
Anti-Imperialist League 184
antimony 3, 121, 127, 190
A.N.Z.U.S. pact 250
ARABIA, Arabs 24, 27, 29, 32, 34, 55, 60, 66, 167, 187, 285
ARAKAN, Arakanese 3, 5, 14, 15, 17, 71, 72, 74, 79, 142, 144, 145, 209, 212, 216, 273, 274, 276
d'Argenlieu 254-6
ARNHEM LAND 90
ARU 40
Asociacion Hispano-Filipino 198
ASSAM 145, 147
Association of South Asian States (A.S.A.) 241, 282
Augustinians 86
Aung San 217, 272
AUSTRALASIA ix-xi, xv, xvi, 3, 5, 91, 110, 111, 249-52, 295
AUSTRALIA, Australians x-xii, xv, 8, 9, 35, 90, 91, 105, 109-11, 125, 127,

319

Index

132, 191, 194, 225, 243, 249-52, 291, 297, 298
Australoid peoples 9
AVA 17, 69-71, 75, 76, 146
AYUTHIA 18, 21, 24, 27, 69-74, 78-80, 91, 108, 133, 144
Azahari 285, 286

B

Ba Maw 215-7, 271
Ba Swe 272, 273, 275-7
BAGDAD 30
BAGUIO conference 246, 282
Bahol Balabayuha 223
Bajaus 128
BALAMBANGAN (JAVA) 50
BALAMBANGAN (BORNEO) 126-8
BALANINI 83
BALI 3, 9, 11, 13, 44, 50, 60, 61, 124, 125, 170
Bali Aga 9
BANDA 3, 40, 43, 49, 52, 53, 90, 127
BANDJERMASIN 44, 50, 52, 56, 63, 113
BANDUNG 168, 169; Conference 246, 282, 291
BANGKA 4, 67, 116, 133, 173
BANGKOK xi, 73, 133, 134, 149, 150, 152-5, 217, 222, 223, 225, 226, 245, 262, 266, 270
BANTAM 39, 41, 43-5, 49-52, 57, 60, 61, 64-6, 166
Bao-dai 234, 254-7, 259, 265
BARAM 130, 132, 190
barangay 33, 85, 86, 195
BARCELONA 197
Barisan Socialis 293
barrio 85
Barwick 250
Basco 194
BASILAN 83, 129, 150
BASSEIN 69
BATAKS 9, 31, 44, 103, 167, 172, 300, 304
BATANG MARAU 129
BATAVIA, indexed under JAKARTA
BATJAN 52
BATTAMBANG 152, 156, 253
BAU 190
Baud 120, 161
bauxite 4
BAY OF BENGAL 3, 73, 99, 112, 114, 142, 143
Bayinnaung 70, 71, 273
BAYON monument 12
BELGIUM, Belgians 115, 119, 120, 122, 159, 220, 298
Bell Act 279, 281
Bendahara (of MALACCA, JOHORE, PAHANG) 32, 63, 137, 139
BENGAL 32, 59, 71, 74, 79, 99, 102, 114, 144, 145, 209, 278
BENKULEN 57, 116, 118
BENTAN 41. See also RIAU
Berg, C. C. 13
BERLIN 197; conference (1884-5) 101, 126, 132
betel 19, 121, 142
BHAMO 75, 147
BHANTUS 208
BIAKNABATO 199
BILA 123
BILITON 4
BINH-DINH 147. See also VIJAYA
Birch, J. W. W. 140
Bismarck 101, 131, 132, 153, 233
Bloch, Marc xi
Blundell 136, 137
Bodawpaya 144, 152
Boedi Oetomo 174
Bollaert 256
BOMBAY 99
Bonham 138
BONI 56, 62
Bonifacio 198
BORNEO xi, 4, 5, 9, 13, 31-3, 40, 42, 44, 62, 64, 67, 80, 82, 102, 103, 108, 116, 118, 124, 126, 127, 129-32, 164, 165, 170, 173, 189, 243, 245, 248, 285, 286, 294-8, 300, 301
Borneo Company Limited 190
BOROBUDUR xiv, 12, 25
Boromotrailokanat 21
Bosch 123, 159, 161, 162
Bose, S. C. 277
Boun Oum 264
BOVEN DIGUL 175
Bowring, Bowring treaty 150, 155, 218, 219, 221, 225
Brahmans 25, 29
BRANTAS 13
Briggs 291
BRISBANE 250
BRITAIN, British ix, x, xiv, xv, 8, 33, 34, 51, 52, 56, 57, 59, 60, 72,

Index

Index

Index

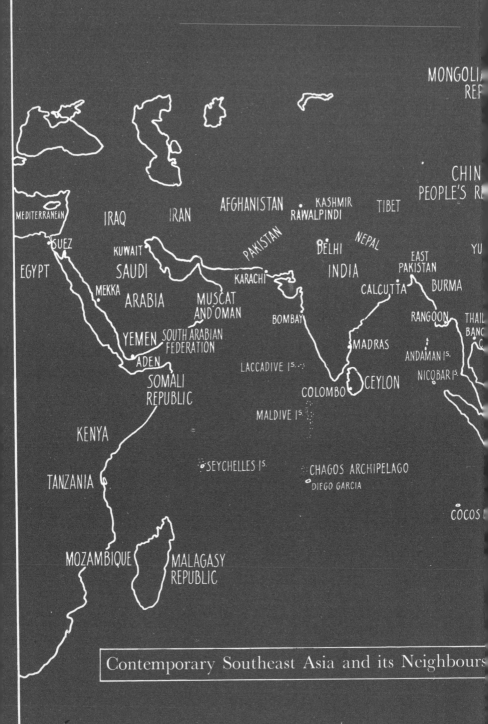

MONGOLI
REF

CHIN
PEOPLE'S R

MEDITERRANEAN

AFGHANISTAN   KASHMIR   TIBET
RAWALPINDI

YU

IRAQ   IRAN

SUEZ

KUWAIT

EGYPT

SAUDI

MEKKA

ARABIA

PAKISTAN

DELHI   NEPAL

KARACHI

INDIA

EAST
PAKISTAN

BURMA

CALCUTTA

MUSCAT
AND OMAN

BOMBAY

RANGOON   THAIL
BANC
C

YEMEN   SOUTH ARABIAN
FEDERATION

MADRAS

ANDAMAN IS.

ADEN

LACCADIVE IS.

NICOBAR IS.

SOMALI
REPUBLIC

COLOMBO   CEYLON

KENYA

MALDIVE IS.

TANZANIA

SEYCHELLES IS.

CHAGOS ARCHIPELAGO

DIEGO GARCIA

COCOS

MOZAMBIQUE   MALAGASY
REPUBLIC

Contemporary Southeast Asia and its Neighbours